Agents of Grace

Agents of Grace

Fulfilling our Destinies,
Blessing the World

Birthing the Luminous Self Trilogy
Book Two

Karen Anderson
and
Barry Martin Snyder

Luminous Self Media

First Edition, November 2011

Front cover artwork by Jean-Luc Bozzoli, www.jeanlucbozzoli.com

Back cover butterfly crop circle photo provided by Remko Delfgaauw,
www.xld-sign.com

Back cover photo of the authors by Martha Ekstrom Wilhelm

Luminous Self Media
http://www.luminousself.com

ISBN 978-0-9835990-2-9
Printed in the United States of America

"I have been wanting to write to tell you how much I LOVED the book. What an amazing book, process and connection."
-- G. G., New Mexico

"I have finished 'reading' your book although that is not how it has physically taken place. It has felt more like expanding my 'true self' while journeying on a path guiding me towards the Light.
When I would begin to read a passage it felt like I was going unconscious, although I know I was uploading more energy. So, I have read some, allowed the expansion and grace, felt the experience taking me into the world to places of new insight and connection then to return to more reading.
There is so much encoded in your 'simple' book that I have savored the banquet of the feast until now I feel fed! So beautiful the sharing, as you both are, weaving a golden thread of consciousness through the words to ignite us all. Thank you for the gifts you continue to bring here to ground the Light and help awaken us all." -- D. S., Oregon

"Just wanted you to know how much I appreciated *Soul Awakening*. It resonated so deeply with much of my own experience -- especially the 'figure 8' experiences, which I've called my 'roller coaster ride.'" -- K. K., Indiana

"What a wonderful sharing! I am enjoying it immensely and commend you two for allowing your own stories to be told in order to draw people in deeper to the personal 'real' side of living spiritual principle. I found this part was the one that kept me reading 'just one more chapter, then just one more chapter...' I found this open sharing also showed how the evolution process is working, or can show up in unique and personal ways. Most of all I feel deep gratitude and joy knowing you are who you are." -- M. A., Utah

What people are saying about *Soul Awakening: The Journey from Ego to Essence*:

"I love your book. It's so heartfelt and personal. It speaks to my heart and opens me to letting go of all the stuff that gets in the way of simply being the LOVE that I am here to express myself as. The guidance is so full of grace and love. Thank you for writing such a pure authentic personal perspective so those of us who read it can see ourselves in it. I will certainly recommend it to everyone I know." -- D. O., Oregon

"Like so many, I have longed to follow Christ by connecting with the God-within – in order to live by the divine will the way Jesus exemplified; however, unlocking that door has always remained a mystery - until now. *Soul Awakening* contains the key we can all use to connect to, feel and receive God's unconditional, immeasurable, gentle Love directly. Words cannot begin to describe the thrilling adventure and joy of connecting directly to the Source! This book is not merely a reflection of Karen and Barry's perseverance and dedication to doing God's Will, but it's a gift of God Grace and Love given to all of us through these two incredible human beings." -- R. S., California

"Just finished your [Soul] Awakening ebook...Man, what a story you have there!! Thanks so much for writing it. I saw myself in so many areas...I'm going through a massive transition myself. From being a money junkie (stock investment guy, private equity, dreaming of the McMansion, etc...) to losing my house to foreclosure and having actually no desire AT ALL to go work and make money. People think I'm nuts ... but it doesn't really bug me (much) 'cause I know there is a good reason behind it all ... Thank you for blazing the trail." -- A. D., Canada

"I wanted to say how much I enjoyed and appreciate your book. It supports me at many levels, probably more than I am aware of or can put into words, and I am looking forward to the next two volumes. I especially appreciate how you weave your personal stories and more general pointers and lessons together. It's also good for me too see how you both have gone through similar phases I have or am going through, and understand better/ confirm what I sense it's about and how I can relate to it in a more nourishing way." -- P. K., Norway

The Birthing the Luminous Self Trilogy

Humanity is in the midst of the most enormous evolutionary shift in its history. For millennia, the veils of soul-amnesia have occluded our consciousness, making it a challenge to remember who we truly are. The litany of wars, unequal distribution of resources, and environmental destruction attests to this fundamental forgetting that as souls, we are all one. Our collective soul-forgetting has brought our species and the planet to the brink of destruction.

Yet in the midst of this crisis, a luminous, soul-awakened human species is being born. Individuals everywhere are beginning to stir from their sleep as the divine light within the core of their being ignites. Birthing the Luminous Self is the process of awakening to, merging with, and expressing our divine magnificence through every facet of our mind, body and world. As this occurs, we shed the thick, opaque skins of the false self to reveal the brilliant radiance of the true, multidimensional Self. This is the process that is underway in those who are at the forefront of human evolution. One day, all of us will shine forth in our true splendor as awakened souls, blessing one another and our planet with our Presence.

Each of the three volumes in the trilogy presents an essential facet of the process of Birthing the Luminous Self. Volume One, *Soul Awakening*, offers an in-depth treatment of the all-important step of reconnecting with our inner divinity -- directly, consciously coming home to our core Self. Once we have reestablished that conscious connection, we are capable of serving as conduits of grace through which the Divine can pour Its blessings. This is the subject of the second volume, *Agents of Grace*. Finally, we reach the ultimate stage in the human experience: transcending all human limitations and stepping forth as a full and complete embodiment of the Divine. Now, we follow in the footsteps of the being who demonstrated absolute freedom from the laws of the physical plane through the resurrection and ascension of his body into an eternal, infinite body of light. Each in our own way, we realize *We are the Awakening Christ*, the title of the third book in the trilogy. Together, the three volumes of the trilogy describe and catalyze the progressive journey into the full realization of the Luminous Self.

Contents

PART FIVE
GraceWork at the End of Time

Introduction

The great philosopher-astrologer Dane Rudhyar stated, "We are each born in answer to a need." At some point in our journey through life, each of us has probably intuited that we have come to Earth to fulfill a purpose that no other soul can actualize in quite the same way. Responding to this need of the Whole for our unique contribution is a deep, primal urge within us all.

The burning desire to discover and fulfill our soul purpose is the voice of our true nature alerting us to the importance of offering our unique gifts to the world. Whether we vaguely sense or deeply know it, each of us has incarnated at this exact time on planet Earth to help our world and humanity through the greatest evolutionary leap in the history of the globe. As we look out at the world, the need for immediate and profound transformation through grace is evident everywhere. Seeing this intensifies the desire to contribute in the highest way possible. Many of us intuit that we are here to contribute more than the capacities and gifts we possess at the personality level. The sense that we have something more significant to offer arises from our soul, the inner doorway to the vast levels of grace accessible through our higher Self.

We can only temporarily put aside what we were born to be and do. A compelling knowing that *now is the time* is emerging in all of us who have come to Earth at this pivotal time to offer our gifts to the Whole. More than anything, we want to relieve suffering and make life more wonderful for our fellow beings in any way we can.

The path to our service is through our own awakening. As we reconnect with who and what we truly are, we become aware of levels of being that transcend our limited, human capacities. We begin to realize we are here to bridge the worlds of spirit and matter. When we invite the vast energies of the Divine to pour into and through us, we discover we are capable of bestowing blessings and catalyzing evolutionary shifts. We come to know that we are here to be agents of grace.

~ ~ ~

Functioning as an agent of grace is not something that lies "out there" someplace in a distant future. We do not need to be "enlightened" or "spiritually advanced" to bring through the Divine to bless one another. Each of us is *already* a conduit of grace, although we may not have thought of ourselves in those terms. Our service might be simple and humble, or large and complex. What matters most is not the apparent scope of our contribution, but the manner in which we perform our service, and where it arises within ourselves. The sincere desire to make a difference in this world, along with the humility to take direction from the Divine and put our own personal will aside to serve the larger Whole, are primary qualifications for acting as agents of grace.

Our heart-and-soul alignment is far more important than any spiritual pedigree we might think we require. After all, being a conduit of grace is not about doing; it is not about being *more* of anything. The most beautiful acts of service occur when we put ourselves aside so the Divine can come through us. Any of us is capable of this in any moment.

Earlier in our own lives, our desire to serve found expression through, for example, sharing garden produce with neighbors, teaching children with special needs, volunteering at food co-ops, and working on community initiatives. While we derived a degree of satisfaction from these endeavors, we sensed more was possible. We did not know how to get from where we were to that eventuality, but we trusted that Life would bring us into our highest service if we continued to follow the inner promptings of our souls.

When we were brought together in 1989, our service went to a new level, and became focalized on a specific contribution to the collective awakening. A journey we could never have planned or arranged led us into facilitating direct, conscious experiences of the soul realms. During these sessions, people accessed the divine magnificence at their core, which came forth to guide them through their challenges and provide answers to pressing questions. We taught hundreds of people how to consciously connect with and deepen their communion with the soul, oversoul and Source levels of being, and to go beyond the limits of identifying with the ego-mind. This phase of our journey is recounted in the first book in the Birthing the Luminous Self Trilogy, *Soul Awakening: The Journey from Ego to Essence.*

After more than a decade of facilitating soul-awakenings, another level of possibility opened up. A multi-year journey revealed entirely new ways we could be utilized by the Divine to facilitate awakenings. As each new pathway unfolded, we shared all that we had been brought into with those who felt drawn to receive it. In the process, we realized ever more fully that we are **all** here to be agents of grace, bridges between spirit and matter who are here on Earth to spark one another into full remembrance of our essential divinity. Personal and planetary awakening is the evolutionary imperative at this time. Nothing else will enable us to transcend the innumerable crises we face and bring forth the Heaven on Earth we all deeply desire and know is possible.

Our experiences left no doubt that the unprecedented levels of grace necessary to catalyze a collective awakening are now available to us all. This book offers an in-depth immersion in the gifts of grace we have been blessed to receive, along with guided inner experiences of each one, so that you can immediately begin to use them in your own life and share them with others. These gifts of grace bring us more deeply in touch with the sacredness that lives within us. As we awaken to who we really are, the inharmony, dis-ease and conflict born of forgetting our essential nature transform into the peace and joy of living from the true, eternal Self.

Anchored in the soul and its larger domain, the oversoul and Source levels of being, we become capable of accessing and transmitting a myriad of "flavors of God" to those in need of divine grace. The Transmissions of Grace are three "flavors" of the Divine that we have found to be enormously helpful in the journey of awakening. They stimulate the conscious unfoldment of the three primary soul centers, an essential element in birthing the luminous Self. Once we have received and integrated the transmissions, they can easily and naturally be passed on, replacing the all-too-prevalent energetic climate of discord and dis-ease with an endlessly expanding atmosphere of "contagious ease."

Transmissions can be shared with the people and animals we love, and that is, perhaps, the most widespread way the Transmissions of Grace are passed on. As satisfying as this can be, though, we don't need to stop there. We can, for instance, ask a transmission to fill a space that many others will pass through. Each soul will "drink" of the energies, taking in what is appropriate and helpful at that time. For instance, we might ask that a transmission fill an airplane that is experiencing turbulence, so that all within it can feel soothed and nurtured by the energies. In a workplace plagued by interpersonal conflict, we can invite a transmission to fill the space and soften the rough edges of ego that are contributing to the friction. The possibilities for using the transmissions in shared spaces are truly limitless. When we work with the transmissions in this way and observe the results over time, we become ever more confident that we are, in fact, capable of bringing through divine frequencies, and that our presence makes the world a more wonderful place.

But even this is not the end of the story. The Transmissions of Grace and other ways of serving as a "secret agent for God" enable us to powerfully and effectively take part in the larger evolution of humanity and our planet herself. This book was written for those who are here on Earth at this time to be conscious agents of grace. Everything we know about functioning as an agent of grace has been poured into this volume to help this specific group of souls to step into their soul purpose and destiny.

～ ～ ～

The first section of *Agents of Grace* affirms that we are all already conduits of grace, and offers in-depth support for stepping into new ways to serve and to deepen our spiritual capacity as agents of grace. This section includes experiential processes that facilitate deepening communion with the soul, oversoul and Source levels of being, the fountains of grace available to us all. Usable, practical information on how to serve as an agent of grace in any situation is accompanied by a sequential, guided journey through the steps involved. Real-life stories describe a variety of everyday possibilities for serving as a divine conduit. This section concludes with the importance of discovering and manifesting our unique soul purpose and destiny, along with stories describing how this has occurred in our own lives.

Part Two relates the inner and outer voyage that led us to the Transmissions of Grace. We were taken to India -- not once, but twice, for an immersion into the radical awakenings of enlightenment. This section of the book delivers a living transmission of the energy~consciousness of enlightenment through clear, potent teachings that activate the state of no-self through the de-clutching of the mind. We became aware that we have entered into a new time, an age of exponential grace in which the means to catalyze a worldwide awakening are here.

As highly effective vehicles to enhance divine communion and awareness of the true Self, the Transmissions of Grace form the core of this book. The Transmissions of Grace assist those who are here to be agents of grace to realize and fulfill their soul purpose and destiny. These infusions of energy~consciousness awaken the three primary dimensions of the soul, an essential aspect of realizing the true, eternal Self. By the time you finish reading this book, you will be familiar with the qualities and attributes of each of these facets of your true nature. At the end of each chapter on a transmission, a guided inner experience of calling it in opens the door so that you can begin to work with the particular nature of that transmission and share it with others.

When we receive and integrate the Transmissions of Grace, they immediately begin to flow through us, directly affecting not only our own well-being and that of friends and family, but also the world at large. When it seems that each day brings news of yet another catastrophic mass event, the transmissions offer us a way to express our love, compassion, and sense of oneness with our Earth Mother and our fellow beings the world over. We transcend ancient feelings of helplessness and hopelessness as we activate our ability to serve as divine conduits and literally bless the world with our presence and intention.

As we each seek to make the most significant contribution we can to a world in the process of dying and being reborn, it is important to remember that virtually all personal and planetary crises have one central cause. Living under the trance that we are separate, physical beings, divorced from one other and the planet and the Divine, has brought us to the verge of extinction. Only when we reconnect with our true nature, rooted in the consciousness of unity with each other and all of life, will we be able create the Heaven on Earth we know is possible.

Thus, there is no greater contribution we can make to assist humanity through the crises we face than awakening to the infinitely intelligent, loving and powerful Self that we already are. As we awaken, which can only occur through divine grace, we become able to access ever more profound realms of grace, which then flow through us to bless all we encounter. Coming to know ourselves as sacred aspects of the Infinite One, we become the fountains of grace that will restore this planet to the Garden it was always meant to be.

During every age, awakened ones have come to Earth to lead us beyond the illusion, delusion and confusion of the egoic condition. They have shown us how to discover the wisdom, love, and peace that are our divine birthright. These souls offer living examples of the freedom and unity consciousness available to us all. Until recently, such beings have been relatively few, but now, all across the planet, a mass awakening is underway. Millions -- and perhaps soon, billions of souls in the human experience -- are realizing their true nature as facets of the Divine.

It is time for each of us to step into the roles we were born to play in this collective awakening. Above all, this book is meant to assist you in making your unique contribution as an agent of grace. Nothing could be more important at this critical time on planet Earth. Beneath and beyond the words in this book, *Agents of Grace* carries a living transmission of grace intended to activate the dormant potentials within you. All you need to do is allow it to happen. Enjoy the journey!

And may the words of a Serbian proverb guide your way:
Be humble, for you are made of earth.
Be noble, for you are made of stars.

PART ONE

✛ ✛ ✛

Opening to the
Miracle of Grace

✛ ✛ ✛

1

Grace 101

What is Grace?

We have all experienced the hand of the Divine touching our lives. It might have happened in a small way: We found a $20 bill on the sidewalk, or a stranger broke through our mental storm clouds with a sunny smile. Sometimes we receive a bigger reminder that a larger, beneficent reality holds our little human lives. A vivid dream or a "chance" encounter may offer just the guidance we need. Or an out-of-the-blue windfall -- a *godsend*, as humans accurately call such gifts of grace -- suddenly makes a long-held dream possible to fulfill. During a time when the two of us often felt forlorn and forgotten by Life, we won an all-expenses-paid trip to Mexico. There is nothing like swimming in a placid, azure sea and resting in a hammock beneath swaying palms to lift the spirits! Benevolent surprises like these give us the reassuring feeling that we are being watched over by a powerful, loving presence that only wants to see us thrive.

Moments of grace happen far more frequently than we sometimes realize. Their gifts are often overlooked or quickly forgotten in the busy, onward flow of our lives, especially if we are subconsciously not sure we deserve them. A friend may call, just to say she loves us. During the conversation, she reveals that she felt compelled to get in touch "for some strange reason," with no conscious awareness of what a hard week it's been on our end. We take shared delight in the way grace moved her to offer just what was needed at the perfect time.

At the larger, more profound end of the spectrum, nearly everyone has either experienced or heard stories of divine intervention. If a miracle has not graced our own lives, surely we know of someone who has received an unexpected boon from Beyond. Who doesn't love to recount a miraculous healing, a near-death experience, or a tale of someone saved from bankruptcy by an unforeseen bonanza that arrived just in time? Such stories remind us that we do know what grace is, through our own experience.

In fact, there is never a moment in which grace is not present, and we are aware of its gifts to the degree that we are paying attention. Life is filled with miracles, but we typically only register the ones that challenge our conditioned beliefs about "the way life is." Deeper consideration reveals that grace is inextricably woven into the fabric of existence. It is so omnipresent, so close to us, that we often don't see it, just as we don't usually notice the air we breathe in its optimally invisible state.

What keeps our heart pumping and our lungs breathing through all the years of our lives, though we have nothing to do with making these things happen? Consider the way a human body grows from the union of two cells, as an amazing intelligence creates a myriad of specialized cells, tissues, and organs, organizing and arranging it all into a vast, interwoven system far more complex than anything a human being has ever even attempted to design. This unfathomable intelligence is also central to the way the path of our life rolls out before us. Can any of us look back over our journey and claim that we arrived where we now find ourselves through our own devices? As much as we like to think that we plan and control our destinies, every voyage through life is full of magical twists, turns, and seeming detours that turn out to be blessings in disguise. Each unforeseen rearrangement, every "chance" encounter leads us into the perfect circumstances for the next stage of our soul's evolution, whether we perceive them as such at the time or not.

We can penetrate the depths of the subatomic world or expand out into the infinity of the cosmos, but we will never find a place where the divine hand of grace is not present. The incomprehensible intelligence that infuses All That Is has kept it all functioning from the beginning of the universe eons ago into a future we can never know. At the level of ultimate truth or reality, grace thoroughly permeates what is, has been, and ever shall be.

When grace enters our lives in a way we notice, we usually focus on its outer effects -- the healing, redeeming, and uplifting beneficence grace delivers. But this is not its greatest gift. That takes place in our minds and hearts, as "miracles" of grace change the way we perceive ourselves, life, and God. Each descent of the Divine into our lives presents an opportunity to reconsider the limited beliefs and world view we've osmosed through our conditioning. Like nothing else, miracles demonstrate that the commonly shared rules and laws of everyday existence are not immutable. They reveal the possibility that the seemingly fateful order of things can be transcended. Ultimately, then, moments of grace offer a doorway to awakening and liberation.

When Karen was repeatedly stung by a Portuguese Man of War, as related in *Soul Awakening*, the outcome most people might have expected was ongoing, excruciating pain and substantial scarring of her arms, back, and chest. Recently, we happened upon internet photos of a man's arm after he'd been repeatedly stung by the same type of jellyfish. Days later, lines of red welts crisscrossed his limb like highways of pain. Yet during the immediate aftermath of Karen's experience of being stung, we found that by joining energies to bring awareness to each layer of suffering, and continuously turning the whole experience over to God, the seemingly inevitable course of dis-ease was stopped. Through opening the vertical connection to the Divine and being present to the physical sensations, the thoughts and feelings, and the underlying layers of identity and separation, we witnessed what many might call a miracle as we watched the rows of inflamed, scarlet stings shrink and all but vanish within a half hour. Once the deeper messages hidden within the experience had been delivered, the accompanying pain and suffering no longer needed to persist.

Perhaps the ultimate understanding about grace, the most essential wisdom inherent within its mysteries, is that grace offers the only means by which we will arrive at the world we know is possible. Grace offers everything any of us could ever dream of, more than a billion Christmases could ever bestow. Grace is the cosmic Joker in the card deck of Life that triumphs over all limiting circumstances and situations.

Grace is our Natural State

While Grace may seem miraculous at times, it is actually the normal, natural expression of universal law. The manifestations of the infinite One through its creation are meant to mirror the divine perfection of their Creator. Although visitations of grace can stun us with their remarkable timing and appropriateness, what is really astonishing is how far we've strayed from the grace that is meant to be ours in this human experience. Conflict, war, disease and even death are all distortions of the way life is intended to be. We tend to view these aberrations as "the way things are," but they, not grace, constitute what is truly abnormal.

Grace reminds us of the way life is supposed to be. The true Self is designed to live in peace, love, joy, happiness and abundance; these divine qualities are its natural state. We all intuitively know that life is meant to be a grace-full dance, not the jagged immersion in suffering that so often characterizes the human condition. To maintain such a distorted inversion of the ultimate truth about ourselves takes enormous effort. We expend a tremendous amount of energy to live in separation from what is real and true. Grace, in contrast, feels easy and natural. It requires no effort at all.

What Gets in the Way of Grace?

If grace is our natural state, why does life so often feel less than grace-full? The fact that earthly life is frequently marked by pain and suffering has led more than a few humans to discount the reality of grace altogether. Some have even concluded that the limitless Divine, the ultimate wellspring of all grace, is a mere human fabrication.

When we enter into earthly embodiment, most of us lose touch with our true Self, which is forever rooted in the One Great Being. Instead, we identify with the physical form -- finite, temporal, and vulnerable to injury and death. For virtually all human souls, the resulting amnesia leads us to perceive ourselves as flawed, limited human beings. We forget that our true nature is inherently whole, complete and perfect. This soul-amnesia begets the chaos, conflict, and suffering that fill not only our personal lives, but the world at large.

When we become identified as a limited, human personality, we enter into a trance state that renders us oblivious to our true Self, God and grace. The ego-mind perceives a strange, darkened inversion of the true reality: Instead of experiencing the Divine as omnipresent, it can only see a world of fear, doubt, limitation, disease, and lack. Controlled by the mind, the small self interprets, to at least some degree, everything that crosses its field of awareness through these ubiquitous filters. Even when it is having what it considers to be a good or even great day, the ego-self is capable of experiencing but a fraction of the peace, bliss, joy and truth that characterize an awakened being's existence.

Because the small self perceives life through the dark filters of fear and limitation, its perception is distorted. Thus, its range of possibilities for creative thought and action narrows and its assessments are often off the mark. The ego-mind reacts to danger when there is none, and conversely does not see grace-filled opportunities even when they are in plain sight. Separated from the effortless knowing of the higher mind, the ego-self lacks the insight and guidance that elegantly, impeccably lead us through life.

Although we humans tend to equate mind with a particular form of intellect, in actuality the mind operates at many levels. The profound Buddhist and Hindu understanding that mind constitutes both the perceptual and formative field and the mechanism by which reality is observed and created might be expressed simply as "what we see is what we get." The unconscious images held in the mind continuously project out onto to the infinitely creative life matrix from which reality as we know it forms itself. Quantum physics reminds us there are no passive observers: The very act of perceiving, of being present and aware, directly influences not only what is taking place now but also what happens next.

Few among us have not encountered the blowback from the ego-mind's dark projections. When a painful emotional pattern plays out again and again, we feel as if we are in a continuously repeating bad dream. One mind may wonder *Why is it that just when I get really close to someone there's a blowup and they leave?* Another mind may endlessly reflect on a different dilemma: *No matter how hard I try, why can't I ever get out from under this never-ending financial pressure?* Addictions offer an extreme example of how the ego-mind's subconscious beliefs and motivations can grab control of our lives. Forgetting we are perfectly sacred souls in the human experience, awareness of our innate holiness can give way to utter degradation and shame when the small self takes over.

How Do We Return to Grace?

Whether we suffer from a painful, recurring emotional pattern or an all-out addiction, the doorway to freedom lies in awakening to the need for an entirely different approach to life. The overwhelming success of twelve-step programs is not random happenstance; the steps echo the core premises and practices of time-honored paths to accessing life-changing levels of grace. The first three steps lay out the problem and its remedy with absolute clarity and truth. The first step is the admission of powerlessness over the addiction along with the inability to create a healthy life. The second is the recognition that a higher power is needed to restore one's sanity. The third is the decision to turn one's life over to God.

These three steps summarize the essence of the path of awakening and transformation through grace. When, through the humble admission of powerlessness, a human being living in the trance of separation and Self-forgetting comes to the end of all resources, solutions, effort, trying, and doing, the path of grace begins. This opens the way for an upward ascent of consciousness, and the awareness that conscious re-union with God and higher Self is the answer to the insane condition of the separated mind. Having faced one's condition and recognized the only obvious answer, the last step is the complete surrender of one's entire life to the Divine. These three steps create the inner alignments necessary to disentangle ourselves from the entrapment of the false self sense and return to our native condition through grace.

The path to grace is really the path of awakening, for in an awakened state we live in a state of grace. For a far more in-depth treatment than this brief summary of the essential steps, we suggest consulting our first book, *Soul Awakening: The Journey from Ego to Essence*, which is devoted to the journey of awakening as a path to, and of, grace.

Grace: Our Last, Best Hope?

As human beings living on a planet rife with extinction-level crises caused by our own species, it is only natural to wonder how the ubiquitous dis-ease of the human condition can ever be transformed into an entirely new way of being. Can grace really heal and resurrect not just our species, but a planet that is also severely imbalanced? To answer this question we must delve into the divine play of God, the source of all grace, and recognize its inexorable outcome.

As the Source of everything that exists, all the Infinite wants is to better know itself through the divine play of its Creation. Like a child playing in a sandbox, God is always dreaming up new ways to experience itself. One of its dreams was to find out what would happen if It created a myriad of individualized aspects of itself and then projected these facets into its Creation. This would enable the One to have innumerable experiences simultaneously as It interacted with the created realms through each "finger" of itself. As souls, we are those fingers of the Divine, and exactly like Source Creator, each of us is finding out about life on our own small stage within Creation. We all exist to experience, express, and create in order for the One to realize itself through and as each one of us.

This is where the "fall from grace" becomes part of our planetary story. A group of souls, exercising their divinely given free will, decided to make a very deep plunge into matter by embodying on planet Earth. Whether they were overly enthusiastic in their mission or rebelling against divine will, the result was a new experiment, a dream in which they became hypnotized by sensory experience and forgot their spiritual Source. In short, they came to believe they were separate beings, isolated from their Creator and all other forms of life, most importantly each other. This provided an amazingly potent opportunity to deeply explore matter and Self-forgetting, which in turn allowed the One to have endless new experiences. The prime directive was being fulfilled in a brand new way. So no sin, no bad; we're all aspects of the One exploring incarnation, as innocent as the proverbial children playing in the sandbox.

As we all know, while this choice was freely made, it has also led to no end of pain and suffering. But since the nature of the One is infinitely spacious, allowing and loving, It never forces anything upon us, even a return to the paradise we never really left at the level of our true Selves. We are loved so much by the Prime Creator that It allows even our nightmare dream identity to continue until we voluntarily give it up and ask the One to take control of our lives. When we are willing and ready to die to our limited, human identity, our awareness of the truth is restored and we are reborn into our eternal, infinite estate. In the midst of this individual and collective death and rebirth that is currently unfolding on planet Earth, we find ourselves on the verge of stepping onto the path of grace.

The end of the story was known from the beginning, for God directs the play of Creation and God is All That Is. No matter how thoroughly we may behave as if we are discrete entities, wholly apart from the Divine, we can never can be separate from the One. Even though this particular version of God's play included forgetting our true nature, in the script it is written that in the end, all of us will find our way back to the Divine. God will realize itself through its soul aspects, for this is the entire reason behind Creation. The manifest world is the stage upon which God realizes itself. Just as the sun will surely rise each day, so, too, will the light in the soul of each human being be rediscovered and blaze forth at the end of the great cycle of its human experience.

Now is that time. Vast cycles of creation are coming to a completion. Ancient timekeeping systems including the Mayan calendar, the Vedic cycle of yugas, and the calendar that chronicles eons of planetary transformation in the Great Pyramid testify that we are at the end of a long cycle of spiritual evolution. The One is stirring again within us, as us, reasserting its Self as the foggy haze of our amnesia lifts. It is time to fulfill the divine plan and re-awaken, as the One realizes Itself fully within its Creation.

Within the center of our being lies the essence of our eternal, infinite Source, omnipotent and immutable. Since our divine core contains all the qualities, attributes and capacities inherent within the One, only Self-forgetting can cause a temporary experience of anything other than That. In essence, we are in every way identical to the Source of all that exists, with the same potentials and abilities awaiting our remembrance.

Living in amnesia as nearly seven billion separate selves, we human beings see our dis-eased, separated state mirrored in the rising tsunami of planetary crises, most of which we have directly caused. They are designed to function as the catalysts for us to wake up and realize how lost we are, both personally and collectively. More powerfully than anything else Creation could come up with, our endgame predicaments beckon us to cease our drunken, egoic stumbling and embark upon a planetary twelve-step program.

Just as an addict's life begins to shift the moment s/he admits there is a problem, as we collectively relinquish all that forms and supports our addiction to the illusion of a separate, egoic self sense, the doors will open ever wider for grace to flow in. There is no limit to what becomes possible as we die to illusion and remember what is and always will be the truth. Since the prime movement of Creation dictates that we are destined to reawaken and realize our true nature, it is assured that we will ultimately manifest our divine capacities and qualities. The story of how this will unfold is still to be written. Will it be a dark, melodramatic tragedy or an uplifting tale of grace-filled triumph over suffering and limitation, or some permutation of the two?

That story is ours to write. How many crises and catastrophes will it take for us to collectively admit we are addicted to acting as separate egos -- out of control, powerless over the self, and in need of the grace of divine intervention as our last and only hope?

The good news is that the omnipotent movement of God is for us to awaken. Now, as humanity's long cycle of egoic sleep is coming to a close, ever more of us are beginning to unfold our unlimited nature in as many ways as there are awakening souls. This birth of the divine human is accelerating with each passing day, even as the calamitous predicaments that are catalyzing it proliferate. As we remember the truth of our being, the dis-eased and distorted circumstances on planet Earth, having served their purpose, will inevitably dissipate, replaced by the outpicturing of our innate wholeness and perfection.

Beneath the seeming smallness and insignificance of our daily lives, some part of us senses there is something vitally important for us to do, far beyond anything we have manifested thus far. When we rediscover the spark of the One at our core, we come to know that we are here on Earth at this extraordinary time for an equally extraordinary purpose: to participate in the healing and resurrecting of humanity and our beloved planet. Knowing how significant our part in the divine script would be, we returned to Earth for yet another physical incarnation -- and promptly forgot all about our divine mission, for a time. Now, the chimes of remembrance are either gently ringing or clamoring for our attention, because we are entering the climactic time and circumstances for which we were born.

What is an Agent of Grace?

Even the simplest tasks transmit blessings when the spirit in which they are performed emanates from the heart and soul. A gas station attendant bestows a radiant smile as he cleans the windshield; a checkout clerk spends an extra minute chatting with an elderly customer who, she intuits, may have spoken to no one else that day; a neighbor leaves a bag of apples from the tree in his yard on the front porch next door. We serve Life as agents of grace when we bless one another in even the simplest and humblest of ways. As small and insignificant as they may seem, their powerful, unseen effects change the world from the inside out.

We bless the world and all of its inhabitants when we live from the love that is our true nature. Following the inner promptings of our heart and soul is the way we are designed to live, and since this feels so natural and effortless, we often don't view our expressions as emanations of grace. Not wanting to feed the ego, we may underplay our soulful contributions to the Whole. Yet the fact remains that when we live from the soul, our very presence is a blessing to All. Whenever we express our true, divine nature, the spiritual blessing-grace we bestow raises the vibrational frequency of our surroundings, ultimately divinizing the Earth and all who live upon it.

Since the beginning of time, there have been humans on fire with spirit, desiring nothing but to fully merge with the Beloved. In songs and poems, they have passionately declared their desire to be a vessel through which the Divine could pour Its blessings, a flute for God to play to bring healing, hope, and joy to the world. Such saints and holy beings are so completely available to God that their individual, personal will is subsumed in the greater Work of manifesting the Will of the One. Sometimes their service is humble and anonymous, known to the world only after their passing. Others carry out projects astounding in their scope and dedication. All serve as agents of grace, here to dispense blessings to a suffering humanity.

Although many remarkable beings have delivered profoundly meaningful infusions of grace to the planet and humanity, we don't need to be fully awakened or a saint to function as an agent of grace. Any one of us is capable of being and acting as a conduit of grace, for grace is core to our very nature. The more we live what we love, the more love we bring to this planet. The more we live from the light within, the more light we radiate to all beings. The more we tap into the peace within our core, the more our lives are an expression of that peace. It's as simple as that. Ultimately, as we penetrate the inner sanctum of the soul and tap into the divine presence that is our deepest nature, the more we emanate its infinite, transformative blessing-grace. The same divine presence that enables saints and adepts to perform miracles lives within each of us, beckoning us to return to our Source.

The deeper our state of union with the soul, oversoul and Source levels of being, the more we are in touch with this inexhaustible fountain of all grace. As human beings, we function as conduits for the grace from these higher levels of being to come through us. This is why the only way to deepen our capacity to be an agent of grace is through deepening our communion with our true, divine nature. And only one thing is ever in the way of deeper communion with our true nature: the separate self sense. Thus, an agent of grace is any being whose outer-acting personality is expressing the soul and higher Self, rather than the separated state of the ego-mind. In these moments, we transcend the egoic tendency to live from the little "me" that acts from a self-centered orientation.

Since most of us are in the process of evolving from ego to soul, we constantly segue from one point to another along the ego-soul continuum. At one end lies the purely selfish act; at the other, selfless, saintly behavior. Living somewhere in the middle range of the continuum, we may occasionally dip into doing things for our own gain, and rise at times to be a pure conduit for the Divine to act through.

As conscious communion with our vast, divine nature deepens, the desire to relieve suffering and assist all beings to awaken grows. When the ego's obsession with aggrandizing the small self falls away, we are no longer as focused on what we can *get* from every situation. Now, we look for what we can *give*. We want nothing more than to see all beings lifted out of separation and suffering into their exalted state of grace.

This burning inner fire of vision and desire to serve at the highest level of possibility is the voice of the soul breaking through the limits of the personality, allowing us to claim our divine inheritance as aspects of God/One/All That Is. That "still small voice" propels us on the inner journey through all the passages of ego-death necessary to come home to who we truly are. We leave the broad way of the world to seek the narrow path back to God, surrendering ourselves more and more fully, dying again and again so that "not my will, but thy will be done" through me. This is what it means to become an agent of grace.

Spiritual traditions emphasize that it is not what we do, but how we do it -- and more importantly, where the impulse arises within us -- that really matters. In this light, no task is too small to be used as an opportunity to dispense grace. Nor is the seeming scope of the service necessarily an indication of its stature in the eyes of God, or of its impact on the Whole. While one person resentfully sweeps the floor, sure that a greater destiny would be hers to fulfill if only she had been able to get a college degree, another lovingly brushes away the dirt and debris from her kitchen, happy that Life gave her a room to cook in and a broom to sweep it with. Through her humble action, the luminous radiance of her soul streams outward, blessing all beings near and far. Mother Teresa embodied this ideal in her often-repeated remark that as she washed and fed the homeless, dying people of Calcutta, she was giving comfort to Jesus in all his distressing disguises. Seeing the world through the eyes of her true nature, all were uplifted and awakened by her love and light.

EXPERIENCE: How Have You Served as an Agent of Grace?

Put this book aside for a few minutes and invite your eyes to close. Now, become aware of your breathing. Feel the sensations of the breath as it comes in and goes back out through the nostrils. Invite your awareness to travel into your inner world.

Invite the breath to carry your awareness into the soul center above the heart. Feel the unique frequencies of your core essence, the individuated expression of the Divine in you. Become conscious of the you that is far more than the body-self -- the you that is often called the soul, the true, eternal Self. Rest in the Self and enjoy the feeling of being at Home within yourself once again.

Agents of Grace

Ask the soul to take you back through your life and show you some ways in which you have already served as an agent of grace. You may be shown images, or even movies, of times when you were a vessel the Divine utilized to benefit other beings. Some may be as simple as cooking a meal for a friend, while others have far more significance. You might even have been given an opportunity to serve as an agent of grace in a profound way.

Begin with the first situation that presents itself, and go on to the next as it is revealed by the soul. Allow the process to continue for as long as the soul determines. Savor each experience, seeing yourself through the eyes of the true Self. Notice the sensations and feelings that are present as you witness times in your life when you were a conduit for the Divine.

When the experience feels complete for now, rest quietly for a time to allow all that you have seen and felt to come into a new level of integration within you. Honor the ways the Divine has come through you to bless the world and those who live within it. Know that you can return to the soul space at any time to be shown more about how you have functioned as a conduit of grace.

Feel your gratitude for being able to serve in these ways. And if you like, invite the One to move through you in new, more expanded and powerful ways, so that you can more fully manifest your soul purpose and destiny.

As you feel ready, allow your eyes to gently open. You might like to record your experiences in a journal or share them with a loved one. As you honor the ways the Divine has poured through you, the realm of possibilities opens wider for more experiences of being a conduit of grace to occur.

2

The Keys to Accessing Grace

Deepening Soul Communion

Because a foundation in the soul is central to serving as a conduit of grace, this chapter briefly recapitulates what we have learned about consciously connecting with the soul, oversoul and Source levels of being. Our first book, *Soul Awakening,* is dedicated to catalyzing the journey of awakening from the amnesia of identifying with the separate ego~personality into awareness of and communion with our true nature as souls. We suggest returning to the Reflections that conclude most of the chapters in *Soul Awakening* for a concise review of the many stages and phases of awakening to the soul.

Awakening to the soul and accessing grace are inextricably linked, for the same energy~consciousness processes that open awareness to the multidimensional Self enable us to access the limitless, divine fountain of grace. Realizing our oneness with God, we simultaneously discover the infinite grace that is the very nature of the all-inclusive, causal realms of perfection. The distortion and imperfection so ubiquitous at the human level result from a breach in energy~consciousness between the higher-dimensional realms of the Infinite and the physical plane. Grace flows into our experience through the restoration of the unity between the divine, transcendental domains and our third-dimensional embodiment.

Most of us, though, have never been taught how to go about restoring this unity; we need more than lofty abstractions to find our way back to the true Self. More than two decades ago, the two of us learned firsthand that it is possible to cultivate direct experience of the unity that is our true nature -- to feel that oneness as a living reality, not just a nice-sounding concept. Yet while we can do many things to prepare the fertile inner ground, we really have no control over how or when we awaken; it occurs through descents of grace. From its omniscient, omnipotent perspective, the Infinite Mind of the Divine knows exactly what is needed to remove the unconscious veils that prevent us from realizing the truth of our existence.

To try to awaken ourselves tends to engage the ego, the aspect of being most defended against awakening. It is only the separate ego self sense that believes it is asleep and is invested in continuing in this illusion and amnesia. Resorting to personal, human efforts to awaken is like turning to the prison warden for assistance in planning an escape. During soul-awakening sessions, this reality was brought home again and again. When clients arrived with predetermined ideas of what should happen, or when their or our minds tried to direct their inner journeys, nothing much happened. But when we all turned the session over to a higher power, grace flowed in to accomplish what we were incapable of bringing about on our own. Learning how to access grace for awakening became our focus in facilitating direct experiences of the soul.

As people awakened through aligning with grace, their communion with the transpersonal Source of all grace deepened. Ever more grace flowed into and through them, further accelerating their awakening and spilling over to bless those ready to receive it. Not only do we awaken through grace -- as we awaken to our oneness with its Source, grace fills us to overflowing.

The Three Inner Alignments

In soul-awakening sessions, infusions of grace seemed to occur most frequently when certain inner alignments were present. These coherencies in consciousness appeared to function as divine access codes that opened the doors to the descent of grace. They circumvented the veils and impediments of egoic consciousness, allowing the light of the soul and beyond to be revealed.

The first of these inner alignments is **sincerity**. Those who experienced powerful awakenings typically held coming home to their soul as the most important consecration in their lives. They realized their suffering had a single fundamental cause: separation from God and their true nature, which are, of course, one and the same. Having looked without for the joy, happiness, peace and fulfillment they knew was possible, they had finally recognized that these divine qualities can only be found within. The Divine holds each of us in such unconditional love that It allows us to continue in the illusion of separation until we un-make the decision to live cut off from our Source. When we sincerely want God more than anything else, the Divine can once again take its place at the core of our experience.

The second inner alignment is the **humility** of realizing we cannot make it on our own; we need assistance from Beyond. Humility requires us to admit that our little, human selves do not have all the answers. This opens the way for larger levels of being to pour in the assistance we need. When we confess just how frustrated, powerless and hopeless we feel in the face of our challenges, we become willing to ask for divine help, and open to receive it.

The presence of sincere, heartfelt humility enables us to turn our lives over to God. The infinitely loving and powerful intelligence of our vaster nature can then take control and lead us home to our sacred core. If we knew how to get there on our own, we would already be experiencing awakened illumination as our permanent state. The Divine alone can bring that about, for Infinite Intelligence knows everything about us. Its omniscient, overlighting perspective reveals the inner resistances and wounds we must face as part of our unique process of awakening. Only such limitless wisdom can possibly know the most elegant, efficient ways to open and realign the inner channels so that grace can infuse our being with divine presence.

Desire is the third inner alignment that opens the doors to the soul and beyond. When we passionately desire nothing more than to awaken, our entire being opens to the Divine to receive the grace that awakens. Desire functions as an attractive matrix that magnetizes spirit to whatever we want most. When desire and consecration unify, awakening is expedited. Our consecration is the sacred focus of our intention, while desire is the fuel that propels that intention upward into the divine domains.

The key alignments of sincerity, humility and desire not only help us to awaken to our true nature, they also enable us to function as conduits of grace. Consciousness made coherent through these three inner alignments opens us wide to the flow of God's grace, energizing the prayers and requests for assistance we call forth for others.

Merging with the Inner Source of Grace

Most people find it easiest to access their divine core by bringing awareness to the center of the chest, just above the physical heart and the heart chakra. This sacred domain has been called the soul center, the Soul Lotus, the heart of hearts, and the Cave of the Heart. This is where the presence of God, individualized as our true Self, resides.

The journey of Self-realization centers on merging consciousness with the divine presence within the Soul Lotus. As our awareness rests more fully within our core divinity, the Soul Lotus blossoms, and the subtle perfume of the indwelling divine presence is released into all the subtle bodies and chakras. As this occurs, an alchemical process transforms the human self into a divine Self. Divine presence suffuses our being, eventually filling it to overflowing and streaming out to catalyze healing and awakening in others.

We serve most effectively as a conduit of grace when we first consciously connect with the fountain of grace within. Bringing awareness to the sacred space in the center of the chest is the key. For most of us, the soul center in the chest is a place that is quite familiar. When something touches or moves us, or when we receive distressing news, a hand often spontaneously rises to cover this sensitive area. During times of great joy, we may feel this part of us bursting with energy. In many spiritual traditions, as people prepare to pray their hands join, fingertips pointing heavenward, over this innermost center of their being.

One of the simplest, most effective ways to deepen soul communion is to regularly bring awareness to this area in the center of the chest and meditate on or contemplate whatever is present there. Breathing and feeling while awareness gently rests at the altar of our being "waters" the Soul Lotus, causing it to begin to unfurl. The conscious breathing and the focus of attention provide a flow of subtle energy that vibrates this area open.

While directing awareness to the inner sanctum of the soul, it can be helpful to consider each of the three inner alignments. Feeling the sincere yearning to deepen into the Divine within, we send a message to our true nature that we want it to come forth. When we humbly surrender, allowing the Self to guide our awakening, we give it the authority to take over. The desire or passion for our most beloved, true Self is the magnetic energy that draws our sacred essence into our conscious experience.

The energy~consciousness of our essential nature, the presence of God residing in the core of the soul, has a particular quality of feeling that is unmistakable once we have experienced it. Just as joy and sadness possess unique energetic qualities that we instantly recognize when we feel them, our divine essence has a feeling-tone that immediately lets us know we are in communion with it. We call this inner feeling **soul signature**. The homing beacon of soul signature calls us back to the true Self and leads us into progressively deeper levels of divine union.

As the Soul Lotus opens, a palpable shift occurs in the field of energy~consciousness in which our being resides. It becomes clear that we have tapped into the most potent and profound transformative force that it is possible for us to access. Bathed in soul frequencies, we receive the direct knowing that our true nature includes everything we could ever want and more. Throughout the ages, a central inner practice of contemplatives, mystics and saints has been to commune with this numinous essence. Basking in divine presence naturally occurs with ever greater frequency as we repeatedly journey into the soul realms. A client described her practice of inner communion as "toasting," while many in the Christian community refer to their immersions in divine absorption as "soaking."

Deepening communion with the soul's essential divinity is core to the process of realizing our luminous nature. This is how the individualized aspect of God that we each are is birthed into full embodiment. An alchemical transmutation guided by the infinitely loving intelligence of the Supreme One raises, resurrects, and illumines mental, emotional, physical and spiritual levels of being into a holy, pure and perfect expression of God. This process transmutes all that we thought we were into all that we are ultimately meant to be. The more we merge with the Soul Lotus and let its energy~consciousness flow through us, the more its unlimited grace uplifts everyone and everything that is open to receive its healing, wholing, and illumining radiance.

The following simple process facilitates deepening communion with the soul. More than a guided meditation, it provides an induction into the energy and consciousness of the true Self. Sincerely, humbly working with this induction over time will increase awareness of the indwelling divine presence. As awareness deepens in the soul, the Soul Lotus gradually vibrates open, releasing its grace-filled "perfume" into all aspects of our lives.

EXPERIENCE~ACTIVATION: Consciously Connecting with the Soul

Invite your body to relax into a comfortable position, either sitting or lying down. Become aware of your breath. Feel the sensations of the breath as it moves in and out of your body, breath by breath. Notice all the subtle feelings as each breath moves through your nostrils and down into your chest.

17

Invite the breath into the soul center just above your heart. You might like to place a hand over this area as you breathe and feel whatever is present here. Become minutely aware of all the subtle sensations moving in and around the breath. Notice any thoughts and feelings that are surfacing. As you continue to breathe and feel, simply allow them to be present, neither going into them nor rejecting them. Rest in the breath at the altar of your being and look beneath the surface level of feelings and thoughts into the quiet, peaceful depths below them.

As your awareness rests within, feel how much you want to experience a deeper communion with the Divine at the core of your being. Ask it to reveal itself to you, to make its presence known. It may manifest as a deep peace, or love, or a quiet emptiness. You may sense a divine presence deep within that tells you this is who you really are.

The soul may also come forth visually, appearing as light. You may see a flame, a golden star, or another form of luminous presence. A sense of excitation, joy, bliss, or a high frequency of pure energy may also be present. You may see a symbol or image, or hear a voice or a sound that is clearly of the soul.

However it presents itself, simply experience the soul in whatever ways it manifests. Feel its radiance. Notice all the subtle sensations and emanations that are present. Realize that this is who and what you truly are -- the flame of the One, a holy, pure, and perfect aspect of God.

Allow yourself to dissolve into this indwelling presence. Merge with it and become one with its essence, for this is who you really are. Allow all sense of a separate "me" to melt away. Feel the presence surround and engulf you, dissolving away anything unlike itself. Rest in this unity for as long as you like.

When this feels complete for now, let your awareness slowly emerge from your sacred core. Gently reconnect with the physical plane of existence. Allow whatever time is necessary to fully come back into the body and feel totally grounded. You may want to rest for some time, or to move around slowly and allow the expanded state of energy and consciousness to integrate.

Know that the true, essential Self is always but a breath away. You can return to your sacred inner sanctum whenever you like.

You may choose to work with this induction over time using our *Conscious Soul Communion* CD. The Resources section at the back of this book details how to order it.

Connecting with the Oversoul and Source

The second major stage in the journey of awakening and opening to greater levels of grace begins as we become aware that the soul rests within a larger beingness. As souls reawakening to our transcendental nature, we remember that we are not confined to the physical realm of existence, after all. We may be gifted with spontaneous experiences of the vast, numinous realms, meet higher-dimensional guides and teachers, and in other ways reconnect with our limitlessness.

As individuated soul consciousness awakens to its larger Home, awareness naturally turns skyward, feeling a vertical pull toward the higher levels. Seeking sustenance from their heavenly Source, human beings instinctively raise their eyes to the realms above. Throughout the centuries, sacred art has depicted penitents praying with heads and eyes turned upward; their hands, too, may be lifted toward the heavens in supplication.

Many people experience heavenly communion through a strong, heart-and-soul connection with a particular form of divinity, whether it is termed God, Krishna, Creator, Buddha, Allah, Source, higher Self, Divine Mother, Christ, or any other name for the Divine. Whichever form of being evokes the strongest inner response and activates your personal connection with ultimate divinity is the aspect of the One for you. The love and devotion we feel for the Divine form the conduit between the higher realms and the soul. This connection is also greatly enhanced via the intermediation and assistance of whatever form of deity attracts us. This devotional approach or bhakti path is a very powerful way to open the connection to the oversoul realms and beyond. Nothing more then fiery love and heartfelt passion are necessary.

Communion with the higher aspects of our being is also enhanced through an awareness of the energy~consciousness circuitry of our multidimensional subtle anatomy. There is a structural, subtle anatomical reason why we humans look above for our ultimate spiritual sustenance. The human subtle anatomy, consisting of the seven primary chakras and subtle bodies, is united by a vertical conduit that is often called the central channel. It runs through the central axis of the subtle body/chakra system, right in front of the spine, linking us both upward and downward to vaster realms of being. Energy~consciousness continuously flows through this channel in both directions. The upward vector connects us with the transcendental or superconscious realms, the abode of the higher Self or oversoul, and beyond that the Source of All That Is. All the information and programming for every aspect of our embodied being flows from these levels. Essentially, our earthly manifestation results from the holographic projection of our soul's being as an extension of the oversoul and Source.

The central channel also proceeds down through the lower chakras and the Earth Star chakra just below the feet into the dark, subconscious realms of the divine feminine. As the higher light descends from oversoul and Source into and through our seven bodies and chakras, it merges with the dark feminine matrix, which gives birth to and makes manifest the higher levels of being. The dark light or shakti provides the substance through which the energy~consciousness from the oversoul and Source come into form. This marriage of the light and dark, yin and yang, spirit and matter forms the basis for the soul's existence.

The same inner alignments of sincerity, humility and desire that catalyze the personality's awareness of the soul are equally effective in opening the central channel upward to enhance communion with the oversoul and Source. The sincere intention to connect with the transcendental levels of being ignites conscious communion between the soul and the higher Self and Source. A heartfelt desire to consciously reunite with the vast Self we never really left provides the magnetic power of attraction that invites the Divine to descend into conscious awareness. Humility disengages the resistance of the ego, allowing the intelligence, will, and power of the higher Self and Source to take over the process of establishing and deepening communion. Love, the basis for all devotional paths, opens the inner channel as it dissolves the illusory veils of separation.

We can also help the central channel to open by utilizing our inner, higher perception. Some people easily become aware of this passageway by asking their soul to reveal it to them. It is also very effective to visualize the central channel as a conduit a few inches in diameter that runs through the center of the body just in front of the spine, with the focal point at the heart soul center, proceeding both upward and downward beyond the head and the feet. Awareness can then travel all the way up and all the way down the central channel with the intention of opening and expanding it.

The central channel functions as an energetic telephone line that directly connects us to the higher realms. When we sincerely, humbly "make a call" through that channel, the Divine responds. The most important communication is letting the higher levels of being know we would like to consciously connect with them, and asking that they make their presence known through our higher sensory perception. The degree to which we are able to consciously connect with the higher levels of being determines the amount and strength of spiritual current that can flow down through the central channel into the soul. Deepening conscious communion with the higher Self, other divine beings and the Godhead also progressively opens the inner circuitry. Divinizing, illumining, grace-filled energies then flow into and through us in ever-greater torrents, accelerating our awakening and increasing our capacities as agents of grace.

The higher we go, the greater the power and illumination we access. We might imagine the transformative power of the personality self to be 1 watt, and that of the soul, 1000 watts. The might of the oversoul might be equivalent to a million watts, while the potency of the I AM Presence and Source levels is infinite. Accordingly, if we are to become super-effective agents of grace, the importance of consciously reconnecting with these levels is self-evident.

A caveat needs to be mentioned here: To process the ever-increasing power and illumination that pours down as consciousness ascends into the higher realms, the subtle anatomy needs to be open and clear. To the degree that the seven chakras and subtle bodies carry distorted, separation-based energetic imprints, the current will encounter resistance to being grounded in and through us. When a big burst of higher illumination occurs, before long that light typically goes to work cleansing and purifying the inner circuits. That process forms an essential part of both the journey of awakening and that of becoming a conduit of grace. The greater the current, the more purity and openness are required to cleanly transduce it into the physical plane.

When we call upon the higher energies to descend to assist others, they also pass through our own energetic anatomy. This accelerates the purification process already underway. Fortunately, our carefully cultivated connection with these expanded levels of grace allows us to access the love, wisdom, and power required to resolve our own unfinished business. And every bit of purifying serves our central goal: to realize our true nature. There may be no faster way to evolve than through consciously accessing and communing with these vast levels of grace, not only for our own transformation and awakening but on behalf of others as well.

The inner process that follows facilitates connecting with the higher-dimensional levels of the Self. The soul-connecting process above and the guided inner journey below provide practical technologies of grace to facilitate awakening into your role as an agent of grace. You may find yourself working with the soul-connecting induction for a time before you feel prompted to expand into the higher realms. As in all things, let your inner knowing be your guide. If now is not that time, simply skip the guided inner experience that follows and go on the next section.

The process below picks up where the soul-connecting process ends, and assumes that you have made a conscious connection with the soul. If you do not feel strongly established in this connection with your inner divinity, we suggest working with the previous process a while longer. Setting aside time each morning or evening to go within and commune with your sacred core invites awareness to rest more deeply there over time.

EXPERIENCE~ACTIVATION: Connecting with the Oversoul and Source

Begin by utilizing the soul-connecting process above until you have merged with your divine core and can easily access a sense of soul-communion whenever you like. Ask the soul whether it is time to connect with the oversoul and Source levels of being. If the answer is a clear "Yes," continue. If not, continue to utilize the soul-connecting process, inviting awareness of the Divine within to deepen.

Feel how much you want to be consciously connected with the higher levels of being and the Source from which you emerged. Feel your desire to deepen the communion with your vastness. This is the path of transcending all human suffering and limitation, the path to fully birthing your true, luminous Self.

Remember that this is not something you can do. It is about total surrender to the vaster levels of being. They know exactly how your journey into full reunion should proceed, for they are the source of the blessings we access as agents of grace.

Ask now to be taken through this journey, guided by the oversoul and Source levels of your being. The process we share here is but a possible template for this inner voyage. Any time you feel guided to go in another direction, simply surrender and follow wherever the path leads.

Let your eyes close as your body finds a comfortable position it can maintain for a while. Invite the breath to carry your awareness into the inner sanctum of the soul in the center of the chest. Breathe and feel the unique frequencies that tell you that you are Home.

As you rest in the soul space, become aware of a flow of energy that proceeds vertically both upward beyond the body and downward into the core of the Earth. Before inviting in higher energies, it is important to be well-grounded. This allows the incoming energies to deeply integrate and prevents any energetic imbalance caused by ungrounded spiritual energies in the aura. From the soul center above the heart, feel the passageway that opens downward through the center of the body. Allow your consciousness to descend through the lower chakras, continuing until you exit the auric field just beneath the feet. Gently continue down into the dark, magnetic realms of Mother Earth until you come to rest in her core. Feel the strong anchoring her sacred womb provides. Rest here as long as you like.

Now, invite your awareness to gently travel back up, carrying the dark, attractive, magnetic energies with you. Continue up through the Earth, reentering the auric field below the feet. As your awareness encounters the base or root chakra, feel your strong grounding through the central channel into the core of the Earth. You may want to visualize a magnetic cord stretching from the base chakra downward, firmly, continuously attached to the Earth's core. When that feels sturdy and solid, let your awareness rise back to the heart soul center and rest there for a few moments, enjoying the sensations of being thoroughly supported from below.

Next, become aware of the central column's upward vector, from your heart soul center through your neck and head, exiting through the crown chakra at the top of your head. Ask the crown chakra to open and sense the central channel continuing upward. Allow your awareness to follow the central channel up into the higher-dimensional realms where your higher Self or oversoul resides. Invite this vaster level of being to reveal itself through inner feelings or images. Continue to commune with these realms above the head, simply experiencing whatever arises in consciousness. Allow plenty of time for this part of your journey.

When this feels complete, turn your awareness upward again to a point somewhere between fifteen and fifty feet above your head. Ask Source or your I AM Presence to come into your conscious awareness, sending your heartfelt desire up the central channel with the request. Continue to project your awareness upward until you sense a presence above you.

Feel the power and magnificence of the I AM Presence and Source. You may sense limitless luminosity and expansiveness. Allow your subtle senses to open to whatever ways this vastness wants to come into your experience. Commune as long as you like with your ultimate Home.

When this feels complete for now, allow the focus of awareness to gently travel back down the central channel, through the top of the head and into the body, coming to rest in the soul center just above the heart. As this occurs, continue to feel the connection through the vertical channel into the vast realms of being above.

You may still feel or sense the oversoul and Source aspects of your being. Rest in the heart of the soul and commune with them as long as you like. Invite all the energy that has descended into your body to gently radiate through the physical form and out into your energy fields.

Allow whatever time is necessary for the higher energies to ground and balance within your being. It may be helpful to feel your connection down the vertical axis into the center of the Earth. Invite any excess energies to flow down and ground into the planet's core. When you feel balanced and grounded, invite your awareness to return to normal waking consciousness.

Communion with the vast levels of Self may occur quickly or unfold over time through many inner adventures. Trust that it will happen in its own perfect way and timing, and continue to periodically work with the oversoul/Source connecting process as you feel guided. Once a conscious connection with the higher realms has taken place, the circuits are open. To stabilize and strengthen the connection to our vastness, it helps to regularly devote time to communing with the oversoul and Source.

3

Becoming a Conscious
Agent of Grace

Consecrating our Lives

The first act in stepping into our roles as agents of grace is to wholeheartedly embrace that this is what we are here for; being a conduit of grace is core to our soul purpose and destiny. This is a very big step, spiritually, for it aligns us with God's will for our lives. There isn't any more powerful way to uplevel the spiritual power that comes through us than to unite our human will with the will of the Source of all power.

Consecration is affirming that the will of God, the soul and the personal self are unified and aligned. Even though we might know that serving the Divine is what we are here for, the actual process of consecration is powerful and important. It is the spiritual act in which we align all levels of our being to fulfill our highest calling. It's a commitment to ourselves, God, and our fellow beings. This act closes the door to many distractions and cul-de-sacs to which we might otherwise give energy. The resulting energetic integrity allows the fullness of our soul to come forth in what it is really here for.

Consecrating our lives to serving as an agent of grace occurs progressively over time, as we face and transcend all that prevents us from stepping forth in this new way. Many of us find it hard to believe we could be worthy or capable of serving God as a conduit of divine grace. Self-doubt may present the single largest impediment to fully stepping into the purposes that bought us back to Earth for yet another incarnation. Unresolved trauma and shadow issues lie at the root of the unconscious unworthiness, guilt, shame and fear that prevent us from fully embracing our destiny path. We go beyond these limitations as we realize two things. The first is that we, as ego-personalities, don't do anything -- God does what is needed through us. That takes the issue of our capabilities right out of the picture. The second is that the heartfelt desire to serve as an agent of grace is the voice of our soul, which is the Divine speaking through and as our true being. We aren't the ones who determine whether we are qualified for the job. God does the choosing, and already knows everything about us. If we feel called to step forward as agents of grace, it's because the Divine is prompting us to do so.

We can embrace our doubt and fear and simply step into our role despite it all, for in truth, none of it has any ultimate basis. The only power it has is that which we give it through believing the voices of the mind. Through the eyes of the Divine, we are seen as we really are: holy, pure and perfect. The personality flaws and distortions we believe are real are nothing but temporal realities with no basis in ultimate truth. We can acknowledge they are there while simultaneously denying that they have any absolute truth or power. Eventually, they will be faced, embraced and brought back into the light, for this, too, is part of the path of being an agent of grace. The very process of reabsorbing these distorted ego~personality aspects into our wholeness contributes to planetary awakening. Each time the light flushes out another shadow so that it can be surrendered to the Divine, more illumination infuses not only our own subconscious but also the collective unconscious. This lightens the load for everyone, making the journey easier for all who follow.

Many of us hold subconscious fears of allowing powerful spiritual energies to come through us. We may worry we will misuse the power, as we may have done in another lifetime, or as we have witnessed others doing. However, two safeguards prevent this from happening. First, the energies of grace don't flow strongly unless we are in a humble, surrendered heart-space. To the degree that we are identified with the ego, the level of being that may be tempted to misuse power, we are disconnected from the soul and beyond, which means the channels of grace are closed down. If not much spiritual power is flowing through us, there is less danger if we express it inappropriately. Second, we can choose to turn the fear of misusing spiritual power into an even firmer intention to surrender into the Divine and stop letting the ego get in the way. A strong focus on keeping the ego in check and letting God do the work and take the credit may be our strongest safeguard against this potential pothole on the path.

Inviting potent spiritual energies to act through us, we may fear being overwhelmed and losing control of our life. We may believe that if we open to higher energies, we will have to give up important, enjoyable aspects of our life pattern, or leave behind those we love. Most of us also operate within an "upper limit syndrome" that affects the amount of joy, happiness and fulfillment we allow ourselves to have, based on how worthy of having it we judge ourselves to be. If, like most human beings, we subconsciously hold residues of self-judgment and unworthiness, these impediments to serving as a conduit of grace will no doubt rise to the surface at some point.

Stepping into being agents of grace can make us aware of all the ways we still use the world's values and criteria as points of reference. This tendency takes us away from our soul's knowing, substituting what our culture deems important for the Self's truth about how best to consecrate our precious life energy. Nearly every achievement the world values has an egoistic basis. The ego-self wants to know things like *Will I receive acclaim for this -- will I be noticed by others? Will this support me financially?* and *Will it boost my sense of self worth?* Meeting the world's criteria for success typically involves doing and becoming more, not less. In contrast, as conduits of grace, we do virtually nothing except offer ourselves as vessels through which the Divine can act. We are largely referencing from beyond this world, working in and from the higher-dimensional realms that are still off the radar for most human beings. Becoming an agent of grace is not about building ego, but about wholly surrendering it to God.

If you encounter fear, conflict or resistance to consecrating your life to what you know you are here for, we suggest taking time to go inside, connect with your soul and ask Infinite Intelligence to show you what is in the way. It will gently, lovingly bring the limiting beliefs causing the conflict to the surface. Seeing them will immediately begin to defuse their power. You might then ask for grace to pour down to dissolve all impediments to stepping fully into your soul purpose and destiny, and expedite the process of doing so.

When examined, not one subconscious belief that bad things will happen to us if we turn our lives over to divine service turns out to be true. In fact, we discover that the opposite is the case. When we consecrate our existence to awakening and allowing Source to pour blessing-grace through us to all of life, the joy of fulfillment is beyond anything we previously knew was possible. Nothing can compare to knowing that the highest level of assistance has been rendered. What else would we want to do with our lives? Any fears that we will suffer loss dissolve as we realize all of our true needs are met when we surrender to serving God's will alone.

As egoic impediments fall away through bringing awareness to them, our consecration to serving as an agent of grace deepens. The rest unfolds on its own, guided by the Divine. The stress associated with "making life happen" disappears. We find ourselves in an actively passive state in which everything we "do" arises from a place of stillness and surrender. When there is nothing to conflict with or oppose it, the movement of divine will is effortless. It encompasses all earthly, human issues and considerations from the most inclusive perspective. No error is possible.

The personal ego is subordinated as it is refashioned into a vessel for God to fill. This is an enormous soul gift, for it greatly accelerates the journey into divine union. It is as though a hand reaches down from above and progressively takes ever firmer control over our lives, lovingly asking us to surrender more deeply into its dominion. In the process, we are more firmly placed on the path of surrender and service, which is also the path Home.

The job description for this service is really quite simple. The first step is to live from the soul, with the goal of increasingly experiencing and responding to everyone and everything from our sacred core. Living from the soul, we automatically step onto the path of fulfilling our purpose, for our very state embodies the essence of grace. The deeper our realization of Self, the greater the grace that naturally wants to pour out to the world through us. The immense love and compassion that fill our awareness impel us to want to be of assistance.

When awareness rests in conscious communion with our inner divinity, there is never a time when we aren't fulfilling our function, even when we are sleeping or working through unresolved psycho-emotional material. During the moments we devote to inner contemplation and communion, the power of our contribution increases. When we meditate while feeling our oneness with the Earth and our human family, immense grace is being transmitted through us to the Whole.

The linear mind tends to devalue contributions that do not involve a concrete, physical interaction with our fellow beings or the planet herself. Yet for centuries yogis, ascetics, and mystics, sequestered away from the world, have made enormous contributions to human evolution, often while few even knew they existed. Remembering this helps us to acknowledge the significant service we render while we sit on our meditation cushions. Devoting sacred time to divine communion forms the cornerstone of our service as conduits of grace.

For years, the two of us have often ended our morning meditations by giving our entire day over to God, asking to be guided every step of the way so that we might awaken and fulfill our purpose. *May I be a blessing to all I encounter today* has become a favorite prayer. Taking a moment to consecrate the day aligns our energies before we go out into the world. It also increases our awareness of specific opportunities to bring light into situations and function as a conduit of grace as they arise throughout the day.

Responding to Opportunities to Serve

The beautiful thing about the path of grace is that we don't have to go looking for opportunities to serve. When we make ourselves available to Life, possibilities for service are magnetically attracted to us and simply appear in the flow of our lives. We are purposefully taken into circumstances in which the Divine wants to work through us. Our ever-deepening surrender invites God to show us what needs to happen in each situation.

Often, we are alerted to a potential opportunity to serve when we experience a lack of ease, peace, oneness, and love in the energetic climate of our experience. But encountering a situation of inharmony is not necessarily a signal to spring into action. It's important to check within before proceeding. For example, watching someone we love succumb to an addiction arouses our desire to serve as a catalyst for change. But an inner knowing may also indicate the person isn't ready to shift yet. Sometimes things have to get worse before they can get better; the person may need to bring awareness to what drives the pattern of addiction before it can transform. When guidance indicates our outer involvement would not be helpful, such situations ask for our peaceful acceptance. We can focus on the inner work of calling forth the highest outcome in the situation, feeling our love for all involved and surrounding the entire matter with that love, knowing love is the ultimate catalyst for healing and awakening.

In another situation, we may sense that this is not the way life was meant to be, and that another possibility is wanting to come forth. Now, we can ask for guidance about whether the matter "has our name on it." Bringing our awareness into the soul space above the heart, we can ask, *Is there something I'm to offer here?*

In response to this question, either a clear *YES* or a definite *NO* will arise in our heart and soul. If the response is not yet clear, we learn to wait for a sense of certainty before acting. Even the best of intentions to want to relieve suffering or add something beneficial to Life may not be the in the highest, seen from the superconscious levels of mind the soul can access.

We've found it is never the part of wisdom to respond to a situation when we've been emotionally triggered and are in a state of reaction. Accessing clear guidance becomes unlikely when the emotional body is flustered. During these moments, the ego often steps to the fore, full of ideas about what needs to happen. Its assessments and strategies, along with its emphasis on the need for urgent action, can sound utterly convincing, and to the degree that we are still ego-identified, we may find ourselves rushing in to implement a seeming solution to pressing outer events. But the ego's perspective is only part of the story, and if we respond based on it alone, we will likely find our actions only add to the problem. The ego-mind is not connected to the overlighting wisdom of the soul and oversoul. It lacks the unified consciousness that can tap into Infinite Intelligence.

Once again, the most useful thing we can do is stop all outer action and go within. Breathing and feeling the sensations and feelings that are present will allow them to empty out so we can reconnect with the soul. As awareness comes to rest within the sacred space at our core, we can turn the situation over to the Divine and ask for help. Until the inner psychic waters are clear and the connection to soul and Source is reestablished, no outer activity, no matter how clever or even wise it may seem, will provide real assistance.

Becoming a truly effective conduit of grace relies on our capacity to be an empty vessel through which the Divine can move. In this space in consciousness, we no longer believe that we, on our own, have the solutions to life's dilemmas. Living in the Mystery, we are never sure what we might be prompted to do or say next. We quietly, humbly wait for our heart and soul to convey the inner *YES* that impels us to take the next steps in the ways we are guided. Receiving this inner "green light" lets us know it is time to move forward. Until it comes, we wait.

The emptier we become, the more the Divine entrusts us with, and the more potent the energy that can be poured through us. When our inner channels are at least relatively unobscured by mental and emotional overlays, higher-frequency energies can easily pass through the clear, coherent inner passageways. This emptying in order to be filled is the opposite of what the world teaches us to focus on. But as agents of grace, we learn that the less we become, the more we are in God's eyes.

This is the true "hero's journey," for as we empty ourselves of all illusions that we can do anything on our own, Life can act through us to benefit the Whole. As the greatest miracle-worker of all time, Jesus the Christ, expressed this, "Of mine own self I can do nothing. The Father in me does all." Utterly no ego remained to take credit for even the slightest act that occurred through his human self.

Bridges of Grace Between Heaven and Earth

As embodied aspects of the Divine, we serve as transduction points, portals or transmission stations that bridge the transcendental realms and the immanent plane of third-dimensional existence. When we sense a situation in the physical world that is in need of higher grace, we are really the eyes of the One peering into its Creation through one of its incarnate extensions. Connecting with the soul and focusing awareness within the vertical channel to the light of Source, we create an unbroken conduit through ourselves from the Ultimate One to the situation in need of Its light. This is the essence of our function as conduits of grace.

Divine light is always flowing into Creation through every atom and molecule of matter. As human souls, though, we possess the unique capacity to realize God as our true nature. This allows us to consciously "channel" the One as we invite its unlimited power, intelligence and love into manifestation from our place within Creation. Inhabiting physical bodies with elegant, refined subtle bodies and chakras, our very presence enables divine energies to be transmitted more effectively to others in our realm who are suffering.

To understand how this process works, consider the familiar tuning fork analogy. If one tuning fork is struck, any nearby tuning fork will resonate and begin to vibrate if it is on the same frequency or note. Because we all have the same energetic system of subtle bodies, chakras, and divine circuitry, we humans are all on the same basic wave length. Thus, even when we are simply walking through a crowd, everyone else's soul is, to some degree, resonating with ours. Those whose energies are very similar to our own may feel a resonance overlap that can manifest as palpable sensations of shared harmony.

When awareness rests in the soul, we serve as beacons of higher, more coherent frequencies, which resonate other available energy fields to uplevel. Distance is not an issue here, for the transmission of frequencies is unlimited by time and space. At times, though, our physical presence in a particular location is needed to assist in anchoring higher energies into the realm of form.

When we become aware of the connection from soul to Source while simultaneously inviting divine energies to flow through us to another, a circuit is created directly from the Ultimate to wherever the energy~consciousness infusion is needed. While we may feel suffused with energy as we ask for assistance for others, the most significant inpouring of energy does not usually come through us and then flow outward to them. Instead, it pours down their own central channels from their higher levels of being. In essence, we are asking that grace come directly from their higher nature to the embodied soul and human self, since the higher Self and Source know exactly what each of us needs. Our connection to our own higher levels of Self as we hold this possibility for another facilitates the dispensation of grace. Again, the tuning fork analogy is relevant. When we are anchored in our own column of light that extends all the way up into Divine Infinity, and hold the same possibility for another, that person's multidimensional subtle anatomy tends to mirror our own.

While grace-filled energies are continuously showering upon us all from the nonphysical levels of being, agents of grace in physical bodies serve an essential function. Higher-dimensional beings usually do not render specific service to those on Earth unless they are requested to do so, either directly or indirectly. Even though they are aware of everything occurring on the planet and are capable of affecting earthly events in major ways, the universal laws of free will and noninterference require that they wait until a request for assistance has been made.

This may explain why we are brought into particular circumstances. We may, for instance, be prompted to watch the news or read e-mails that alert us to a need for blessing-grace. For whatever larger reason, we agree to take the responsibility of witnessing the pain, suffering and discord of the human condition in this specific situation. Observing suffering naturally generates the soulful response of wanting to see healing occur and harmony be restored. Because we are in a body and part of the human soul family, as an integral aspect of that totality we are able to ask for that for the whole. In the highest, most inclusive sense, we *are* our brothers and sisters who are suffering; when they suffer, we suffer, too. Because this is so, divine law confers upon us the right to request assistance on behalf of others.

Optimally, when we are functioning as divine conduits, we are able to ask others if they would like our assistance. If they respond in the affirmative, we can offer our services without creating karmic consequences. But asking for permission isn't always practical or even possible. We may feel called to act on behalf of large groups of people, those at a distance, or animals or other aspects of the natural world that can't directly communicate. At times, we are impelled to do more than simply ask for divine help on their behalf; we want to offer our own services in a more direct way. What do we do then?

Our core essence connects us to all of Life, for every other life-form is also animated by a spark of the Divine. In our souls, we are one. We might imagine all of these seemingly separate souls uniting within one Universal Soul, which contains sub-components such as the human group soul and the soul of all terrestrial life. Because we are each an integral part of the human and planetary group soul, we feel in our own soul what others and the planet are experiencing. This felt-sense of oneness not only motivates our desire to be of service, it also allows us to receive requests for assistance directly through our own soul-knowing. In such situations, we can ask within our heart of hearts whether we have permission to render assistance. If we receive a strong, clear *YES* from the soul, we have satisfied the condition of honoring the free will of all involved. In essence, at the level at which we are all one, the souls of those directly involved have asked for assistance, and we are responding to that call, which we experience as a simultaneous inner prompting to participate.

Conversely, even when we receive a direct request for help, it may not be appropriate to provide the asked-for assistance. If the inner knowing that it is appropriate to do so is not forthcoming, we are wise to refrain from action or even inner work. Larger factors unknown to us may make it inappropriate for us to become involved in any way. This may place us in a difficult position on the personality level, but to override our inner knowing would not be in the highest. We may choose to stay in touch with those concerned, for things may shift and our participation might feel right at a later date.

For example, some time ago we received a group e-mail requesting healing prayers for an acquaintance whose cancer was now advanced. We were all asked to visualize Carmela in vibrant health. People at her bedside prayed she would be healed from the cancer, and Carmela herself felt she was being healed. Nonetheless, the two of us sensed she was heading toward the Great Transition. Since we couldn't know for sure that physical healing was in the highest for Carmela, and had nothing against her leaving the body if that were her next step, we prayed that this situation further her awakening to her true nature as fully as possible.

Despite her adamant assertions that she would be physically healed, Carmela's soul left her body a month or so later. It did seem that she was being healed of what lay behind the cancer, for her final communications indicated she was transforming rapidly on mental, emotional and spiritual levels. But her path was to leave her physical body, and many of those around her had difficulty seeing beyond their attachment to the outcome of physical healing. Detachment and living in the Mystery allow us to truly assist what is wanting to occur, rather than overlay a situation with our human self's preferred outcome.

If we do feel to pray that a person receive whatever s/he is requesting, whether it is the means to make a trip, to be healed of dis-ease, or to experience the resurrection of a relationship, we always add the qualifier, *if it is in the highest and best for all beings.* Another way to state this is *if this be God's will.* By including such phrases, we are releasing the power back to God, which is where it always ultimately rests. This guarantees that our request will be in alignment with the larger will.

Ultimately, the key to Right Action is to completely subordinate any personal desires and impulses to the will of the Divine. We may think we know what is best for another, but only the Divine can know for sure. Two phrases summarize this approach to life. The first is *Thy will be done,* which affirms our willingness to submit to divine will. We add the second phrase whenever we make a call or request of the Divine, whether for ourselves or another: *This or something higher.* Even when we are praying for something as innocuous-sounding as healing for another, we cannot know if that healing is part of the Divine Plan for that life. These two simple phrases express the spiritual maturity that keeps us in integrity as agents of grace.

Making the Call for Divine Assistance

Often, when we feel the call to serve as an agent of grace, the knowing of what is required in the situation arises from within the depths of our being. This sense of knowing is the soul speaking to the human self. We can trust our inner knowing to the degree that we are familiar with the signature of the soul, the unique quality of its presence at our core. When questions or unclarity are present, it simply means we haven't arrived at the clear knowing that can only come from the soul. If we are not sure whether the communication is arising from the mind or the soul, we can take it into the soul space and ask the Divine for clarification. We can also ask what the One would like to bring to the situation through us. This usually results in a clear sense of what wants to happen next.

When we do not receive a definite indication of what would be most helpful in a particular situation, we can simply ask the Divine to pour in whatever is needed. Tremendous assistance can also be rendered through asking Source to pour forth its divine qualities, for they are the highest attributes of being and can bring only blessings into the world. Love, peace, stillness, harmony, and grace are just a few of the facets of the Infinite One, along with any quality of being that blesses and sanctifies. We can ask that the divine qualities that would be most helpful to resolve the situation pour in to lift it into its next level of integration and wholeness.

Sometimes we sense a specific divine quality would be helpful. If two people are quarreling, for instance, we might feel a deep desire for them to experience greater harmony and compassion, and request that those qualities energetically bathe them both. Or we may feel prompted to ask that peace envelop them, absorbing all discord into itself. Calling for divine love is rarely inappropriate, for its inherent intelligence knows exactly how to promote healing and awakening.

A primary objective in the journey into Self-realization is to ever more fully embody attributes such as compassion, patience, peace, harmony, and wisdom. Each of these is an unfoldment of our essential nature. In any circumstance where dis-ease and suffering are present, calling in qualities like love, understanding, and truth can only have a positive effect, for they are universal soul needs and characteristics. Everyone involved will receive an assist in more fully incarnating the qualities requested.

When discord or inharmony arises and we feel to be of service, we might begin by tuning in to the situation as a whole, as well as the people involved. What is taking place? We can ask to see it all through the eyes of the soul, which will reveal a more expanded perspective on what is unfolding. Then, we can ask what kinds of divine energies are most needed, and wait for a clear response. As we discern the elements that might be most helpful, we can ask to be a conduit for them to pour through to lift the situation and all involved.

Discordant outer conditions are the inevitable byproduct of disconnection from our true nature. The highest outcome we can call forth for those who are suffering, then, is realization of the true Self, to the degree that is possible here and now. Consciously reconnecting with who we truly are offers the ultimate solution for any form of conflict, disease or suffering. Ultimately, it also promises our final release from all human limitation through liberation.

In any situation, one of the most helpful things we can do is to look beyond the surface appearance of distortion, dis-ease, suffering and ignorance, giving it no ultimate reality or power, while also not denying that it is there. We can view what is present as a temporary, relative condition brought about by the fundamental forgetting of the true nature of everyone involved. We can then call forth the remembrance of the essential Self and do our very best to see the luminous presence that is always residing in the depths of each being involved, whether s/he is aware of it at the moment or not.

When the actions of others appear to arise from egoic forgetting of their essential oneness with all of life, the two of us often make one simple call: *May they awaken.* We then include ourselves: *May we all awaken.* In response to outer situations that seem saturated with the suffering of amnesia, we often find ourselves making a call to the Divine to come forth and unfold the God-nature of all involved, so that It can take control and do whatever is necessary to bring about a peaceful resolution. Sometimes we feel guided to ask that the Divine act to help perpetrators of suffering go beyond the separated egoic state: *May the soul take dominion here!*

When all levels of ourselves are coherent and aligned within our vertical connection, in union with soul and Source, we see through the eyes of God and perceive with divine mind. With this perspective, we do not get caught in seeing distorted human manifestations as real and true. Instead, we view them as the products of sleeping souls, and it is easy to forgive those souls because they are unconscious of what they are setting into motion by their actions. From this place in consciousness, we can pray as Jesus did on the cross: *Forgive them, for they know not what they do.*

It feels unimaginable to offer this prayer when we are viewing the situation through human eyes. Seeing those involved as evildoers and believing they are willfully causing harm to life as an expression of who they really are makes it impossible to hold them in forgiveness. But when our consideration goes to a deeper level, we see that they *must* be asleep, for no one who is awake could possibly commit the horrendous acts that are perpetrated daily. From this perspective, we only want the perpetrators' awakening, for we know that this is the ultimate solution to all earthly dilemmas. This alone will break the chain of suffering that binds souls to the wheel of the human condition.

In serving as an agent of grace, we can always make one final, universally applicable request. As we turn the entire matter over to the Divine, emptying ourselves of all ideas and concepts about what might be helpful, we can simply pray, *God, do everything you can for all involved in this situation.* Our sincere appeal, aimed like an arrow into the Heart of the One, releases the hold of the human on the situation and turns it over to the level of being that can most effectively respond.

The Steps to Calling Grace into Action

In making the call for grace to pour into a situation, a series of specific steps has proven to be useful. This sequence summarizes everything that has been discussed above. After we present the steps, you'll have an opportunity to put them into action through the guided inner experience that follows.

As with all new endeavors, this method of calling in grace may seem complex at first, but through repeated experiences of summoning grace into action, the process will feel increasingly comfortable and natural. Eventually it will become automatic, so that whenever an opportunity to serve as an agent of grace arises, the steps will easily unfold, without thought. As you utilize them over time, you'll find that these steps evolve into your own way of calling in grace, as unique as your soul signature.

1) Contemplate the situation at hand. As you breathe and feel any bodily sensations and feelings about it that are present, you are preparing the ground for grace to flow into the circumstances calling out for divine intervention.

2) Now it is time to drop deeper into soul communion, the foundation of all else that may unfold. Invite your awareness into the heart soul center. Feel the presence of the Divine within you. Bask in that presence until it feels strongly anchored in your awareness. Ask that the Soul Lotus fully open so you can feel your union with the flame of God within.

3) As your consciousness rests within the soul space above the heart, become aware of the vertical axis that unites you with both the deep, dark realms of Divine Mother below and the illumination of the vastest levels of Source above. First, immerse within the dark feminine realms beneath the physical body. Feel and visualize the vertical channel going down from the Soul Lotus through the center of the body, continuing down between the legs and into the core of the Earth. You may find it helpful to visualize a dark, magnetic cord connecting the base chakra to the core of the planet.

4) From this deeply grounded foundation, turn your awareness upward, traveling back into the heart soul center. Invite your consciousness to extend up the central channel through the crown chakra and into the higher-dimensional oversoul realms. Continue on into the vastness of the I AM Presence and ultimately the Source of All That Is. Feel the presence of the Di-

vine, with its bright-white luminosity, power, and infinite love. Ask that its frequencies pour down the central channel and anchor in the Soul Lotus. As this occurs, you may feel or inwardly see a pillar or column of light extending from your soul center to Source, uniting these levels of being.

5) The primary circuit through which grace can flow is now open and operational. Before continuing, once again feel the strong, clear alignment and connection from your personal self sense to the soul, oversoul and Source of All. Being consciously connected and unified at all levels of being is essential to function most effectively as an agent of grace, for now it is possible to transduce the highest levels of intelligence, power and love.

6) Since grace does not originate with us, we need to call to these larger levels to act through us. The truly active part of being a conduit of grace is to make a request or decree that calls God into action. In addition to asking the Ultimate One for help, you might like to call to specific ascended masters and higher beings such as Babaji, Quan Yin, St. Germain, Mother Mary, the Universal Christ, and Lord Maitreya. You can also call in the assistance of your angelic guides, teachers, and spirit helpers. Whomever we ask, the essence of this step is to open and invite the Divine to descend and "do the work."

7) Now, ask to be shown precisely what would be most helpful in this situation. Ask the Divine to give you a clear understanding of what the highest and best would be. You may hear something simple like "peace" or "compassion." Or you may be shown an image of an outcome. For example, if two people are arguing, you may feel to ask for love and harmony to envelop them, and envision them reconnecting and embracing.

8) Formulate your request as clearly and completely as you can. If you receive a vision or inner knowing that something specific needs to occur, use images, feelings, and clearly stated thoughts so the Divine can respond in an equally precise and powerful way. For instance, if you sense peace is what is most needed, feel how much you want those involved to be immersed in peace. Visualize and feel what they and the situation might look like if peace had already entered and taken command. In your own body, feel the quality of peace you would like to have descend.

9) Feel your energies totally aligning with your request. The stronger the intention and desire, the more potent the response. When a clear inner alignment is present, you will feel your heart light up with a strong sense of desire and commitment to seeing divine grace bless the situation and all involved. You will feel a resounding, unequivocal *Yes, this is what I want to ask God for in this situation.* If this inner *Yes* is not yet present, take the time to get completely clear on what is right for all.

10) Finally, make the request. Feel your sincere desire to have God send forth Its infinite love, intelligence and creative power to bring about the wished-for result. Send that request up the central channel, your connection right into the heart and mind of God.

From here on, the prime creative intelligence of the universe does the rest. Remind your human self that God will take over now, and since God is omnipotent, the matter is already handled at the absolute level and the results will soon come into manifestation. You might sense light and energy descending, along with divine qualities such as peace, love, or other energies associated with your request. Usually, a clear sense of a response is also present, or at least an acknowledgment that the request has been received and an activity of grace has begun.

At this point, the basic function of a conduit of grace is complete. Now, it's in God's hands. All that remains is to give thanks to all the higher levels of being for their assistance, and offer love and gratitude up to them.

EXPERIENCE~ACTIVATION: Calling in the Grace of Love

Create a quiet, undisturbed place for yourself. Close the door, turn off the phone, and get comfortable.

Take a few minutes to consciously connect with the soul, oversoul and Source. Once you feel connected, ask the soul to make you aware of someone who could use an infusion of love. If you feel called to, contact the person and ask if s/he would like an infusion of love and would be willing to let you know what the experience was like later. Setting a specific time will help the recipient be more conscious of what happens. If you don't feel to make contact, it is important

41

to ask the person's soul and higher Self for divine authority. If you don't receive it, try someone else.

Envision the person and feel yourself connecting with this individual, soul to soul. Feel how much you would like to see this being infused with love. Visualize and feel this happening. You might even feel and see the transformation that occurs through the inpouring of divine love. This is the result you are requesting.

Hold it all in your consciousness -- all the thoughts, feelings and images that are part of the vi-sion~request. Bring it all into the center of your soul. Ground yourself to the Earth's core, and then feel the connection up to the oversoul and Source. Offer the request up the central channel, the communication linkage to the Divine. You may find it helpful to envi-sion the request drifting upward in a bubble or sphere.

Now, ask that this request be made manifest. Use these or your own words: "Beloved higher Self and Source, please pour forth divine love to (person's name). Infuse and saturate this person with the heal-ing, raising energy of love. Transform anything unlike love within this being into love. Please do this or what-ever else is in the highest good."

Continue to feel the vertical connection while simultaneously maintaining your connection with the person. You may begin to feel divine love infusing yourself and the individual. The infusion may continue for some time, and may include other energies de-scending and transformational processes unfolding. Your only job is to be a hollow reed for all of this to pass through, witnessing, experiencing and holding it all in the embrace of your heart and soul.

When the process feels complete, acknowledge that it is done and offer up your gratitude to the higher levels of being and any divine beings who have as-sisted.

As the experience ends, notice how it feels to be a conduit of grace in this way. Be aware of any sensa-tions and feelings within your own body and emotions.

You might like to journal about your own experiences as an agent of grace.

Why is Grace Elusive at Times?

Sometimes, our prayers and requests for grace don't seem to be answered. When the principles of opening to grace are followed and the manifestation doesn't happen as we had hoped, subconscious doubt and fear may have prevented the full expression of grace in the situation. Life responds to all that is held within both the conscious and subconscious realms. If we don't believe we're truly worthy of having grace descend, it may not happen. When we doubt the words we're saying, or believe we lack access to the power to fuel them, grace may remain elusive. Whatever we *can* allow will take place, and that level of allowance expands as we awaken. As the conscious mind registers the definite, positive effects of calling in grace, its belief in grace increases, and some of the subconscious fear and doubt is converted to greater faith.

For many humans, discovering the power of faith is where the process of opening to grace starts. But faith is not the end-all. As we experience the effects of grace in our lives, faith rapidly transitions to knowing. Instead of hoping, which relies on the faith that is a supposition of the thinking mind, we come to *know* with absolute certainty that grace is something we can count on. That knowing comes from the alignment of our human self and subconscious mind with universal truth. And when the subconscious becomes fully aligned with Infinite Intelligence, instantaneous manifestations become possible.

Yet another limit on how much grace can pour onto planet Earth is found within transpersonal beliefs. Virtually every religious cosmology includes a separate, dark or evil force that acts in opposition to the will of the Divine. This sets up the ubiquitous, classic struggle between the forces of good and bad, light and darkness. A quick scan of the day's news headlines certainly seems to confirm the existence of this fundamental polarity, but deeper consideration brings the idea into question. Believing in an anti-life, anti-love presence that is opposed to God's inherently loving, wise and perfect nature implies there is something other than God in existence. But if God is All That Is, that simply cannot be. Even physicists tell us universal oneness is an indisputable fact.

All relative appearances of a force opposed to the living, loving, perfect Creator are the result of illusions created in the dualistic state of mind. The illusion of separation creates the misperception that there could be God and another that opposes God. The fundamental belief in separation induces a deep, very powerful hypnosis that operates not only at the human level, but also within the next two higher dimensions to a lesser degree. The collective unconscious contains a vast reservoir of this fallen, "evil" or "anti-life" consciousness, and it plays out through each of us to some extent. Occasionally, out of the collective arise potent individual embodiments of this darkness, such as Hitler and Pol Pot. Lesser manifestations include autocratic rulers as well as those who act only in self-interest at the expense of the well-being of billions of other humans. Anti-life unconsciousness expresses through us when we abuse our bodies with addictive substances or lash out and injure another, whether physically or emotionally.

This consciousness has existed for a very long time and is now woven into the fabric of our world so ubiquitously as to be largely unnoticed, or even considered "normal." At vaster levels of consciousness, our imaginations collectively create the im-age~presence of an evil being such as Satan, in the West, and the asuras and demons of the East, who supposedly possess Godlike powers and oppose the good and the light. However, the dominion of such beings is a relative reality with no ultimate basis. While the relative manifestations can be horrific, they are nonetheless night-mares created in the illusion of separation. God is All That Is. Only the darkened collective mind of billions of sleeping souls could create such an illusion. The only reality it has is within this dark-ened mind. But when many, many drops of the ocean dream this nightmare, the collective trance can take tangible form in the outer world.

The conflicts and crises that pervade the human world form self-reinforcing feedback loops that convince the darkened mind its world view is true. Thus, the nearly universal belief in a dark, evil power separate from God continues to this day. Like a roll of film looping through a projector, this virtual image is empowered by the divine light that flows through each of us. When we wake up to the fact that it is an illusory image in the mind, we free ourselves of its destructive power.

For awakening souls who are here to function as conduits of grace for humanity, this understanding is crucial. The degree to which we are caught in the hypnotic trance of a separate, material or evil power limits the grace that can pour through us. Miracles could and would occur instantly through any one of us who is awake to the reality that there is no force or condition that opposes God, the ultimate reality of all truth, perfection, love and eternal life. Throughout human history, God-realized beings have demon-strated this awareness through instant healings, raising the dead, and other miracles. The minds of such beings simply perceive anything that is not held in the luminosity of the love, power and creative intelligence of the One as an illusion. The great healings and miracles that have occurred throughout the spiritual history of the planet are the demonstrations of beings whose consciousness is anchored in truth. The source of the miracles is their consciousness, which sees through all relative appearances of disease, limitation and even death, to the perfect, divine being temporarily asleep to its true nature. More than healers, these miracle-workers are potent awakeners, capable of snapping others out of the trance-state of separation and all its attendant, relative manifestations.

Many spiritual traditions, including the Judeo-Christian, Hindu and Buddhist religions, teach that hell realms exist. It is true that within the relative experience of this dimension, some people do encounter dark, lower realms. However, when the light of the soul shines upon these convincing relative realities, they are revealed to have no ultimate basis or power. During the two decades we've accompanied people on soul journeys into the deepest, darkest realms of the subconscious, no one has ever encountered a dark, evil presence that turned out to be a real threat. Even the most disturbing images and thoughts have invariably dissolved away when brought into the light of the soul, which reveals them as the illusions they truly are. When the Divine is present, the apparitions of the lower realms simply vanish.

As souls in the human experience, we are like fish who do not know they are swimming in the ocean, unaware that we exist within a false, limiting psychic atmosphere. It may take some time for the light to shine into all the darkened corners of the mind and dispel all illusions forever. But one day, the mind will be free to view the world through the eyes of God. That outcome is assured, through the grace of the Only One That Is, which has no equal to oppose its totally loving intentions for all its aspects.

When Jesus asked for divine grace to manifest, he often ended his prayer with "Thank you, Father." These three simple words expressed his gratitude to God, the wellspring from which all grace flows. They also conveyed his understanding that what he had asked for was already accomplished. In his oneness with God, no separation existed between the knowing of what needed to occur and when and how it occurred. His consciousness was one with the omnipotent, omniscient Creator. Not a speck of doubt marred his subconscious; no thought that anything could happen but what he envisioned and requested was present. Simply put, Jesus was God acting. Until we realize this ultimate level of being ourselves, we can learn from his example, giving the entire process over to God and being aware of any doubt or disbelief that divine grace will do what needs to be done.

Many people believe they need to repeatedly pray about something or call for the manifestation of a vision again and again, energizing the call with a lot of emotion. This indicates the presence of the belief that we are making it happen, which takes us right back down to the human level. We believe repetition is needed because we don't fully trust the omnipotent activity of divine grace, or we think there's some force out there that is opposing it. Once the divine alignment is in place, though, and the matter has been turned over to God, it is done.

Once it is done, all that remains is to accept it is so. The urge to pray or reaffirm a request for grace repeatedly is usually a sign that doubt is operating at a subconscious level. The real issue is to face and deal with the doubt, by uprooting the underlying belief that anything can oppose the activity of divine grace.

That said, it is perfectly fine to pray repeatedly when the prompting to do so is present. If an inharmonious condition persists or seems to need greater assistance to come to resolution, guidance may indicate that it would be helpful to pray or call forth grace on an ongoing basis. As the situation moves toward resolution, the path it takes and the issues that need to be dealt with may shift and change. Additional energy from beyond may be required. But the underlying reality remains: Once grace is called into action, the highest possible outcome will occur if the level of allowance permits it to unfold. One day, we will all arrive at the completely clear state of mind in which only God exists. Then, our level of allowance will be complete and total.

Becoming a Zero

When the two of us first began to facilitate soul-awakening sessions, we had no professional training, and our vocational backgrounds gave us little help. Our minds often wondered, *What do we have to offer?* Our lack of outer preparation turned out to be exactly the catalyst that drove us deeper into our souls. This took our personal selves out of the equation, which allowed the Divine to do everything without our interference.

Being present during sessions taught us that fulfilling our soul purpose and destiny isn't anything we can "do." In fact, the more we give up the egoic "doer" and surrender to the movement of the Divine, the more easily and serendipitously all will happen through the movement of grace. When we *let go and let God* ever more fully, our awakening and our service to the planet are expedited by this radical surrender.

A line from the ancient Advaita text called the *Astavakra Samhita* sums this up: "You who have been bitten by the great black serpent of the egoism 'I am the doer,' drink the nectar of the faith 'I am not the doer,' and be happy." Committing our lives to serving as agents of grace asks us to release the ego's control so the Divine can step in. We won't be able to lay out linear plans and expect definite results; we may be asked to serve in ways that stretch the edges of what we thought we were capable of being and doing. Each of these challenges results in a small death and rebirth as we face and surrender more of who and what we thought we were.

Eventually, as layer after layer of not-self peels away, what remains is a "hollow reed" through which the Divine can blow its grace-filled breath, accomplishing in and through us what It alone can do. The more we have died to all that we believed we were, the emptier we become -- empty enough to at last be used by the One for its purposes. Ammachi, the great hugging saint of India, expresses this with startling conciseness: "When you are a zero, you'll be a hero."

But the ego can be slippery, and it loves to grab the credit for the blessing-grace that pours through us. The acknowledgment and adulation we may receive water the seeds of ego, especially the spiritual ego, who believes its "specialness" is what allows grace to occur in our presence. It may try to convince us that because we are awake, powerful and attuned, "miracles" happen in those who come to us for help. We hear the spiritual ego in remarks like, "I healed a woman of migraines."

Because the spiritual ego uses the language of spirituality and often sounds wise and astute, it can cause us to believe we are hearing the true Self. When we hear someone enumerating their trainings, travels, and healing gifts, we are probably listening to a spiritual ego attempting to impress us with its "credentials." In contrast, the soul knows it has no need to present qualifications. Its presence is enough, and it has no reason to convince others of this fact.

Since grace flows most freely through those who are free of the false self, becoming a zero is central to being an agent of grace. And, of course, becoming a zero is not something we can "do." We can, though, stand guard over the mind, observe its games, and offer them up to the Divine for transformation through grace. Whether the ego tends toward self-aggrandizing or self-deprecating, feeling wise and powerful or inept and powerless, all are expressions of the separate self. In the end, becoming a zero means going beyond all self-definitions, all identities -- and all limitations. This is how we become a clear, open vessel in which only the love, peace, wisdom, and knowing of the soul remain.

God Does the Work

An attorney who came to us for soul-awakening sessions liked to say that he was here on Earth because his higher Self had sent him down into this dimension as a "probe." In the same way, as conduits of grace, we are each an extension of the One Infinite Creator currently visiting this earthly realm. While, as individualized aspects, we are wholly pure and perfect specimens, each of us is but an infinitesimal fractal subset of that One. While a drop of water in the ocean is identical in essence to the ocean, it is still but one of an infinity of drops. If the drop moves, it is the ocean that moves it. The drop, then, is an extension of the ocean's creative movement, but it is the power of the ocean that determines all.

Christ Jesus elucidated this principle through his statement that he, the human being named Jesus, did nothing. He always attributed all power and will to his Father in heaven. Only the One Source of everything is truly omnipotent, and any power, will or intelligence we possess as holographic fractals of that One arise from within the larger field of being of which we are an inextricable part. Christ Jesus' ability to walk on water, raise the dead, and manifest anything desired arose from his 100% orientation from the Source level of consciousness. At this level, we tap into the omnipotence of the Ultimate. Beings like Christ Jesus, Babaji and Krishna not only operated from but existed at that level, as does the Christ or God Self of each of us. The only difference between us and these great ones is that we haven't yet realized the fullness of our God Self.

Only as self dies is Self born. As the human, body-identified sense of self dissolves and the personal ego is revealed as an illusion, the vast luminosity of the divine Self shines forth. This Self is one with the Absolute, the empty fullness of pure consciousness out of which all of Creation unfolds. The Self lives in unity with the One, as an extension of it, without will, power or volition of its own.

All creative manifestation through a fully Self-realized being occurs as a unified movement of the One through its extension as the individualized Self. The moment a sense of a separate "i"dentity arises, the moment a self that forgets it is fully unified with God emerges, delusion's dark veils begin to settle over the mind. This sense of a separate self is the misperception that results in the "fall" of the soul into suffering, limitation and imperfection. Our true estate always lies within the "garden" of our divine origin, where the living fabric of all things is the luminous light of the One in all its glory. We can't get back to the garden until we ascend out of the matter-identified illusion of the self.

As long as we think our little human selves are doing any-thing at all, the level from which we are creating occupies the low-est, least inclusive part of the matrix of our multidimensional being. We perceive the cosmos upside down if we think our infinitesimally small human self can ever be the source of transcendent grace. Thus, if we, as human beings, think we are the source of our ac-tions, their power is minimal. When we consciously unify with Source and fully surrender to that level, we ascend the ladder of being into the infinite power that creates universes.

Each of us could experience divine creation, as did Jesus and other realized masters, were we fully established within their levels of communion with Source. The subconscious limitations most human minds hold prevent that level of power and grace from manifesting. All aspects of ourselves need to be ready for increas-ing levels of grace and want that upleveling. Since the Divine never does anything against our free will, the limitations held in our minds restrict what is possible -- but only until they are released.

4

Practical GraceWork

Once the commitment is made to step into serving as an agent of grace, opportunities to fulfill this function begin to appear in the context of everyday life. During the course of our workday or out for an evening walk, we suddenly find ourselves called to be a bridge between the peace and perfection of the transcendental domains and the conflict and crisis of the physical plane.

In the preceding chapters, we've presented the principles that enable us to consciously act as agents of grace. Here, we demonstrate the principles in use by sharing examples of ways we have been utilized as divine conduits. As the following stories illustrate, there are as many opportunities to serve as an agent of grace as there are moments in the day.

Barry: Grace for Relationships

Years ago, our neighbors at the time were in the midst of a difficult passage in their domestic life. Although they were still living under the same roof, Evan and his wife, Leslie, had become estranged. Evan sometimes came by to discuss what was going on and receive emotional support.

They hit a particularly difficult period where it seemed Leslie might be involved with another man. The couple's unresolved issues escalated to the point where they were no longer able to communicate. Leslie was so full of painful feelings that she often blew up when they tried to talk. Evan was concerned about the effects of these outbursts on their children.

We began to include the family in our daily prayers, and hoped the parents could resolve things in the best way for all involved. On the rare occasions we saw Leslie, she looked to be brimming over with rage. One day, Evan confided that a very important discussion about the legal status of their children would be happening the next night. He was deeply concerned about what might happen when Leslie arrived. She had not been home in a number of days and all communication had become hostile.

Early that evening, I was out for a walk when I saw Leslie's car heading toward their home. As the car went by, the expression on her face troubled me, and I felt the palpable tension emanating from the vehicle. I walked into our backyard, which had visual access to their home, just as the car pulled into their driveway.

Evan walked out to meet Leslie -- in order, I guessed, to begin the discussion there instead of in front of the children inside the house. Within seconds Leslie began to yell at Evan, and I wondered if the situation might become physically violent. It felt way beyond anything I could deal with a personal level, and it wasn't my place to become involved, so another way of meeting the situation was needed.

I sat down on the ground, turned within, and merged fully with my soul. I then projected my consciousness up the central channel and connected with Source and all the higher beings working with this family, requesting their assistance. I asked that peace and harmony rain down upon Leslie and Evan so that they could stay centered in who they really were and communicate from their souls. My prayers continued: *May the highest and best unfold. May the Divine take control of the situation and stop all attack and violence. May their higher Selves rein in their ego-personalities.*

As Leslie continued to rage, I began to feel a strong, powerful energy building above them. It was very bright and very, very potent, and it rapidly descended like a bolt of lightning. It shot down toward the two of them and entered Leslie's crown chakra.

In less than a minute, the decibel level of her voice dropped. The screaming ceased, and now Leslie was simply talking very loudly. A minute later, they were both speaking in normal voices. As they went on talking, a different quality of energy descended. A strong presence seemed to be holding them both, controlling their outer expressions. While this energy was immensely potent, it also felt calm and peaceful. Suddenly, to my amazement, they reached out and hugged each other. They then got in the car and drove away.

Later, we learned just how intense the situation had become. A few nights before, fearing for their safety and well-being, Evan had left the house with the children. This prompted Leslie to lock them out. There were threats of divorce and taking the children away from one another. That was where the situation stood when I happened to be nearby as Leslie came home that day. While we didn't know all the details, I could certainly feel the intensity of the situation. Now, at least for the moment, the possibility of a violent crisis had passed.

There is no way to know what would have happened had I not been directed there to open up that doorway of grace. Would the situation have become violent? That looked like a definite possibility. What I knew for sure was that a profound shift had occurred. From months of no physical contact and frequent verbal abuse to a hug in a matter of minutes certainly seemed miraculous.

A few days later Evan stopped by to tell us that things had taken a radical turn for the better. Whereas it had seemed highly likely they would go apart, they were now living together again as a family and at least carrying on the normal household rituals of family life. Evan was clearly extremely grateful for this turn of events.

Nothing was ever said about the higher-dimensional assistance that poured through on that fateful day. We've learned the wisdom in the ascended masters' saying that it is best "to dare, to do, and to be silent." And as we've emphasized above, there is really nothing any of us can take credit for. The soul prompts us to be in the right place at the right time, and all that flows through is from the higher levels of existence. We humans feel grateful to play our roles as conduits for this to occur, a role that blesses us as much as the recipients of the divine grace.

Karen: Grace Through Creative Expression

During the 1980s, I made beadwork and gemstone jewelry and sold it at craft fairs. Sitting down at my work table each day, I prayed to be shown the arrangements of colors and shapes and semiprecious stones that would bless the person who would eventually wear each piece of jewelry. Then, I'd launch into the day's creating.

Sometimes the combinations surprised me. They weren't what I would have chosen, and occasionally the resulting pieces seemed a bit discordant to my sensibilities. But I trusted my inner knowing and went on creating in this way, building up my stock so there would be plenty to display the following summer.

That was when the second part of the process unfolded. One after the other, my customers looked everything over and zeroed in on the piece for them. They often said, "This is just what I've been looking for!" Their remarks were especially gratifying when I knew the combination of elements was not what I would have created on my own. I felt deeply satisfied to be a conduit for the Divine as I custom-made jewelry for those who were meant to receive it.

Many years later, after being profoundly moved by a show of the members' work, I joined a women's creative arts collective. At the beginning of each meeting, one of us led a short meditation designed to focus and center our energies. Then, we all went into the silence, immersing ourselves in the creative process. At the end of our time together, we showed one another what had come through. In this welcoming space, what incredible creativity emerged from these otherwise modest, unassuming women! The group energy created a field of such open allowance that we were all amazed at what lay within us, just waiting to emerge.

Years before, I had read the words of Jesus in a Gnostic text. They went something like, "If you bring forth what is within you, what is within you will save you. If you do not bring forth what is within you, what is within you will destroy you." The words returned with new urgency and meaning as I contemplated the trajectory of my mother's life.

Doris grew up in New York City during the Great Depression. She had considerable intelligence and ability, yet her big dream for her life was thwarted at a pivotal moment in her youth. Although my mother was awarded a scholarship to a prestigious high school which would have solidly placed her on a college and career track, her mother, worried about her youngest daughter's safety traveling alone across the city each day, would not allow her to accept the coveted prize.

Instead of going on to college and becoming a teacher, as she had hoped, my mother entered a vocational program and became a legal secretary. Although Doris worked for attorneys who recognized her intelligence and gave her entire cases to manage, her real abilities were never fully utilized. And her vocational dreams never came true.

Was this part of the reason she went on to kill herself in her early 50s? Her suicide note contained this tragic, riveting sentence: "A flower that is stepped on never has a chance to bloom."

In the wake of Mom's death, which occurred when I was 28, I knew it was upon me to go beyond the pattern of self-destruction that had not only claimed my mother, but her father as well. I had to find out what lay within me and bring it out, so that it didn't implode. Although calligraphy and jewelry making had provided creative outlets, neither of these forms expressed what lay within me in a deeply meaningful, original way. It wasn't until the collage group that I felt this level of expression beginning to come forth, and that was what made each meeting such a deeply thrilling experience.

Although many stunningly exquisite collages came into being, not all of our creations were pretty. In our quest to be true to what wanted to come forth from within us, we explored all sides of life and the psyche. As we worked through our horror at the disregard for life that occurred around the planet in countless ways, making collages became cathartic and transformative. Personal issues, too, found resolution and expression through combining images on paper.

The collage group provided a nurturing, sacred vessel that welcomed out what lay within each of us. Within this safe energetic container, nothing was disallowed or shamed. To the contrary, all members of the group waited in receptive expectancy to witness what had emerged from within each of us. Just as the Great Mother brings forth endless expressions of life for the pure joy of it, we delighted in experiencing both the creative process and its results, the divinely inspired creations that came through our sisters. In those moments, we came to know that there is nothing more marvelously transformative than bringing forth what lies within us.

In the collage group, I learned that within me, as within each of us, is an inexhaustible wellspring of creative inspiration. I came away knowing that the ability to create is not reserved for professionals, or those with artistic training. Every one of us can serve as an agent of grace through creating. The beauty we bring through from higher levels of inspiration is the Divine expressing through us. That expression blesses this realm, no matter how many or how few people see what we've created. When our creations flow out from our core, they lift the vibrational level of this earthly dimension. And when others witness our creations, their energies are enhanced and expanded into the subtle, soulful levels that infuse what we have brought forth.

The most divinely inspired creations confer sublime blessings to all who are available to receive them. Recently, our friend Amad in Pakistan has begun to send us his favorite poetry. What a delight to discover, among the quotidian matters of each day's e-mails, a poem from Rumi or Hafiz, or a quotation from Meher Baba's chalkboard. This agent of grace, half a world away, blesses our lives by sharing what he loves.

Barry: Grace at Work

A decade after I left banking, I decided to dust off my financial consulting skills and briefly reentered the work world. The noble endeavors of a small company that served the developmentally disabled attracted me to work with them. The executive director indicated he needed to get a better handle on the company's financial situation, and realized a solid budgeting and financial planning process was essential.

I set about gathering the necessary information and developed some future projections. When the data came together, they painted a rather gloomy picture. In the absence of regular financial reports, no one knew the company had been losing money for some time. No wonder they were having difficulty paying their bills! When I plugged all the data into my computer, it became clear the company was hemorrhaging, and projections indicated it would run out of working capital in the very near future. It didn't help that the ability to borrow and raise capital was nonexistent under the circumstances.

I called an emergency meeting with the executive director and a few of the top people and explained that the situation looked dire. I strongly suggested looking at some possible scenarios to deal with the crisis as quickly as possible. During the next week we held a series of meetings to discuss what could be done. Although I tried to find a way to approach each meeting with some form of optimism, I just couldn't see any way out. They had been losing money for so long and had depleted their capital so badly that it seemed impossible to reverse the trend before they hit bottom. All projections indicated bankruptcy was the company's most likely option.

The mission of the company was so heartfelt that I couldn't bear to tell them their dream might be ending. This was a particularly warm, caring group of people. They had assisted their developmentally disabled clients to experience the fullest life possible for more than a decade, and now their efforts seemed doomed to failure. With great trepidation I went into the final meeting and expressed my perceptions. While I talked, I could see the director was very upset by my words. I explained that the last thing I wanted was to be the bearer of bad news. But my job was to present the truth as I saw it, which would ultimately be best for all involved.

I suggested emergency measures be instituted immediately, starting with cutting every nonessential expense. I recommended that we meet with the board of directors and suggest looking into some form of reorganization. I had prepared a written report that I wanted to present to the board at that meeting.

I concluded by offering the hope that there is always a possibility for grace, and suggested that those who felt inclined should pray for help. A few nodded their heads, breaking the numb silence in the room. I closed the meeting by saying there is always hope if we ask for help both from above and from those who have an investment in seeing the company continue.

After the meeting, I told the director I would call him to set up the meeting with the board. When I phoned later that week, the director wasn't in. The financial officer told me the meeting with the board had already occurred, and my report had not been mentioned. Instead, the director painted a much rosier picture of the company's finances.

A letter soon arrived announcing that I had been discharged; the consulting contract was over. This was difficult news; I felt I had started something I couldn't complete. I felt conflicted because the board of directors hadn't receive my report. Should I contact them directly? I only wanted the best for these people, but now I had become the enemy of the director.

I felt sad and depressed for a few days until I realized there must be an opportunity, even in this. One day I stopped everything and went into deep meditation to pray and ask for assistance. What was I to do?

What came in was to let it all go and completely give it to God. I had been purposefully removed, since my task was done. As images of all the beautiful young adults I had met when I visited the facilities bubbled into my awareness, my heart burst open. It just didn't seem acceptable for them to lose their homes and jobs.

More than anything, I wanted this company to be saved. When I asked for guidance, I felt it was my task to call in grace for this to occur. I sent all the emotional energy I felt with my request up the vertical channel right into Source. For quite some time I prayed for a miraculous resurrection. And then a palpable sense of a response arrived. The golden-white light of the Christ descended, carrying the feeling that I had been heard and the request would be answered. Along with this came the knowing that what I needed to do had been done.

More than a year later, I happened to meet the company's chief financial officer in a store. He confided that things had been pretty rough for the first few months after that last meeting. But then a series of very fortuitous events had begun to unfold. A number of creditors agreed to reduce or even forgive the company's debts because of their allegiance to the mission of helping the developmentally disabled. They were able to obtain financial assistance from some unnamed sources that stepped forward in their hour of need. Several people who had been sources of internal problems for some time voluntarily left the company, which improved morale among those remaining. One of their small companies got a large contract that assured future income. The top offi-

Agents of Grace

cers also took sizable pay cuts. This sequence of events could never have been predicted. After skating on the verge of bankruptcy for six months, the company slowly started to turn around. A decade later, it is still in operation.

In retrospect, I recognize that I was called into the situation to be more than a financial consultant. My larger role was to be an agent of grace. It was difficult to be the one to assist those in charge in facing their denial, but that opened the door for grace to pour in. The crisis that ensued brought them all together to align themselves to save the company. I'm sure many employees were praying quite strongly and regularly for divine assistance. And the universe responded to their urgent call.

I'll never know what effect my calls for grace had on that fateful day. But I do know that the energy that poured in was very strong, and that shortly thereafter grace descended in previously unimaginable ways. I feel fairly certain that this company would not have survived had it not been for the events that unfolded after I was brought into the situation. In all my years in banking, I had never seen such a miraculous turnaround.

I see now that my financial expertise played a very small part in what happened. At the larger level, the outcome had nothing to do with my capacities. I was cosmically "used" by the Divine to be the physical point through which higher levels of energy~consciousness could be transduced into the situation. More than ever, I was reminded how little our human capacities really mean in the larger scope of things.

Grace During Earth Changes

During this time of massive purification and cleansing on planet Earth, the frequency and severity of earth changes and other so-called natural disasters continues to escalate. These events provide potent evolutionary catalysts for large groups of human beings, who respond to the crises from their current levels of consciousness. While some perceive themselves to be victims of a capricious God, others use the challenges to leapfrog up the evolutionary ladder. For more than a few, such mass events spark soul-awakening as little else can.

Our own experience with earth changes and severe weather events included minor earthquakes and significant floods before our strongest initiation, a major hurricane, arrived in 1992. Our experiences during Hurricane Iniki are related in great detail in *Soul Awakening*, but this story is such a powerful example of the grace

58

that is available in even the most intense of circumstances that we feel to again touch on it here.

One morning on Kaua'i, we were awakened by a very early phone call from the owner of the home we were caretaking, who was on retreat on the other side of the island. Her message was succinct and potent: "The island will be struck by a Category Five hurricane around 1 p.m. today. The winds are estimated to average 160 mph with gusts in excess of 200. Do everything you can to save yourselves and the house. May God be with you, and all of us!"

This woke us up in a hurry. The situation felt overwhelming, far beyond the capacity of our human minds to cope with it. This served to immediately shift us into our connection with God. The vertical axis to Source opened, and we felt our oneness with All That Is. We lay in bed a few moments longer, giving it all up to God and asking that the Divine take complete control of the situation.

The response was immediate. Our minds became totally quiet; all we heard was the still, small voice instructing us. We were told to drive to the hardware store, and on the way there, a complete list of the items needed magically dropped into our consciousness and onto a shopping list. At the hardware store, we tore the list in half, got two shopping carts, and proceeded to fill them with the supplies we would soon need.

Back at the house, we found sheets of thick plywood, the window coverings we would nail up to create a fortress we hoped would withstand the storm. The corner bedroom was secured just as the winds began to pick up. Before we entered our makeshift bunker, we found ourselves standing in front of the house, surrounded by the lush vegetation that would soon be reduced to mulch. As we stood face to face, we joined hands and felt a strong vertical column going straight up to Source. Briefly, powerfully, we called in divine assistance and felt it descend. A golden pyramid of Christ Light came to rest directly over the house, along with the strong knowing that we were being watched over by many Christed beings.

During the ensuing storm, virtually everything standing was leveled. A row of huge, heavy ironwood trees stood right outside the bedroom we had turned into our survival bunker. Many of those stalwart trees fell, but not one hit the house. When the eye of the hurricane passed and the wind changed direction, with equal ferocity it battered the side of the house we could do nothing to protect, for the windows were too high to reach. It seemed likely these big picture windows would be blown out in seconds. Then, the extreme pressure would blast the walls of the house outward, leaving little of the structure intact. There was nothing we could do about that -- nothing, that is, but pray. Once again we asked God to take control.

As the winds escalated, we went into the bunker bedroom, closed the door, and lay down on the bed. We had done all we could; now, our lives were in the hands of the Divine. As we affirmed this truth, we were lifted into an exalted state of grace, suffused with bliss and light that raised us to a level in which absolutely no fear remained. In this space, nothing but peace and divine communion existed. Beyond all doubt, we *knew* we were held in complete grace. It no longer mattered whether our physical bodies survived or not. In this sublime space in consciousness, that was not even an issue.

In the middle of the storm, Barry found himself leaving our bedroom shelter and walking out into the unprotected living room. Outside, mature acacia trunks were snapping like matchsticks, while the wind blew directly at the unframed plate-glass windows. Barry could hear them gently rocking back and forth in their loose frames just as they would on any afternoon that the trade winds caressed them. The violence of the storm, just a few yards away, had no effect on them. Barry watched in absolute awe as the laws of physics were cast aside. Then he sensed the presence of the golden Christed pyramid hovering just beyond the windows, and the explanation was clear.

The next day, we investigated the condition of the house. A few roof tiles and two small jalousie panes were missing; that was the extent of the damage. Immensely relieved, we gave thanks and got on our bikes to journey into the nearby town. There, more than half of the homes had been leveled. We saw plumbing pipes sticking out of foundation slabs, front walls peeled back as if by a giant can opener, bathroom fixtures, furniture, and shattered wood strewn about, and personal belongings scattered across muddy yards. Mercifully, miraculously, missing from the scene were the expected stretchers bearing damaged or deceased human bodies.

We rode back home in an altered state from observing more devastation than either of us had ever seen. As we approached the house, the denuded garden and fallen ironwood and acacia trees made it clear the same forces had been equally hard-hitting here. But there in the middle of it all stood the house, looking no different than it had before the storm arrived. Gratitude and reverence for the awesome love and power of the Divine welled up in us. Where could we ever put our faith and trust but in the infinite, invisible One, which had once again demonstrated its omnipotence?

Karen: Grace in Unexpected Places

During a financially challenging time, Barry and I briefly worked for a psychic hotline. Little did we imagine the poignant, if not tragic, cross-section of suffering humanity we would encounter. Some people simply wanted a yes or no to their questions, justifiably nervous about that $3.99 per minute charge showing up on their credit card bill. Others poured out a litany of pain, detailing the sorry state of their lives -- jobs lost, homes forsaken, children taken away, relationships interrupted by jail time, good health an unknown. I'd empathize with things I'd never been close to experiencing, happy to provide some human warmth. At some point I'd remind people about the cost of the call, and encourage them to pray for help -- which, I'd point out, was free of charge.

Late one night, a caller with a strong Texas accent began to recount her woes. It didn't take a psychic to figure out that her loud, slurred delivery reflected an advanced state of inebriation. One after the other, she detailed the current conditions of her life -- business failures, a husband who had left her for a younger woman, property disputes, ungrateful grown children.

Finally she revealed that earlier that day she had driven into town to pick up the 357 Magnum she'd ordered a week ago. She was planning to end her life with it this very night. I registered this new piece of information with more than a little alarm, profoundly grateful for her steady stream of words that seemed as if it would never end. Part of me hoped it never would, for I had no idea what I would say when it did. I wondered whether anything I said would cut through the thick haze of her drunken state.

Help me, Guys, I implored my Friends Upstairs. Had I ever felt so desperately in need of their assistance?

My belly had knotted up with trepidation. This woman's life was in my hands! What if I said the wrong thing and she ended it all after we hung up? I tried to calm myself, breathing into the fear and releasing it on the outbreath as I had so often counseled clients during soul-awakening sessions. No Earth-plane assistance was available; there was no time to ask anyone what they would do in this situation. I was on my own. I had always relied on the guidance that poured in from Beyond, and I trusted it above all else. Had there ever been a moment when I was more in need of divine help?

With most callers, I attempted to cut to the chase and save their money. But this was no time for economy. No matter what this call was costing a minute, I needed to keep this woman on the line. I still had no clue what I was to say. I waited, hoping for some kind of inspirational response to come in. Nothing happened.

Agents of Grace

The woman's recitation droned on and on. Her slurred words ran together in my mind like a finger-painting left out in the rain. A part of me felt desperate; I wished I could call the psychic hotline myself and get some guidance on how to handle this life-or-death emergency call. Another, deeper part -- a level of myself I was not very in touch with at the moment -- watched the drama unfold from its place of calm certainty.

"And then there's the Baba-ji' thing," the woman said. She pronounced the Hindu name with the accent on the last syllable, Texas-style.

The words sliced through my mental fog and yanked me right back to here and now. I was fully present, my attention riveted on what was unfolding.

"The Baba-ji' thing?" I repeated, matching her intonation, hoping for more.

"Yeah, this guy who says his name is Baba-ji' keeps showing up in my dreams," she elaborated. "I don't know who he is or why he keeps showing up. I'm afraid if I tell anyone, they'll think I'm crazy and lock me up. You're the first person I've told."

She stopped talking, and her breath seemed to hang in the air in suspended animation. I could feel her waiting to see how I would respond. Would I think she was crazy?

I calmly, quietly said, "I know who Babaji is."

"You *do*?" She was obviously flabbergasted. "You know who Baba-ji' is?"

"Yes, I do."

I went on to tell her that Babaji was a great, immortal being who had lived in the Himalayas for centuries, and that my partner had met him in his most recent form as Herakhan Baba during the 1980s. Barry had spent time at Babaji's ashram, I continued, and had told me many amazing stories about his experiences there.

The woman listened, drinking this in.

She responded, "I can't buh-*lieve* you know who Baba-ji' is. I just can't buh-*lieve* it." The information I had shared seemed to be sobering her up.

"Well, it's true," I replied. Several seconds of silence went by.

"I can't buh-*lieve* you've heard of him," she reiterated. Contrary to the words, her capacity to trust what she was hearing appeared to be growing with each repetition.

I then told the woman that many people view Babaji as a manifestation of the Hindu God Shiva, who presides over the death and destruction that have to happen so we can be reborn into who we really are. I reflected that, from the things she had told me, it sounded as if she was going through just such a process. Even though everything seemed to be in ruins, this must have needed to happen so something truly new could happen in her life.

With that, the steady stream of words stopped. I let out a slow exhale. Things were going well, I told myself. Of all the "psychics" her call could have been routed to that night, she got someone who had endured a few bouts of death and destruction herself, and who had fervently prayed to Babaji for help on more than one occasion.

"Well, that may be," she responded, "but I still don't get why Baba-ji' would be coming to me in my dreams."

Help me here, Guys, I pleaded with my Friends Upstairs. *This has to be right.* I felt my breathing opening up a space within me that could receive whatever might pour in from Beyond.

"I don't know for sure, but I can tell you one thing," I heard myself say, as interested as I hoped she was in what that might be.

"He doesn't waste his time," I heard my voice continue. "If he's coming to you, there must be a good reason, even if we don't know what it is yet. He just wouldn't waste his time on anyone he didn't think was worth it. And he certainly wouldn't bother with you if he thought the best thing for you to do was kill yourself."

There's no way I could have thought that up. The argument sounded convincing to me. But would she buy it?

She took the words in, absorbing their import.

"Are you sure?" she finally asked.

"I'm sure."

My breath slowly exhaled. We sat in silence for a few moments.

"He must be coming to you to help you through this awful time in your life," I suggested. "And that is an incredible blessing. He wouldn't do that for just anyone."

The intense sense of urgency that had tensed my body and filled the room began to dissipate. I felt my breathing normalize, though some residual tension remained. Our conversation continued awhile longer as the woman integrated what had been delivered. From her remarks, it was clear the information was having its desired effect.

At last I felt that she had accepted the gift of grace that had come through for her. Before we said our final goodnight, I made sure she had a plan for disposing of the gun. I made her promise to follow through with it.

I'll never know what became of that woman. But it would be nice to think that somewhere in the Lone Star State, there is somebody still marveling that, during her darkest hour, there was at least one person in the world who knew exactly what she was talking about.

Is there a better feeling than being utilized by Life in this way? Years may pass while our life feels like an arid desert, and we wonder what on Earth we are doing here. We may ask the Divine when we will ever experience the fulfillment we know is possible, and pray to be shown the way into that eventuality. And then one day, when we least expect it, the opportunity we have awaited appears.

It is easy to give all credit to God when we know we are not the ones acting in such situations. I could never have come up with the things the Divine gave me to say to that woman. To this day, I feel blessed that I was in the right place at the right time to offer what came through me to someone facing the ultimate pain of incarnation, the sense that our very existence has no meaning or purpose. Is there any question about who, exactly, was routing the calls that evening?

Barry: Grace that Empowers More Grace

After a year away, Allen, a friend and client, came by for a visit. He arrived just before dark on a cold, wintry day with eight inches of snow on the ground and more on the way. With the approaching weather, the snow tires still in the trunk of his car, and dark settling in, it was obvious he was to stay for the night. The decision was cemented when the car would not start when he attempted to move it closer to the house to unload his things.

The next morning, some of Allen's painful relationship dilemmas bubbled to the surface. Soon Karen and I found ourselves holding space as his soul took him on a journey to explore the issues more deeply. The mysterious path of the soul's grace took him into his belly, where he faced the unresolved childhood patterns that were the source of his current suffering. As Allen prepared to leave a short time later, his childhood vulnerability was written on his face and carried in his body movements.

I helped him jump-start the car and install the snow tires. As he left, I warned Allen to keep the car running, since it seemed likely there was a problem with the car's electrical system. Off he went into the grey, overcast day.

Within fifteen minutes, we received a phone call: Allen had arrived at the gas station on the main highway. He had forgotten not to turn the engine off, and now he couldn't get it started. Clearly, Allen was reliving the childhood insecurity, self-doubt, and powerlessness that had arisen during his session, as part of the process of healing his core wounding.

Although we could feel how much Allen would have liked us to come and help him, the deep inner knowing arose that we were not to drive to the gas station and assist him. Instead, we felt prompted to call in divine assistance for him so that he could align within himself, connect with the Source of all grace, and allow It to take control of his situation.

Still on the phone, we deepened into the stillness together. I found myself in the familiar inner position of being immersed in the golden-white light of the God Self. I felt the light pouring down and enfolding Allen as I envisioned him standing next to his car at the gas station. The light carried with it the instructions I then verbalized: He was to go inside, connect with the Divine, and turn to It for assistance and resolution. "The light never fails," I assured him, adding that this was a great opportunity to build his faith and trust. Allen thanked me for my support and we hung up.

We didn't hear back from Allen, so awhile later we called his cell phone. Sure enough, within minutes after our call, someone had come along and jump-started his car. Now, he had safely arrived at his destination, after stopping at an auto shop where someone tightened a loose battery terminal and sent him on his way.

Sometimes, the most powerful way we can serve as a conduit of grace is to access the grace that will empower others to function as agents of grace in their own lives. The grace descending into Allen knew exactly what to do to align and center him in his soul and higher Self. He was led from within through a practical experience of calling grace into his own life, and his newly discovered capacities met with total success. Now, he carries the potent awareness that was imprinted through this experience: He is directly connected to a Source of omnipotent grace that he can call upon at any time. This awareness makes it much more likely that the next time he faces a challenge, he will remember that the ultimate source of resolution lies within, in his God Self.

〜〜〜

The stories above illustrate just a few of the countless ways we may be utilized as conduits of grace in everyday life. Our capacity to serve in this way continually expands and deepens as we consecrate our lives to being available for the Divine to work through us. We can also invite the One Great Being to assist us in opening wider to Its inpouring blessings. The following inner experience is designed to facilitate that.

EXPERIENCE~ACTIVATION: Expanding the Capacity to Be a Conduit of Grace

Once again, open up a sacred space. Sit or lie down, invite the physical body to become comfortable, and bring your awareness to the breath. As each breath comes and goes, feel your energy and consciousness settling into a peaceful state. Invite the breath to carry your awareness into your sacred core, the soul space above the heart.

Feel your desire to expand your capacity to function as a conduit of grace. Now, from within the soul space, extend your awareness up the vertical channel. As your consciousness rises into the levels of the oversoul, enjoy the expansive vastness of those realms. As awareness continues to rise beyond the oversoul levels toward ultimate Source, make your intention known. Ask to be utilized in the highest possible ways to be a conduit of grace on a day-to-day basis.

While you continue to feel your deep desire to be used more fully by Life as an agent of grace, notice whether any promptings arise regarding current situations in your life. Do you sense any communications from the soul, oversoul, and/or Source? Allow some time to simply be present and receptive.

Reflect on your recent opportunities to be a conduit of grace. Maybe you encountered someone who was upset about something, and you found yourself inspired to say things that seemed to help. Or you came upon a sick or injured animal, and gave it loving care. Perhaps you shared an e-mail that tickled your funny bone with several friends, knowing it would lift their spirits. You might have felt moved to brighten your work space with a bouquet of flowers that everyone would enjoy. Allow some time to continue reflecting on how you have recently served as a divine conduit.

Now, ask to become even more aware that opportunities always exist to invite the Divine to pour through you to bless the world. Ask to be made aware of the particular opportunities that Life is putting in front of you each day, and to respond to them more fully. If you feel that certain divine qualities would help you to function more fully as an agent of grace, invite the Divine to strengthen them within you. For one person, more patience might be helpful, while another might sense a need for greater physical energy and stamina. Someone else might call for deeper compassion and tolerance of differing views.

Ask the Divine to shower you with the frequencies of energy~consciousness that would be most helpful. Bring your awareness to the vertical axis, feel your natural, innate communion with God, and ask for the qualities you desire to flow down into you from the limitless One. Allow some time for this to take place, and notice what you experience on all levels of your being.

Finally, ask the Divine to show you a specific situation in your life that would benefit from your serving as a conduit of grace. Breathe open a welcoming space within you for the awareness of this circumstance to be present. Now, connect with the situation from the soul level. Bring the entire matter into the soul space above the heart and call for grace to be poured into the situation, right now.

As your awareness continues to rest within the soul space, observe what happens. Notice any new perspectives or orientations toward the situation that are now present within you. Ask if there is a specific way you might function as an agent of grace in your outer expression, or if it is sufficient for you to work on the inner planes with the situation. Often, a combination of the two is most effective.

Allow this experience to come to its natural conclusion. Breathing and feeling whatever is present, notice any new sensations within your body and energy field. Feel your gratitude as your capacity for being a conduit of grace enlarges.

Gently bring your awareness back to the outer world, and invite your eyes to open when they are ready. How does the world look to you now? And how does it feel to sense your place within it?

This basic inner process can be used with any life situation that arises, from relationship issues to financial challenges and health concerns. Before the mind has a chance to get busy with the matter, turn it over to the soul and beyond, asking for divine help. Be sure to ask if there are specific ways you can serve as an agent of grace in the situation. Allow plenty of time to receive whatever pours in, whether it arrives in the form of information and understanding, energetic infusions, or a sudden upwelling of a divine quality such as love. Then stand back and watch what unfolds.

You might enjoy journaling day by day to track the changes in your life, paying special attention to the situations that present ongoing challenges. Observe what happens and record the shifts, noting how things are changing. The action of grace will reveal itself -- if not immediately, then over time. Often the effects are instantaneous, while in other situations they accrue gradually and result in subtle, pervasive changes. Consciously observing and recording what unfolds builds faith and trust in the effectiveness of making ourselves available as agents of grace.

5

Our Grace-Note
in the Planetary Song
of Awakening

Each of us possesses a unique gift, a quality of being that only we can bring to the world. As individualized aspects of God, we need to sound our particular note or tone in order for the planetary song to be complete. Our irreplaceable offering also plays an integral role in the planetary transformation, especially when we know that participating in the collective awakening is the biggest reason we are here on Earth at this time. Since no one else in all of Creation possesses our exact combination of energetic frequencies, there is no substitute for it. That is why it is imperative that we each reconnect with our essential Self and let our note clearly ring out from the center of our being.

Our true soul gift can only come from the core of the soul itself. The form the gift takes is important, but less so than the release of divine presence from our sacred core. The presence alone is what awakens and transforms. When it flows out into the world through our particular soul gift, it resonates the divine core in others. Ensouled art and music are powerful examples of this, for while the form may be beautiful and uplifting, an intangible essence enters the center of our being in the presence of a spiritually empowered song, poem, dance, or painting. The form both carries and expresses its unique frequency pattern, which travels into us and acts beyond the level of the senses and the mind.

We may have spent decades looking without for what can only be found within, finally realizing it is impossible to discover what we're here for in the outer world. Yes, the ways we express our purpose will most likely involve the things of the world, as will the tools and devices we need to make it manifest. But the essential nature of our unique note is hidden within the depths of our soul. To uncover the highest expression of our life energy, we must journey within.

The passage into our inner sanctuary is the journey we must make to unfold our divine gift, for it lies in the abode of the soul at the altar of our being. This gift is what we have been prepared for, lifetime after lifetime. Countless experiences and awakenings have sculpted our soul to be ready for this moment. Creation has been working for thousands, if not millions, of years to prepare agents of transformation for this exact time in human evolution. That is how divinely organized and planned the process is, and your particular role in it is irreplaceable.

Most of us carry many layers of conditioning that overlay and obscure our true, divine nature. As we grow up we try to fit into what our parents, schools and society expect us to be, even when it goes against the inner voice of the soul. To avoid being judged or punished, we unintentionally pave over the pathway into the inner sanctum where our unique, essential nature resides, and expend our precious life energy on activities that are not resonant with our soul frequencies or life purpose. That's why it's essential, if we are to fulfill our soul purpose and destiny, to journey back within. Along the way to our sacred core, we will need to face all the levels of false self we've laid atop our essential nature in a veneer of accommodation to outer forces. All the ideas about who and what we think we are and what we are here to do will eventually be surrendered as we travel toward the truth of our being. Again and again we will die to our conditioned self-images as we return Home to the true Self and discover deeper levels of our soul purpose and destiny.

Barry: Leaving the World, Finding the Divine

The journey of discovering my unique gift involved completely dying to the "me" I thought I was. I had to leave the worldly context that framed my identity and watch as one layer after another of my false self was shredded.

It may sound paradoxical that the path to discovering who I really was began just as I was becoming who I thought I really wanted to be. My idealized self-image was to be a successful businessman, and my career was the central focus of my life. Everything I valued most -- money, power, prestige, a sense of purpose and accomplishment -- came from what I did. For a while all of this seemed fulfilling and satisfying; it was what I believed life was all about. But when I saw what happened to those above me on the career ladder and contemplated the effects of some of my business dealings, it became clear that where that path led was not a path of soul.

Though just a short time ago I had seemed to be standing on secure, solid ground, now I found myself thrust into the Mystery. I seemed to have no choice but to jump off the highest cliff I had ever stood on into a vast emptiness, with no sense of support, no idea where the path might go. All that I had known had to be left behind -- the money, power, prestige and privilege, the safety and security, the career that had seemed to offer everything I had ever wanted.

As I stepped off the cliff into the void, I was carried into a whole new octave of existence. I quit my job, got a backpack, and went to Asia, with no plan or idea where the path would lead. I discovered ways of living that matched my soul frequencies more than anything I had ever known, and experienced the greatest possibility for my life in the form of God incarnate as demonstrated by Mahavatar Babaji. What I gave up paled in comparison to what I was given. The giant step of faith and trust was rewarded with equally enormous gifts of grace. I learned that the more we surrender and the bigger the ego-death, the greater the grace we receive in return. Over time, I surrendered one dimension of my existence after another to the inner divinity that was coming forth. And as this occurred, the vast, inner presence of the soul swallowed up more and more of what Barry thought he was.

As described in *Soul Awakening*, the process continued until the Lotus of the Soul opened and "i" merged with the inner divinity that was the true source of my being. The world I had known had virtually disappeared, because the consciousness that created that seeming world had largely dissolved. I found myself living with no objective. What arose in this empty fullness was a feeling of compassion for all sentient beings and especially my fellow humans. It was readily apparent they were suffering, just as I had. I knew how difficult it was to be where I saw most people in the world, because I had been there. I saw that the planet and humanity were heading toward a great crisis, precipitated by living in a separated state of consciousness.

The only thing left to do was to assist others to come out of the ego's dream-state, the nightmare of separation. I was finally dead enough, surrendered enough to want nothing more than to do God's will and help others. I was finally ready to serve.

With my Soul Lotus open, higher-dimensional consciousness had become a normal experience. My meditations were journeys into the vast realms of the oversoul and beyond, where I began to remember many previous incarnations. The core of the soul opened, revealing an inner temple in which I began to merge with the previous incarnations, especially those pivotal to my soul destiny and purpose in this life. One by one they reintroduced themselves, and the gifts and capacities developed during that particular lifetime again became available. The wisdom and understanding that had arisen during those lifetimes began to flood back into my awareness.

The pivotal lifetimes included one as a priest in Egypt and another as a sacred scientist in Atlantis, where I actively worked with advanced technologies for Self-realization and ascension. Other lifetimes devoted totally to the inner path emerged: a lama in Tibet and several incarnations as a yogi in India, where much knowledge was gained on the inner path of realizing the true Self. As I remembered these lives and harvested the soul gifts from many lifetimes, I also found myself avidly reading books on the subtle energetics and inner processes of awakening. I attended workshops and studied sacred geometry, crystals, light work, and other technologies to activate the light body. Much of this information seemed very familiar and obvious, since I was remembering what I had known in previous embodiments. Slowly it all braided together into a composite that was perfect for this lifetime, when I would be put to service in assisting in the planetary awakening and ascension process.

At the right moment, I was asked if I would be willing to work with a grouping of higher beings called The Office of the Christ to assist in the planetary awakening. Shortly thereafter, the Universal Christ presence began to descend into and through me whenever I connected with Christ Jesus on the inner planes. People began to show up with a wide variety of human dis-eases and conflicts. In the absence of any healing or therapeutic training, I found myself asking them to lie down. Then I would call in the Christ presence to do whatever could be done for them. As the Christ presence descended, a healing and transformational process would ensue. My only role was to be a conduit through which this grace could flow.

As I stepped into this new level of service, higher-dimensional beings delivered an intensive on the energy~consciousness processes that occur in the multidimensional subtle anatomy during the process of birthing the Luminous Self, the Christed being we are all destined to become. Once I understood the processes involved in awakening, I was shown designs for creating an energetic space incorporating crystals, pyramidal energetics, sacred geometry, magnetics, and more. This multidimensional energetic matrix was intended to unify the oversoul and Source levels of being with the human subtle bodies and chakras. This would accelerate embodying the transcendental levels of being, which is the essence of realizing the Luminous Self.

As it all unfolded, it was a marvel to see how perfectly this and all my previous lifetimes had been orchestrated over thousands of years to bring me to this moment when the journey at last bore fruit. The satisfaction that had eluded me in this lifetime was now so fully realized, my heart and soul felt like they had been set on fire. All I wanted was to carry out my purpose, and each moment I was engaged in it felt ecstatic. The momentum escalated when Karen and I were brought together and another phase of soul destiny unfolded. For two decades our lives became a university of the soul, guided by higher beings for the purpose of expanding the scope of our service.

It was a long way, both in distance and in consciousness, from the skyscrapers and ego-driven banking world in Los Angeles to merging into the higher dimensions with people during our sessions in a small bungalow in Hawai'i. Little from that former life could have prepared me for this new phase. It would have been impossible for me to chart the path that took me to my soul purpose and destiny. Only the mysterious journey of following the pathless path my soul laid out before me could have taken me there. And only this path could have peeled away all the layers of not-self, all the illusions and ego limitations, that had to be let go so the divine gifts could come forth.

Karen: The Garden of the Resurrection

My journey of awakening had contained a considerable amount of emotional suffering. As I found my way through it to a place of greater freedom and inner peace, I yearned to assist others so they would not need to experience as much emotional pain as I had. As an astrologer, I was fascinated by Chiron, the heavenly body that had been discovered on my birthday in 1977. In astrological symbolism, Chiron is said to represent the wounded healer, someone who has transformed the greatest travails into healing gifts. Could all that I had been through somehow be alchemically transmuted into the ability to facilitate evolutionary transformation in others?

In *Soul Awakening*, I shared the story of how my soul symbol transformed over time. For weeks, each morning in meditation I had brought my awareness into the soul space above the heart, where I saw a tiny flame barely glowing within a vast, dark cave. That minuscule fire seemed about as tenuous as my awareness of my soul.

Gradually, over many weeks, the little light grew stronger and more stable. Then, one day, I went within to find that the flame had migrated. Now it blazed forth from a standard outside the cave, next to its entrance. As I stood there amazed at this new development, I looked around and realized the cave was adjacent to a beautiful garden. Moved by the beauty and refinement of this living sanctuary, I inwardly heard, *This is the Garden of the Resurrection.*

As I continued to absorb the blessings of this exquisite place, a life-changing communication arrived: **You** *are the Garden of the Resurrection.* These words spoke to my deepest longing to assist others in going beyond their suffering and discovering the divine magnificence that lay within them. I had often despaired of ever overcoming enough of my own suffering to serve in this way.

In that moment, self-doubt was replaced by the realization that *I already was* everything I had sought to become. There was nothing I needed to learn, or develop, or strive to be -- *my very beingness* facilitated resurrection. All that I had endured had transformed into the ability to be present while others experienced their deepest pain turning into wisdom, acceptance and forgiveness. This was soon borne out by a series of sessions in which women dove to the bottom of the trauma of sexual abuse and experienced the miracle of divine resurrection for themselves. The great dream for this life had suddenly come true!

Through grace, my own suffering evolved into the capacity to facilitate the transformation of wounding into awareness of the inherent wholeness that always lies beneath it. All that my own life journey has contained and all that I have become as a result uniquely prepared me for this particular way of being a conduit of grace. In the same way, each of us goes through the exact preparation and "training" needed so that our innate soul qualities can blossom into gifts of grace. If our readying process contains trauma, it may seem we are victims of an unfair universe at the time the hardships occur. But if we can ride our suffering all the way to the bottom, we will be carried back up and out into the realms where the meaning in the suffering and the evolutionary gifts hidden within it are revealed.

When John Lennon said, "Life is what happens while we're busy making other plans," he could just as well have been taking about grace. When things are going well, we have no problem opening to receive the divine blessings that are pouring in. But when the opposite of all we had hoped for has arrived, it is not easy to see through the distressing disguise and find the gift of grace in the situation. The challenges may be so enormous that we might simply be focused on getting through each day. Only in retrospect does it become evident that this training period was honing the exact divine qualities that would later be needed to fulfill our soul destiny.

My life had presented me with much in need of resurrection. From my mother's suicide to the family pattern of addiction, decades had been devoted to overcoming deeply limiting programs and the residues that remained from traumatic events. Although I had found help along the way, I often felt alone with these challenges, while those around me seemed to have carefree lives free of emotional hardships. Just as it is often said that we teach what we most need to learn, our ultimate service often takes the form of exactly what we ourselves have yearned to receive from others. Being given the opportunity to function as a Garden of Resurrection for others who are suffering has been satisfying beyond words. My prayer that my challenges could be transformed into healing presence had been answered in a way that transcends anything I could have imagined. Whenever I am utilized in this capacity, I am saturated with the sense that *This is what I was born to be and do.* The feeling that fills me is *It doesn't get any better than this!*

It may be the ultimate gift of grace to be able to view whatever befalls us as a blessing, however disguised it may appear to be. Reading even the most exalted spiritual accounts cannot confer this ability; we must live into it. Often, it is only in retrospect that we recognize the perfection of our past: the day-to-day, in vivo training program that has brought us into this current moment. When we can meet our situation with gratitude and acceptance, we are more likely to discover the gifts that lie hidden within the thorny dilemmas we face. As our faith in the Divine deepens, we come to know that each and every circumstance we encounter offers an opportunity to evolve beyond fear into greater trust that God has our best interests at heart.

The One only wants to see each of us blossom into the fullest expression of our soul gifts. Knowing this, we can view our current situation as an opportunity to flower a little more completely, day by day, until at some point we realize we are living in the fullness of our soul's expression.

Discovering Our Unique Note

Recognizing the deeper purpose that only we can bring forth -- our unique note in the planetary song -- is a pivotal initiation in the evolution of the soul. Whether it occurs all at once or over time, as the soul steps into fulfilling its destiny, it brings forth the highest possible manifestations it was designed to contribute to Life. The desire to discover the essence of our unique purpose can become a burning fire in the heart that propels us into an outer quest to find out the reasons we have taken embodiment this time around. Our search may lead us down a variety of avenues we feel impelled to explore, as we study, research, and experiment to find out what really fascinates us. We know we are being guided from within when we feel a strong energetic pull we cannot resist. Some people zero in on one primary endeavor and devote years to it, while others pursue a series of soul-interests over a lifetime. In either case, an underlying energetic signature alerts us that we have found a pursuit that resonates with our soul.

Some people discover that the unique flavor of grace flowing through them wants to express in specific, defined outer ways. This was the case for us when we were led into facilitating soul-awakening experiences. Many others are here to embody particular divine qualities such as compassion, peace and joy. Their outer lives may look much like everyone else's, as they go to work, raise children, and so on, but all the while their luminous essence is emanating divine grace, uplifting everyone they touch. Although they may seem largely unnoticed by the world, their contribution is just as valuable as that of those with a more specific form of service.

While our outer preparation goes on, an even more important inner preparation occurs as the deeper and vaster dimensions of the soul unfold. The inner program or script to guide us, as well as our unique qualities and gifts from many lifetimes, come forth from within our heart of hearts. When, above all else, we focus on deepening our soul communion and commit to living from the soul's guidance, we can trust that we will fulfill our soul purpose and destiny.

This fulfillment is part of an immensely vast and complex transpersonal process that our human selves are incapable of discovering or carrying out on their own. As both of us have experienced, ego~personality patterns and identities must die in order for our soul purpose to be born. These false identities veil the soul's deeper nature. As they fall away, we begin to hear the first murmurs of our particular note in the planetary song. We transcend the veils of consciousness taken on during this embodiment as we remember and recover abilities and gifts from other incarnations. The stream of many lives opens to us and the skills, capacities, knowledge, wisdom and soul qualities developed previously become available again. Discovering our soul purpose and destiny is very much based in harvesting all that we are as an eternal soul that has sculpted itself over many lifetimes.

The ego must be substantially subsumed in order for the soul to reconnect with the nonphysical sources of guidance that make themselves known when we are ready. To fulfill our purpose, it is quite possible that we are now going to be working not only with other human beings, but also in concert with higher-dimensional presences. Our function may be part of a larger plan involving many beings, some in bodies and others working at transcendent levels. To be dependable in carrying out our part of the plan, we need to be guided by the soul, not the ego-mind.

As we are raised into our soul purpose, ever more higher-dimensional energy descends into and through us and out into the world. This is especially true when angelic presences, ascended masters, and other higher beings overlight our contribution and pour their vastly expanded energies through us. Consciously opening the vertical axis into the oversoul and Source levels fuels our expression with infinitely larger quanta of spiritual power. How we qualify that energy is of utmost importance, because whatever we imprint it with, whether a sublime state of peace or one of internal chaos, will have a much greater impact because it is empowered with potent higher energies. Cultivating inner calmness, harmony and balance so that we do not muddy the higher energies with mental and emotional distortion is critical.

This doesn't mean we must be completely empty and free of ego-distortion for the soul's purposes to emerge. Even those who are intensely involved in fulfilling their soul destiny find shadow material arising, sometimes powerfully, and the remaining ego-patterns occasionally attempt to take control. When unconscious material comes up, though, our ever-deepening soul communion allows us to witness and contain it instead of giving it energy and acting it out. Our deepest soul gifts are not activated until we have reached a steady, dependable level of awakening and grounding in the soul. We must demonstrate the capacity to consciously observe, rather than act out, any remaining ego distortions so they do not affect our service. This fail-safe seems to be built into the evolutionary programming, providing a necessary safeguard.

Sculpting the soul like a diamond to reflect the particular qualities of divinity each of us is here to emanate is the process of many lifetimes. During each embodiment, new dimensions of what we are evolving into come forth. For many of us, this is the culminating lifetime after a journey of millennia, the life during which the Lotus of the Soul blooms and the fullness of the soul's nature comes forth. The promise of this fills us with a sense of expectancy and a deep desire to get on with what we came here to manifest. Many of us know that this is the pivotal lifetime we have long awaited, when the fullness of who and what we are will blend with the frequencies of many others to lift the planet to new levels of coherence and remembrance of truth. This knowing is the precognition of what is unfolding, a vision and promise of what is surely to come.

PART TWO

✦ ✦ ✦

The Age
of
Exponential Grace

✦ ✦ ✦

6

The Promise of
Mass Enlightenment

For decades we, along with countless others, had held the vision of a collective awakening. Within our hearts and souls, we knew that participating in this evolutionary upleveling was why we had returned to Earth at this pivotal time in human history. All around us, we witnessed many signs that this planetary awakening was, in fact, underway. More and more people seemed to be waking up, both in the sessions we facilitated and across the planet, and the process appeared to be easier and quicker for many than it had been for us.

After years of traveling up and down the spine of the Rocky Mountains and among the islands of Hawai'i facilitating soul-awakening sessions and groups, we had entered into a quiet, simple time in our lives. Life had planted us in the midst of a large, extended family on a farm that we liked to say was either in the middle of nowhere or the middle of everywhere. We spent summers working as fire lookouts on even more remote mountaintops. Through literally chopping wood and carrying water, the openings in consciousness that had occurred over many years were deeply grounding and integrating.

At our fire lookouts, we gazed out over vast expanses of beautiful, spacious stillness and sent forth prayers and requests for divine intervention on behalf of humanity and the planet. As we considered the state of the world from our remote remove, we often felt saddened by the pervasive conflict, inequity, and suffering that continued to color most human lives. We longed for a large-scale breakthrough that would indicate a substantial new wave of possibility was rippling through humanity's consciousness.

The two of us had often felt there were far greater possibilities for serving as conduits of grace than even those we had experienced. Having learned to trust the Mystery, we felt at peace with however our journeys continued to unfold. At times we wondered whether this quiet, isolated existence would be the final chapter in the story of our lives.

And then, when we least expected it, we received an intimation that there was more...

A New Possibility Arrives

The first clue appeared in an e-mail from our spiritual brother, Kiara Windrider. After more than two decades in the U.S., Kiara had moved back to India, his motherland. A few months after he and his new wife, Grace Sears, left the country, Kiara e-mailed that Grace had become "enlightened." It had happened through something called a "deeksha," a spiritual transmission of energy that had precipitated an intense, three-day kundalini eruption and awakening process in Grace. Kiara added that thousands of others, mostly Indians, were experiencing profound awakenings at this ashram, and that programs for Westerners would soon be offered.

Kiara went on to explain that the spiritual leaders of the ashram, called Kalki Bhagavan and Amma, were said to be dual avatars of enlightenment. They intended to "give" all of humanity full, permanent enlightenment by 2012, if not sooner. According to Bhagavan, when 64,000 people "made it," or became enlightened, that would constitute a large enough percentage of humanity to trigger the "hundredth monkey effect." Collective awakening would be the inevitable result.

On the ashram's web site, Kalki Bhagavan stated that mass enlightenment is the only thing that will save humanity from its self-destructive path. We knew that enlightenment is our natural condition, revealed when the veils of mind are stripped away. We had also read texts about awakening that insisted since enlightenment is our true nature, no one can give it to us. Yet Bhagavan asserted he could do just that, guaranteeing that everyone would "make it" after receiving deeksha -- if not right away, then soon. While what we read sounded a bit grandiose, it also struck us as very real and possible. The report from Kiara, a trusted friend, seemed to confirm everything the web site promised.

What really got our attention, though, was Bhagavan's description of enlightenment. It is not a spiritual phenomenon, he insisted, but a neurobiological event. Bhagavan emphasized that the deeksha physically transforms the brain, restoring its originally intended structure and function. When this occurs, suffering ends, replaced by the joy, happiness and peace we were always meant to experience.

The idea that enlightenment arises as a result of physiological changes in the brain made perfect sense to us. As the film "What the Bleep Do We Know?" demonstrated, the neural networks that govern our behavior start to become wired in during childhood. These habitual pathways largely determine how we respond to the stimuli that enter our world. And they are self-reinforcing: The more frequently we respond with a particular emotion, the more likely it becomes that the next time a similar stimulus appears, the same feeling will arise. For instance, if we are in the habit of reacting angrily whenever another driver cuts in front of us, the neural "groove" for the anger response becomes ever more deeply ingrained, until it seems we have little or no choice about our response. Some researchers go so far as to surmise that we literally become *addicted* to our emotional responses, because similar neurological effects result from both emotional habits and physical substances.

Bhagavan's claims that the deeksha leads to changes in the brain also spoke to issues that had arisen in our work with people. During sessions, after diving into unresolved feelings and beliefs and turning them over to the Divine, most clients easily and naturally entered into communion with the true Self. But some time afterward, the ego-mind often attempted to reestablish itself. It might negate the awakenings that had occurred during the session, or point out why they could not be lived out in the person's life.

In one woman's initial session, the soul-communion she experienced sent her into superconscious states of rapture. As the wisdom of her higher Self poured in, many challenging life issues were clarified, if not resolved, within a very short time. A few weeks later, not feeling well, she returned for a second session. Some of the same issues she had received illumination about were up again. When we asked whether she remembered what her soul had revealed about them during the previous session, the blank look on her face indicated that most of the revelations had receded into the depths of her subconscious. The ego-mind had managed to pave over the memory of the luminous opening she had experienced, including the rapturous bliss and wisdom that were beyond anything she had ever known. This revealed just how potent the mind can be in resisting awakening to the soul.

We really wanted to discover what would free people from the egoic patterning that obscured soul-awareness and led to nothing but suffering. We had long sensed the roots lay deep within the brain, but we didn't know how to get at the distortions there that perpetuated the egoic control mechanisms that made life miserable. How could the tangled neural nets that seemed to drive so much human behavior ever be unraveled? Kalki Bhagavan's message sounded like an answer to our prayer. The key to freedom lay in the brain, and here was someone referred to as an avatar of enlightenment offering to alter our brains through grace. Is there anything a sincere spiritual seeker wants more than the permanent, unbroken state of awakening Bhagavan promised would follow?

The name Kalki also seemed significant. In Hindu cosmology, the Kalki Avatar is the prophesied last incarnation of Vishnu, the aspect of the threefold God who most closely corresponds to the Christ, or God incarnate. Vedic scripture asserts that Kalki will come at the end of time, just as many Christians believe Christ will return, to liberate humanity. *Could this man called Kalki Bhagavan be the Kalki Avatar?*

"You might want to come over and check this out," Kiara had said when we responded to his provocative e-mail with a phone call. Soon we were heading to India to see what all this "enlightenment" stuff was about.

Our First Visit to Golden City

In February of 2004, we arrived in south India. As our taxi entered the ashram campus, we were greeted by a swirl of Westerners from many nations, all clothed in white. The cultish overlay of spiritual glamour inspired little enthusiasm in either of us.

What have I gotten myself into? Karen wondered. Barry somewhat sarcastically joked that what he really wanted was to stick his head out the window of the cab, receive the deeksha, and head right back to the Chennai airport. After years of dissolving spiritual mask identities, we had landed in a place that seemed rife with them.

Yet the young disciples, or dasas, of Kalki Bhagavan who taught our classes were as calm and self-possessed a group of beings as we had ever come across. One dasa was big and jovial, with sparkling deep brown eyes and a James Earl Jones voice. His large body swathed in a sea of white cotton shook with laughter as he gently poked fun of our cherished spiritual beliefs.

A quiet, slender dasa also teased us Westerners about our concepts of enlightenment. "Do you think you will leave here with a halo around your head?" he'd ask with a sly smile.

84

A third dasa insisted, "We are no different from you. We have all the same thoughts and feelings -- the only difference is that in us, there is no place for them to stick."

Oh, how we longed to have Teflon-coated brains, like these ever-peaceful, ever-joyful dasas!

The dasas' teachings emphasized that the vast majority of human beings possess little or no free awareness; consequently, most of us believe whatever the mind says is true. Until there is a "de-clutching" of the mind -- until the mind lets go of its tight grip and stops controlling our consciousness and behavior -- there can be no true freedom. Throughout history, a few fortunate ones have been propelled into the state beyond the mind's dominion, usually after years of arduous spiritual practices. Now, the dasas insisted, such methods were no longer needed -- the deeksha would do everything.

"Go on meditating, if you enjoy it," they counseled, "but know that it is not necessary."

Some of the dasas' strong, sharp statements were eerily reminiscent of an est seminar. "Fear is who you are!" they would shout. "The mind is nothing but a garbage pit!" One elaborated on this point: "You keep a golden lid over the cesspool beneath it, pretending you are 'good' and 'nice' when all the time there is nothing but rotten, smelly garbage underneath."

We hoped the other participants, many of whom appeared to be relative spiritual beginners, would not take this to heart, for it had the potential to severely depress anyone who believed that fear and garbage were fundamental to their true nature. While we understood the dasas' goal must be to break down identification with the mind and its contents, we felt sure there must be another way. Our own experiences had unfailingly demonstrated that what lay within each of us, hidden beneath the mind and ego, was sublime beyond description. But when we attempted to question the dasas' harsh statements during class, we were told we weren't yet ready for discussions about the soul.

Preparing for the Deeksha

Before receiving the deeksha, our group first experienced five days of karma clearing processes, which turned out to be a synthesis of modern Western psychological techniques and ancient Indian enlightenment teachings. The leaders seemed to know just what to say to unleash torrents of unresolved feelings in the participants. During the inner processes, nearly everyone in the large hall wailed and shrieked, moaning and crying out as long-buried emotions roared to the surface.

Karen wrote in her journal: "After days of listening to people screaming out the pain of a lifetime -- if not the suffering of countless earthly embodiments -- I fully felt that all I really care about is seeing people wake up. My heart was so wide open that I'd look into a person's eyes and burst into tears at the preciousness of that life -- all that has transpired, all that is aspired to. I consciously turned down the intensity so I'd be capable of getting up and leaving the hall at the end of each session."

Our time at the ashram seemed to be progressing in a way that was strikingly similar to most of the soul-awakening sessions we facilitated. First, we dove into unresolved egoic material, thoroughly feeling whatever arose. Then, once we had fully met what was present, its charge dropped away as it naturally found its place within our wholeness. No longer burdened by as much egoic baggage, openings in awareness inevitably followed.

The processes at the ashram were as thorough and unrelenting as anything we had ever experienced. We'd been emptied of everything within us that was ready to release. Glimpses of new levels of consciousness had begun to occur. Within a very short time, the ground within us all was being thoroughly prepared to receive the deeksha.

Barry: "Me" Dissolves

During one process, the crown chakra opened and white light infused the field of awareness until that became all there was. No sense of the body remained, just pure awareness. I could hear everything going on in the room, yet there was no "connection" with any of it -- it was all just sensory input passing across the screen of the mind.

The session ended and everyone got up to leave. There I lay, no connection with the body, no sense of a personal will to make anything happen. I wondered how long it would be before someone noticed my immobilized form and came to inquire, but the hall was empty by then and there I continued to lie.

The deep body identification had been dissolved to the degree that I was unable to even exert my will over the physical form. There was absolutely no fear, but a sense of relief, a tremendous feeling of freedom. Clearly I was not the body, nor was the body mine.

Then there was a sensation -- the first, as a fly landed on what I remembered as "my" arm. Somehow, this awakened the body and it remembered itself. A few moments later the body got up without my volition and walked out the door. As the feet made contact with the hot, bare earth, it was as though I had never felt the pulsing, living being under my feet before. I stood there in awe at how alive everything was.

With the veils of ego-mind so deeply dissolved away, physical sensations were experienced as never before. It didn't seem strange or supernatural, but the way the senses were meant to be -- the way it is to be truly awake and alive.

A day or two later, the light again descended and the top of my head seemed to disappear. The group process was about feeling emotions, and the one that surfaced was a sadness about the state of my left index finger. A saw had severed a nerve in it the previous spring, and sensation had been lost in the fingertip. While it was a small issue, I felt sad about the loss of the luscious sensation of touch. Now, all I experienced was numbness, not the warmth and texture of skin when I massaged or touched another.

As I allowed myself to fully drop into the sadness, what arose was how deeply I missed this and how sad it would be to go without it for the rest of this life. A particularly strong sadness arose for the body itself, that it was now damaged and less than fully functional. As my heart opened, feeling gratitude for all that I had experienced previously with that finger, and lamenting having lost it for life, a current descended through the head, down the arm and into the finger.

I sensed something had shifted. In touching that finger to the woven mat beneath me, it was immediately apparent that most of the feeling had been restored. The knowing arose that this was a gift from Kalki Bhagavan, an acknowledgment that "God" cares and that miracles happen. This, along with everything else we were experiencing, shattered deep levels of doubt and conditioning. Something truly amazing was going on here. We had never before encountered this level of power and grace.

Barry: The Long-awaited Deeksha

I was already floating in the higher worlds when it came time for the big event, the one we had all come to India for...the deeksha. The hall was crowded with three hundred people when Kalki Bhagavan walked down the center aisle separating the men and women. The spiritual power he emanated was so strong that even my visual impressions began to alter. I struggled to keep my head upright to watch the procession of dasas behind Bhagavan. A glee as I had not experienced arose with the knowing that this was **the** day, a supreme moment in my journey.

Seated on a dais with five male dasas to his right and five female dasas to his left, Kalki Bhagavan answered questions for some time. Then he arose, and one by one the male dasas stood before him with their arms outstretched, palms up. Bhagavan gently and quickly placed his hands, palms down, over those of each dasa. As he did this, the dasa slumped to the floor, caught by two others who supported him back to his position on the stage. Next, the women dasas received Bhagavan's transmission. They burst into gales of laughter but were able to walk back to their places without assistance.

One by one, the men in the group went up to the five male dasas, lined up side by side. They were still so overcome by the transmission that each had another dasa behind him, holding up his arms. Knocked out by the energy, I was unable to walk, so I crawled toward the stage to wait my turn.

One dasa held peacock feathers, another a large bowl with a handle, and a third had a whisk and a container of water. As those ahead of me moved down the line of dasas, many needed help after they had passed the second or third. By the time they had received the transmission from all five, they either needed to be carried or assisted to an empty space on the floor where they could lie down.

Kneeling before the first dasa, I looked into his eyes and found myself peering into eternity, the Void itself. I immediately began to drift beyond this world. When the second splashed water on the crown chakra, the bliss became almost overwhelming. With each dasa, the light and ecstasy peaked until the now-thin shell of primal containment, the contracture of mind that comprised "me," could no longer be held on to. The level of bliss pegged on the bliss-o-meter and then it broke, dissolving "me" into everything and nothing. Drunk on bliss, I was assisted down the aisle laughing and smiling, full of love for everyone.

To describe the state is impossible, for it was more an absence of than an experience of. Complete emptiness that is paradoxically full might be a try. Suchness, oneness -- we have all heard the words, and they turn out to be inadequate to describe this state that is utterly simple and natural, the way things are without overlays.

The sense of being altered and hugely expanded, the infusion of bliss and light began to subside, more quickly at first, and slowing over the weeks and months thereafter. Even now, years later, they have not gone completely away, but have become integrated and normalized as the base-level experience of being. Most importantly, the thinking mind had "de-clutched," as Bhagavan had promised. The incessant background noise of the thought-stream interfering with awareness and obscuring clarity had virtually stopped.

Karen: The Everything and the Nothing

When Bhagavan entered the hall, an aura of composure and peace radiated from his short, rather rotund form as he strolled to the stage. Many in the group began crying, while others swooned in ecstasy, overcome by the joy of being in Kalki Bhagavan's presence. Bhagavan answered questions from the audience in an extremely economical, incisive way that left no doubt in my mind that I was in the presence of an enlightened being. I marveled at my good fortune to be in this room, where the very atmosphere was charged with exaltation.

Then, suddenly, it was time for the deeksha.

When the female dasas received the energy from Bhagavan and began to laugh uncontrollably, the effect was contagious; about half of the people in the room erupted into gleeful gales of laughter. I love to laugh, yet I found myself dropping into a profound stillness that only deepened as those around me were carried away with cosmic hilarity. As the uninhibited laughter subsided, only to resume with even more abandon, it got quieter and quieter within me. Something astounding was happening, and the deeksha hadn't even officially begun!

Michelle, a new friend from Mexico City, stood next to me, her entire body shaking uncontrollably as it did whenever the spiritual energies became intense. As the dasas began giving deeksha, I maneuvered Michelle to the front of the line and whispered to one of the helpers, "I think Michelle needs to receive her deeksha now." She nodded, instantly registering Michelle's state, and I returned to my spot near the back of the room.

For the next hour or more, I watched as nearly everyone else in the hall received deeksha, feeling as though each transmission was happening to me, too. The joy of witnessing so many beings lifted into their true magnificence filled me with gratitude for having been brought to this amazing place. Weaving and listing like a drunken sailor, here came Barry, leaning on his helper's arm as he grinned and waved to those of us still waiting our turn, as if to say, "This will soon be yours." Other faces radiated the brilliant beauty of their true natures, unencumbered by mental and emotional baggage.

And now it was my turn. As I took my place before the first dasa, someone whispered, "Look into their eyes." With one or two, I seemed to be gazing into Infinity. There was no one home; not the slightest residue of a personal self remained in those fathomless depths. In the eyes of others, I saw the great, goodhearted bliss of no further concern for anything -- the absolute knowing that all is taken care of, forever. Reaching the end of the line, I noticed that, unlike many before me, my body still seemed capable of walking. Grace, Kiara's wife, escorted me to my place on the floor, and I lay down.

And there I remained for the next few hours -- or eons -- all sense of residing in a physical body having totally disappeared. Pure consciousness was "all" that remained. There was no "I" -- no thought, no feeling, no anything localized. What was left was vastness -- without quality, without attribute. Floating in vastness, as vastness. No forms existed in this vastness, yet it was not empty, but rather immeasurably full: of Presence, of Life, of Isness.

In this state of pure being, there was nothing to do and no one to do it. There was not even anyone who could possibly think that thought. Words can never do justice to the experience, for they are a distant shadow of a reality far more vibrant than anything this consciousness had previously experienced. In the empty-yet-full vibrancy, beingness simply *was*, for a length of clock-time that shall forever remain a mystery.

An eternity passed in that ocean of pure beingness. And then, out of the infinite vastness, sensation unexpectedly returned, as people nearby began to stir and make their way to the exits. Stepping over my outstretched legs, more than a few bare feet bumped into them. This occurred with such frequency that a thought arose out of the endless spaciousness: *Maybe they don't see these legs. Has this body become invisible?*

As provocative as the thought seemed, there was no way to test it out, since movement remained impossible. Even to open the eyes required a level of volition that had utterly vanished.

As this first thought floated in the vastness, absolutely no preference accompanied it. Either way was fine -- whether the body had, in fact, disappeared, or whether it still remained lying on the floor. There was no "me" to care! All that existed were a bemused wondering, a detached curiosity, and a realization that knowing the "answer" was totally unimportant.

This state went on and on, in the timeless expanse of pure being. Eventually, the eyes slowly and effortlessly opened, and they noticed that the room was nearly empty of people. Now, enjoyment of the faculty of sight began. The marvelous patterns of the roof thatching seemed endlessly fascinating; the evanescent loveliness of the flower garlands over the doorways touched a place of deep tenderness. *Ah, the incredible, impermanent beauty of this realm!* Tears flowed, but there was no one crying.

Joy arose, replaced by peaceful stillness, which segued into the thought that it might be nice to lie down on the bed, back in the dorm. After some time, the body, of its own accord, slowly rose to a sitting position. Much later, it completed its ascent into the upright world. After another eternity it found itself back in the dorm, and collapsed onto the bed, where it remained until morning.

Upon awakening, the body seemed perfectly capable of doing whatever was necessary, but at a fraction of its normal speed. It proceeded, snail-like, to the shower house, and even ate a bit of breakfast. The minutest, most "ordinary" experiences -- a hand picking up a fork, water flowing over a dish to clean it -- seemed to take place in a surreal, somewhat psychedelic realm. Acutely sensing the unique expression of Life in each person who passed by had become the prevailing perceptual mode.

Back in the dorm, my new friend Michelle's deeksha had resulted in a return to babyhood. Smiling, she slowly explained that she now needed to learn how to do everything all over again -- walking, eating, dressing herself. When she expressed a desire to take a shower, two or three of us accompanied her to the bathhouse, supporting Michelle from each side as her feet slowly shuffled along. As we progressed, whenever a dear friend -- and for Michelle, even the slightest acquaintance had become inexpressibly precious -- hugged her, Michelle's entire body began to shake as it had before the deeksha. So much love seemed to be coursing through her veins, the physical form seemed barely able to handle the intensity.

It was amusing to be "helping" Michelle, when the level of functionality going on here was not what anyone would place within the parameters of "normal." But while my experience of life had been seriously altered by the deeksha, and Michelle's had been even more affected, others seemed to be going about their lives with little or no change. This was puzzling, for I had witnessed the profound effects of the transmission on their faces right after they had received it. I had seen the Divine shining out from their eyes, and felt the presence of the true Self beaming out from their heart of hearts. Beholding the essential beauty and magnificence shining forth from hundreds of people after the deeksha had miraculously stripped away superficial identities and preoccupations had been one of the most profound experiences of this life.

Now, the ego-mind had apparently reasserted itself en masse, for these same people talked on and on about travel plans and other mundane matters as if the deeksha had never occurred.

Responding in kind, or saying anything about the state I was experiencing, proved impossible. I could only gaze at people from the depths of the inner stillness, amazed they were able to function "normally" at all. I knew who they really were; I had seen the core Self exquisitely radiating from within each of them! Sadness that they had so quickly lost touch with what had been present just a short time earlier arose and passed by. There seemed to be nothing I could do about that.

Still, it was odd to walk around the campus and see people as they were now, so rapidly veiled and obscured once again, when I had seen them as they truly are. I seemed to be carrying around a secret, something I would have loved to share with them, but preoccupied with earthly matters, they seemed utterly unavailable to receive it. Why had the deeksha had such a potent effect on some of us, while most seemed to immediately revert to former ways of being? Was it simply the strength of the mind, as the dasas had often discussed? Were some of us more ready than others to be catapulted into a totally different way of experiencing reality?

Over the next few days functionality slowly returned, yet an undercurrent of something very different was always present. Simply put, I felt altered -- in a major way. A deep sense of inner quiet was ever-present, right behind whatever was taking place in the outer world. Little arose to say, with even less desire to say it.

The pervasive feeling of calm, quiet happiness was beyond anything I'd ever experienced. Throughout the day, a deep feeling of gratitude often arose. I could hardly believe my good fortune in having been brought to this place to receive the blessings of the deeksha. From our brief contacts, it was clear that Barry's consciousness, too, was undergoing a similarly radical rearrangement.

When, in a couple of days, we left the ashram to travel throughout south India, nothing seemed to have the power to upset us in any way. Learning that our train would be four hours late, we simply sat down and relaxed, thoroughly enjoying sitting on a bench in the train station, watching the passing show. The 100-degree temperatures plastered our clothing to our backs, but it was merely the experience of heat, and sweat, and rumpledness. Everything simply was what it was, and there was no desire on our parts to have it be different. Freed of the heavy burden of preferences, wherever we went and whatever unfolded we were delighted with what we found.

The transformative power of the deeksha was octaves beyond anything we had previously encountered. People from all over the world were traveling to this remote part of India, drawn by the promise of enlightenment, the prospect of being freed from their earthly suffering by the changes in the brain we had all heard about. To our knowledge, nothing like the deeksha phenomenon had ever occurred before on such a widespread basis. Yes, great beings had given transmissions of awakening to their followers, with results that were often powerful and at times life-changing. But seeing hundreds of people catapulted into the enlightened states we had witnessed left no doubt that something extraordinary was going on.

After what we had seen and experienced, Bhagavan's promise of a soon-to-occur mass awakening kindled by a critical mass of people "getting it" seemed plausible, if not inevitable. If enough people were blessed with the kinds of experiences we had received, the collective morphogenetic field would automatically be infused with their new states of consciousness, and the hundredth monkey effect could most certainly occur. This was what so many of us had waited for -- a concrete manifestation of grace that could avert planetary catastrophe by catalyzing a massive awakening.

Barry: The Mahavakyas of Kalki Bhagavan

Now that the programs had ended and we had received our first, life-altering deeksha, it was time to leave the enveloping womb of the ashram campus and immerse ourselves in the colorful, teeming tumult of Mother India. I wanted to share with Karen all that I liked best about this beloved country I had spent a year exploring two decades before. As we toured south India's grand temples, the events at Golden City were alive and percolating within.

At a shop on the campus, I had come across the lone copy of a small pamphlet entitled *Mahavakyas of Kalki.* During our week at Varkala beach in the steamy, palm-upholstered state of Kerala, I delved into this intriguing little booklet. Upon opening it, the experience was far beyond reading -- it was a direct revelation from the "Supreme One" or "Parabrahman" (equivalent to the Godhead, in the Judeo-Christian tradition), as the verses referred to the source of the writing. The booklet indicated that on the cusp of a major epoch of human spiritual evolution, this aspect of Source descends, emanating revelations to guide humanity.

The transmission and words of the little book, coupled with the impact of our experiences, engendered a knowing that the Kalki Avatar was the presence overlighting everything unfolding at Golden City. Hindus believe the Kalki Avatar is the last incarnation of Vishnu, who is equivalent to the Holy Son or God incarnate in the Judeo-Christian pantheon. Bhagavan's relationship with the Kalki Avatar wasn't completely clear. While he allowed himself to be called Kalki in the early days, he denied he was the Kalki Avatar. During public addresses he made it clear the Kalki Avatar is a cosmic presence that will incarnate through many beings, not just one.

This spoke volumes to me, as I knew this to be true of all the divine incarnations of this time. The Cosmic or Universal Christ presence -- whether it manifested as Kalki in the East, the Christ in the West, the Hebrew Messiah, the Islamic Imam Mehdi, or the Maitreya Buddha -- would never be confined to only one human being. That is what makes this time so special: The Godhead is descending into all of humanity, not just one avatar or divine incarnation. From the power and magnificence that manifested through him, it seemed likely that Kalki Bhagavan embodied some portion or aspect of the Kalki Avatar. This intuitive sense brought home the profound scope and magnitude of the expansions in consciousness we found ourselves experiencing. The possibilities for planetary awakening had suddenly zoomed to a whole new level, and enlightenment on a grand scale now seemed feasible -- and, quite possibly, not far off.

Returning to America

As soon as we came home to our comfortable nest on the farm, the deeksha energies went back to work on us. We didn't know it at the time, but months of dissolution lay ahead. Our biological rhythms entered a state of continuous flux. One day we'd find ourselves sleeping for twenty hours, only to be awake nearly all of the next. Barely able to leave the house at first, we ventured to town only as necessary. Neither of us had any interest in reading or watching TV or using our laptops. We floated through the days in a seriously altered state, and what needed to be done somehow happened, with little thought or "doing" involved.

Much of our identification with our previous life pattern had been erased. Our brains had been so thoroughly rearranged that very little sense of who we had been remained. When friends called, few words arose to describe what had happened. Our radically altered presence undoubtedly communicated all that we were unable to find words to express. More than a few people seemed incredulous when we did our best to describe our experiences and articulate how utterly transformed we knew ourselves to be.

If either of us had been on our own, the adjustment to post-deeksha life might have been a lot more challenging. We felt tremendously grateful to have one another as a companion on this journey through an entirely new landscape. Luckily, while there were ways we were each fairly nonfunctional, our remaining areas of functionality dovetailed with each other's inabilities to carry on as before. For many weeks Karen found it impossible to even imagine driving a car. Barry was fully able to drive, but found it a challenge to talk with friends or attend to financial matters. Karen handled the bill-paying and returned the phone calls. And so it went, as together we formed a more or less functioning unit that got us through life while the deeksha energies deepened and embodied in us both.

Sizable chunks of mind, memory, and self sense had completely dissolved away. This was brought home for Barry when he was nearly knocked off a high ladder while attempting to prune a tree limb, something he had done many times. The subconscious programming that automatically judged the cut angle necessary to have the branch fall the right way was gone. The limb hit him, dislodging the chain saw from his hand, but somehow he remained on the ladder. Virtually no adrenaline ran through the body; all he experienced was a slight increase in heartbeat and breathing rate. What could have been a crippling fall didn't happen.

Barry later said, "In that moment, I knew to the bottom of my feet that I am safe. Grace is looking after me." This experience revealed just how deeply the brain/mind had been altered. Even the deeper, biologically programmed responses had been affected. Yet an umbrella of grace seemed to be overlighting every moment of our experience. The occasional brushes with catastrophe were apparently breaking down very deep mental programming, including some of the psyche's instinctive survival responses. As Bhagavan had promised, a comprehensive, all-pervasive de-clutching of the mind was underway, and it seemed to be going deeper than even traditional ideas of what enlightenment is about. In this state of conscious being, aspects of the human experience deemed universal were being transcended. Reality itself was morphing in profoundly beneficent ways.

Somehow, life went on without all those programs, even better than before. Short-term memory was virtually gone, yet in some mysterious way, everything got done. When we needed to know something, we did -- not from the retrieval of linear information stored in memory, but through the direct knowing that arose in the moment. If the car keys were not in their usual place, the knowing that they would appear at the right time was invariably borne out by subsequent events. Mind had entered into a whole new level of operation. Functioning from conditioned memory patterns had been replaced by the clear, direct knowing that comes from universal mind.

7

Enlightenment Teachings
and the Deeksha

The 21-Day Program

During the next year, Bhagavan's ashram began training people to give deeksha. We couldn't imagine anything more joyful than facilitating the kinds of awakenings we'd both experienced through our first deeksha, so back we went to Golden City in February of 2005. Happy to be back in our beloved India, we felt excited about what might unfold during the 21-day program we had anticipated for so many months.

Krishnaraj, the dasa that would be teaching our course, had a delicate presence and an angelic voice that carried many of us into exalted states when he sang sacred chants. His discourses were gentle yet penetrating.

"You receive deeksha," he said on the first day, "to the extent that you realize you can do nothing to bring about your enlightenment." Take your hands off the process, he counseled; that is the best thing you can do.

Krishnaraj then enumerated the three phases of the enlightenment process: recognizing the garbage pit of the mind, emptying it, and opening to receive the descent of the Divine. When the mind is filled with egoic debris and distortion, he added, we cannot expect to be clear channels for the Divine to pour into and through us. The process of emptying the mind, then, is crucial if we are to become conduits for God to express through us.

Krishnaraj described how the Christ had come into Jesus, but not until he endured the purification process in the desert, during which he faced his biggest mental obstacles. In a similar way, Shiva did not enter Ramana Maharshi until the personal self had been obliterated. When Krishnaraj himself experienced the divine

97

descent, the sixteenth-century poet and singer Mirabai had infused his being with her spiritual and musical gifts. This explained the refined, feminine presence that emanated from our gentle teacher.

The next day, Bhagavan's closest disciple, Anandagiriji, spoke to our class. "Passion is one step before madness," he asserted. "That is what we want from you here."

Addressing an age-old conundrum, he went on, "You must be *filled* with desire before you can be *free* of desire." He recommended focusing on how much we want to become enlightened. This, he said, would open the way for that blessed state to arrive.

Self: The Root of the Human Malaise

Anandagiri's focus then shifted to the source of all suffering: the small, egoic self. We human beings don't want to face how self-centered we are, Anandagiri insisted. We'll do anything to avoid looking at the ugliness of the small self, which is synonymous with mind. We distract ourselves in a thousand ways so that we do not have to face the harsh truth that most of what we do is for ourselves.

As he spoke, the word *selfish* came to mind. Had we ever really noticed the root of that often-used word? It suddenly became clear that all selfish behavior arises out of the self. And all that the self perpetrates is, no matter how it may initially appear, nothing other than selfish.

Now Anandagiri began to describe how the self perpetuates its existence. "The self needs an issue," he elaborated, "something out there that it can get busy with, to continue: a question, a fear, a worry. Fear and doubt are how the self propagates its existence. When these disappear, the self disappears."

We knew just what he meant. After our time at the ashram the previous year, we had traveled around India for several weeks. As we traversed that nation of endless minor inconveniences, none of it seemed to have any power to upset us in any way. After our first deeksha, the self had dissolved, and in its place blossomed calm, happy acceptance of whatever was present.

"As long as self is there, misery is there," Anandagiri continued in his charmingly accented English. "Separation is there. 'Me' is there. 'Me' equals pain and conflict. 'Me' and 'not me' is the cause of all war and conflict."

He paused to let this sink in, then succinctly summed up: "Self is the cause of all problems."

Wow! Could it really be that simple? "Self is the cause of all problems." We sat contemplating the world situation, from hunger and racism to war, environmental destruction, and the rampant greed and corruption that continue largely unchecked. Yes, all could be traced back to self. A relatively few people acting from selfishness had the power to bring about suffering in many, many others.

This seemed just as true on the personal level. We thought about our lives, and the times we had contributed to the suffering of others. Where else had our actions originated but in the self? Self-interest, self-concern, self-obsession, self-aggrandizement... was there any end to the possible permutations of self in action?

And where else did our own suffering arise but from thoughts that revolved around the self? *I want, I need, I have to have, I am angry because I don't have*...on and on the litany of self goes. Yes...every bit of the human dilemma reeked of self. When we act from self, we perpetuate the pain that has permeated the human condition for millennia.

While we all continued to digest Anandagiri's pithy summation, he offered a welcome juxtapose: "Liberation from self is the Golden Age."

This, too, made immediate sense. We cannot move forward into the New World dragging the baggage of self behind us. Humanity will not bring forth liberated ways of being until we drop all of our self-immortalizing strategizing and scheming.

Who among us has not dreamed of a Golden Age? Getting from here to there has not always seemed as easy as envisioning what we hope it will be like in that far-off time and place. Now, suddenly, it didn't seem as far away. If the deeksha obliterated the self, then we were all closer than we thought.

The two of us had tasted a bit of this radiant state after our first deeksha the year before. Traveling through India, all resistance to What Is had vanished, replaced by an easygoing acceptance of whatever presented itself. This carried through to our on-going lives when we returned to the U.S. A mind emptier of self certainly led to a happier life!

Another day, the teaching revolved around suffering. The previous year, we had heard the dasas insist that *self is suffering* so often that the phrase had engraved itself upon our consciousness. Now, our dasa gave suffering a new twist.

"The only thing that makes the heart flower," Krishnaraj asserted, "is suffering. Look at all the great ones -- they all became saints through suffering."

Suffering, then, was not something to avoid at all costs. Suffering could make us great, if we met it fully.

The dasa had frequently reminded all of us to not hold on to our concerns, but to ask Bhagavan and his wife, Amma, to resolve them as only they could. Today, Krishnaraj advised us to not simply turn our suffering over to Amma/Bhagavan.

"*Feel* it, too," he recommended.

His words offered a refreshing counterpoint to the prevalent New Age advice to not focus on "negative" feelings, but instead visualize and affirm what we want, in an effort to avoid our suffering altogether. Having facilitated countless soul-awakening sessions in which people spontaneously dove to the bottom of their suffering and were then blessed with direct experiences of the exalted state beyond it, we appreciated the wisdom in Krishnaraj's discourse. We had learned that the way beyond whatever loomed in awareness was right through the center of it. And the key was to feel whatever was present, all the way to the bottom.

That afternoon's teaching zeroed in on enlightenment. "When you are enlightened," Krishnaraj promised, "the mind will not interfere with your experience." If we feel happy, we will smile; if sadness is present, tears may fall. No internal voice will insist we should be having a different experience, or try to convince us that one experience is better than another.

"You will know that everything is perfect as it is," he emphasized.

Krishnaraj then delivered a pithy revelation: "Mind is not good or bad. It simply gets between you and your experience."

How often had we demonized the mind, blaming it for our suffering, when it was we who went along with what the mind insisted was true? Here was a statement of fact: *Mind gets in the way of direct experience.* It labels, judges, interprets, quantifies, classifies, objectifies...the list of ways mind responds to What Is suddenly seemed endless.

After our first deeksha, we had begun to experience life free of the veils of mind. We knew how much more fun life is when we simply let mind do what it does best, generate thoughts, without giving those thoughts any credence. Once again, the dasa had elegantly, efficiently summarized what we knew to be true.

A Gentler, More Gradual Deeksha

During the rest of the program, the teaching continued through deekshas, discourses by Krishnaraj, small-group discussions, and occasional darshans with Bhagavan himself. We felt disappointed that Bhagavan no longer directly empowered the dasas before they gave us deeksha, especially because the transmissions felt considerably less potent than that first blockbuster deeksha the year before. Yet we had to admit that, day after day and deeksha after deeksha, a subtle, deep shift was clearly taking place.

When asked why the deeksha energies were not as strong as they had been the year before, Bhagavan told us he had altered the way the deeksha worked. The goal now was a more gradual awakening, instead of the immediate, powerful shifts many of us had experienced previously. Bhagavan asserted the end result would not change. He fully expected that those who received the deeksha would become enlightened before 2010 or 2011, and planetary enlightenment would occur before the end of 2012.

Bhagavan went on to explain that it was simply taking people too long to integrate the extreme reorientations of consciousness the deeksha had delivered. He felt they needed to be able to carry on with their lives as functional human beings. That made sense to us, in light of the many months we had been more or less nonfunctional after our last visit to Golden City. Most people did not have the luxury of several months to wait for the brain-mind rearrangements to integrate. The jobs, families, and other commitments that filled most lives precluded that. If a mass awakening were to occur, it would have to accommodate these realities.

The two of us, though, felt nothing but gratitude that our experiences had been so potent and life-altering. Despite the occasional inconveniences resulting from the thorough dismantling of our minds, neither of us would have traded our experiences for a more gradual transformation. The absolute, sudden potency of what had been delivered decimated countless limitations about what was possible, simultaneously demonstrating the level of grace currently pouring in and the states of consciousness now available.

To a radical degree, we had been released from the clutches of ego-mind. How often had we asked for divine assistance in getting to the root of that? How many approaches had we tried, only to feel there was still more? Through grace, our wish had been granted. The unresolved egoic material that remained had lost its power to overtake our awareness and subject us to its tyranny. The ego-mind was no longer the default mechanism that ran our lives. What more could we ask?

Enlightenment: Our Natural State

Bhagavan often repeated one fundamental assertion: Enlightenment is our natural state. We are born without the veils of the mind, he explained during one discourse, with no sense of a separate self. After a few years of earthly life, we begin to individualize, and that results in the temporary experience of separate-ness. In the natural order of things, this illusory sense of apartness is surrendered back into the unity state when we reach mature adulthood. That's the way the process was originally designed to work, Bhagavan maintained, and it did work this way for a very long time until humanity went to sleep. The identification with the sense of being separate began to warp the mind and even the brain, until the gray matter itself became hardwired into the state of separation. Thus, the state of separated consciousness continues as we mature, instead of being surrendered back into our natural state of unity. Furthermore, Bhagavan emphasized, this is why it's impossible to reach the enlightened state without a major shift in the brain itself.

At present, most people function primarily through the lower three brain centers, which are related to our lower, "animal" nature. In the normal, awakened state, the brain functions with more energy focused in the frontal lobes, the most developed part of the brain from an evolutionary standpoint. The activation of the frontal lobes imparts the sense that everything is arising as one integrated whole within a unified field of experience. More simply, the subject-object orientation no longer exists. This is experienced as a state of oneness.

As we were aware, brain research has demonstrated that the neural webs in the brain act as antennae that respond to specific mental and emotional energies. During childhood, these neural patterns form based upon the nature and frequency of particular thoughts, feelings and mental images. The more often the same kinds of experiences repeat, the more the resulting neural pathways are reinforced, making it ever more likely that similar experiences will continue to happen. This explains the human tendency to recreate the same patterns again and again, and why the challenging ones seem so intractable when we attempt to change them.

Bhagavan explained that each mind is connected to the collective unconscious, which he called the Ancient Mind. In his view, the collective unconscious forms a repository for the separate "i" sense of humanity, along with all its thought patterns. Ancient Mind is a vast ocean of consciousness upon which each small, individual sense of separation rests like a bubble.

"The mind has no thoughts of its own," Bhagavan declared. Although we each believe we are special because of the interesting and unusual thoughts that occur to us, "there is nothing unique about any of your thoughts," he insisted. Each seemingly individual mind is continuously tuned in to and "downloading" content from the collective unconscious. All thought, then, is shared. This is illustrated by the recurring themes that color great literature, drama, and song, subjects that engage many, if not most, human beings, since we are all drawing from the same well of collective experience and interpretation.

Are we doomed, then, to be forever ruled by the Ancient Mind? Not at all, Bhagavan promised, adding that grace is the only way we can be released from the immense pull of the collective unconscious. Only when the very biology of the brain itself is altered does it become possible to experience free awareness.

This, of course, is where the deeksha comes in. Through grace, Bhagavan explained, the deeksha has the capacity to rewire the structure and functioning of the brain, including the neural webs that endlessly recreate human suffering. In the process, the brain's natural, intended functioning is restored.

The deeksha, Bhagavan asserted, changes the brain in such a way that it no longer resonates with the Ancient Mind. In a way, it's like changing the channel on a television. The mind will always be turned on, just as the TV in many homes is perpetually on these days. Try as we might, we can't escape the mind itself, or turn it off; it's part of what we are. We can, though, "change the channel." This, Bhagavan emphasized, is the miracle of the deeksha.

All our years of trying to get to the bottom of distorted mental-emotional patterns had resulted in relatively little progress. Though their impact had lessened, it still remained. Yet after one very potent deeksha, the job had largely been accomplished. Clearly, a basic wiring issue in the brain itself was the root cause of our inability to completely transcend the suffering of the ego-mind.

The Illusion of "Me"

What came next sounded even more radical. As we listened to Bhagavan speak, we felt the mental glue that had seemed to hold our minds together dissolving. Reality as we had known it was ending.

Although human beings constantly refer to *their* minds and *their* thoughts in the most matter-of-fact way, in truth, Bhagavan insisted, "my mind" and "my thoughts" do not exist. They do not exist because *there is no real and separate "me."*

Ripples of amazement traveled through the hall as the impact of this startling statement landed. Separate minds that did not know they actually do not exist struggled to absorb this shocking remark, processing their responses in dozens of languages. All expressed the same astonishment: *What? No me?*

The dasa's statements from the year before floated to the surface: *Self is suffering. Without the self, there is no suffering.* One-stop shopping -- or, more accurately, its reverse: one-stop divesting! When the self vanishes, the suffering it inevitably spawns naturally dissolves away along with it.

The next days' teachings and deekshas revolved around seeing the self in action, for identifying the self in its various guides and expressions disables its all-pervasive effects.

"Start watching the ways the limited, small self is involved in all activities," Krishnaraj dasa suggested. "See how self-centered it is -- without judging that as good or bad. There's no need to condemn. Just watch!"

He continued, "Each of us has a dark side we don't want to see. At first we most easily see this self when fear, anger, or other so-called negative emotions are present. Later, we see it in even our noblest acts, those we feel best about."

Many in the room seemed to be chewing on this last statement as though it were a tough piece of gristle. *Could it really be that self is not just the origin of our negativity -- it also spawns acts we deem good and positive?* This was almost too much to fathom for some, judging by the puzzled looks on their faces. Yet all of us have undoubtedly performed virtuous acts for effect: to impress someone, to demonstrate our merit, to win favor or outdo a perceived opponent. One way or another, we've all tried to prove that we are "good" people. If our minds have harbored the belief that we are inherently bad or evil, we may have spent our lives attempting to convince ourselves and others that the opposite is true.

Radical Acceptance of the Self

But seeing this self was not the end of the story. Now, Krishnaraj introduced the second part of the process of self-awareness: "Having seen this self, *accept it,* wherever you are. This is not the same self-acceptance psychologists talk about. Bhagavan's acceptance is of the whole process. It's a stopping of fighting against the self."

He paused to let this sink in, then continued, "Now, for the first time, you know love, not the running from the self or trying to cover up the darkness, but the love that comes from loving the self and accepting the self-centeredness completely. Anything else is not love."

"Love yourself with all your jealousy, all your anger -- not because you're trying to be saintly," Krishnaraj went on. "It's not about becoming beautiful so we can love ourselves. This is the intent of

---

today's deeksha -- to help you see your self-centered existence completely, accept it and love it."

Krishnaraj then showed a video of Anandagiri talking about what he called inner integrity. "Awareness is not a means to an end," he began, "but an end in itself. The journey begins with awareness of where you are. In striving for something higher, we don't see ourselves where we are."

"When we do," Anandagiri went on, "a miracle happens. It's not enlightenment, but it's the next best thing to enlightenment to completely accept oneself."

To illustrate the power of this shift, Anandagiri shared a story from his own life. "All my life, I was labeled a 'good' child and student. In the ninth grade, the internal conflict I felt about this came to a head. Bhagavan, who was the headmaster at our school, suggested I should go sing to a boulder at the edge of the schoolyard about who I am. As I sang and sang, the inner conflict dropped away and all that remained was complete acceptance of myself, exactly as I was. I have not known conflict since that day."

Having been in this calm, quiet man's presence, we had no trouble believing his claim. Through grace, he had reached this place of inner coherence early in his life. But it was not too late for the rest of us; our hope that we, too, could experience true, lasting inner peace had brought us halfway around the world to this campus on the arid plains of south India. We went on listening to his discourse.

Anandagiri stated, "The common belief nearly every human being holds is that we have to change in order to experience freedom and joy. But Bhagavan says that joy and freedom lie in seeing the mind's content *as it is*, not in changing the content."

This reminded us of Byron Katie's teachings, which center on the simple-sounding approach of loving whatever is present. Having worked with her teachings for several years, we knew that although this sounds straightforward enough, it is not always easy to put into practice. However, after our initial deeksha the year before, our ability to "love what is," as Katie often puts it, had dramatically increased. In fact, it had become the ground of our beings.

The End of Self-Escape

Believing we are not all right as we are, we humans do any number of things to try to change what we find within. Judging, criticizing, or rejecting What Is leads to a tremendous amount of busy-ness. An awful lot of human doing seems to have originated in not liking what we find within ourselves.

"We try to escape ourselves," Anandagiri continued, "by three methods. The first is naming our condition; for example, admitting, 'Yes, I am full of hatred.' There is nothing auspicious here, whereas *accepting* it leads to spiritual gifts."

"The second method is denying and running away from what is there -- for instance, pursuing love instead of accepting the hatred. Or refusing to pay attention to what is there, or striving to be content. Bhagavan likes to say, 'The journey begins with awareness of where you are. It also ends there.'"

Anandagiri went on, "The third method we use to escape from ourselves is by justifying our shadow, not taking responsibility for it. We might say, 'It's Kali Yuga, a dark age; the world is full of hatred, so I cannot help it if I also am full of hatred.'"

In contrast to these self-delusions, Anandagiri then explained that inner integrity "is seeing the deeper reasons we are upset -- being authentic with our true feelings that may go all the way back to the core event that triggered them in the first place."

"Seeing is an end in itself," he emphasized, "not seeing, hoping for a change. See for the joy of seeing."

This inner seeing brings clear benefits, which Anandagiri went on to elucidate: "Those who confront the self become confident; the burden of trying to be someone else is lifted. Confronting the self brings a kind of peace and calmness. No one can progress spiritually with conflict, and all conflict arises from the self."

Dismantling the Self

Now Anandagiri addressed the fundamental desire of the small self. "The self wants to be somebody," he stated, "in your life, your town, and the world. It wants to get recognized, to feel superior to those around you, or to be humbler than others, or to be sweeter and more loving then they are, or more spiritual. In all of this, the other person is not important. You are only making sure you have the recognition and feeling of superiority, the love, or whatever the self is hoping to receive."

Murmurs of self-awareness rippled through the hall as Anandagiriji continued: "What makes the self feel most secure? That's what the self will perpetuate. This creates identities -- the noble son, the dutiful daughter. We take refuge in these identities."

"To fill the emptiness, what do we do? What noble actions do we perpetuate so we don't feel the void?" He paused to allow us to consider his questions.

"We are afraid of these images of ourselves being destroyed," he continued. Then he said, "You are a zero when there are no more images to be protected."

The two of us listened in amazement. This was an exact echo of the statement we had heard Ammachi make many years before! During a discourse at her ashram in the San Francisco Bay Area, she had said, "When you are a zero, you will be a hero." Of course, the joke is that by the time you have become a zero, there is no one left to care that you are a hero.

Anandagiri elaborated on the theme: "The self has such fear of losing something, it does everything it can to make sure that never happens. When there are no more things to be protected, we're free. All falsehood is gone. Being emptied of all this equals enlightenment."

Bingo!

But there was more. Anandagiri continued, "An unenlightened person is a leech, using every opportunity and experience for itself. It is highly destructive. Unenlightened people see a thousand problems and a thousand solutions. Amma/Bhagavan see only one problem -- the self, and only one solution -- enlightenment."

Could a more economical explanation of the human predicament and its ultimate solution possibly exist?

Karen: Deeksha to See the Self

As several male and female dasas silently filed into the room, Krishnaraj told our group, "Amma/Bhagavan will make you aware of the self in today's deeksha *if you are willing to see.*"

After receiving deeksha and lying down, the patterns that have shaped this life -- and this self -- came to the surface to be seen and accepted. Later, I wrote them down:

I have to be good, smart, better than others, outstanding.

I have to be what my parents want.

I have to be what others want -- a good listener, someone they can get energy from, someone who will love them and be there for them.

The first belief led to a near-complete lack of confidence in myself. I got approval for what I *did* that was noteworthy. I had little sense of being approved of for my *being*. I always felt insecure, on shaky ground: If I couldn't produce, if I didn't excel, what then? The upshot of this fear seemed too scary to even imagine; its unexamined presence led to a great deal of efforting and struggle, for my sense of self-worth was dependent on outer validation.

I wrote a bit more about the difference in the love I felt from my parents:

> Dad loved, no matter what. Mom's "love" was far more conditional. My fear that others' love would go away stems from our relationship, and from my belief that she loved me less when my brother was born. "If only I could earn it back..." became a yearning and a motivation throughout my childhood years.

Finally, I saw the pervasive effects of the childhood patterning:

> What did I ever do because I really wanted to? How can I even begin to know?
> All I can do is love that girl who strove and struggled and did everything as well as possible, hoping someone would finally see her and fully approve. [And, I can add now, hoping someone would completely love her for who she was, not what she did.]

In this and other exercises, the 21-day program skillfully blended the via negativa and the via positiva. Some processes and deekshas thrust us into the realms of the unfinished business that lay within each of us, so it could finally be faced and fully felt. Other deekshas and discourses provided a glimpse of what lay ahead as all of this emptied and we could at last see reality as it is. This was one of the simple, straightforward definitions of enlightenment the dasas often repeated: "Enlightenment is the ability to see reality as it is!"

What is "Enlightenment"?

During his occasional darshans, Bhagavan's spontaneous discourses often focused on dispelling illusions about enlightenment. He sought to demystify it, insisting enlightenment is not exotic and elusive, but our natural state. Our experiences the previous year confirmed this: The deeksha had propelled us into a place in consciousness that seemed far more real and natural than any way of being we had previously known. The deeksha had not added anything new; instead, it instilled a refreshing absence of mental content that had no real purpose or value. Just as a sculptor carves away everything that is not an elephant, the deeksha had stripped away enough of what had obscured free awareness that an effortless ease was present nearly continuously.

The idea that enlightenment bestows spiritual fireworks, elaborate visions, and supernatural powers, Bhagavan emphasized, is an illusion. The ego, intent on self-aggrandizement, is sure we will morph into some sort of powerful, super-intelligent divine being when enlightenment happens. It believes all our problems will vanish and life will become what it considers "perfect."

But it isn't like this at all. When the mind "de-clutches," as Bhagavan liked to put it, we are free of the effects of mental conditioning. Said another way, the ego-mind no longer has the capacity to control awareness. Now, consciousness is not circumscribed by beliefs, concepts, and judgments. It is simply present, open and available to whatever the next moment brings.

As we experience the dissolution of all that has comprised our sense of self, we arrive at a place in consciousness that is commonly called "no self." All identification with the fixed images and roles that formerly constituted who and what we thought we were simply evaporates. We step into a vast emptiness in which the core thoughts and feelings that formerly defined our self sense are rendered null and void. As the two of us experienced during our first visit to Bhagavan's compound, even the identification of self with and as the physical body may dissolve.

After such experiences, all thought, all feeling arises in the empty sky of the mind, and these temporary apparitions are no longer experienced as aspects of who and what we are. They are simply the result of mind doing what mind does, with no binding or lasting effect. There is no need to do anything with it, react to it, attempt to make it go away, or in any other way engage with it. Everything simply arises, stays for a while, and then passes away. No sense of "I," "me," or "mine" exists in the context of that experience. There is only oneness, unity of being.

According to Bhagavan, all human suffering originates in the mind. All conflict, crisis and war, all that plagues humanity individually and collectively, results from the illusory sense of the separate I. The only way the world can experience peace and move into a new way of being, then, is for collective enlightenment to occur. Only when we directly experience that we are all one, in unison with the Earth, the natural world, and one another, will the distortion so common on the planet today disappear.

How is Enlightenment Experienced?

We all wondered what it will be like when we are finally and permanently established in the enlightened state. One morning Krishnaraj announced that, for the next four or five days, all deek-shas would revolve around enlightenment -- the end of the little self. This, he stated, could manifest in a variety of ways.

The first sign he mentioned was the end of conflict, some-thing Anandagiri had previously discussed at length. Krishnaraj then described a second manifestation of the end of the small self: the loss of a sense of a controller of the body and/or the thoughts. A day or two ago, a woman in Karen's dorm room had been thrust into this, when all ability to govern her body had seemingly van-ished. She had to be helped, if not carried, to the program hall, the dining hall and everywhere else she wanted or needed to go. Like Michelle the year before, Carla had reverted to babyhood, and at the moment she lay on thick padding at the back of the hall, unable to move of her own volition.

Krishnaraj elaborated on this manifestation of enlightenment: "You will be merely a witness, not trying to pull something to you or push it away. Bhagavan says that an enlightened person is one who does not pull or push, because there is no one there to pull or push. He doesn't reject so-called negative thoughts and feelings, or try to hold on to beautiful ones."

"Identification with thoughts, and the idea that we create the thoughts," Krishnaraj went on, "is gone. The thoughts themselves, though, do not go away. Mind is not absolutely absent, but for mo-ments or hours it might be possible to have no thoughts."

Reiterating a now-familiar theme, Krishnaraj continued, "En-lightenment alleviates the cause of suffering: the identification with the self." He elaborated, "An enlightened person can suffer, but it is not *personal*. Christ suffered, for humanity. An enlightened person suffers what others are suffering."

Krishnaraj then offered several examples of what it will be like to be enlightened. "There is no carry-over -- when an event ends externally, it ends internally." *There goes Monday-morning quarterbacking in all its guises -- thinking about what I could have said or done, what someone else should have said or done, ad nauseum. It will be quiet around the water coolers of the world!*

"An enlightened person is able to disagree with others when that is the case, and say so, without trying to protect his or her own opinion. Such a person is willing to submit to the truth."

Addressing the prevalent idea that enlightenment means never expressing emotion, Krishnaraj declared, "A person who is enlightened can become irritated and angry at others' behavior.

The anger is short-lived -- it doesn't carry over. There is no more mental process of 'How can she or he do or say that?' And there is no more guilt. The feeling simply is what it is, and when it passes, it is over."

Adding to this, Krishnaraj explained, "In an enlightened person, anger arises when there is something to correct; there is no hatred in it. It is there when the person sees something that harms others. Ramana Maharshi," he went on, referring to the great awakened one who lived at the base of Arunachala Mountain, "rarely spoke. But when people at the ashram weren't well-treated, he shouted at those responsible. The anger comes out of love, and feeling others' suffering."

Offering yet another example of the way enlightened behavior differs from typical human reactions, Krishnaraj asserted, "In an enlightened person, physical suffering will not be translated into psychological suffering. The person just stays with the pain. An unenlightened person doesn't stay with the pain. It goes into psychological suffering and then into meaninglessness, existential suffering, and back to the physical pain. The person is unable to stay with the pain, so attention goes to the mind. Unable to stay with the mind, attention goes back to the physical pain."

In an enlightened person, Krishnaraj continued, "old patterns may still exist and come up occasionally, with no sense of 'my' patterns." Overall, though, there is freedom from much that previously vexed the human self.

"Enlightened people don't care about maintaining an image. Unenlightened people may be feeling some inconvenience around them, though. If patterns remain in an enlightened person, they may be gloomy or get angry. They will feel no need to improve themselves. Enlightened people *cannot* prevent the unenlightened from feeling 'hurt.' They do what they do, and others do what they do with that. Their reactions have nothing to do with the enlightened person!" Krishnaraj spoke with a tone of certainty likely born of experience.

Finally, the physical, bodily effects of enlightenment can be considerable. "Ayurvedic physicians can tell if a person is enlightened by checking their pulse," Krishnaraj claimed. In a normal person, the pulse is around 72, but in an enlightened one it slows down to between 56 and 62. Also, changes in the physical heart can manifest on other levels: "There is more ability to forgive and love, and less tendency to possess. Jealousy will vanish -- there is no one there to compete or fight."

It was easy to see why Bhagavan insisted enlightenment was the answer!

Stop Trying to Change the Mind!

In another video, Anandagiri described what it is like to be around the being he and many others revered as an avatar of enlightenment: "Living with Bhagavan is intense. He has a mission -- to bring in the Golden Age, to give enlightenment, to set man unconditionally free -- that is so intense it sometimes feels like an obsession."

He continued, "Bhagavan has a thousand ways to speak about enlightenment. One is, 'When the impossibility of changing the mind strikes you, you are enlightened. There is no time or effort involved.'"

"Thoughts come from the thought-sphere," Anandagiri went on. "There is only thinking, but no thinker. That's why we say it is an automatic process. It all goes on, on its own, like your hair growing. The same is true for the body -- did you create it? Bhagavan will give you the experience that the body is not 'my' body."

"With thoughts, it's not the *thought* that's the problem, it's the *resistance* to the thought. For example, someone could say, 'I feel bad when I get angry.' The effort to change the mind and thoughts gives rise to suffering. When I *know* my thoughts are not my thoughts, I make no effort to change them. There's no struggle."

Anandagiri paused, giving us all a moment to digest what he had just said. Then he continued, "Changing our thoughts is impossible. We don't know what caused them -- the food, the satsang (spiritual gathering), the astrological and meteorological factors, and many more, are responsible for the kinds of thoughts we are having at this moment. Trying to change our thoughts will not relieve our suffering. Only seeing our thoughts are not our thoughts will do that."

Then Anandagiri repeated the message he had previously delivered: "If you are a big zero, you cannot suffer at all." Had he heard Ammachi talk about the benefits of becoming a zero? The resemblance between their statements seemed uncanny.

A bit later he delivered yet another intriguing statement: "When you know it's not yours, mind becomes yet another beautiful experience, like watching a bird." We had glimpsed this state. Watching the mind instead of giving credence to all that arose there *was* entertaining, in its own way. We hadn't quite arrived at the place of seeing mind as a "beautiful experience," though. Maybe these minds were not yet as empty as they seemed.

As the video came to a close, Anandagiri summed up:

Your body is not yours; it is an automatic response.

Your thoughts are not your thoughts; they are only Ancient Mind.

There is no thinker or controller. That is illusion.

After a break, Krishnaraj launched into a discussion of the reality that the Cosmic Will is the only will. "A person gripped by the self is compulsive and automatic," he asserted. Believing the self is who s/he is, "such a person will be shocked to find out *nothing is there.*"

All across the cavernous hall, nervous, disbelieving laughter broke out. Hands waved in the air as participants raised question after outraged question in response to this take-no-prisoners declaration. The general tone could be summed up thus: *How dare you tell us the self is an illusion!*

Finally, with the awakened clarity that unfailingly characterized his communication, Krishnaraj put a halt to it all: "The mind is just trying to prove it does exist."

"When you start to feel the self being wiped out, all kinds of questions will arise," he explained. "When we see what a burden it is to continuously ask these questions, magic can happen."

Then he delivered yet another bombshell: "The mind doesn't pose questions to get answers, it poses questions to keep itself alive."

But even that was not the end of the story. Krishnaraj needed to point out one more thing: "Even the craving for clarity and understanding is not yours."

Karen: The Fruits of Devotional Surrender

I have never been drawn to seeking or having a guru, so I was as surprised as anyone by my behavior during the 21-day program. The year before, I had found it awkward and inauthentic to bow to the Sri Murti, the life-sized photograph of Bhagavan and Amma at the front of the hall. Chanting the unfamiliar Sanskrit syllables of the moola mantra along with the dasas at the beginning of each session felt strange and uncomfortable. Yet now, each morning I found myself prostrating at the feet of the Sri Murti. As tears of fervent longing streamed down my cheeks and onto the floor, I'd implore Amma/Bhagavan to do whatever it took to get me awake. With no conscious intention, I'd somehow been catapulted beyond deeply established identities and ways of being into an altogether new state in the quest for enlightenment.

Things really began to get interesting on the eighth day, during the ceremony called the Phala deeksha. One by one, we were escorted by female dasas to the front of the hall, where other dasas placed highly charged silver slippers called padukas atop our heads. We had been told that deeksha with the padukas symbolized complete submission to the Divine, since the padukas were charged with the energy of Amma/Bhagavan.

"The more we praise the Divine, the more we are submitting to It and relinquishing the ego. God is subjective; as you relate to God, God will relate to you. More than even enlightenment," Krishnaraj had said, "a characteristic of the Golden Age is this oneness with the Divine -- one call and God is there."

Returning to our places after the deeksha, we lay down. I asked Bhagavan to do whatever he could through me, and drifted off into a state of sublime peace.

When, sometime later, we were told a meal awaited us in the dining hall, I silently followed the crowd next door, aware that something magnificent had happened within. As I filled my plate with food, I could hardly believe how beautiful it all was. Life force intensely radiated from the rows of gleaming tomato slices, the piles of cucumber rounds, the bunches of grapes. Slowly making my way to a table, I sat, marveling at the visual feast before me, too enraptured to eat. I smiled and smiled at the unspeakably magnificent plate full of Life while everyone around me consumed their food as if nothing out of the ordinary had occurred.

Then my eyes were drawn to the woman sitting beside me. How incredibly precious was her face, her very being! Tears cascaded down my cheeks as I beheld the divinity shining through the eyes looking back at me in amazement. The tears continued to flow as I turned to look at the face across from me, then those at the next table, and finally all of the unbelievably beautiful beings, their every movement so perfectly exquisite, filling the huge dining hall. Had I ever really seen anyone before? The splendor of it all -- the glory of Life itself -- was overwhelming.

This sacred communion marked the beginning of an exalted state that progressed over the next few days to the point that writing was no longer possible. There was no one left to write, no way to get the hands to perform the mechanical functions that had so recently been automatic. The extensive note-taking during each session abruptly stopped. Since Krishnaraj had asked us to submit daily reports about what we were experiencing, friends kindly took dictation as I did my best to describe the remarkable things that were occurring. Even that was a challenge!

During a group meditation called Ananda Mandala and the deeksha that followed, the third eye opened into a vast field of brilliant, deep blue. It felt as if the top of my skull had come off and was now wide open to this infinite expanse of dazzlingly blue space. Living streams of gold extended out into infinity, framing the indigo sky-field in brilliant illumination. The splendor continued for an eternity.

The next Ananda Mandala found Michelle, who had become a friend the previous year, sitting beside me. As we all began the focused breathing, her whole body began shaking uncontrollably, as it did whenever higher energies poured in. In contrast, I was feeling an immense stillness that only deepened as the energies built.

At some point it began to feel as though warm, golden honey was being poured with utmost gentleness onto the top of my head. Slowly, inexorably, the honey slid over my hair, down onto my forehead, and along the right side of my face. It slithered over my shoulder and continued down my right arm, as I blissfully enjoyed being tenderly slathered with divinity.

While the cosmic honey continued to ooze downward, Michelle's body, seated to my right, shook with ever greater intensity. I tightened my grip on her hand, to no avail. Her form continued to shudder and vibrate.

Now, the molten honey slowly flowed down my right arm and gradually began to envelop the fingers of the right hand. Suddenly, the moment I'd known was coming arrived. I felt the divine nectar travel across the infinitesimal divide between Michelle's physical form and my own, like a neural impulse jumping a synapse.

Instantly, all shaking in Michelle's body ceased. I felt her enter into the same profoundly immovable peace that was present in me. Of its own volition my head turned to look into her eyes, and we silently communed in the depths of gratitude: *Thank you, Bhagavan.*

Karen: The Search is Over!

Throughout the rest of the 21-day process, each day deepened and grounded the state of oneness. Although Barry and I rarely communicated, preferring to maintain silence, during one morning's presentation we shared a moment of realization that let us know our paths were exactly parallel.

Both Bhagavan and Krishnaraj had often reminded us that there truly is no self; the solid personage we think we are is merely a collection of personalities that come and go. On this pivotal morning, Krishnaraj elaborated: "Since there is no self, there can be no seeker. Furthermore, since enlightenment is our true nature, there is nothing to seek!"

Suddenly, profoundly, one simple realization blazed forth: *The search is over!*

Elation rose up and overflowed. My head turned to look at Barry, who "happened" to be looking right at me from his spot across the room. A huge grin lit up his face; the light of crystal-clear awareness shone from his eyes. As we left the hall after class, our eyes again met and Barry said, "The search is over!"

The mind's incessant questioning ceased; there was no one left who wanted to ask anything. What remained: floating in the eternal now, empty of mentalizations, happily resting in Infinity. After each of Krishnaraj's discourses, I listened in wonderment to the queries of class members, amazed at the lengths to which mind will go in order to remain in control. What wouldn't it do to sabotage true presence and open-ended awareness?

What was left of this mind was barely able to track some of the participants' thought-processes; they originated in a realm galaxies away from the one I now inhabited. Instead, I sat in the back of the hall with others who were similarly God-intoxicated, including dear Michelle. We passed around a vial of rose oil and anointed one another between amused giggles at the complexities of mind.

What a relief mindlessness was! It felt far more joyful to share love and intense gratitude for all the blessings than to attempt to follow the verbalizations of those whose minds generated endless questions. With no more sense of self, each day passed in an infinite succession of *now, now, now* moments. What would show up next? It didn't matter -- one thing was as interesting as another.

After our initiation on the final day of our program, it was time to go out into the world as deeksha-givers. Our first stop was Amma's ashram, where we gave deeksha to the thousands of Indians who gathered for darshan each day. Many touched our feet; a few kissed them. Placing our hands over the heads of wide-eyed infants in their mothers' arms, we asked Amma/Bhagavan to bless each baby through us. *May this little one have a beautiful, awakened life!*

Karen: A Dark Night

The initial joy of sharing the deeksha was soon unexpectedly eclipsed by another kind of experience altogether. As we traveled back across the Pacific, a nameless, content-less heaviness descended upon me. When we reached home, I learned that my beloved father had been diagnosed with three kinds of cancer. Then, while I was in the Midwest helping Dad and his wife move into a smaller home, our dear neighbor, the matriarch of the farm where we lived, died of lung cancer. Alongside these outer shocks, childhood patterns and wounds arose, along with guilt and shame over the results of past unconsciousness.

No matter where I looked, not only my own life but the world as a whole seemed to be permeated with pain and suffering. Why did it all have to be so awful? A dark, gloomy storm cloud enveloped me, every bit as intense as the illuminated, exalted states at the ashram had been.

Bhagavan had said that each of us would, at some point, go through a dark night of the soul, but no part of the 21-day program had prepared me for this immersion in the depths. I seemed to be on my own, with no guiding light other than the inner soul-flame that had led me through life for as long as I could remember. It was remarkable to experience no resistance to the process. A vague memory of past preferences for happiness and joy surfaced, but now, wishing it were different, hoping it would pass quickly, and preferring one state to another never arose.

Everything simply was what it was, existing right alongside the absolute faith and trust that it must be serving a purpose, or it wouldn't be happening. For decades I'd inwardly heard, *You are being prepared for a time when large numbers of people will be in crisis.* Now, all that arose was, *This must be yet another part of that preparation.* Submitting to it was clearly the only option.

This experience did not seem to be the same as the traditional Dark Night of the Soul, in which God appears to have forsaken the sufferer and existential aloneness eclipses all else. As deep as the emotional pain went, I never felt apart from the Divine; instead, the immersion into the remaining shadows of the personality and the grief that my father would not live forever provided poignant demonstrations of the dasa's oft-repeated reminder that *self is suffering.* A lot more self clearly needed to empty out so the Divine could fill that space.

Each day, I learned more about the particular flavor of suffering that results from human attachment. Contemplating my father's cancer diagnosis and eventual passing filled me with sorrow, in stark juxtapose to the utter peace that had been present in that blessed state of No One Home. Wondering why the world was so filled with misery alternated with submitting to What Is. This internal tug-of-war went on and on until the new state of being gradually won out over past patterns and habitual neural grooves. Personal suffering fell away as consciousness increasingly came to rest in accepting What Is without question. This process took place in one area of life and consciousness after another.

While all of this unfolded, a part of me observed the whole thing as a curious yet detached witness. Some time before, Barry had experienced a Dark Night of the Soul that overshadowed a number of years and became particularly intense for a few months. This experience seemed to be passing through far more quickly; within just a few weeks I began to emerge from the heaviness that had blanketed my awareness.

The radical willingness to fully surrender into the process seemed to mitigate the need for it to go on indefinitely. Decades had been spent exploring the inner terrain; before meeting Barry I had done considerable shadow work through a variety of modalities. Facilitating so many soul-awakening sessions during which people dove into their deepest pain and suffering had also prepared me well. Now, the purging could take place with little or no obstruction.

And the many potent deekshas I had received in India were apparently at work even now, affecting the usual progression and duration of the dark night experience. Since the deeksha had, in its mysterious and comprehensive way, rewired the brain, the dark night apparently did not need to be as long or intense as others had experienced. The grace that poured through the deeksha seemed to have performed precision microsurgery on the fundamental energy~consciousness matrix of the separate self sense. As the brain transformed, the underpinnings of the egoic sense of self evaporated. With the core illusion contained within the neurobiology of the brain now dissolving, there was no need for a slow, arduous ego-death process. Now that the primal seed of the separative egoic condition had been deactivated, all the roots and branches it had sent out no longer needed to be pruned one by one. With amazing efficiency, the deeksha had gotten to the bottom of it all.

This was clearly an evolutionary acceleration; with the deeksha, it was no longer necessary to go through a lengthy, difficult ego-annihilation process. It appeared that what once might have taken months or years could now occur swiftly and be integrated simultaneously. The journey of awakening seemed to be compressing, which only made sense in an era during which time itself is speeding up.

As we had found the previous year, spending the summer at our fire lookouts offered a perfect opportunity to integrate and embody all that had occurred during our time in India and its aftermath. Most of each day was devoted to floating in the vast, spacious silence of our mountaintop vistas. Resting in oneness, we never tired of drinking in the beauty of the forested landscapes that surrounded us. Long morning and evening walks in the high country grounded and stabilized the shifts in consciousness that continued to blossom.

8

Sharing the Deeksha

The Seven-month Groups

Although we were now initiated to share the deeksha, neither of us felt impelled to go out into the world and get something going, as some other deeksha-givers were apparently doing. The self had dissolved to such a degree that there wasn't anyone left to make things happen. With the demise of the self, the "doer" had also largely vanished. If something was to unfold, it would simply have to occur on its own as part of the arising and passing of the great play of Life.

And it soon did. As a stream of deeksha-givers passed through our area offering evening events, we sensed a need for a more in-depth approach to sharing the great, transformative blessings of the deeksha. The people with whom we discussed this idea responded with enthusiasm, so we began to offer seven-month groups in which, along with the deeksha, we shared the inner processes we had found most meaningful during the 21-day program.

The power of the deeksha presented a variety of evolutionary doorways to those who received it, some blissful and others not as easy to be with. Once again we found ourselves in a living laboratory, just as we had with facilitating soul awakening years before. A whole new level of grace was now flowing through us; as Bhagavan had made clear, it was the grace of enlightenment, and it wanted to go forth and bless everyone.

The joy and bliss the deeksha engendered often sent people into rapturous states, and spontaneous gales of laughter often erupted in the groups. The deeksha delivered strong infusions of light with a yang, electrical quality, and many people experienced upper chakra openings beyond anything they had ever known. They felt freed from the clutches of the small self, and with mind deactivated, the light, love, and joy of the One could pour into and through them unimpeded.

Most people thoroughly enjoyed the state that typically followed the deeksha, for it brought them into ecstasy and deep peace. At the same time, many participants encountered challenges in integrating the energies. We hoped the ongoing format of the groups would support the process of grounding and embodying the awakenings the deeksha catalyzed, so they would not merely provide a transitory state of bliss but would weave into the fundamental fabric of being as thoroughly as possible.

Dropping in, Dropping self

As the deeksha went to work within the brains and minds of its recipients, many found challenging emotional patterns and core childhood wounds surfacing for deeper levels of healing. After the initial heights of blissful spiritual transcendence, some felt alone and adrift on a stormy sea, believing God had abandoned them. A few found themselves in the midst of a full-blown dark night experience, just as Karen had after returning from India.

We encouraged everyone to fully be with what was present, and recommended feeling the feelings to the bottom and surrounding whatever was going on with love. We reminded people to pray for help in the ways that felt right to them. "Breathe, feel, and turn it over to the Divine" -- the mantra that had come in handy during so many soul-awakening sessions -- now found new usefulness during group excursions into the inner realms of suffering.

It seemed that, even in our culture of self-help, therapy, and twelve-step groups of all kinds, most people had never learned the basics about meeting whatever arose within them. Group participants tended to talk *around* what they were feeling -- analyzing, giving reasons for their feelings, and expressing their thoughts about whatever the issue was -- all the while believing they were feeling what was present. None of this got them any more free.

We therefore started at the beginning, teaching people how to simply become aware of their breathing. This initial step gave their awareness a place to land and gently, safely led them out of their heads and into their inner worlds. Then, we focused on feeling the sensations in the body -- a tingle here, an ache there, a thick, congested feeling somewhere else. Most people had never consciously focused on bodily sensations to this degree before, and some were amazed at the way their inner landscape revealed itself. One sensation would lead to another, winding through the inner world from an elbow to the belly, up into the head and back down into the heart. As each sensation was fully felt, it could then be let go on the outbreath. This created a freer and more open space within.

More often than not, body-sensations gave way to the feelings stored within them. A tight, clenched sensation in the throat might lead to strangled, frustrated crying; throbbing in the legs could segue into a sense of emotional paralysis and helplessness. As feelings arose, we encouraged people to simply feel them, allowing the emotional charge to be fully felt and then released on the outbreath. Each wave of feeling that could be felt and surrendered back to Life led to a sense of greater interior spaciousness.

As feelings arose and moved through, the thoughts that fed them often came forth. We suggested witnessing these ideas and concepts without giving them credence or power. Simply observing them without identifying with them, or, conversely, making them wrong, allows thoughts to dissolve, easily and naturally, with no resistance. This in itself was a revelation to many group participants.

At times, people continued the process of self-investigation by spontaneously delving into the identities and "reality bubbles" within which they lived. A few traveled all the way to the core of the matter, becoming aware of the primal separation -- from their true Self, others, all of life, and the Divine -- at the root of all other "symptoms" of dis-ease. As this ultimate layer was felt and released, they naturally and easily entered into the state of oneness that is all that remains once everything else empties out.

The Gifts of the Deeksha

The deeksha's catalytic impact brought to the surface whatever was ready to be faced, felt, and eventually embraced. Troubling thoughts, discordant feelings, and limiting patterns arose in nearly everyone who received a series of deekshas over time. This in itself was a major blessing, one that was welcomed by those who really wanted to get free and were willing to go wherever that journey took them. As mental-emotional content arose, the heightened awareness brought about by the deeksha could now shine upon long-standing issues and reveal the way through them. Patterns that might have taken much longer to work through were now being resolved more quickly and easily, without the lengthy processing necessary in the past.

Alongside this internal cleansing and purgation, the effects of the potent neurobiological changes Bhagavan had promised began to manifest. Nearly everyone reported significant, permanent shifts in consciousness, including far less mental chatter and negative self-talk. Where worry, anxiety and fear once occupied awareness, now calmness and equanimity reigned as a steady, underlying state. Many reported the mind simply did not "get busy" with things anymore, and everyday life unfolded far more smoothly and effortlessly.

With the thinking mind quiet, the eternal witness emerged, which enabled viewing the contents of mind from a detached perspective. Awareness of the beliefs and judgments that had been causing suffering increased significantly. Many group participants found relief from self-criticism and perfectionism, along with greater self-acceptance and freedom from the personality patterns that had dominated their experience of life. When egoic material arose, it was viewed as simply passing through for another chance to bring awareness to it, or perhaps as one last, dramatic appearance on the way out. Where buttons would have been pushed and emotional reactions automatic, serene composure now prevailed. As group members learned to feel and accept whatever arose, they found it increasingly easy to be with every aspect of the human condition.

Most participants found that a quiet undertone of reasonless joy and happiness was now present, whatever the outer circumstances. As heads got quiet, hearts were clearly opening; nearly everyone appeared to be enjoying the first stages of enlightenment as defined by Bhagavan. Looking around the groups after several months, we saw the shining eyes and radiant faces of the true Self beaming out into the world.

The body language of many participants expressed a new comfortableness with themselves -- a radical acceptance of whatever they were feeling, a deepening compassion for self and others, a willingness to release into the Mystery, a level of trust previously only dreamed of. Together, we celebrated stories of breakthroughs in situations that once looked hopeless. Workplaces altered, relationships were reborn, and new healing gifts came through. Beneath these outer manifestations, a simple, quiet peace formed the foundation of it all.

When someone entered into a rapturous state of stillness, we all silently shared in the blessing-grace. Looking into one another's eyes, the same unspoken message was wordlessly transmitted again and again: *We are so, so blessed.* Hearts flowered; minds quieted; deeply felt oneness with self, others, and Life replaced isolation and separation. As the groups continued to meet and the months effortlessly rolled by, the promise of the Golden Age Bhagavan had described was beginning to manifest before our very eyes.

The Limits of the Deeksha

Bhagavan had warned that the Western mind was a "tough nut to crack." He had admitted his surprise that full enlightenment seemed elusive for those of us from the Occident. Although we had hoped that the promise of enlightenment would be widely realized in the groups we offered, instead, they bore out Bhagavan's warning. Nearly everyone felt very excited about what their newfound state portended, not only in their own lives but for humanity and the planet. We witnessed considerable openings in awareness and a pervasive flowering of love among group participants. But no one appeared to be getting fully enlightened.

While the deeksha transmission powerfully activated the upper chakras and the heart, it seemed to have little effect on the three lower chakras. This left a lot of people in blissful, ecstatic states that often led to the same kind of giddy laughter that had filled the hall in India during our initial deeksha. While ecstasy is a supremely pleasurable state, and many people seemed convinced that experiencing it equaled enlightenment, a complete awakening includes far more than states of bliss.

Those ecstatic states presented another challenge: Some people developed a craving for the spiritual high they felt from the deeksha. A few began to attend every deeksha event they could find, even if it meant driving many hours to distant towns. When the inevitable cleansing reaction set in and the next mental-emotional material to be addressed arose, some believed all they needed to do was get more deekshas. If meeting whatever was present with full awareness was the goal, more deekshas would not necessarily provide the means to that end.

Grace does not offer an easy escape from the exigencies of the spiritual journey. For every activation of spiritual energy we receive, a corresponding purification of all that is not resonant with the higher vibrational state it engenders will take place. The figure 8 "conveyor belt" of transformation carries consciousness up into the transcendent realms of perfection and down into the unresolved parts of the human self, weaving all levels and facets into wholeness. To experience that unity of being, recovering the shadow and integrating the wounded, fragmented aspects hidden in the dark recesses of the psyche is just as essential as opening to the light.

Spiritual discernment and maturity were needed to frame the deeksha as an aid to awakening, not the end in itself. The grace of the deeksha was considerable, but to give one's power away to it in seeking yet another hit of bliss was just a subtler form of enslavement. We did not want to participate in anything that would bind or imbalance people instead of liberate and unify them. We often cautioned against receiving too many deekshas, and made it clear that awakening involved far more than the powerful head-center activations the deeksha delivered. Above all else, we strove to keep the focus on the unfoldment of inner divinity as the goal of it all.

That brought up another caution: We were not sure that those who had received the deeksha were any more in touch with the true Self than before. Although their minds seemed more open and available to Life and their mental suffering had dropped off considerably, were they any more aware of their essential nature? As much as we had always loved seeing people shed the not-self, which receiving deeksha clearly catalyzed, we also wanted to facilitate their reconnecting with the true Self, something the deeksha did not necessarily accomplish. Since directly experiencing the soul had been the focus of our work for so long, we felt a spiritual imperative to keep the inner divinity of the essential Self at the core of whatever we offered in the world.

Asking for clarification on this issue, we were given the understanding that the Western psyche is significantly different from that of Easterners. Reflecting an evolutionary vector of individualization and mental development, ego development is typically more pronounced in the West. Thus, as they go about sculpting a clearly defined sense of self, Westerners tend to have busier, more complex lives than those of their Eastern counterparts. The pressures and requirements of modern society require strong egos and well-functioning intellectual minds. This is not wrong, nor does it indicate an evolutionary error. It simply means the Western psyche is less likely to allow the mental~egoic self sense to completely dissolve in a rapid enlightenment experience. This explained why, in our groups, we were not seeing an abundance of the sudden awakenings we had both experienced and witnessed in others during our visits to Bhagavan's ashram.

The psyches of those in the West are more inclined to realize the indwelling divinity of the soul first, before they experience the empty mind of enlightenment. On the path of God-realization, the false self slowly transforms into an expression of the soul's essential divine nature. It does not dissolve as much as resolve into the God within. As surrender to the Divine deepens, the false self is gradually absorbed into the true Self. Rather than experiencing the pure emptiness of enlightenment as they awaken, Westerners are more likely to immerse in the rich plenum of the Presence of God. In contrast, many Indians experienced pure states of enlightenment when they received the deeksha. The Eastern psyche tends to start with enlightenment and then move toward God-realization, whereas in the West awakening most often occurs in the opposite order.

We came to understand that for Westerners, awakening would most likely occur as a progressive process of absorption into the Divine, within and without. The heart-openings and quieter minds in many group participants may have signaled the initial stages of a gradual, organic flowering of Christ Consciousness, which is the ultimate synthesis of the two prongs of awakening: enlightenment and God-realization. However, we still yearned to see people directly experience their inner divinity, for this remained at the core of what we felt was our true purpose in life.

During Anna's pivotal session in Hawai'i, which is recounted in *Soul Awakening*, she perceived the light of the One shining within her chest, and knew that she *was* that pure light, not her suffering. From that moment on, it was clear to us that experiencing the true Self, more than just about anything else, had the capacity to transform lives. Facilitating direct communion with the soul, the inner wellspring of divinity, became the primary focus and purpose of our existence. Even now, many years later, we knew we couldn't go on offering anything that didn't support this above all else.

Our experiences in the seven-month groups brought us back to the central importance of the Divine as the foundation of any and every spiritual exploration. This and this alone, we felt, must be the guiding force in the spiritual journey, and union with our essential divinity the ultimate goal to be realized. Nothing we can receive from without should ever be confused with this. More than ever, we were convinced of the necessity of approaching any spiritual activation or initiatory process *only* from the guidance of the soul.

Through it all, we continued to hold the vision that awakening -- both the opening into enlightenment and the flowering of God-realization -- could occur as easily, as gently, as beautifully, and as inevitably as the unfurling of a rose. Our years as fire lookouts had taught us that within the natural world, thunder and lightning are rare events; far more often, life unfolds in a gradual, integrated way. Although our own awakenings had often occurred through spiritual lightning bolts that zapped our consciousness into entirely new realms, we knew that might be too disorienting for many people. We wanted all that we offered to be in harmony with the effortless, natural processes of Creation, so that awakenings could be easily integrated and lived. With all of this in mind, we asked the Divine if the energies of the deeksha could be modified, so that its effects could be more easily and organically grounded and embodied.

Personal Considerations

The two of us had always been "free agents for God," unaffiliated with any organized spiritual path or structure. The majority of our spiritual training had not been received from other human beings; it had occurred through infusions of energy~consciousness from Beyond. We were shown how to facilitate soul-awakenings through our own direct experience during hundreds of sessions in the Chrysalis, the highly coherent energetic space Barry had been guided to construct.

The deeksha was the first outer assist to awakening we had added to our work, and its humble beginnings at Bhagavan's ashram had mushroomed into a vast, worldwide Oneness Movement. Even though we had traveled to India twice, first to receive the deeksha and then to become deeksha-givers, we had never seen ourselves as part of a movement, even one dedicated to world oneness. While many seemed overjoyed to be part of this global organization and willing to abide by its strictures, we felt increasingly alienated as the movement became ever bigger and more regimented. After so many years of voyaging ever deeper into the realms of the soul, we were unable to sacrifice our inner truth and freedom to outer authorities.

Instead of letting us indulge in the apparent security of becoming part of a mass movement, the inner knowing we had learned to live by threw us back on ourselves, insisting we examine every belief and circumstance through the lens of the soul. Although many in the Oneness Movement saw Amma/Bhagavan as God incarnate and shared the deeksha exactly as they decreed, we felt the need to dis-identify from the collective belief that we are separate and imperfect and need a Godlike human savior or guru to lift us beyond our limitations. The dissonance between what felt right and true to us and what the movement advocated forced us into a deeper unity with the inherent divinity that was and is our ultimate guide through life. More clearly than ever, we saw that nothing can be placed above that, not even "avatars of enlightenment."

In retrospect, we recognize that Bhagavan and Amma did attempt to let everyone know that each of us is one with the Divine.

On one occasion Bhagavan said, "You all are Amma/Bhagavan." While a few seemed to grasp this, the wonderful and potent structure of the guru relationship continued to provide helpful spiritual sustenance for many.

But this was not our path. Just as children leave the sheltering nest of their home of origin and become self-sufficient adults in the wider world, we were being asked to release all "spiritual parent" projections onto Amma/Bhagavan and recognize that their capacities are available to us all. Letting go of the perceived need for intermediaries brought us into greater spiritual maturity, deepening our capacity to directly commune with Source. That, for us, seemed far more important than following the dictates of others, however "enlightened" they may seem.

9

A New Octave of Possibility

Barry: A New Direction

Our inner process of differentiating from the Oneness Movement inevitably spilled over into the groups in which we shared the deeksha. We hadn't felt comfortable with the idea that the deeksha energy came through Bhagavan and not directly from God. Abundant experience had made it clear that each of us is directly and eternally connected to and wholly part of the One, and that realizing and embodying this reality was the very goal of earthly existence. The last thing we wanted was to create another subtle layer of veiling for ourselves or those who received the deeksha.

Shortly thereafter, we received a response to our soul's desire for a different way. Preparing to give deeksha in a group, Karen and I closed our eyes to connect with Bhagavan on the inner planes to receive the deeksha energy. I then inwardly saw Bhagavan point upward, above his head. I instantly knew he was directing us toward the ultimate source of the deeksha -- and all other forms of grace. Responding to the evolutionary vector of this time, he had no need to act as an intermediary, beckoning us to move beyond him to the source. As consciousness ascended, the source of the deeksha began to pour forth the transmission directly.

During the following months, as the origin of the deeksha shifted from Bhagavan to our individual connection with Source, we felt as though we had come back Home. The deeksha's blessing-grace did, indeed, flow directly into us, without the need for an intermediary, making it clear that the source of the deeksha energies was accessible to all. It, like the source of all things, was one with our essential being. *If the truth is oneness,* we realized, *how can there be other than one source, and therefore how can we not have access to it?*

In experiencing the deeksha freed from its ties to a particular individual, we had broken through into a new level of realization and empowerment. We only wanted to see others experience the same level of spiritual sovereignty. But this was not the end of the story.

For some time I had strongly felt that the Universal Christ energy and consciousness could somehow infuse the deeksha. The Christ was so central to my path of service that it felt unnatural for the deeksha to be split off from this profound source of blessing-grace and resurrection. In soul-awakening sessions, the most powerful shifts had always occurred when the Christ Presence was involved.

Once again, as soon as we asked, the Universal Christ began to overlight and infuse the deekshas we gave. Many people commented on seeing the Christ in our eyes during transmissions, just as we witnessed the individualized divinity at the core of the soul -- often referred to as the God within or the holy Christ Self -- instantly begin to flower in recipients of the transmissions.

Because the fundamental nature of the true Self is love, group meetings were increasingly colored by easy, natural outpourings of love. As a group soul whose primary fabric was divine love came into being, we devoted more time to looking into one another's eyes and witnessing the truth of who and what we each are. After one group, I found myself staring in rapture into the eyes of a participant. As she returned the infinite love through her gaze, the words "Christ Consciousness" arose from within her as an acknowledgment of what we were experiencing. Whatever one called it, experiencing the vast, universal love of this field of embodied divinity was beautiful and fulfilling beyond words.

As the resurrecting power of the Christ came through the deeksha, evolutionary shifts that might have once taken years were now occurring in months, weeks, or moments. Our long-held vision that awakenings could unfold as easily and naturally as the unfurling of a rose was beginning to manifest. Some people went through immense changes, and challenging moments arose, but for the most part the transformations seemed to be relatively easily assimilable and self-integrating. An empty fullness of divine presence and peace was increasingly reflected in eyes and outer demeanors. Ego-minds were dissolving into the infinitely welcoming fullness of the true Self. Nearly everyone seemed delighted with what was occurring.

And yet...

Bhagavan had promised that once people received a few deekshas, they would spontaneously be able to access the energies and transfer them, just like those who had attended a 21-day program in India. Thrilled by this possibility, we consecrated the seven-month groups to its unfoldment. We wanted to see the blessings of the deeksha spread all across the planet, catalyzing the mass awakening Bhagavan had promised would occur.

But despite our encouragement, no one seemed ready to claim the ability to transfer the states of awakening they had experienced to others. This was disappointing; we had no desire to be part of yet another priesthood dispensing proprietary grace.

We felt grateful for the core gifts of the deeksha, the capacity to de-clutch the mind, rewire the brain, and open consciousness to enlightened states. The deeksha decommissioned the ego like nothing we had ever experienced, and we recognized the immense value of that. Serving as conduits of grace through sharing the deeksha had felt deeply satisfying. Yet we continued to sense there was something beyond even this, something that would feel even more right to us. In our hearts and souls, we knew that anything we offered needed to resonate with the deepest truths our journeys had revealed. The deeksha offered part of the picture, but not the entire package.

We envisioned a transmission that would be as effective as the deeksha but free of all identification with and attachment to a particular path or organization. We felt sure it was only a matter of time until such a transmission could be passed from person to person, freely and without limit, igniting the mass awakening Bhagavan had so often insisted was coming. We weren't sure how this would occur, but we trusted it was inevitable.

Just as the One creates a multitude of varieties of flowers instead of a single type, the possibilities for divine expression through us all are forever multiplying. The grace from Source is always seeking new outlets and manifestations. When we, as souls, acknowledge our inherent divinity and step into fulfilling our divine purpose as embodied aspects of All That Is, we discover the scope and variety of the expressions that can occur through us are unlimited. The two of us felt more than ready to experience more of this unlimitedness. Once again, just as he had with the deeksha, our spiritual brother Kiara Windrider provided the key to our next step.

PART THREE

✢ ✢ ✢

The Transmissions
of Grace

✢ ✢ ✢

10

Ilahinoor

Kiara had recently moved to Turkey. During a retreat he was conducting on the Aegean Coast, the group realized they had been together in Egypt during Akhenaten's reign, when adepts were delving into the mysteries of immortality and ascension. Along with these memories, Kiara and his new friends became aware of an exalted energy that none had ever experienced before.

The Egyptian God, Ra, then communicated that the energy emanated from a consciousness field built by many beings who, over the ages, had achieved physical immortality and ascension. Access to the field had been severely limited over the last few thousand years while humanity passed through a very dense period in consciousness. This was all changing, Ra indicated, for now the human species was awakening and being prepared for personal and planetary ascension.

Over the next several days, as the little group continued to experience the energy, a name for it arose: Ilahinoor, which means *divine light* in Turkish and Arabic. Kiara pronounced the word in four syllables: ih-lah-hee-noor, with the accent on the second syllable. During our next phone conversation with Kiara during the spring of 2007, he described Ilahinoor as a soft, feminine energy that was very helpful in integrating the deeksha. He happily described the easy, effortless way people spontaneously shared Ilahinoor with one another after receiving the transmission.

This was what we had all been waiting for -- an energy transmission that not only brought great blessings to those who received it, but could also be passed on immediately, free of hierarchical organizations, rules, and control. We all felt thrilled that, with no limits on its use, Ilahinoor could go viral in no time, bringing its gifts to all who were interested in receiving them. The radical new possibility the deeksha had introduced was going to its next level of unfoldment!

We couldn't wait to experience Ilahinoor. After we all hung up, Kiara transmitted Ilahinoor to us from his home in Turkey. Karen describes her initial experience:

The energies came in through my face, then descended into the body, primarily on the left side. They came with a great deal of whirling turbulence, like an unstable solution or the action of a washing machine. The energies swirled for some time in the face and head, then in the heart / throat / soul center area. They eventually moved down the left side of the body into the second chakra area, where they stayed for a long time.

As the turbulence continued to churn, it left in its wake a feeling of absolute stillness in each area as it moved on. It finally came to rest in the base chakra in the form of a bubbling bowl, gently curving: a container in which the energies could be deeply embodied. It felt lovely.

The deep, rich stillness intensified and rooted more firmly as I continued to invite Ilahinoor to land within me. There was an unmistakable sensation of the energies' presence, and I knew that they would always be there, for they had become part of me. They would also be able to be transmitted, if that were the intention.

I was pulled very deep within as the energies took root, and I stayed immobile in a deep, rich space for a long time. The energies went down the legs and into the feet, where I felt them take residence. I sensed the full grounding of Ilahinoor would manifest over time.

As all of this occurred, a strong impression of the Middle East was present. I felt a sense of oneness with the land, the people, and the ancientness of it all. The image of figures wearing long robes and walking on the earth barefoot arose, along with a quiet, subtle yearning for, or maybe a remembrance of, this simple, grounded, integrated way of being. Perhaps the energies of Ilahinoor somehow carry this template of the human experience.

Since the Ilahinoor energies went down the left side of my body during my first experience, I was curious what might happen with a second transmission, so I asked Kiara to send Ilahinoor to me again a week later. This time it went straight to the area around the right eye where a serious case of shingles had occurred a few years before. The energies rooted around in there for quite some time, and then subsided, and I felt the experience was complete.

Sharing Ilahinoor

Ilahinoor immediately felt like the breakthrough and next step we'd been awaiting. The transmission contained the same level of transformational power as the deeksha, with different and complementary effects. Whereas the deeksha strongly stimulated the upper chakras, Ilahinoor went deeper, grounding the higher energies within the lower chakras. We sensed that, like the deeksha, Ilahinoor altered brain physiology, and that a series of transmissions over time would decommission the ego-mind. Ultimately, we felt, both transmissions would contribute to the dissolution of the separate self sense.

Our initial experiences of Ilahinoor prompted us to share the new transmission in our groups right away. We felt sure Ilahinoor would help people to integrate the expansive, brain-rearranging effects of the deeksha, and we had a feeling it would offer other benefits as yet unknown. Would others feel capable of passing it on after receiving it, as we hoped?

Kiara had offered some tips on sharing Ilahinoor. He suggested inviting the transmission into the head by placing the hands over specific areas in sequence. First, as with the deeksha, the hands were placed over the crown chakra to invite the energies to pour in. Then, one hand covered the forehead while the other cupped the occipital ridge at the base of the skull. Finally, Kiara had discovered that an area at the center of the back of the head just above the base of the skull was key.

We found ourselves adding additional movements to this sequence of head positions. The soul center above the heart, which we had come to regard as the center of an embodied soul's being, naturally wanted to receive Ilahinoor's imprint. After our hands had completed the head positions, they moved to the upper chest area until the transmission there felt complete. Since, during our own experiences of receiving Ilahinoor, the energies had descended to land deep within the belly, we then found our hands moving to the belly soul center area, below the navel. Acquiring a life of their own, the hands remained there until we sensed the transmission had taken hold deep within.

With many recipients, the transmission of Ilahinoor ended there. But sometimes, the hands then traced a path down the sides of the legs to the feet, and occasionally hovered over the chakras in the feet to deeply ground the transmission. These additional steps occurred most often with those who seemed especially un-grounded or imbalanced by a strong focus on the upper chakras and higher-dimensional energies. Finally, our hands traced a path from the belly soul center back up through the heart area, over the shoulders and down the arms, encouraging the energy of Ilahinoor to stream into the hands so it could be shared through them with others.

During teleconferences and private sessions with those at a distance, we first envisioned each person sitting before us, and then went through the same sequence, our hands moving from one position to the next. Feedback overwhelmingly indicated that these distance transmissions were no less powerful or palpable than those delivered in person.

Our first opportunity to share Ilahinoor came with the ongo-ing group in Eugene, Oregon. After giving each person the Ilahi-noor transmission, we suggested they lie down and allow the en-ergies to "cook" for some time, until the process felt complete. After a break for a snack or a brief walk outside, we returned to the room and had everyone find a partner. Each pair took turns being the "giver" and "receiver" of the Ilahinoor energies. Rather than having recipients lie down this time, we suggested they simply continue sitting quietly, eyes closed, feeling the effects of the transmission working within themselves. When they felt complete, they then be-came the transmitters, sharing Ilahinoor with their partners.

It was deeply moving to observe everyone stepping into their new role as divine conduits so easily and naturally. Rising into their true identity as sacred aspects of the One Great Being, they treated one another with the dignity and grace of their essential selves. A feeling of holiness suffused the room as everyone in it entered into directly experiencing their oneness with the Divine.

We returned the following month to hear that those who had experimented with Ilahinoor during the intervening weeks had found its nature to be very feminine and deeply healing. Some felt the transmission deepening and grounding the openings in con-sciousness that had occurred through the deeksha. This feedback confirmed our own experiences with Ilahinoor, but the best was yet to come.

A new, very joyful face beamed out from among the group members. DeeDee revealed that for years, a debilitating case of Lyme disease had severely limited her ability to move freely, making her full-time massage practice nearly impossible to continue. After she received Ilahinoor from a member of the Eugene group, she shared it with a friend. Strongly intuiting that Ilahinoor could really help her, DeeDee asked her friend if she would be willing to give Ilahinoor to her as often as possible for a few weeks. The friend happily obliged.

After almost a month of near-daily transmissions, DeeDee found herself miraculously set free from the pain and immobility that had curtailed her activity. Her formerly intermittent sleep became deep and long, and she felt rested for the first time in years. She resumed taking long walks and hikes and eventually began to cross-country ski again. As her energy increased, her bodywork practice was once more infused with ease and joy.

DeeDee's story deeply affected everyone in the room. Now we knew for sure the Ilahinoor transmission could be passed on. DeeDee said she had begun to share Ilahinoor, finding it eminently comforting to bodywork clients recovering from stress and trauma. Some of them were no doubt passing it on to their friends and family. The transmission was already on its way around the world!

Before hearing DeeDee's account, we had some sense of the nurturing effects of Ilahinoor. But we had not anticipated that the transmission could precipitate such a profound physical healing. Kiara had mentioned nothing about this possibility. DeeDee's story galvanized our commitment to share Ilahinoor whenever possible.

As news of Ilahinoor spread, we received e-mails from people all over the globe asking us to share it with them. To expedite this, we began to offer bimonthly teleconferences. What a joy to sit in our little living room on the farm, sharing this wonderful transmission with people all around the planet! As they related their experiences with Ilahinoor, we heard many stories of its healing blessings. Mental, emotional and physical conditions, many of which had eluded other therapeutic approaches, were brought to the surface rapidly and gently for healing.

Here is a sample from an e-mail:

> I transmitted Ilahinoor to my daughter, who definitely has an active, stressed-filled and ungrounded life at this time. She told me that she felt movement from the left side of her rib cage and under and around her heart, like when you hold a slinky in your hands

and move it back and forth from one hand to the other. It was beautiful, she said.

Since that time she does feel more grounded and is handling the difficulties in her life with a quietness and calm that transcends what she ever dreamed of. She is so very grateful, and knows that what she is feeling is radiating to those in her immediate family.

I don't want this to sound like some kind of "high" that I'm on or that I've been converted to something -- it is all very surreal, grounding, joyful, and nurturing ... I am so grateful to both of you and Kiara and those who help you for bringing in this energy of Divine Light and passing it along to others, allowing "us" too to pass it along.

The Deep, Dark Light of Ilahinoor

The word ilahinoor is composed of two root syllables: *ilah,* which refers to the Divine, and *noor,* which means light. Again, to pronounce ilahinoor, divide it into four syllables as follows, placing the accent on the second syllable:

IH or EE

LAH'

HEE

NOOR

This is an extremely sacred word in the Islamic tradition. Feel the magnificence and grandeur of the word and its meaning as you say it aloud. Know that giving voice to the word literally calls in the light of the Divine.

As we continued to share Ilahinoor, we found that the transmission "delivered" the divine light in a very different way from the deeksha or meditation practices that access the transcendental realms. While many people experienced illuminations with Ilahinoor, the light did not remain in the head centers, but penetrated deep within the body. The embodied nature of the transmission prompted us to refer to Ilahinoor as the Divine Light of the Goddess, for its energy is often experienced as deeply feminine -- soft and gentle, yet pervasive and powerful.

Experiencing and sharing Ilahinoor over time carried us ever more deeply into the mysterious realm of the divine feminine. We were reminded of the twofold nature of the awakening process, which embraces both the masculine and feminine qualities of Life. Ilahinoor opens the deeper realms of the soul's embodied nature. This fertile, feminine darkness magnetizes the white light of spirit into the physical body, enfolding it and giving it form and substance.

Within the realm of the divine feminine, we encounter the "dark light," the luminescence within form itself. We have all seen this luminous darkness shining out from pupils of deepest black in eyes that are alive to spirit. As the dark light and the white light unify within us, the clear light of consciousness shines forth.

The bright, white light so often sought after by spiritual seekers is only half of the equation; without the dark light, awakening cannot be complete. As we become aware that we are composed of light that is both white and dark, masculine and feminine, we may directly experience these qualities endlessly blending and merging within us, as the yin-yang symbol illustrates. We may also perceive our very cells lighting up with radiance, held within the deep, dark, womb-like matrix of the Mother. When the energy~consciousness of Ilahinoor lands and integrates within us, it can catalyze a deeply embodied experience of the fundamental, inextricable unity of the divine masculine and feminine forces.

Deep within the belly, just below the navel, lies the soul center known by many terms: the hara or tan tien, the sacred womb or egg, the abode of Divine Mother or shakti, and the seat of the feminine or mother aspect of God. While Ilahinoor affects all the chakras and soul centers, it primarily focuses here, in the belly soul center. In men and women alike, Ilahinoor is typically experienced most strongly from the heart down, helping us to embrace the lower chakras and whatever they are holding that has not yet been loved and included in our totality. As it descends to our very depths, Ilahinoor supports the process of sinking into the dark light of the divine feminine: the endlessly flowing fountain of Life, which nurtures and supports all living beings.

As this aspect of Self awakens, our very bodies are seen as sacred. We come to know that these forms we inhabit are fully divine, no less God than the transcendental realms of spirit. The perception of the matter worlds as merely maya or illusion dissolves in the full opening of the hara center. One's body is seen as a manifestation of Self, and all forms, all "other" bodies, are perceived as part of the Self. One way this might be expressed is *I AM One with the sacred womb of the Mother, birthing and holding all life in all universes.*

The image of the Egyptian Goddess Nut bending over the cosmos, enfolding it all in her vastness, illustrates this level of realization of Self. Ammachi, the hugging saint and avatar of south India, often says that all she wants to do is embrace as many of her children as possible while she is here. Her embodiment of the Divine Mother is so complete and total that she views every single human being as one of her children. All are equally lovable, unfathomably cherished simply because they exist.

Ilahinoor awakens the realization of our embodied divinity and our oneness with all of life. This transmission reveals the unified consciousness of life itself -- the innate, omniscient, omnipresent presence that pervades all of Creation. The prime purpose of this intelligence is to further life, to see every form of beingness flourish and become more abundant. Here is how one woman expressed this:

> To me, Ilahinoor has a dark light, moist inner earth/plant vibrating quality that feels ideal for growing. The plant kingdom called to me after being introduced to Ilahinoor, too. ... Even lumber on the side of a store under construction communicated.

As Ilahinoor helps the belly soul center to open, enhancing our ability to perceive this unity, we begin to see it at work everywhere, within and without. Walking through a forest, we marvel at the symbiosis of the plants and animals that live there. Watching a bee gather pollen for its hive, we become aware that it also pollinates the plants it visits, allowing them to flower, bear fruit and reproduce. We marvel at the innate intelligence that causes migratory birds to know when to fly south for the winter, and the unerring guidance system that leads them to their destination. The instant reaction that prompts us to flee in the face of danger, to cuddle and stroke a frightened baby, to eat when our energy dips, to sleep when the body needs rest -- all are manifestations of the intelligence of life.

We are born with this inner knowing at the core of our embodied being, our natural soul. It does not always remain accessible, though; psycho-emotional traumas can diminish our communion with it. As we judge, deny and separate from aspects of the psyche, and thus lose touch with the innate intelligence of life, addictions and other life-destroying behaviors arise. We can restore the psyche's wholeness through recovering these wounded aspects and bringing them back into conscious union with the soul. This can occur through inner consciousness work intended to reconnect and reintegrate them. It can also take place when Ilahinoor is received over time in a setting supportive of healing and integrating what has not yet been loved and enfolded within our wholeness.

How People Experience Ilahinoor

Ilahinoor is most often experienced as a soothing, nurturing energy that is easily assimilable by virtually everyone. This soft, descending energy often feels like gentle waves moving through various parts of the body, down into the abdomen, pelvis, and sometimes the legs and feet. It brings a deep sense of relaxation, a peace within the body that makes one feel comfortable and at home within it.

Who among us could not use an infusion of deep peace, gentle comfort, and healing nurturance? Ilahinoor assists those with active, stressed-filled lives to drop back into the body and re-connect with the natural rhythms and intelligence of life. People who tend to feel ungrounded or "spacy" find Ilahinoor helps them to get back in touch with their innate sense of earthy, organic flow and grounding. It is particularly helpful for those who spend a great deal of time in the mental realms.

Since Ilahinoor works to unify all of the life intelligence in the body, it can help in reuniting split-off aspects of the psyche with the soul. Transforming separation into inclusivity and oneness is the underlying dynamic that promotes all healing. Many who have received the Ilahinoor transmission report healings on all levels -- spiritual, mental, emotional and physical. Some are relatively minor, while others, like DeeDee's described above, border on the miraculous. People often report that distinctions between the various levels of being dissolve in the awareness of unity Ilahinoor imparts. Similarly, its healing benefits are often experienced in a holistic way that transcends categorizations and permeates the entire being.

Of course, no one can know what, if any, direct healing will occur after an Ilahinoor transmission, and it is important to remember that Ilahinoor doesn't do the healing or create the results. Through grace, it assists in restoring the preexisting wholeness and integrity that have been obscured. Although healing can and does occur, no one knows what the soul of each person is meant to experience as part of the divine plan for their unfoldment. As with all modalities and transmissions, we can hold the intention that Ilahinoor go where it is needed and do what is most beneficial for all involved.

Ilahinoor provides foundational support for the process of

awakening, for it assists in healing and making whole the human psyche and natural soul. Without this foundation, even the most exalted spiritual energies will have no place to land and be expressed. In fact, as the higher energies pour in, they tend to amplify any distortions in the psyche, which can exacerbate their symptoms and manifestations. If, as we climb the spiritual path, we continually focus on the purification, healing and wholing of our humanness, we are far more likely to experience our divinity as fully embodied and eminently livable, active and effective in the world. A life of joy, happiness and fulfillment is more apt to take root and flower when we have provided the tender plant of our beingness with plenty of rich, moist compost, in addition to light and water and fresh air.

If we have held spiritual judgments on ourselves, Ilahinoor can help us to relax these impossibly high standards and accept ourselves as we are. A woman who attended many Ilahinoor calls reported:

> *Usually spiritually exciting things don't happen to me, but when I just think of Ilahinoor my tummy heats up, especially right before I sleep. I also feel such peace and love inside I want to pinch myself to see if it's real.*
>
> *I feel so close to the plants. I feel one with them. I always loved my garden and now the feeling has deepened into a joy even greater than before.*

This woman went on to infuse her gardens with ilahinoor so they would bless all who passed by with comfort and peace. She felt delighted with this simple, natural contribution to her neighborhood.

Disconnection with the innate intelligence of our human soul results in the ubiquitous dis-eases of our times. Addictions, for example, are a sign that we have lost touch with what truly nourishes us, as is our attraction to eating and drinking things that harm the body. Overuse of stimulants such as sugar and caffeine, too, reflects a basic disengagement from our belly wisdom, as do emotional issues including fear of intimacy and codependency.

Ilahinoor is especially helpful for those who feel lost and disconnected from their human self. If pressing issues involving relationships, home, family, and money are present, the lower chakras and belly soul center are probably in need of greater awareness. When people accumulate an excess of unintegrated higher energies -- for instance, from receiving a lot of higher light transmissions or infusions in a short time, or meditating for hours a day --

they are often flooded with an immediate sense of relief as the Ilahinoor transmission helps the higher energies to descend and land. As the lower chakras are bathed in the light from above, consciousness openings can be integrated and embodied, and the subtle body and chakra systems can come back into balance.

An overcharge in the upper chakras may impart transcendent bliss and a sense of rising above the difficult feelings and issues of the world. This is almost always a temporary state, which will be followed by an equally strong descent. As Taoist philosophy teaches, life continuously moves from one polarity to its opposite, seeking balance. Staying connected to the hara center and the lower chakras and experiencing Ilahinoor on a regular basis can help us to welcome the descent rather than experiencing it as a painful crash. In fact, Ilahinoor reminds us that each ascent into the higher realms must be followed by a corresponding deepening and integration period, if it is to be fully embodied and lived.

Ilahinoor may bring to the surface feelings and memories that have not yet been fully faced and felt. It shines attention on the belly center and whatever has been held there that is now ready to be seen, felt, and accepted more deeply. When such material arises, we suggest reminding yourself that facing and embracing it is an integral aspect of awakening. You can invite the breath into the belly, and feel it penetrating right into the core of the sensation or feeling there. As you fully feel it, remember to just as fully release it on the outbreath. Turn it over to the One who knows how best to bring it all into healing and wholeness. Rest in the arms of Divine Mother as She comforts you through the emotional storm. Feel Her sustaining love and caring enfolding you. Listen as She whispers the messages She alone can give you.

A woman who received Ilahinoor described her experience of this process:

> This morning I thought about Ilahinoor and called it in. The most beautiful, loving energy filled me. It was so gentle. It allowed more of my pain and brought it out. I cried for joy, for the whole thing. My vision feels different. It's like I can see more of what's love peeking through what goes on out here. I'm ecstatic in the most mellow sort of way.

Contagious Ease

Many people reported that working with Ilahinoor seemed to make facing the remaining unintegrated emotional content easier.

As the belly soul center flowered, resistance to the more challenging aspects of awakening faded away. "I never knew it could be so easy to feel things -- even the things I thought would be the hardest -- and let them go," became a common refrain, as the following report from a woman in Europe expresses:

> I experienced a wonderful sense of lightness and groundedness, very in my body, and the miracle was that although it was very cathartic, it was not ungrounded in any way, and I never felt overwhelmed in any way, which was great.
> In fact I felt after a few hours quite liberated, in that I felt in touch with myself, and very authentic, which I have not felt in a long time -- a sense of being able to not only feel my feelings, but express them! So it helped me to feel grounded enough to express my feelings!
> Truly liberating, and in essence, therapeutic. It is a wonderful energy.

Another woman wondered whether her experience was appropriate:

> [I'm] not sure if this is what "should" be happening -- lots and lots of grief bubbling up; deep tears. And now a strong desire to have my body physically loved. This is really disturbing me as I am not familiar with this feeling...and I don't have anyone that I feel I can trust to allow this with. I've been happily alone for a year and suddenly I have to have loving touch and NOW. (I don't mean sexual.) So many tears. Perhaps this is just myself waking up in my body but it's scary. Can you recognize this feeling? Have others gone through this?

As we are all discovering, there are no limits on or rules about what "should" be happening -- with Ilahinoor or in life as a whole. Here is where Ilahinoor really shines, for this transmission helps us to be present with What Is, within and without. Saying "No" to what is present in our mental-emotional world not only comes between us and our experience, it postpones awareness of the true Self. When we can say "Yes" to whatever arises, we are one with the soul, our inner divinity, which accepts and embraces everything, without exception.

The more comfortable people became with facing and embracing whatever was present, the more gently and tenderly they treated themselves and one another. *We are one*, they seemed to be seeing, *even in our unhealed emotions. We all have the same "stuff" -- the greed, envy, anger, and sadness; the yearning to be free. The story may differ, but the underlying feelings are the same.*

After they had received Ilahinoor, people reported a new sense of inner quietness and peace, and a relaxation into and acceptance of themselves, their lives, and their awakening process. Many saw that struggle only occurs when we resist what is present and think that something different should be happening. The actual emotional content was not so hard to face, they realized; it was the judgment that it was wrong or bad to be feeling what they were feeling that had filled the process with conflict.

Suffering had been compounded by spiritual beliefs such as *I should be beyond this emotion. If I were truly awake, none of this would be present. I need to hide these feelings and pretend that everything is calm and clear.* As Ilahinoor opened up an allowing space for everything that was present, these judgments were replaced by greater self-acceptance and equanimity. Emotional tempests might continue to rise and fall, but deep within was a place that could contain them all and allow them to pass through, without the damage that can occur from holding back and then venting strong feelings.

Daily life was flowing more smoothly for many, as they discovered a quiet, simple joy in the everyday tasks that had once seemed boring, meaningless, or irrelevant to what they had thought awakening was all about. Feeling isolated and alone in a separate little bubble gave way to a palpable sense of unity with all forms of life, from trees and rocks to the birds out in the yard.

We were especially happy to hear from those who had become imbalanced from receiving too many high-light activations without enough corresponding attention paid to the embodiment of the vaster energies. These people usually expressed a great need for grounding, nourishing support for their human selves, and found what they sought in Ilahinoor. A Scandinavian man's e-mail described his feelings of despondency after months of finding himself lost and adrift. The many deekshas Erik had received had apparently dismantled his sense of self so thoroughly that he no longer had a clear sense of the meaning of his life. After his first experience of Ilahinoor, he wrote:

> *It feels very wonderful to see and feel the changes that happen with ilahinoor. It is like a gentle*

*mother coming and comforting and showing everything
is going to be all right.*

Erik's depression lifted and he went on to share the blessings he had received from Ilahinoor with others in similar situations.

A woman who found Ilahinoor so resonant she later joined
nearly every teleconference we offered had this to say after her
first experience of the energies:

> Since the transmission, the refrain I-laaaaa-hee-
> noor has moved through me spontaneously accompa-
> nied with the down flow of a wide stream of bright liq-
> uid light that enters the crown, zips down to the belly,
> splits down the legs and out the soles into tiny light-
> filled roots. Quite amazing. The energy feels so right/
> needed/good/balancing.
>
> The Ilahinoor energy feels to me like that com-
> plete relaxation that occurs when falling into a big soft
> chair after a long hard day. The chair provides deep
> rest and support as I realize I didn't know how tired
> and out-of-balance I was. Or how a long drink of fresh
> water tastes after not realizing how thirsty I actually
> had become. Ilahinoor really does enlifen/enliven.

If there is one thing Ilahinoor seems to impart to the human
self, it is this sense of being at home in our own skin. As we sink
into flowing more easily with the rhythms of life, we find ourselves
responding to what comes with the carefree abandon of a child
playing in a sandbox. As Ilahinoor continues to be passed from
person to person, circling the globe, it is helping the focus of humanity's attention to shift from contagious *dis-ease* to contagious
ease. What would any of us rather do than spread ease? It is a joy
to envision a world full of people relaxed and at ease, happy to be
themselves, just as they are.

Endless Opportunities to Experience Ilahinoor

Skandar's creativity with Ilahinoor (and the other Transmissions of Grace we will describe in the next two chapters) has endlessly delighted us, along with everyone else on our calls who has
heard him relate his adventures with animals, birds, trees, and
places. At various times, he has been guided to send the transmissions into abandoned mines, a golden eagle that had been suc-

cessfully rehabilitated and was being released, a city park, and even holes in the ground. Of the latter, he explains:

> I dug holes all around the area, and put Ilahinoor into the holes in liquid form. Gaia was really happy, and gave me the opportunity to send the animals to these springs of healing. They can lap it up however they want. I put in 179 holes over the winter. Last year we [the rehab center] took in 150 injured animals. This year, nine.

"You can plant it like a seed, without any intention," Skandar says of a transmission, "and let it go. This energy is playful. It's so beautiful, you have no idea where it's going to take you, and that's the beauty of it!"

Another time, Skandar shared Ilahinoor with several aggressive dogs at the animal shelter.

> They were biters, and weren't adoptable, so they were going to be euthanized. I did the transmission at 10 a.m. and 2 p.m. one day. The next morning, they had completely turned around. Now they have a chance of being adopted.

"Most people are a little too strong with their energy fields with animals," Skandar cautioned. "Pull your energy field in to around 16 inches from your body. Then, ask for their permission. Look into their left eyes." He then shared more from his vast accumulation of animal wisdom:

> Animals have protection coding that is essential to their survival. They let this relax to receive transmissions. I sit in an open area and talk with them: 'If you want a transmission, you'll have to come over and sit and behave.'
>
> I use the image of turning on a faucet: 'Okay, we're going to have some flow between us.'
>
> If you can get close enough, hold your hands six to ten inches away from them and stroke or pet their bodies without touching. They will give a signal when they've had enough.

Skandar's relationship with the transmissions is clearly unique and multifaceted. Yet he takes no credit for what happens when he shares the energies with others. "I'm just the conduit," Skandar humbly insists. "I take directions really well."

Since Ilahinoor is particularly helpful in the ongoing process of embodying the divine light in daily life, it can easily and naturally permeate all aspects of our earthly existence. Maryval, who has also participated in many of our calls, related the way Ilahinoor infused her yoga practice:

> While meditating one morning, I called in the ilahinoor energy. When that finished, I started my yoga practice. In some of the asanas, I felt moved to chant "iiiiiiiiii-laaaaaaa-hiiiiiiiiiii-nooooooooor," and was surprised at the releases that occurred, deepening the asanas. The next day, I chanted ilahinoor in all the asanas and was surprised at how much yummier each one became. It felt as if an inner yoga teacher was gently touching areas that I'd thought were soft but which still could release more.
>
> The following day, I got in the asana to the best of my ability and then chanted ilahinoor three times in each asana, only to discover each time that there was always more energy that my body wanted to let go. I also chanted ilahinoor during the transition between the asanas. When I finished and began to move about my day, I felt as if I was liquid light flowing.
>
> Ilahiyoga (Divine Yoga) or Yoganoor (Yoga of Light)? Try it yourself and decide. It feels to me Divine Light Yoga - Ilahinooroga!

During another call, Maryval described the ways Ilahinoor was weaving itself into the very fabric of her being. She reported:

> Ilahinoor is chanting itself through me even when I don't call it forth -- in Home Depot, in the midst of traffic jams. It's singing itself into situations where it wants to be.

Healing Addiction with Ilahinoor

An infectiously enthusiastic physician we'll call Dr. R regularly attended our Ilahinoor teleconferences. He was the medical advisor at an addiction rehabilitation facility that, until now, had not been a calm and peaceful place. We'll let Dr. R describe what unfolded when he began to share Ilahinoor there:

Thank you both for your phenomenal presentation and transmission last night. I still feel the waves of Light flowing through my body and soul. I had an unusual dream experience last night which I want to share. I awakened in the dream surrounded by Light. I heard a voice come out of the Light saying, "I am Ilahinoor. I am the Angel of Light. Call upon me by my name and I will transmit my Light to you and to all you call upon me to touch. I am the Ilahinoor, I am the Angel of Light."

This is unusual because I am a man of science. This is the first time I have ever had such a dream. I don't often even remember my dreams. This morning I awakened feeling like I was glowing. I think I know what "luminous" means now.

This morning I did group therapy for 40 alcoholics/addicts in our Recovery Home. With their permission I did my first transmission of Ilahinoor. (I asked Ilahinoor to touch each of them.) There was an immediate visible change. The normal addict negativism lifted. There was a feeling of lightness and almost joy.

The next day, all 40 transmitted Ilahinoor to each other. All I could do was break down in tears. Then, on Family Day, 100 people gave the energy to each other. The same thing happened. The entire Universe stopped -- was in between breaths -- nothing and everything at the same time. It makes me weep with tears of joy.

Conflicts have been reduced by 75%, and this is the week of the full moon. Everything was so peaceful, everyone went around the grounds in silence, like monks in a cloister.

Eighteen people are in detox now, and usually they go through excruciating pain. They still have pain, but they were almost peacefully transitioning. The detox usually takes a few days, and it took a few hours!

We don't touch each other at the house. All of this was done by sending Ilahinoor with intention and by name. As everyone joined in chanting "I-la-hi-noor," it just went where it wanted to go, in waves. It is such a beautiful sound, to hear 100 people chanting -- the vibration is tremendous. Then this holy hush comes over them.

When Dr. R spoke about the "holy hush" during subsequent calls, he often teared up, overcome with the glory of what he'd experienced. We felt deeply touched by the blessings pouring through this man to the community of souls recovering from addiction. As he described the magnificent changes he was observing, a sublime stillness, a peace that is not of this world united us all, however far apart our physical bodies may have been.

Several months later, Dr. R began to receive reports that Ilahinoor had migrated to other treatment facilities in his state. There are now more than a thousand people receiving and sharing Ilahinoor in addiction recovery programs there, and the transmission has recently been declared an approved treatment modality.

Who among us is not aware of the pain and suffering caused by drug and alcohol addiction? Ilahinoor seems to address the root of the issue: the lack of soul-nurturing that leads people to turn to substances, seeking the solace they have been unable to find elsewhere. In light of Dr. R's testimony, the potential for similar benefits with other types of addiction -- eating disorders, caffeine and nicotine addiction, and all other forms of seeking without what can only be found within -- immediately comes to mind. A vast realm of possibility lies as yet unexplored, just waiting for those who feel called to participate in a grand experiment.

The Grace of Ilahinoor

The advent of Ilahinoor made it clear that Source wanted to include everyone, everywhere, in the descent of grace. It was no longer necessary to travel halfway around the planet and pay thousands of dollars to be initiated to give a transmission. Unlike the deeksha, Ilahinoor could spread from person to person in the context of daily life. (2011 Update: The deeksha initiation in India is now offered at far more reasonable rates, and deeksha givers are able to initiate others to give deeksha now. Neither of these changes had occurred when Ilahinoor arrived in 2007.)

Everyone who receives Ilahinoor can immediately pass it on to anyone who would like to experience it. Some people may require a few transmissions to lock into the source of the energies, but with repeated exposure it naturally flows through. Stepping into sharing the transmission with others constitutes a major upleveling for those who have thought some sort of spiritual pedigree was required to access the Divine. A radical shift in identity occurs as we realize we are capable of inviting sacred energies to pour through us to bless others.

Since Ilahinoor has no rules or limits, no long training programs, and no hierarchies or organizational structures, it is available to all. People are free to share Ilahinoor with friends, coworkers, animals, pets, plants, trees, and birds. Anyone can ask to be a conduit for Ilahinoor to fill a building, an airplane, an area of a city, a nation, or whole regions of the world that might benefit from its soothing, healing vibrational frequencies. And, of course, it is a great joy to envision the planet and all its inhabitants bathed in the healing, nurturing grace of Ilahinoor!

We will always feel grateful to Amma and Bhagavan for opening the doors of possibility that eventually led to Ilahinoor, and for all the grace they bestowed upon us. While their work continues to assist many, the One Source had expanded and differentiated its expression even further. Now, the blessing-grace is flowing forth not only through avatars, but through people that would consider themselves very ordinary. Anyone who wants to be a conduit for Ilahinoor can invite that to happen!

EXPERIENCE~ACTIVATION: Ilahinoor

Find a comfortable place in which you can remain for a time. At first, you will be sitting, and later it will be best to lie down. As you sit quietly, allow your eyes to close and become aware of your breathing. Feel the breath coming into the body and then going back out. Letting your awareness sink into the breath, feel yourself traveling into the inner world.

Contemplate all that you have read about Ilahinoor. What deeply spoke to you about this transmission? What does it offer that would be food for your soul? Allow a few minutes to consider this.

Now, feel how much you would like to directly experience the blessing of Ilahinoor. Feel your willingness to receive this gift of grace, and breathe open a space within yourself that can be filled with the energy of Ilahinoor.

From the sacred space in your heart of hearts, call to the One Divine Presence out of which everything in creation emanates: I open myself now to experience the grace of Ilahinoor. I am ready to receive it now!

*Chanting the sacred word Ilahinoor three times aloud is a powerful way to open the channels for the grace of Ilahinoor to pour in. The word ilahinoor is composed of two root syllables: **ilah**, which refers to the Divine, and **noor**, which means light. To pronounce ilahinoor, divide it into four syllables as follows:*

IH or EE

LAH'

HEE

NOOR

This is an extremely sacred word in the Islamic tradition. Feel the grandeur of the word and its meaning as you chant it aloud. Know that giving voice to the word literally calls in the Light of the Divine, and raises the divine light that already lives within each of us.

After you have chanted or spoken the word Ilahinoor aloud three times, feel yourself opening like a flower to receive the transmission. You may feel it pouring down from above, or coming alive within you, or both.

Another powerful way to access the presence of Ilahinoor, is to repeat a series of phrases that convey the dimension of being that Ilahinoor unfolds within our soul. Speaking them aloud can be very effective to call in the frequencies of Ilahinoor. In some situations, it may be more comfortable or appropriate to silently repeat the three sentences to yourself.

God is Life

Life is All That Is

I AM That

To be fully realized and embodied in this state of consciousness is to have a relaxed, open belly soul center and to experience complete, conscious union with God as all of Life.

After calling in Ilahinoor, welcome the energy of Ilahinoor into your being. First, invite Ilahinoor into the crown chakra on the top of the head. Feel the energy pouring down into the center of the head, the head soul center or Cave of Brahman. Allow whatever time is necessary for the energy to fully anchor there. An intelligence within the energy will tell you when it is complete.

Next, call the energy of Ilahinoor into the soul center just above the heart. Allow the energy to fill this space until it, too, feels full and complete. Finally, welcome Ilahinoor into the belly soul center and invite it to take root there.

Each experience of Ilahinoor has its own quality. At times, the transmission may want to go only into the head center, while at others it easily flows into the heart soul center and down into the belly. Feel the transmission going wherever it is most needed and doing whatever is necessary so that the frequencies of Ilahinoor can fully live within you. Allow plenty of time for this, until it feels complete.

Then invite Ilahinoor to flow into your arms and settle into your hands, so you can transmit Ilahinoor to others. Let this take as long as it likes.

When the sitting portion of the transmission seems to be complete, and you feel the frequencies of Ilahinoor are alive within you, lie down and allow the transmission to continue to deepen and integrate on all levels of your being. Allow plenty of time for this.
After that feels complete, and you feel yourself returning to waking consciousness, ask to be shown anything else that will help Ilahinoor to deepen in you. A glass of water, a walk in nature, or connecting with a beloved pet are some ways this transmission may want to be assisted into a richer, fuller level of integration.

Be gentle with yourself after the transmission has landed within you. Resist the temptation to get busy, and allow the grace of Ilahinoor to continue to settle in over time.

You may want to repeat the above inner experience at regular intervals to invite the frequencies of Ilahinoor to be most fully experienced and grounded. Some readers will find the above induction brings them into a living experience of Ilahinoor. Others may want a more direct, potent immersion in the energy~consciousness of the transmission. In either case, we suggest joining one of our teleconferences. The powerful group energy field that is created by our combined energies acts as a tuning fork, helping all involved to have a stronger experience of the transmission. During the calls, there is time to ask questions, hear from others who have worked with Ilahinoor, and most of all, bask in a potent induction of the frequencies.

NOTE: Before sharing Ilahinoor with others, we recommend a thorough reading of Chapter 13, "Utilizing the Transmissions of Grace." There you will find basic guidelines that support an optimal experience for everyone. This chapter also contains instructions and suggestions on how to share Ilahinoor, including specific hand placements and their sequence.

11

Love~Oneness

*Those who don't feel this Love
pulling them like a river,
those who don't drink dawn
like a cup of spring water
or take in sunset like supper,
those who don't want to change,
Let them sleep.*

Rumi

Receiving Ilahinoor from Kiara had begun a whole new chapter in our lives. As we shared Ilahinoor with each other, our pets, and many other people, the great blessings of this transmission came forth. Witnessing rooms full of people easily and naturally sharing Ilahinoor with one another after receiving the energy demonstrated that it was no longer necessary to go to spiritual teachers or gurus to receive highly transformative spiritual transmissions. These frequencies are continuously pouring into the planetary energy field, blessing anyone available to receive them. And these places in consciousness lie within us, awaiting their activation at the appropriate moment in our soul-evolution.

The advent of Ilahinoor hinted that the morphogenetic field, the consciousness "soup" that surrounds us all, might well have other possibilities floating within it. Thrilled with the effortless way Ilahinoor was spreading, and feeling wide open to any other blessings of grace that wanted to pour in, we wondered what they would turn out to be.

One afternoon we were sitting in our living room when we sensed that something new was trying to come through. As an energy began to descend, we noticed it felt somewhat similar to the evolving flavor of deeksha we had begun to transmit that carried the Universal Christ vibration.

We found ourselves taking turns placing our hands on each other's heads to direct the flow of energy. A bliss that reminded us of the deeksha was accompanied by a very strong expansion and deepening in the heart area. As the warmth intensified, the flow of divine love increased, spilling over into our energy fields. At times we needed to consciously release and surrender into the heart expansion as it melted through our limits to experiencing love.

We inwardly asked, *What is the nature of this energy? What do we need to know about it?* The answer that immediately arose in Barry's mind was:

God is Love.

Love is All That Is.

I AM THAT.

We sensed the core of the brain being rearranged, and particularly the limbic system, the center for psychic "feeling" perception or clairsentience. In most humans, this brain center begins to shut down in early childhood as we unconsciously suppress the flow of feelings, especially those from the nonphysical, spiritual levels. We quickly learn which kinds of emotional expression are acceptable to our caregivers and which are not. In the process, our perception of fear, sadness, pain and other discordant feelings dims, along with our full appreciation of states of love, joy and happiness. Now, we felt the inpouring energy unlocking the shutdown, allowing the vibrational frequencies of love to be more fully felt. The love was not confined to one particular expression; it felt universal and omnipresent, the fabric of all that exists.

It seemed that yet another "flavor of God" wanted to be experienced and shared. When we considered what to call this new transmission, the name **Love~Oneness** arose. While Ilahinoor most often traveled into the belly soul center, this new energetic infusion powerfully stimulated the opening of the heart soul center. In Sufism this center is called the Heart Latif; in Taoism, the heart tan tien. The Vedas of ancient India refer to it as the Cave of the Heart. Other esoteric traditions term this soul center the Heart of Hearts, the High Heart, and the Heart of the Soul.

No matter what it is called, when the heart soul center opens, we experience God as Love. We have all heard those words, but an immersion in their living reality delivers a powerful, unforgettable spiritual opening. As we go deeper, we realize that not only is God love; *everything* arises in the fabric of love, whose warp and weft weave through all of Creation. As this awareness takes root and blossoms, we realize the core nature of the Self is one with God and love. Now, this is no longer an abstract spiritual concept; it becomes a living reality as we are absorbed in the experience of Love~Oneness as All That Is.

As we had with Ilahinoor, we began to share Love~Oneness, wondering what others would experience. Our first opportunity came with a group of people who had experienced Ilahinoor some months before and had continued to regularly share that transmission with one another. We called in the energy of Love~Oneness and joined with the group in reciting aloud, "God is Love. Love is All That Is. I AM THAT." Then we walked around the circle, placing our hands first on each person's head and then over the heart soul center. To complete the transmission, our hands traced a path from the heart over the shoulders and down the arms, inviting the energy to stream into the hands so it could be shared with others.

A potent field of love infused the room. It wasn't only an ethereal, transpersonal love, although it did contain that component. This love felt as deep as it was vast, and seemed to just as powerfully embrace the human level as the rarefied, nonphysical component of our existence. It was simply Love, with a capital L.

All around the room, hearts melted open. Tears fell for some, while others were transported to an interior place they had yearned to visit for a very long time. Love~Oneness was having precisely the same kinds of effects among the group members that we had experienced.

After everyone lay down for half an hour to allow deeper integration and then took a short break, we reconvened. It was now their turn to share the transmission with one another. The group members paired off and entered a sacred space of stillness. Relieved of the role of dispensers of grace, we watched as all present called in the frequencies of Love~Oneness. In awe and gratitude we witnessed the blessing-grace that flowed through those who were the "givers" standing before their partners waiting to "receive." Each seemed perfectly capable of being a conduit for the same level of grace that had come through us moments before. As with Ilahinoor, no special initiations or preparations were needed.

What a deeply fulfilling moment! For nearly two decades, the purpose of our work had been to awaken the realization that we are all divine beings, aspects of God/One/All That Is. Now, as the group shared Love~Oneness with each other, the radiant glow that filled the room attested to each soul's direct connection with the Source of the transmission.

When divine energies flow through us, they leave no doubt that we are one with God. As we reverently place our hands on another and witness that being lighting up with sacredness, the reality that we are conduits for divine frequencies to pour through becomes self-evident. In that moment, the deeply embedded beliefs and stories of limitation, separation, sin and unworthiness held in the collective unconscious of humanity are proven false, as the truth is revealed through direct demonstration.

What could better serve to close the illusory gap between ourselves and God? Could anything more effectively take us beyond the search for "special" intermediaries than finding out we all possess the capacity to serve as vessels for the Divine? As more and more of us make this discovery, we birth not only our own Luminous Selves, but a new, Golden Age in which all beings will know their true, divine identity.

When we began to offer Love~Oneness through teleconferences, participants' feedback expanded and confirmed what we were learning about the nature of this transmission. One woman shared her excitement in an e-mail:

> *A lot happened to me during the transmission of Love-Oneness. Activation! Emotional connection! Visual of a warm golden light in the sacred heart area. Mother Mary's presence! Visual of a golden thread connecting all that were on the conference call...the thread pulled us in together tightly. At the end when you said you were sending Love, i felt my heart really accept that.*
>
> *It appears to me that this area has been closed off for a long time and needs a lot of opening! I have not experienced feeling energy in this area before; i think a lot of us have shut down that area of feeling and experiencing. There's a real awakening happening here!*

Another woman who was a deeksha-giver reported:

> *Absolutely wonderful! I felt so at home with this transmission. It was so full of God, so full of Christ-Love! So heart-centered. I was intoxicated with Love and Oneness all day. My deeksha meeting that night was like a Golden supernova of Love from the heart. The next day, I was totally hung over, could hardly wake up and get out of bed, like the early days of receiving deeksha before my body had adjusted to it.*

Today I am clear and integrated. Thank you! This is profound.

The Nature of Love~Oneness

It is impossible to separate the sense of oneness from the experience of love, for they are one and the same. If, as has often been stated, love is the "glue" that unifies all of Creation, then love cannot be experienced apart from the oneness of All That Is. We use the term Love~Oneness to express the indivisible unity of the two.

Everything is healed and made whole when it is bathed in love. Fragmented, denied aspects of the psyche weave back into wholeness and are reincorporated into the soul when they are embraced within the heart of Oneness. Parts of our experience we have held outside the embrace of love are welcomed back to live within our totality. All are invited to sit at the table of infinite love, where no one is a stranger and nothing is excluded from the banquet of Life.

As the heart soul center opens, we transcend limited ideas and concepts about love through directly feeling and coming to know the oneness that is the essence of love. This all-encompassing love widens its embrace ever more until it includes ourselves, others, all of life and the divine Source of it all in the epiphany that nothing, not one iota of Creation, exists outside of love. All that arises within us, no matter how painful or disturbing, likewise floats in a sea of love. Even the most difficult, painful circumstances are seen to be but temporary conditions in which love has been forgotten or denied. Fear and separation and all the desperate acts they engender are revealed as based in illusion, the result of temporary amnesia to the all-encompassing love that is the true nature of everything. When we see and know this, all can be accepted and forgiven.

Once we have directly experienced the reality of love that underlies all surface appearances, our ego defenses rapidly begin to melt. Relationships heal as we feel the love~oneness that unifies us with everyone and everything. This occurs in a deeper, more embodied domain than the non-dual realization in which the mind perceives the truth of oneness. During a heart-centered opening, realization takes place within the realm of feeling, expanding the capacity for warmth, intimacy, and communion with all of life.

The direct, living experience that love is the fabric of all of Creation and the perception of the inherent unity of all things may occur all at once or gradually unfold over time. In any event, fully integrating and embodying this state of consciousness involves a complete psycho-spiritual and physical conversion. All in need of healing in the mental, emotional and physical bodies will be brought to the surface at the appropriate time to be transformed into its original state of love and oneness.

Many mystics and saints have been blessed with a profound experience of unity that forever changed their lives. In that moment, they realized there was nothing they would rather do than consecrate their existence to serving God through loving all within Creation. From that day forward, they were carried into an ever-deeper absorption into that field of universal love. Whether or not we are blessed with such a sudden epiphany, most of us will live into this realization over many years, if not decades. The accompanying task of facing and transcending all that prevents us from living each moment in the awareness that All is Love may become the consecration of a lifetime.

From the moment poets and troubadours began to describe the human experience in all its dimensions, the ineffable essence of love has pulsed, glowed, and often ached in their songs and lyrics. Throughout the centuries, one of the most beloved of these has been Rumi, the 13th century mystic poet of Turkey. For an immersion into the mystery of love in all its guises and states, read this man's odes to his Beloved, the Divine, and to the human he found most lovable, his dear Shams.

We began this chapter with an evocative excerpt from one of Rumi's poems. Here is another taste of Rumi's great gift, acknowledging that beneath all our earthly preoccupations, we are all lovers:

Oh lovers, lovers, it is time
To set out from the world...
Beneath this water-wheel of stars
Your sleep has been heavy.
Observe that heaviness and beware
For life is fragile and quick.
Heart, aim yourself at Love!
Friend, discover the Friend!
Watchman, Wake up! You weren't put here to sleep!

Rumi

Experiences of Love~Oneness

Virtually everyone finds that the Love~Oneness transmission activates the heart and soul. Many report seeing everyone and everything through the eyes of love, and becoming aware of the perfection of others exactly as they are. Aspects of self and others that have previously been hard to accept are now viewed compassionately, free of the mind's judgments.

The Love~Oneness transmission appears to dissolve, at the perfect pace and in the perfect way, the barriers or illusions to the experience of love~oneness as our true nature. As the heart soul center opens, it becomes increasingly clear that the fabric that unites everything is love, which forms the substratum of all Creation. It cannot be otherwise, for love is apprehended as God's most essential nature. Impediments to surrendering to the Divine melt with this realization, as does the ability to separate from and judge oneself and others. When everything, however distorted it may appear, is experienced as being held and based in love, the capacity to embrace all circumstances, conditions and people with an all-encompassing, all-transforming love becomes second nature. Here is how one recipient expressed this:

> *Love~Oneness (first experienced a week ago) continues to work its magic. Initially I felt it as a contraction, but after two days it started to feel as if I was on an intravenous drip of love! Not a new feeling at all, but way more constant than it has been before.*
>
> *I was called to the transmission because I felt I needed all the help I could get in a difficult situation with my elderly parents, and Wow! it's really worked. What I was experiencing as potentially upsetting, tedious, restricting, frustrating, etc. has now been reframed as an opportunity; a powerful initiation of the heart. It's all still the same on one level, but it's held within this all-embracing field of love, and it feels like my parents and I are magnifying mirrors for each other's love.*

Recipients of Love~Oneness often report experiencing a quieting or stopping of the mind along with a progressively deepening and expanding heart-opening. As awareness comes to rest in the heart, the mind finally ceases its chatter. We simply know what we need to know, moment to moment, as the heart soul center assumes its intended role as our guide through life. When awareness rests in the soul's peace, the mind naturally follows.

As we realize that all that once seemed to prevent joy and happiness is simply not based in reality, the peace deepens. We come to know that serenity, bliss, ecstasy, love, and all other divine qualities are aspects of our true nature, not states that need to be sought or acquired externally.

The heart soul center unites our embodied humanness with the levels of ourselves that reside in the nonphysical realms. Since the Love~Oneness transmission primarily focuses in the heart soul center, it effectively bridges and unifies absolute, transcendental states of consciousness with the imminent, human levels of experience. During the transmission itself, the frequencies of Love~Oneness may both ascend and descend, traveling where they are needed to heal the upper-lower split and fragmentation experienced by many on the spiritual path. The Love-Oneness transmission also penetrates the illusions of the mind and undoes blockages that have prevented the free flow of love. Therefore, this transmission may be especially effective for those whose hearts have been shut down, who feel alienated from others or life itself, or who seem to be caught in the suffering of the mind.

During or after the Love~Oneness transmission, some people experience a temporary intensification of the knot in the heart that is nearly ubiquitous in the human condition. This may be felt as physical pain, tightness, aching, or other sensations. Emotion, particularly unfelt sadness and grief, may also arise. This may at first be hidden beneath surface layers of "hard-heartedness" and feelings such as anger, resentment, and irritation. When feelings arise during or after receiving a transmission, we suggest breathing into the sensation that first presents itself, fully feeling it on the inbreath, and then just as fully releasing it, turning it over to the Divine on the outbreath. When this layer of sensation is fully felt, it will give way to another, beneath it. Staying present to each sensation through many breaths may be necessary to help the contraction to release. In this way, it is possible to be present to whatever has clouded the ability to greet life with love.

The following account illustrates the way Love~Oneness can bring feelings that have been stored in the heart to the surface, so they can be felt and embraced:

I have the last years felt a deep attraction (maybe the wrong word, but can't come up with any other right now) towards Christ, so this could be what my heart has been longing for. I felt very good for 3 days after the transmission of Love~Oneness. Yesterday evening I started to feel very tired, and today I have been feeling very heavy and sad. A feeling of meaninglessness entering my being. Could not stay at work, went home after an hour, felt like I will not get anything done today, and I don't want to stay there doing nothing. It is easier to just be in the experience of what is happening at home.

When such challenging feeling-states arise, it is important to remember that they are not permanent, but are merely showing us what has been stored within, waiting for this moment to reveal themselves. When we have no resistance to what is present, we can be with any and all feelings, no matter how intense they may temporarily become. If we can simply allow the feelings to be what they are and feel whatever is there, they will pass through and something else will then be present.

Life never stands still. Its unending flow only stops when we say "No" to What Is, preferring that it be different. Then, the feelings and conditions we have rejected persist until we can love them, just as they are. Once they have been embraced, they have no reason to continue in their previous forms, and something new can happen. The irony is that once we are able to love what is within us or in front of us, we no longer need it to change. It is fine as is!

The Love~Oneness transmission offers a potent assist in this process of opening to love All. Working with it over time enables us to welcome in layer after layer of what has been stored within, just waiting to be loved and accepted as it is. The frequencies of Love~Oneness also help us to embrace what we see all around us, to accept that each of us is where we are in the never-ending flow of human evolution.

Many people find that the Love~Oneness transmission deepens their connection with the energy and consciousness of the Christ, and the living reality that the Christ lives within them as their essential Self. This can be a profound experience of coming Home. Seeing the world through the all-loving eyes of the Christ, we easily and naturally forgive what had previously seemed worthy of judgment and condemnation.

Especially when the term "Christ" or the historical Jesus have had little resonance in the past, directly experiencing the frequencies of Christ consciousness can be a life-altering event. The Love~Oneness transmission may lead to experiencing the presence of God as omni-universal love, identical to one's own core nature. For millennia, saints and God-intoxicated beings in all traditions, Eastern and Western, have expressed this universal revelation.

A recipient of Love~Oneness described sharing her experience of the Christ level of being with a friend:

> *I just had a wonderful experience with giving Oneness-Love to a friend who was not feeling well. I called her and said I would sit for a while and send her a healing prayer from the Christ Light or Christ Consciousness. I invoked the light of Christ and saw this in her as well. She e-mailed me and said it was very powerful.*

Sometimes it takes more than one experience of a transmission before we feel we have received its full impact. When we sense there is more we have not yet experienced, we can meet ourselves with love and acceptance. What a great opportunity to choose between loving ourselves and judging ourselves! Why not trust that all along the way, we are experiencing each transmission exactly as we are meant to?

Here is how someone who didn't feel she "got" the Love~Oneness transmission the first time expressed this:

> *The Love~Oneness experience was so profound for me, i feel enveloped in love still for my self and all. i finally feel able to connect this to others more confidently. i felt like i didn't "get it" in some way the first time.*

As with cultivating the ability to meditate, several immersions in the frequencies of a transmission may be needed to experience its full energetic effects. Are we all expert cooks the first time we make a meal? No one would presume that, yet in the spiritual arena we often expect superhuman things of ourselves. Sometimes the issues that arise *around* the transmissions offer just as much evolutionary stimulation as the transmissions themselves. When self-judgments and perfectionism arise, we can meet them with compassion. In the process, our impossibly high expectations will release into greater self-acceptance and inner peace.

Some of us are able to perceive the inner energetic changes the transmissions engender in others. After a telephone transmission of Love~Oneness to a man in Asia, Barry described his perceptions of what had taken place in the recipient:

> *The transmissions operate at the most causal levels of being, bringing about changes within the very core of the soul itself. Tonight during the transmission*

to S, I inwardly saw the Love~Oneness energy go right into his soul center. I saw a very rough, sharp-edged rock within his soul center, which represented his separate ego sense. The energy went right around this seeming obstacle into the very center of his soul, revealing a small, clear white light within the Lotus of the Soul. Then that light began to expand out, irradiating and illuminating that knot. Then the knot began to dissolve.

Once the transmissions are in there, the person's entire lifestream changes, backwards and forwards in time. This means that, as the energy ripples back and forth in time, the basis of past experiences is transformed and the future possibilities also shift.

The healing, transforming power of love is one of the most meaningful gifts the Love~Oneness transmission imparts. As we share this transmission with others, we need not limit ourselves to those of our own species, as the following account illustrates:

This evening I was able to give Love~Oneness to a little hummingbird to coax it back to "life" after my cat caught it. It wasn't noticeably injured, but seemed to remain a bit "lifeless" for a good 5 minutes, not wanting to fly when I tried to coax it. So, I sat quietly with it for another 10 minutes, stroking its tiny head, and feeling its tiny heartbeat strengthen. I just asked for Love-Oneness to give it some energy. Before the daylight was gone, I took it out to a large bush over my back fence, and as I opened my hand, it flew off perfectly!

Like all Transmissions of Grace, the Love~Oneness transmission can be shared with beings of all species, as well as buildings, yards, highways and other public spaces, and landscape features. There is no limit to the ways and places the transmissions can be shared! As we step into this infinitely vast realm of interconnection, we discover that our creativity is activated along with the energetic nature of each transmission.

During a teleconference, Skandar, whose experiences with Ilahinoor were featured in the previous chapter, described the effects of Love~Oneness on the atmosphere at a hot springs he often visited. When he arrived, the energy was discordant. Children shouted and ran around, while the adults talked loudly. As Skandar invited Love~Oneness to infuse the water through him, shifts began to happen:

> *I opened myself to be a conduit for the intelligence [of the Love~Oneness transmission]. It was remarkable to watch the hyperactive kids calm down. Everyone went into a quiet space. Before we all left, we thanked each other for a beautiful time together. That's the first time that has ever happened!*

During another call, Skandar related another application of Love~Oneness. At the wildlife rehab center where he volunteers, a male red-tailed hawk was too badly injured to heal. Skandar continued:

> *We asked what we could do on his way out. His one request was to be bathed in Love~Oneness before he was euthanized. The director, who was holding him, got a good dose. She lit up!*
> *From the hawk came the message, "Okay, I'm ready to go now." The divineness of it was over and under and through us; he was letting go of one life to start another. It was very heart-opening for me.*

As Skandar's example illustrates, Love~Oneness can not only be shared with individuals or specific places; we can also invite it to infuse entire situations. For instance, if someone we know is about to make the Great Transition at the end of this life, we can ask Love~Oneness to surround that person's passing, easing the way and helping the person to accept and embrace all aspects of the journey. We often send Love~Oneness into areas of the globe where people are rising up to claim their freedom and sovereignty, asking that all unfold in the spirit of love and unity. Holding specific regions of the world in Love~Oneness allows us to have an impact on situations we may never encounter on the outer, physical level. And surrounding the entire globe with Love~Oneness offers an evolutionary assist to people everywhere.

A Cautionary Note

Because in most people the Love~Oneness transmission goes straight into the spiritual heart area, it can deliver a powerful burst of energy to the etheric heart as well. Since the etheric body is the nonphysical blueprint of the physical body, any input it receives can directly affect the physical level. If you or your recipient have a history of heart issues, we suggest that you both check inside to determine if it is appropriate to invoke Love~Oneness, and how to go about that. You may receive specific guidance on how best to invite the transmission to enter the energy field so it works harmoniously with the body's particular needs. It may be wise to call in the energy without placing your hands on, or otherwise focusing on, the physical heart area. You can also ask that the energy influx be governed by the soul and higher self of everyone involved, so that it is beneficial in light of the particular situation. In every case we've encountered, if the heart responds with symptoms after a Love~Oneness transmission, they signal a healing process in which blockages and dysfunction are being purged.

In our experience, the Love~Oneness transmission offers healing to the heart area and the physical heart, as the following description indicates:

> I'm 54 with a history of tachycardia and irregular (heart) beating. During the [Love~Oneness] empowerment my heartbeat slowed, steadied, became deeper and more powerful. It has remained this way with no more irregularity. I also feel much better physically.

As with all the Transmissions of Grace, and, for that matter, any other type of spiritual activation, it is always wise to consult the intelligence of the soul and oversoul to be sure it is in the highest for all involved to share the energy. However beneficial a transmission may sound, if it is not in right timing within one's overall evolutionary journey, its greatest gifts will not be experienced. We have learned to wait for an unqualified "Yes" before proceeding with any spiritual activation. If that "Yes" is not present, there is undoubtedly a very good reason. And if it **is** present, it assuages the human doubts and concerns that often arise when considering a new spiritual direction.

EXPERIENCE~ACTIVATION: Love~Oneness

> Find a quiet, comfortable place in which you can sit at first and later lie down. As you sit quietly, become aware of your breathing. Feel the breath coming into the body and then going back out. As your awareness sinks into the breath, feel yourself traveling into the inner world.

Invite the breath into the chest and the heart soul center deep within it. Breathe open a space into which you can invite Love~Oneness when it is time for that to occur.

Contemplate all that you have read about Love~Oneness. What deeply spoke to you about this transmission? What does it offer that would be food for your soul? Allow a few minutes to consider this.

Now, feel how much you would like to directly experience the blessing of Love~Oneness. How would this change your experience of life? What would it be like to see everything through the eyes of love and oneness, instead of fear and separation? Allow some time to imagine what your life would be like.

Now, read aloud the three sentences that summarize the essence of Love~Oneness:

God is Love

Love is All That Is

I AM THAT

Repeat them if you like. Feel their truth reverberate within you.

Then, from the sacred space in your heart of hearts, call to the One Divine Presence, the Source of all gifts and blessings: I open myself to experience the grace of Love~Oneness. I am ready to receive it now!

Feel yourself opening like a flower to receive the transmission. You may feel it pouring down from above, or coming alive within you, or both. Welcome Love~Oneness into the crown chakra at the top of the head. Allow it to fill this center. When this feels complete, call Love~Oneness into the heart soul center. Again, allow the transmission to fill this area until the knowing arises that it is complete.

From there, feel the transmission going wherever it is most needed. Notice any body sensations and feelings that may arise. Feel each one and turn it over to the Divine. Allow plenty of time for this, until it feels complete.

Then invite Love~Oneness to flow into your arms and settle into your hands, so you can share this transmission with others. Feel the frequencies of Love~Oneness coming alive in your hands. Let this take as long as it likes.

When the sitting portion of the transmission seems to be complete, and you feel the energy and consciousness of Love~Oneness living within you, lie down and allow the transmission to continue to deepen and integrate on all levels of your being. Allow plenty of time for this part of the process.

After this feels complete, and waking awareness is returning, ask to be shown anything else that will help Love~Oneness to become well-established within you. Let the energy and consciousness of Love~Oneness be your guide, and trust your inner promptings. Does a glass of water sound good? A walk outside? Listening to a piece of music that resonates your heart energies?

Be gentle with yourself after the transmission has landed within you. Resist the temptation to get busy, and allow the transmission to continue to settle in over time.

Working with this activation over time will progressively deepen your embodiment of the frequencies of Love~Oneness. For some readers, the above induction will lead to a living experience of Love~Oneness. Others may want a more direct, potent immersion in the energy~consciousness of the transmission. In either case, we suggest joining one of our teleconferences. The powerful group energy field that is created by our combined energies acts as a tuning fork, helping all involved to have a stronger experience of the transmission. During the calls, there is time to ask questions, hear from others who have worked with Love~Oneness, and most of all, bask in a potent induction of the frequencies.

NOTE: Before sharing Love~Oneness with others, we recommend a thorough reading of Chapter 13, "Utilizing the Transmissions of Grace," which includes basic guidelines that will further an optimal experience for everyone. The same chapter also contains instructions and suggestions on how to share Love~Oneness, including specific hand placements we have found effective.

We close this chapter with one more poem that expresses the essence of this gift of grace:

Both light and shadow
are the dance of Love.
Love has no cause;
it is the astrolabe of God's secrets.
Lover and Loving are inseparable
and timeless.

Although I may try to describe Love
when I experience it I am speechless.
Although I may try to write about Love
I am rendered helpless;
my pen breaks and the paper slips away
at the ineffable place
where Lover, Loving and Loved are one.

Every moment is made glorious
by the light of Love.

12

Spotless Mind

An Unexpected Gift of Grace

Few among us have not experienced the pain of being whipped around by the tormenting voices and images of the mind. Is there anything we want more at those moments than to be free of suffering? It was just such a moment that brought forth the gift of grace we call the Spotless Mind transmission.

We had just finished a weekend group in Oregon and were on our way to the coast for some rest and relaxation. Although it was a bright, sunny winter day, our inner worlds were a bit stormy. An old relationship pattern had been triggered, and its remnants were still present, threatening to create a full-fledged hurricane if we let it. We drove in shrouded silence as we both inwardly addressed the feelings and thoughts that were threatening to ruin the first day of our vacation.

We made it through dinner in much better spirits and enjoyed the evening. As morning broke, we lay in bed together reflecting on the previous day's challenges. We both admitted our frustration with the occasional eruptions of mind that still occurred. Even after all the years devoted to clearing the suffering of childhood patterns, at times "stuff" still surfaced. The deeksha had done quite a bit to detach our awareness from the content, but whirlpools of thought and feeling still arose at times. *Wouldn't it be wonderful,* we thought, *if that never happened again?*

Experience had powerfully demonstrated that it was possible for the mind to be completely clear. We felt a deep desire to live free of the mental patterns that remained, or at least to never again become entangled with them. This yearning for freedom lit the fire in our hearts to ask Source to completely cleanse our minds of any remaining attachment and identification with their contents.

We found ourselves doing what we always do when we come to one of these places of feeling hopeless and wanting a change. We went inside, felt the sincere desire in our hearts to have our minds completely cleared, and sent a strong request to God for this to occur NOW.

Within a moment of launching our "i-mail," or "inner net" message to the Divine, a cascade of clear, light energy began to pour into each of our head soul centers, the area within the core of the brain that has been called the Cave of Brahman. Everything in our inner and outer worlds dissolved. Quite some time passed as the energy shower continued.

When it was again possible to speak, we both observed that a major shift had occurred. Our minds felt as completely clear and sparkling as diamond or crystal. No thoughts obscured pure awareness. Our brains felt as though they had been instantly transported from a smoggy city to a high, clear mountaintop.

We regained outer awareness with just enough time to shower, dress and leave the motel by check-out time. Heading south along the coast, we noticed that wide-open, pure awareness had become our state of being. Not a thought was arising; we were simply, wonderfully, present.

A few hours later, we were still witnessing the passing scenery, the noises of the car and wind, and the emptiness of mind. The lovely spaciousness between our ears filled us with joy. No more messy minds, messing up our experience of life!

It suddenly became clear that we had received another gift of grace, a new transmission. Barry blurted out, "This is the Eternal Sunshine of the Spotless Mind!" The movie title perfectly described our new experience of life. We laughed out loud with the joy of it.

The unclouded luminosity we were experiencing was clearly the true nature of mind. Darkness and veiling, we soon came to understand, only occur when awareness attaches to or rejects certain contents of the mind. When attachment or resistance is present, mental constructs automatically stick, rather than move through, obscuring the light of pure consciousness. When the veils fall away, the utter simplicity of the way things are shines forth, clearly revealed.

During the next few days, the empty, clear mind state continued. It didn't so much recede as normalize. Thoughts again arose, but they rarely obscured the clear lens of the mind. In the months that followed, old, unfinished business occasionally revealed itself, but we knew it was simply making an appearance on its way out, as the past patterns or samskaras of the mind emptied.

Barry: Spotless Mind, Part Two

The three days after Spotless Mind descended on us were revelatory indeed. Although the deeksha had catalyzed profound transformation, I had never experienced such a state of clarity and emptiness of mind. When content did arise, it stood out in stark relief against the lucidity of the mental field. Certain subtle processes of mind that I had never noticed now became apparent.

Yet despite the obvious benefits of Spotless Mind, we didn't feel we were to share it with others right away. Something felt incomplete; the cake wasn't quite ready to be taken out of the oven. I didn't know what it was until nearly a year later. While looking around in a store full of wonderful Tibetan goods, my eye was drawn to a card depicting a black buddha and his white consort. The inscription on the back revealed that the figures were called Samantabhadra and Samantabhadri, who together form the Adi Buddha, the primordial buddha from which all other buddhas originate. The nature of the Adi Buddha is pure omniscience, pure knowing.

The card had so much energy that I, who rarely shop, found myself buying it. A few weeks later, I began to meditate with the card, calling to the Adi Buddha to make its presence known. Over a period of two days, I became enveloped within and merged into the Adi Buddha during my meditations. Clear fields of mind opened, bringing clarity across many dimensions, vast and deep.

Then, out of Adi Buddha came Maitreya Buddha, the next buddha who will be coming to Earth to birth a new age. A rapid succession of insights followed, revealing that the Adi Buddha and Maitreya Buddha had come to overlight the Spotless Mind transmission. This was the piece we had been waiting for.

It all made sense. Adi Buddha is the buddha, or enlightened one, most directly related to absolute Source, the limitless fountain from which the Love~Oneness and Ilahinoor transmissions had also poured forth. As the Buddhist avatar of the incoming age, Maitreya Buddha is akin to the Christ, the Christian avatar of the new age who, I had come to understand, overlights the Love~Oneness transmission.

A few weeks later on a quiet Sunday afternoon, we felt ready to connect with the Spotless Mind energies again. I placed pictures of Maitreya Buddha and Adi Buddha on a nearby table and we opened our awareness. There was no need to place our hands on each other's heads. The infusion was so rapid and strong we were transfixed in our chairs. The energy built and continued for almost an hour.

Any attempt to describe what happened must come up short, as the experience was more about the absence of content than anything that can be defined. Veils of mind were very rapidly lifted. The most fascinating and ecstatic moments occurred as the shrouds that had obscured the nature of mind itself dissolved. It became absolutely clear that everything is mind -- all that we experience, inner and outer, is simply formations of mind-stuff.

There was no sense of an objective "me" anywhere to be found, only consciousness and mind. Awareness was suffused with a sense of absolute freedom, the "unborn" as Buddhists call it -- that which is never blemished or even touched. From this perspective it became clear that there is nothing objective, everything being purely subjective; there is only experiencing, without the definitions of mind called experience, experiencer and that which is experienced.

Karen: Spotless -- Literally!

During the first transmission of Spotless Mind, my mind felt like stainless steel, completely clear and pristine. Through the months that followed that first spontaneous experience, we often thought back to the moment when, tired of all the mental folderol, we had asked Life to cleanse our minds of every bit of it. As the words of Jesus Christ remind us, when we ask, we receive. We wanted nothing more than to see the world and each other without any filters at all, and presto! It happened.

Now, months later, we were ready for a second immersion in the frequencies of Spotless Mind. Before Barry began to ask for the energy to pour in, strong sensations began in my head. It felt and looked as though a weather front, a "storm system" of brilliant, powerful light, was moving through my brain from front to back. As the "weather pattern" of light moved through, it dipped way down into the brain, clearing it out vertically as the "front" continued on its path. The "storm system" of light seemed to be dredging out everything that was not needed in the brain/mind. It felt very potent, extremely thorough, and not at all unpleasant. No content of any kind accompanied the process.

As the beneficent "weather front" of light reached the back of the head, curiosity arose about whether it would continue down the back part of the brain. As if in response, the "front" seemed to slow down and then stop at the top back portion of the head. An energy moved through the back of the brain, but felt muted, far less strong and light-imbued than on the top of the head. This area of the brain seemed to contain a lot more density, and I sensed it would require another session at a later date.

While this muted process was going on in the back brain, I was given a humorous demonstration of the effects of the Spotless Mind transmission. Inwardly, I saw a dog that resembled a Dalmatian, but its spots were of many colors. Then a downpour of rain began, and I watched with fascination as all of its spots washed off. As the multicolored hues ran down the pavement with the rain, I smiled with delight as I inwardly watched the spotty dog turn pure white. The smile turned to laughter with the realization that the dog was now literally spotless. The Divine has such a sense of humor!

This experience of Spotless Mind felt as powerful as the blockbuster deekshas that profoundly altered my consciousness during the 21-day process in India in 2005. I would rank it second only to the original deeksha we received in 2004, when Bhagavan himself directly empowered the dasas before they gave us all deeksha.

I felt completely happy and blessed at the thought of sharing such a potent, yet gentle, transmission with others. Now that the final pieces had fallen into place, I felt sure that time would come soon.

The Nature of Spotless Mind

What would your life be like if your mind were not attached to and identified with limiting beliefs, judgments and illusory images about yourself and life? Take a moment to imagine your everyday existence, free of the mind's interpretations of reality. Let the images and impressions float in on their own. How does it feel?

Here's a clue: When all of that is gone, happiness, joy, and peace are what remain, for these are our inherent nature.

Rigorous, prolonged examination of mind is one path to freedom; another is opening to grace. Through grace, the veils of mind are dissolved, revealing what is always there beneath the limited sense of who and what we are: the inner truth and radiance of the divine Self. Eternal Sunshine of the Spotless Mind, or Spotless Mind for short, is a Transmission of Grace that dissolves the veils of mind to reveal our absolute nature.

It has been said that all suffering arises in the mind. Sages of all eras, seeking to go beyond suffering, have examined the mind and found it cluttered with illusion. Through an ongoing search for the truth, these illusions dissolve. What remains is the spotless mind, clear of the lenses and filters that obscure the direct apprehension of truth. Here is how one woman experienced this:

It seemed like the stainless (stain less, without stain) steel mind was so bright and shiny that it was a gleaming, pure, silvery white. The next day, when thoughts did arise, there was no place for them to stick on the stainless steel mind, so they just slid away. Fascinating to be aware that similar thoughts used to turn round and round, tenaciously embedded and unable to release. Truly amazing to experience.

The central illusion holding all other illusions in place is the perception of the separate "i" sense -- believing we exist independent of all other forms of life, and identifying with the body-being who has a finite, impermanent existence. Awakening from this false identification is the doorway to freedom, the escape from the hypnosis of being "of" the world of pain, suffering and death. Seeing reality as it is, all awakened beings have confessed that there is no separate self who suffers the conditions of the world such as disease and death. All is merely a play, or maya, a dance of mind.

That all sounds wonderful, but it can feel like a fabled, faraway oasis that may or may not even exist to those caught within the tangled shrouds of identification with mind. Suffering arises from unconsciousness, but the difficulty with being unconscious is that we are, by definition, asleep to the source of the suffering: the identification with the beliefs, judgments and false images in the subconscious mind. Fortunately for us all, through the grace that is flooding the planet at this extraordinary time in humanity's evolution, Spotless Mind and other consciousness technologies are here to help us wake up out of our trance.

The Spotless Mind transmission is a potent catalyst. At the right time in our journey, it offers a doorway to greater mental freedom than we may have ever known. Along the way to this new state of being, we may encounter much that has been stored away inside, waiting for the day when we are ready to deal with it.

Opening to receive Spotless Mind may set into motion a powerful process of purgation and cleansing of the mind. Mental and emotional patterns that have been repressed in the subconscious may bubble to the surface, asking for our attention. We may also need to face aspects of the shadow that live in the mind. Thoughts that disturbed us so deeply we have banished them to the basement of our subconscious may arise to be witnessed from the place of clarity and equanimity Spotless Mind typically instills. People often report that beliefs that once seemed all-powerful now have little or no effect on their consciousness, for they can finally see through them and realize they are not real or true after all.

Like hypnotic subjects enthralled by a pocket watch swaying to and fro, most human beings have entrained to Descartes' famous statement, "I think, therefore I am." We tend to identify so thoroughly with the contents and processes of mind that it can seem terrifying to imagine life without them. The mind may insist that we risk nonexistence without its comfortingly familiar presence. Never mind that this constant stream of mentalizations leads to far more suffering than we realize when we buy into it.

A participant on many of our calls described her apprehension before receiving Spotless Mind:

> I was quite frightened at the beginning -- "Oh, I'll be a vegetable," I thought. Clearing the mind was scary. Now, my brain is pretty empty. I have more access to information I've experienced than ever before. I'm dramatically enriched: The more empty I get, the more gifts I have.

Since this transmission goes to the core of the illusion of the separate self sense, it can be highly catalytic in dismantling the ego self. When egoic material arises, we suggest stopping outer activities to go within and fully experience and observe what is occurring. Repressed patterns of mind are surfacing, and through simply witnessing the thoughts, images and feelings, they will continue on their way. When we do not consciously engage this process of meeting what is there, we are more likely to identify with the content and become the unconscious actor in its pain-play again.

As Byron Katie likes to say, our thoughts are not the problem -- *believing* them is. The process of witnessing thoughts disempowers their hold over our consciousness. For most of us this is a long-term endeavor, one that requires a strong, sustained commitment to getting free. The same thought may arise repeatedly, trying to get us to take the ride into the suffering that follows when we believe it. We may have heard it so often that it has acquired the ring of truth -- until we stop believing it long enough to question its veracity. When we look right at a thought, rather than simply accepting it as true, we finally see through it to a place beyond its hold on our awareness. That place contains all the peace, serenity, and happiness we could ever hope to find. For in that place, thoughts have no power over us. We are free.

A teleconference participant put it this way:

I say thank you every day for having been brought to a place without judgment. [The Spotless Mind transmission] is the most powerful experience I've ever had. It's stunning, and it doesn't diminish. I cannot stir up a judgment!

Experiences of Spotless Mind

As with the previous transmissions, we began to share Spotless Mind in groups and teleconferences. Just as we'd experienced, others reported that this transmission went straight into the head soul center and got to work, rearranging the brain and removing the veils and confusion of ego-mind. Like us, many people felt thrilled to be emptied of so much mental baggage so quickly.

One woman expressed her newfound freedom using these words:

It seems so clear to me that all is Mind and/or Thought and everything we have in our reality comes from that. The more I surrender and let things flow as they may, the easier it is. The more I resist, the harder and more frustrating -- thus headaches, pains, weakness, anxieties and tiredness.

When I sent the transmission to my friend, I really felt the strength and power in giving it, and experienced what A Course in Miracles *means by "ideas increase by giving them away."*

My pattern of neediness in calling people is so apparent to me, that I am looking for approval when I really need to go within more, and the approval I seek is right there inside of me.

Giving the transmissions can result in a more potent experience than receiving them, as this woman discovered. And the more we share them with others, the deeper and stronger their effects tend to be, for both givers and receivers.

Many people receiving Spotless Mind for the first time experience an immediate cessation of mental chatter and a diminishment of suffering from fear- and doubt-based thought patterns. The games of the mind stand clearly revealed, and we recognize the mind as the source of our suffering.

I have been more focused with greater clarity and purpose since the Spotless Mind transmissions.

*All the mindless chatter, when it occurs, is just seen for
what it is -- mindless chatter. I feel my whole brain has
gone through a thorough spring cleaning.*

Although we had begun to share Spotless Mind with many
people, both in person and at a distance, no one seemed to be
experiencing any deleterious aftereffects. On the contrary, the
Spotless Mind transmission integrated as smoothly and easily as
Ilahinoor and Love~Oneness had already proven themselves to
do. The Spotless Mind transmission continues to reveal itself as a
potent catalyst on the path to enlightenment, as the following succinct account demonstrates:

*Extreme silence...a very deep transcendence
...complete unboundedness, almost without attribute.*

The Transmissions of Grace have an intelligence and a life
of their own, and often continue to act upon our consciousness
over time, as the following description illustrates:

*After the Spotless Mind telecon ended, I rested
for about 15 minutes as I usually do. Then I felt drawn
to get up and take care of a few matters. Thirty minutes later, after completing various tasks, I moved toward resting again. The moment I reclined, my task-
oriented mind shifted to Spotless Mind. There was
such a clear distinction between the two minds/Minds
-- one so beneficially active to help the human body
exist on this plane, the other such a beneficially still
True Nature.*

*Then it felt as if Spotless Mind began to breathe
itself deeply into my entire body. With very pronounced
downward pressure toward my belly, Spotless Mind
breathed an energetic pulse that had a different quality
from my regular breathing pattern. It seemed as if
Spotless Mind was making itself more fully present,
not solely in the head soul center, but throughout the
body. It seemed as if Spotless Mind was giving this
body the opportunity to shift to and really know what
the human body experience is like when the grace of
Spotless Mind enters the DNA and cells.*

*I watched that process for 45 minutes and then
was moved to get ready for bed. After those chores
were completed, I lay in bed. The same process unfolded: Spotless Mind energy field took over from the*

*task-oriented mind, and again, Spotless Mind breathed
itself down into my body core, strongly filling me with a
feeling-knowing of how the Spotless Mind energy field
exists not only in the brain center but also throughout
the body.*

As is true of the other transmissions, the possible applications of Spotless Mind are endless, and as our sensitivity to inner promptings increases, we may be surprised and inspired by what unfolds. As always, Skandar brought his unique perspective and experience to the teleconferences devoted to Spotless Mind:

*I use Spotless Mind with pets -- then I can communicate without any distortion. It's part of the healing
ritual, and [with Spotless Mind] the animals can sense
I'm approachable.*

Spotless Mind Within the Larger Context of Awakening

Spotless Mind functions to unfold the dimension of being associated with the head soul center, the Cave of Brahman. This is a way of experiencing life that is often described as absolute or non-dual consciousness, the place beyond all states. Eastern spiritual paths traditionally refer to this as enlightenment, for as the light of the One shines down into the head centers, it illuminates not only these regions but also our entire experience of life.

Many Western spiritual seekers have made enlightenment their primary goal, and pursue it above all else. Working with all three Transmissions of Grace has brought us to a different perspective on this. We no longer view it as the part of wisdom for most Westerners to seek enlightenment first, or to hold it as the exclusive end-all of the spiritual quest. Our appreciation of the Transmissions of Grace continues to deepen as working with them reveals ever more about the journey of awakening. We will have much more to say about this in subsequent chapters.

People often ask us which transmission they should work with first. Our sense is that the optimal order to approaching the transmissions is revealed in the way they were received. First came Ilahinoor to awaken the belly soul center, the hara or tan tien, which anchors us into our humanness and the earthly, embodied experience of being. In the organic process of a plant's growth, its first stage of development involves putting down roots and growing a strong trunk or stalk, so its ensuing maturation is supported by a sturdy foundation. Many people find that Ilahinoor,

Spotless Mind

when repeatedly experienced over time, imparts an analogous sense of grounded nurturance and rootedness. This transmission provides a comforting sense of being held in the arms of Life itself.

When a firm grounding in the belly soul center has been established, it feels natural to invite awareness to travel up into the heart soul center. A radiant, open heart can blossom and thrive when it is supported by the sturdy stem of reverence for life that develops through cultivating belly-consciousness. Right on schedule, the Love~Oneness transmission arrived to awaken the heart soul center. At this stage in its evolution, as identity shifts from the human self to the soul-Self, humanity's consciousness is discovering its multidimensional, spiritual nature and realizing its union with God, whose primary nature is love. The Love~Oneness transmission catalyzes and supports this shift.

The last evolutionary stage, which the Spotless Mind transmission activates, occurs with the full flowering of the head soul center, as individual consciousness merges with its Source. A fully opened head soul center brings the experience of that which exists prior to all manifest being, before even God, which, in this light, becomes another feature of Mind. This final flowering ultimately brings about the dissolution of the sense of a separate "i." Head-center awakenings strike at the root of body identity itself, even while we may continue in the experience of manifest existence for some time.

When the belly and heart soul centers are engaged and activated, head center awakenings can stabilize and last, rather than dissipating as quickly as the lightning bolts they often resemble. What began as a temporary state can become the ever-present ground of existence, the endless, transparent sky through which the events of everyday life effortlessly float. The profound revelations and realizations that can accompany head-center activations are far more likely to be embodied and lived when they descend into and are incorporated within well-developed belly and heart centers.

In Chapter 14, "The Three Dimensions of Awakening," we describe some of the distortions that can arise with an imbalanced unfoldment of the three soul centers. Many Eastern paths, for instance, focus on opening the head soul center first. While that may work well for those who are able to live simply, sequestered from the world, it might not be the approach of choice for householders with worldly responsibilities. We typically recommend starting a journey with the transmissions by establishing some internal grounding first.

The ultimate outcome, the goal of the earthly experience, is the fully awakened, fully embodied, God-realized human being. Humanness forms the foundation for this flowering; all other dimensions seek expression through this tangible, third-dimensional level of reality. If our grounding here is not strong and highly functional, the other levels will either not be fully expressed or will manifest through various fields of distortion.

Because no one way or path is right for everyone, we encourage people to follow their inner knowing above all else. Along with being attentive to inner promptings, it may be useful to deeply consider these issues, along with your current state of being, as you engage with the transmissions. Unless you are clearly guided otherwise, we recommend experiencing Ilahinoor first, progressing to Love~Oneness, and finally opening to Spotless Mind. Accordingly, that is how we have presented the three Transmissions of Grace in this book.

When all three transmissions have been received and integrated over time, their synergistic effect can be far more powerful than the sequential impact of each individually. As all three soul centers awaken, we experience a far more complete unfoldment than when any one is activated in isolation. For a window onto the combined effects of the three phases of awakening, please consult Chapter 15, "The True, Eternal Self."

A well-rounded awakening includes unity of mind; the realization of universal love as the true, divine nature of All, including the Self; and the healing and wholing of the human psyche. Together, these create the optimal conditions for the Luminous Self to be born.

Spotless Mind and the Deeksha

With the arrival of Spotless Mind, we now had three freely available, open-architecture transmissions to share with others, one for each of the three soul centers. During this time, many deeksha givers participated in our events and teleconferences. Some felt torn: Were they being disloyal by opening to receive transmissions other than the deeksha?

The great danger of aligning with a spiritual organization is that we may give our power to it at the expense of our free, sovereign inner knowing. Even though it would seem such groups are intended to take us deeper into our own soul-awareness, the opposite may turn out to be the case. When we are afraid to go toward something that draws us, fearing the disapproval of those in authority, we must question whether participating in the group honors the truth of our hearts and souls.

A woman who had become a Oneness Blessing (the new name that replaced the term deeksha) giver was prompted to attend a teleconference for Spotless Mind. She was quiet throughout the call, but in an e-mail the next day she shared the process Spotless Mind had catalyzed:

> When you started the Spotless Mind transmission I noticed that I felt unfaithful to Amma/Bhagavan for seeking a different transmission than the Oneness Blessing. Then a voice within said, "Good fathers always want their children to have every good thing, even if it surpasses what they had in their lifetime."
>
> Then the guilt about "being unfaithful" lifted away. I felt myself accept this truth about Godhood/fatherhood.

There is a place in this world for all that facilitates evolution and awakening. At this pivotal time on the planet, we human beings need all the help we can get! It is our great joy to share Spotless Mind and the other Transmissions of Grace with all who feel they may be helpful as they awaken. We enjoy introducing the transmissions to deeksha or Oneness Blessing givers, for their sincere intention to support awakening is already well established.

It is tremendously freeing to discover that we all have direct access to the Divine -- that this is not reserved for a few "special ones." As we open to receive the endless blessings of the One ourselves, not through an intermediary, our realm of possibility is enlarged and expanded beyond all we previously thought possible. To witness others stepping into their divine birthright through sharing the transmissions with them and then seeing them, in turn, pass them on is satisfying beyond words. We love to envision the blessing-grace of all three transmissions circling the planet in an endlessly expanding spiral of contagious ease, joy, and freedom.

Readings That Convey the Essence of Spotless Mind

During the years of sharing Spotless Mind, we have come upon many passages in spiritual texts that eloquently convey the essence of this transmission. Reading these aloud, slowly and with conscious presence, can induct the state of Spotless Mind, for they are words that impart the flavor of the ultimate wordless reality. During groups and teleconferences devoted to Spotless Mind, we

Agents of Grace

like to read a few passages aloud as a prelude to opening to experience the transmission itself. In truth, the transmission begins with the readings, for the words of these sacred texts float within the vast field of space and silence from which they originated. These writings emanate the mysterious, ineffable essence of Spotless Mind as we have experienced it.

After the awakening, there is only vast Emptiness;
this vast universe of forms ceases to exist (outside one's Self).
Here, one sees neither sin nor bliss, neither loss nor gain.
In the midst of eternal Serenity, no questions arise;
The dust of ignorance which has accumulated
on the unpolished mirror of ages,
Is now, and forever, cleared away in the vision of Truth.

Yung-chia Ta-shih

I am neither created nor uncreated, for I have always been here.

I am neither deluded nor undeluded, for I have always been here.

I am neither of light nor of darkness, for I have always been here.

I am the Bliss, I am the Truth, I am the Boundless Sky.

How can I speak of having desires or not having desires?

How can I speak about attachment or non-attachment?

How can I speak about God as being real or unreal?

I am the Bliss, I am the Truth, I am the Boundless Sky.

That One is everything --

How can I say it is one?

How can I say it is more than one?

How can I say it is eternal or non-eternal?

Spotless Mind

I am the Bliss, I am the Truth, I am the Boundless Sky.

It is neither solid nor subtle.

Neither appearing nor disappearing.

It is without beginning, middle or end.

It is neither above nor below.

This is the secret of the Ultimate Truth.

I am the Bliss, I am the Truth, I am the Boundless Sky.

All your senses are like clouds;

All they show is an endless mirage.

The Radiant One is neither bound nor free.

I am the Bliss, I am the Truth, I am the Boundless Sky.

Dear One, I am not unknowable or hidden.

I am not imperceivable nor lost.

I am not near nor far.

I am the Bliss, I am the Truth, I am the Boundless Sky.

I have no actions that bring regret or misery.

I have no thoughts that bring pain or suffering.

I have no sense of "me" or "mine."

I am the Bliss, I am the Truth, I am the Boundless Sky.

Avadhuta Gita by Dattatreya

Agents of Grace

≈≈≈

Pleasure and Pain are only aspects of the mind.
Our essential nature is happiness.

Ramana Maharshi

≈≈≈

In a Zen koan someone said that an enlightened man
is not one who seeks Buddha
or finds Buddha,
but simply an ordinary man
who has nothing left to do.

Thomas Merton

≈≈≈

Oh, I am spotless, tranquil, Pure Consciousness,
and beyond Nature.
All this time I have been merely duped by illusion.

Astavakra Samhita

≈≈≈

I no longer spend time in reverie,
worry, conceptualization
and the other kinds of thinking
that most people do when they're alone.
My mind is only engaged when it's needed,
for instance when you ask questions,
or when I have to fix the tape-recorder
or something like that.
The rest of the time my mind is in the de-clutched state.
When it's not needed, there is no mind here.
There is no thought; there is only life.

The Mystique of Enlightenment

U. G. Krishnamurti

≈≈≈

Why are you unhappy?
Because 99.9 per cent
Of everything you think,
And of everything you do,
Is for yourself --
And there isn't one.

Ask The Awakened
Wei Wu Wei

~ ~ ~

The wisdom of enlightenment is inherent in every one of us.
It is because of the delusion under which our mind works
that we fail to realize it ourselves,
and that we have to seek the advice and the guidance
of enlightened ones.

Hui Neng

EXPERIENCE~ACTIVATION: Spotless Mind

Once again, invite your body to find a comfortable, seated position it can sustain for a while. Allow your awareness to move toward the breath. Feel each breath coming into the body, moving about inside, and then leaving through the nostrils. Imagine the breath opening up a space within you to receive the Spotless Mind transmission.

In preparing to receive Spotless Mind, you might enjoy reading one or more of the passages in the section above aloud. Allow the words to be enveloped in plenty of time and space as you read them, to better convey the essence of this transmission. After reading each passage, pause awhile, to let the words permeate your consciousness. When the effects seem to be complete, go on to the next.

At some point, you may find you are no longer able to read words on a page. That is a sign that the transmission has gone into its next phase. Go with it

191

into the silence and open wider to receive its blessings.

Feel how much you would like to live this life with a spotless mind, a mind free and easy, open to the infinite Mind of God in each moment. Feel your great desire to be free of all that has seemed to entangle you in the past -- to be empty of all mental clutter and suffering.

Call to the Divine now, asking to be filled with the frequencies of Spotless Mind. The following three phrases act as access codes to directly link to the field of Spotless Mind. They open the channels so the transmission can more easily flow into your energy~consciousness. These three simple statements succinctly summarize the consciousness realization that Spotless Mind engenders and deepens over time. This realization is the essence of Enlightenment.

God is Light

Light is All That Is

I AM That

After you have stated the above as a call for the transmission to commence, open to receive it. You might also invite the transmission to go into the center of the brain, the Cave of Brahman, and light up the head soul center. Allow plenty of time for the transmission to do whatever is needed in the brain and mind.

When that process feels complete for now, invite the frequencies of Spotless Mind to pour down from the head soul center, travel through your arms, and enter into your hands, so you can share the transmission with others. Allow some more time now for the transmission to go where it needs to go and do what it needs to do within you.

When the sitting portion of the transmission feels complete, lie down for some time so Spotless Mind can continue to integrate and deepen. If you notice the mind generating thoughts, simply observe them with-

out getting involved in them, and they will float by like clouds within the big, empty sky of the mind. You may be shown the kinds of mental processes that have obscured awareness of the inherent spotlessness that is mind's true nature. Physical sensations sometimes accompany this emptying-out process. If they arise, breathe into them, fully feel them, and release them on the exhale, inviting Spotless Mind into the space that energetic congestion and distortion once occupied.

When the period of integration seems to be over and you feel prompted to move about, we strongly recommend refraining from activities that engage the mind for some time. Enjoy the sense of spaciousness and freedom that is present. Ask it what it would enjoy and move in that direction, slowly and consciously. Experience life from the perspective of Spotless Mind...and enjoy!

Repeating this activation over time will progressively deepen your immersion in Spotless Mind. For some readers, the above induction will lead to a potent activation of Spotless Mind. Others may want a more direct experience of the energy~consciousness of the transmission. In either case, we suggest joining one of our teleconferences. The powerful group energy field that is created by our combined energies acts as a tuning fork, helping all involved to have a stronger experience of the transmission. During the calls, there is time to ask questions, hear from others who have worked with Spotless Mind, and most of all, bask in a potent induction of the frequencies.

Final Notes on Spotless Mind

As with the other Transmission of Grace, please read the Transmission Guidelines in Chapter 13, "Utilizing the Transmissions of Grace," thoroughly before sharing Spotless Mind with others. There you will find suggestions for creating a conducive energetic atmosphere, hand placements we have found effective, and other information that will enable you to feel prepared and confident in transmitting this blessing-grace to others.

Sharing the Spotless Mind transmission often leads to the deeply satisfying experience of hearing from others that, perhaps for the first time in memory, the mind is quiet, peaceful, and undisturbed. This transmission can be highly effective for those plagued by a relentlessly busy mind. It also offers a healing balance to people who work with the intellect a great deal, and those who tend to strongly identify with the thinking process and the thoughts themselves. Receiving Spotless Mind typically leaves the mind feeling as clean and fresh as a spring day after a rain shower, although a number of sessions over time may be needed to fully open to this transmission's blessings.

As mentioned above, when the Spotless Mind transmission enters the brain, it does not always result in an immediate feeling of clarity and peace. The energetic frequencies may stir up the tensions and stress that have become habitual in the brain/mind. Symptoms including the sensations often called a "headache" may arise. These sensations may be sharp and stabbing or dull and throbbing, localized or pervasive. However they manifest, uncomfortable sensations in response to the transmission reveal the underlying mental stress that has accrued from an over-reliance on the brain without a corresponding focus in the heart and soul.

When such symptoms arise, it is most helpful to do what is effective with sensations anywhere in the body: Invite the breath into them, feel the various components of sensation that are present, and invite them to spread out and take up more room. The sensations we call a headache nearly always include feelings of compression, tightness, and/or pressure, all of which indicate the presence of energetic contraction. Breathing into and feeling the sensations within the contraction automatically help it to decompress, release, and ultimately pass through the energy field on the outbreath. We can participate more fully in this process by consciously letting go of the uncomfortable sensations as we breathe out.

Has anyone ever seen a drugstore without headache remedies? The predominance of products intended to treat this condition attests to the scarcity of mental relaxation in our world. That many people find little or no relief even from these strong medicines further indicates the cure lies elsewhere, on another level of reality altogether. Contraction in the brain frequently occurs within a culture that is heavily mind-focused and believes the solutions to all our problems will be found by "thinking things through" and "figuring it out." There is nothing wrong with "using our heads," but if they are not aligned with and guided by our hearts and souls, our lives may end up feeling technically perfect but energetically cold and lifeless. Inner chaos, confusion and conflict often ensue when life unfolds in a way that is far different from the script the linear, concrete mind has concocted.

Spotless Mind loosens us up. It pries us free from the embedded context of thoughts, concepts, and world-views in which we have existed and possibly become stuck. As the transmission calls into question all that we thought we knew about life -- all that seemed real but ultimately stemmed from illusion, delusion and confusion -- we see the world through fresh eyes, and apprehend it with a mind that no longer thinks it has all the answers. We happily, innocently inhabit the realm of "don't know."

Before we are able to see the world through a clear, spotless lens of perception, we may need to witness the fear-based beliefs and judgments hiding behind sensations of pain and contraction. Often, the physical sensation simply subsides through being with it and fully feeling it. If it doesn't, there is probably a charge of fear underneath it. You might ask yourself, *What am I afraid to look at? What have I been trying not to see?*

Being willing to face the fear and the thoughts that give rise to it -- thoughts we have believed were true -- is key. Sometimes mental material dissolves as soon as we recognize it for what it is. By simply witnessing the thoughts that arise, the fact that they are not true often becomes self-evident. But when we are convinced the thoughts are real, we may need to witness layer after layer of mental content before we can see it in the light of truth. We can practice standing back and looking at the thoughts from a distance, asking if they are true at an absolute level. For example, we might ask, *How would God or my soul view this idea? Do I know with absolute certainty that this thought is true?* These are good questions to ponder when a limiting belief or judgment seems to possess an inordinate amount of power.

Ultimately, the Spotless Mind transmission opens up the brain/mind so it can experience oneness with the Mind of God. When the thinking mind is quiet, we are available to receive impulses from Infinite Intelligence. This is how dramatic discoveries, inventions, and creative masterpieces come into being. They often occur to the mind that brings them forth when it is not busy thinking at all; we've probably all read stories about famous revelations that took place while the recipient was showering, driving to work, or walking the dog. We may even have experienced this ourselves. When all efforts to remember where we last saw the car keys have come up empty and we have given up on finding them, a flash of knowing about which pants pocket they are in suddenly arises while we are mowing the lawn. And voila -- there they are.

These experiences remind us that when the mind is empty of all extraneous thought, it becomes a vessel into which Divine Mind can pour the exact intelligence we need to accomplish our objectives, whatever they may be. Try as we might, most of us find it impossible to volitionally empty the mind. Although we may have meditated for years, attempting to stop thinking, nonetheless thoughts go on arising, for generating thoughts is what mind does. But through grace, transmissions like Spotless Mind and sudden breakthroughs in consciousness reveal a mind-field that serenely flows out into infinity.

This awareness may not become permanent and ever-present right away, but over time it establishes itself as the ever more reliable substrate beneath the passing show of the world. Beneath and around all that comes and goes, when we stop a moment and breathe and feel, there it is: the consciousness of the unchanging reality that lies within and behind all ephemeral forms. The deepest intention of the Spotless Mind transmission is to carry us all into that awareness so we can live there in more and more moments.

13

Utilizing the Transmissions of Grace

General Guidelines for All Transmissions

After experiencing the effects of a transmission, many people feel a natural urge to share its blessings with others. Transmissions can be imparted to other humans, animals, plants, bodies of water, and other landscape features. We can ask that buildings, workplaces, trains, airplanes, and other human-created environments be filled with the energy~consciousness of the transmissions. We might also be guided to send them into specific locations, to ask that particular areas of the globe be so blessed, or to envision the entire planet bathed in their frequencies. When a particular place or an entire region is infused with the energies of a transmission, those who pass through the area will absorb the frequencies that will enhance their soul evolution. This is a simple, anonymous way we can give to the world in a manner that may, in fact, result in a potent and wide-ranging impact.

Experiencing and sharing the Transmissions of Grace offers a radical departure from thinking and reading about evolutionary transformation to actually participating in it. When we actively engage with the transmissions, we graduate from *talking about* "spiritual growth" to *directly experiencing* it. And each time we pass along a transmission to another, we are helping to catalyze the evolutionary shifts that being is ready to experience. All of this is, in itself, a big evolutionary step!

In this chapter, we offer what we have found helpful in the joyful process of sharing the Transmissions of Grace. The first, most basic thing to remember is that the transmissions don't give us anything we don't already possess in a latent, unrealized form. These infusions of energy~consciousness help us awaken to what has always been present within us, waiting to be experienced. The Transmissions of Grace accelerate the unfoldment of the three soul centers, the primary dimensions of our divine beingness. As these centers unfurl like flowers opening to the sun, the true, eternal Luminous Self emerges in all its magnificence.

The second thing to remember is that we do not need to possess special spiritual abilities in order to experience or share the transmissions, because they do not originate from within us. We cannot possibly *make* a transmission happen. In fact, we of our own selves are doing absolutely nothing, so there is no need to worry about doing anything wrong! We are simply, yet profoundly, *inviting the Divine to pour through us*, asking to function as a sacred vessel for God to pour God into God. When we leave the egoic "doer" behind, we discover how easy and effortless it is to act as agents of grace.

Remnants of the "doer" may arise in the form of expectations in the giver and/or receiver of a transmission. Since the Divine works in mysterious ways, it is impossible to guarantee a particular result from any of the transmissions. Each experience of a particular "flavor of God" will be unique, since the transmissions do whatever is needed at the time they are received. We can't assume that since we had a certain type of experience one time, the next will be similar. Until we have fully surrendered into the Mystery of Life, expectations can bind the mind, preventing us from experiencing what is actually present and happening right now.

Before receiving Love~Oneness, for example, we might imagine that the transmission will confer a profound experience of universal love, only to find that very little occurs in our conscious awareness; we might even find ourselves overflowing with anger or sorrow. Unless we remind ourselves that the transmissions do what is needed, whatever that may be, and that all that occurs ultimately supports our soul-evolution, disappointment and disillusionment may take over. When we welcome the opportunity to face and embrace the emotions that are surfacing, we clear the way for unconditional love to pour forth. That love may, at first, be most needed within ourselves. Once it has bathed the places inside us that are in need of its healing balm, it can then overflow to bless others. When, in contrast, we judge and separate from our experience, thinking we know what should be happening, we may mistakenly conclude that the Transmissions of Grace work for others, but not for us.

Like a mirror of our internal world, the transmissions show us exactly where we are within ourselves. To the degree we are unwilling to accept what is present, this can be hard to face. But if we are willing to simply be with whatever arises, the transmissions can expedite the process of accepting What Is and awakening to what lies beyond resistance and self-criticism. Working with the transmissions over time offers us unlimited opportunities to deepen in self-love and compassion. As we become comfortable with the reality that whatever is happening within us must need our awareness and acceptance or it would not be present, our level of allowance and our self-empathy increase. And every bit of self-love we bring to our own journey naturally extends to others. Ultimately, it becomes possible to receive and transmit these energies in a state of absolute, joyful surrender to the Mystery of God. In open-ended anticipation, we can hold the inquiry, *What gifts of grace does the Divine want to pour through me today to bless myself, others, and the world as a whole?*

When we place no limits on what can unfold, miracles of grace can, and often do, occur. Surrendering to the movement of the Divine is easy when we admit that we do not know what would be most helpful for ourselves or another, but Infinite Intelligence does. When we ask that a transmission be a blessing to the recipient, we can trust that whatever unfolds will contribute to that person's highest good.

The most effective way to deepen in the transmissions is to share them with others. The more we make ourselves available as a conduit, the more potent the energies we are able to transduce. It's a wonderful aspect of grace to realize that to give is to receive. Often, the person "giving" receives a stronger transmission than the person "receiving." Knowing that our own evolution is being expedited along with that of our recipients is a potent incentive to share the transmissions. It is important to note that there is no loss of energy in "giving" a transmission; in fact, it is quite the opposite. Our energy uplevels each time we allow the Divine to pour its unlimitedness through us to bless the world and one another.

Since it is a human tendency to project high hopes for spiritual advancement on any new modality that comes along, it is important to be honest with yourself about any unrealistic, inflated expectations you may be holding about the transmissions. Similarly, it is wise not to evaluate the effectiveness of the transmissions based on your initial experiences of them. Give them time; cultivate patience. The transmissions plant "seeds" in the energetic field that blossom organically over time. They are designed to operate this way so the results are deep, stable and easily integrated on all levels of being. Although the ego loves clear-cut, demonstrable results, big blasts of energy are not always the best for us. They may make a noticeable impact on our minds, but do not necessarily offer the greatest long-term spiritual growth. Awakening frequently occurs through a series of gradual, subtle changes that are noticeable only in retrospect.

It can also be helpful to remember that people come to the transmissions at all phases of soul-evolution. At some points in the transformational process of awakening, the ground has been prepared and we are ripe for a substantial activation. During these phases, we may well receive a potent blast of energy that catalyzes radical shifts in consciousness. At other times, when we are engaged in clearing and purification, our energetic need is to go deeper into that part of the process. To the degree that we are aligned with the phase we are currently traversing, any incoming energies will go to support the particular needs of that part of the cycle. The requirements of our outer life circumstances also affect the way transmissions are received into the subtle energetic system. Each soul is aware of all these factors and adjusts the distribution of incoming energies accordingly.

For all of these reasons, we strongly recommend adopting a long-term approach to working with the transmissions. Most people find that they get to know the nature and effects of a particular transmission by opening to receive a series of energy transfers over time. Inner guidance may indicate the optimal timing is every week or two, or once a month, or another interval indicated by the soul. After receiving three or four infusions of one transmission, it can be revelatory to look back and notice the changes that have occurred, within and without. Journaling also helps in tracking the evolutionary shifts taking place.

Experiencing each transmission on its own for a period of time not only familiarizes us with its unique energetic nature, but also helps to clarify the dimensions of being that are opening within us. As the next chapter makes clear, each transmission stimulates a facet of the soul's triune nature to come forth more fully into our experience. Rather than being an end in themselves, the transmissions are but a means to enhance the conscious unfoldment of each primary aspect of the Self. If two or more transmissions are mixed together within a short time, our inner experience may become a jumble of factors that are hard to sort out and process. Above all, the transmissions are intended to facilitate the inner journey in consciousness. We are much more likely to observe and understand the effects of a particular transmission on the unfoldment of a dimension of being if we make this inner exploration our number one priority.

It may be tempting to rush into experiencing all three of the Transmissions of Grace as quickly as possible, but that desire would most likely reflect a mental concept that there is a race to get somewhere -- and the belief that there is a "somewhere" that is somehow better than where we find ourselves right now. This tendency to want everything right now echoes the dis-ease of the modern age of excess that shapes our lives in countless ways. As it turns out, the antithesis of our hurry-up culture is, more often than not, far more beneficial for all levels of our being. One thing experienced deeply and purely provides the soul with something it can digest and assimilate more easily than a conglomeration of energy~consciousness inputs. As with gorging at an elaborate buffet that appeals to our sense desires but leaves us feeling glutted and queasy, stuffing ourselves with transmissions and other spiritual input may actually slow down or sidetrack the evolutionary process.

When it comes time to share the transmissions, some people will be enthusiastic about receiving them, while others may seem guarded or show no interest. There are valid reasons why not everyone responds with wholehearted receptivity. Some people simply aren't ready to process the evolutionary stimulation the transmissions bring. Without a sufficient soul connection to deal with the transformation that results, it might not be in their best interest to receive them.

While some are not currently psychologically stable enough to withstand the evolutionary shifts the transmissions can catalyze, others may be in a healing process, whether emotional, mental or physical, that the transmissions may not further. There are also those who are heavily engaged with the outer world and know they need to remain grounded in their life circumstances. For such people, dealing with a lot of inner transformation may not be helpful or appropriate. As always, trust the knowing of each person and listen to your own soul for a strong *YES* before you share a transmission with anyone.

Specific Guidelines for the Transmissions of Grace

Many of the following guidelines elaborate upon what has been stated above; others offer new perspectives. All are intended to stimulate your own inner knowing to come forth. We encourage you to trust that above all else. Please listen within and follow the guidance of your own soul. In this way, you will be brought into your own unique, ever-evolving relationship with the Transmissions of Grace.

1) Give each and every transmission only with the recipient's permission.

For us, it is of utmost importance to honor the sovereign free will of every human being. Since a transmission delivers a substantial dose of stimulation into the energy field of its recipient, we want to be sure this is in alignment with the person we would like to share it with. When we receive permission, our energy fields then join around the same intention, and a wider opening is created for the Divine to pour through. Additionally, transmissions can catalyze a great deal of inner change. We need to be sure the recipient is ready for whatever unfolds and willing to go through the process that ensues.

The first step, then, for each person involved is to connect with your indwelling divinity, the soul, to make sure you both have divine authority to share the transmission.

An exception to this guideline occurs when the recipient is unable to communicate permission. This may occur when the person has advanced Alzheimer's or dementia, is in a coma or heavily sedated, or has another condition that prevents giving assent. It is also an issue when we intend to share a transmission with plants, animals, buildings, or areas of the Earth. In such cases, go within, feel your soul connecting to that of the recipient, and sincerely ask if a transmission would be in the highest good for that being or place at this time.

2) All transmissions can be shared in person or at a distance.

Later in this chapter, specific details on both methods of sharing the transmissions are presented.

3) The Transmissions of Grace are NOT intended to treat physical conditions. They are not a substitute for medical care. The Transmissions of Grace are intended only to catalyze shifts in consciousness, which may or may not affect the other levels of being, including the physical body.

4) Pay attention to caution flags.

Transmissions may not be appropriate for people with heart conditions, previous strokes, mental/emotional instability or psychiatric history. The incoming energies may intensify conditions and symptoms by accelerating their healing and resolution. For a person who is already having difficulties coping, a transmission may introduce so much stimulation into the energetic system that overload results. Ask for guidance and proceed only when both people receive the absolutely clear knowing that a transmission is appropriate at this time. Praying together is a wonderful alternative when divine authority to share a transmission has not been received.

Directly touching the recipient during a transmission is not always advisable. When in doubt, ask for permission before touching. You may want to discuss the recipient's comfort level with physical touch before proceeding. Cultural differences may also arise; be sensitive to them and proceed carefully. In some cultures cross-sex touching is not considered appropriate, while same-sex touch is fine.

IMPORTANT NOTE: In many states it is illegal to place your hands on another person without a massage license or minister's certification. The latter can be obtained with relative ease online. Follow inner guidance, and consider transmitting with hands slightly above the surface of the body, rather than touching it. (See Specific Instructions section below for more on this.)

5) Before each transmission, go into a meditative state and ask to be brought into the experience of the energies you wish to transmit.

Allow the state to heighten until it feels clear, strong and imperturbable. Think of yourself as a fountain that is being filled by the Divine. When you feel full to overflowing, the energies naturally want to flow out of you to others. You are ready to transmit!

6) Refrain from making any claims or predictions as to outcome.

This is prudent both from a karmic and a purely legal standpoint. No one can predict what will happen when Source energies are received, or know how the Mystery will unfold. We cannot know what "should" happen, or what would be best for another or ourselves. And although a majority of people experience each transmission in ways that are generally similar, exceptions do occur. Be prepared for them! This is how the collective body of knowledge about these transmissions is expanded and deepened.

7) An influx of higher, more coherent energies will bring to the surface that which cannot coexist with them.

Things may temporarily "get worse" before greater ease is established. Ilahinoor seems to be the least stimulating in this way, and requires the shortest period of integration, whereas Love~Oneness and Spotless Mind seem to catalyze "healing crises" more often.

Each of the transmissions can "clean house" when it descends into the physical and energetic bodies. Symptoms may intensify temporarily as the energetic pattern that created them goes to a new level of healing and wholeness. It can be helpful to view these temporarily heightened symptoms as feedback that is letting us know about the imbalances that have been present within us. This awareness may play a central role in the healing process.

With Ilahinoor, issues related to grounding, embodiment, and the feminine side of our being may arise. The more tender emotions including sadness, grief, and loneliness might be present, along with the nurturing and mother-love themes of the belly soul center. We may become aware that we have not been giving our human self what it needs and wants to feel happy on Earth. If we have been seeking nurturance and comfort in ways that actually harm ourselves, we can ask to be led to more authentic belly-center nourishment.

The Love~Oneness transmission may bring up whatever we have been holding outside the embrace of the heart soul center's all-encompassing acceptance. It can also stimulate the physical heart and the heart chakra and soul center to release emotional pain and suffering related to the absence of unconditional love in our lives. Relationship issues may arise, with their attendant feelings. Emotional release is common.

With Spotless Mind, we may observe and acutely feel how the mind's beliefs, judgments, and separative world-views have led to suffering. Head sensations including sharp, stabbing pain and throbbing may occur as tension and contraction intensify and then release while the transmission does its work. We may be shown the palpable results of our distorted thinking patterns so we become aware of what mental limitations can do to our physical bodies. "Headaches" and other painful head sensations show us the suffering involved in believing what the mind generates. They offer a barometer of how well we are remembering to witness thoughts without giving them power.

With all three transmissions, it is helpful to hold the perspective that all "symptoms" and sensations, all thoughts and feelings, are part of the healing process. When we are present to them, fully meeting them and opening to their messages, they can move through and release. This creates a freer, more open energetic space that was once occupied by limiting mental-emotional content.

There are times during the transformational process when symptoms can become so intense that we feel overcome by them. During these phases, it may be wise to seek professional help. Underlying mental, emotional and physical dis-ease patterns may seem so deep and pervasive that they require outside assistance to deal with them. If healing crises start to feel overwhelming, a series of sessions with someone skilled in facilitating all aspects of the transformational journey can be extremely helpful. During challenging times, it is highly reassuring to have someone hold a safe, stable, and supportive energetic container for your process.

8) Transmissions of Grace assist the natural unfoldment process of the soul, but are not a substitute for fully facing, embracing and experiencing the thoughts, feelings and inner dynamics that are occurring.

We grow spiritually through being present to What Is, moment to moment. The journey of awakening is not about escaping our pain or looking for something to take it away. Rather, we evolve through transcending the resistance to our experience and going beyond externally seeking the happiness, joy, fulfillment and peace at the core of our inherent nature.

While transmissions can stimulate an increasing revelation of these qualities, they are not the source of them. Confusion about this may lead to an addictive response of seeking more transmissions. Instead, deepen into the knowing that the true Self is, and always has been, what we seek. Enjoy directly experiencing That!

9) Allow plenty of time and space between transmissions for the process of purification and integration.

After the immediate impact of a transmission, the next layers of whatever has blocked the experience of our true nature often surface to be faced and felt. When disowned, "shadow" aspects of ego-mind arise to be loved and accepted, we may encounter fear, emotional pain, and other challenging inner experiences. When we can fully embrace and experience whatever arises, we are led through whatever we need to be with, step by step. As it all empties out, we are carried back into the peace, joy, love and happiness of our true nature. Instead of seeking another transmission in hopes of lessening the pain, it is far more effective to turn inward and fully embrace the experience, asking for help from the Divine. In many cases, another transmission will only intensify the symptoms, for it may bring even more unresolved material to the surface.

10) Every time you serve as a conduit for the transmissions, you also receive the energies.

Cultivate inner wisdom and mature spiritual groundedness regarding the number and frequency of transmissions you experience and share. If you feel spaced out, ungrounded, or out of balance, or if your heartbeat becomes faster, erratic, or more pronounced, you may want to slow down or stop sharing the transmissions for a while, until your being stabilizes at a new level of integration.

11) More is not necessarily better when it comes to transmissions.

While we are hesitant to give guidelines on frequency since everyone is different, you might start with receiving or calling in a transmission no more than once a week for three weeks. When this initial immersion in the energies of a transmission feels complete, the interval between subsequent transmissions can be every two weeks to a month or more. Follow your inner guidance, and be aware of the tendency toward overindulgence and "more is better" that pervades our culture.

12) Honor your common sense and belly-wisdom.

If you receive a transmission and something doesn't feel helpful or resonant, it may be that this particular modality is just not right for you at this time. Other aspects of the awakening process may need attention. Also, not everyone feels called to transmit these energies to others, although they enjoy calling them in and receiving them. Trust your inner knowing and be at peace.

13) Please pass on these transmissions suggestions, or your own, to recipients, particularly those who intend to share them with others.

This will assist them in both integrating the energies and knowing how to safely and effectively share them. You are free to copy and distribute our guidelines; we ask only that you include the name of this book, together with our names and web address, www.LuminousSelf.com, on each document. The transmission instructions are also available on our website.

Specific Instructions for Each Transmission of Grace

The following information is intended to give you a starting-point from which your own ways of interacting with the transmissions will evolve. Our greatest wish is for each person to discover uniquely wonderful methods of sharing the transmissions, guided by the soul's infinite creativity and wisdom.

With each of the transmissions, it is most important to develop a relationship with the energies and their Source, and allow them to guide you. The more regularly you devote sacred time and space to calling them in and registering their effects, the more deeply you will come to know the aspects of your being each transmission activates. Over time, you will become increasing familiar and at ease with all that the transmissions awaken within you. With experience, you will also feel more natural and comfortable as you share the energies with others.

For all transmissions: We begin by sitting quietly, closing our eyes, inviting our awareness to go within, and calling in the frequencies of that particular transmission. When the energy of the transmission is palpably present, we place both hands on or slightly above the top of the recipient's head, over the crown chakra, holding the intention that the transmission permeate the recipient's head centers. From there, the amount of time at each hand placement described below varies with each recipient; usually 15-30 seconds or so is enough, although we may feel to move on more quickly or to linger.

Standing or sitting in front of the recipient seems to result in a stronger, clearer transfer than positioning yourself behind the body. You may need to stand to the side or move to reach around someone's body at times, but in general, it's best to remain before those who are receiving the energies, not behind them. We humans naturally want to know who is touching us, and when that touch is about to happen. Even when we are not making physical contact with the recipient, people prefer to be aware of someone else entering their energy field. Honoring this comfort level helps everyone to relax, feel safe, and open to receive the energies.

During transmissions, our hands may touch the body, or hover slightly above it. Sometimes a stronger transmission seems to pour through with direct physical contact, while at other times it can be more powerful to not touch the physical form at all, instead keeping our hands just above the surface of the skin or hair while the energies pour through. (See general guideline #3 above for more on this.) You will develop the facility to "feel" when the transmission is complete in each part of the body and will know when to move on. Often, people find their hands moving of their own voli- tion. As always, allow your inner knowing to be your guide.

Unless a physical condition prevents doing so, it's advisable to receive the energies in a sitting position, with hands on lap, palms facing up. If this is impossible, you and the recipient can determine another body position that will work. Transmitting can be done from a sitting or standing position, whichever seems most comfortable and convenient.

After the transmission feels complete, it is beneficial for the recipient to lie down and allow the energies to "cook" within the physical and subtle bodies for some time. Receivers may feel a succession of sensations, go into a deep state, be taken on an in- ner journey, and/or release emotions. Transmitters can assist by holding the sacred space for this process for 15 to 30 minutes or so, sitting in a meditative state. This not only benefits recipients, it also enhances the spiritual evolution of transmitters, carrying them ever deeper into the energy~consciousness of the transmission. It also strengthens the ability to be fully present in holding energetic space for others.

Ilahinoor

After we have placed both hands atop the head for some time, we move our hands around the sides of the head so the fin- gers are touching on the back of the head, with the palms over the base of the skull just above the occipital ridge. Next, we often place our hands over the heart soul center, which is about 2" above the heart chakra. This can be helpful, but is not essential; if heart issues are present, you may want to avoid stimulating this area of the body and energy field.

Transmitting Ilahinoor into the belly soul center, also called the hara or tan tien, forms the deep, powerful core of this energetic transfer. This soul center is located about 2" below the navel, deep within the body, and is distinctly different from the second or navel chakra. Placing one hand on the sacrum, at the lower back, and the other on the belly encompasses the belly soul center and en- hances the transmission's effectiveness. If this is not possible, placing the hands over the front of the belly soul center also works well.

To help receivers prepare to be transmitters, we invite the energies into their outstretched hands, palms facing up as the hands rest on their upper legs or lap. After the belly center trans- mission feels complete, Barry places his hands first on the minor chakra points on each shoulder, then the elbows and the wrists, and ends with his hands palms-down on the person's upward-facing palms. Karen's hands glide up the center line of the body from the belly center to the heart; then they slowly continue over the shoulders and down the arms, ending face-down over the person's outstretched palms. Whichever method you use, hold the intention that the channels be opened throughout.

To deeply ground the energies of Ilahinoor, we often find ourselves moving our hands down the outsides of the recipient's legs, ending at the feet. Sometimes Ilahinoor even wants to be sent into the chakras below the feet. Focusing on the legs and feet is especially helpful for those experiencing ungroundedness or physical health challenges.

When we transfer Ilahinoor at a distance, we visualize the receiver sitting before us and transmit just as though we were together, which, in fact, we are at a higher-dimensional level.

Since it is so grounding and gentle, Ilahinoor can be shared quite often, more frequently than the every-two-weeks rhythm that might be prudent with the other transmissions. It is important, though, to allow each transformational cycle to run its course; refrain from giving more transmissions when a person is going through a purification or clearing, unless you and the receiver feel strong, clear guidance to proceed. It's usually better to allow the clearing process to continue than to introduce more stimulation that could end up feeling overwhelming.

Love-Oneness

We begin by placing both hands on top of the head, inviting Love~Oneness to infuse the brain/mind and the head soul center. Next, the hands move to the sides of the head, just above and behind the ears, over the parietal area. When that feels complete, the hands move to the person's upper chest area. We notice where they seem to want to go, and follow the flow of energy. We may be guided to place the hands over the physical heart, the heart chakra, or the heart soul center, about 2 inches above the heart chakra.

We typically avoid energizing the heart area if the receiver has heart or previous stroke issues. In these cases, we do not use our hands to transmit. Instead, we join intentions with the recipient and call to the Divine to pour Love~Oneness into the person in the way that will be best. We sit together quietly and allow this to unfold. When it feels complete, we suggest that the recipient lie down for some time to allow the process to continue and integrate.

To initiate the receiver so s/he can transmit to others, after placing our hands on the upper chest, we trace the hands up to the shoulders and down the arms, inviting the energies to flow out through the hands so that they can be shared with others. See the ilahinoor description, above, for more on this.

Eternal Sunshine of the Spotless Mind

As with the other transmissions, we begin with both hands on or over the crown chakra. Next, we place one hand over the brow or third eye (ajna) chakra on the front of the head and the other opposite it on the lower back of the skull. We typically hold this position for some time, until we feel the transmission taking hold in the brain/mind. We then finish by placing both hands over the parietal-occipital area. Finally, we invite the energy to stream into the hands as in the previous two transmissions.

Transmissions of Grace: A Summary

Our culture tends to engender a "quick and easy fix" mentality. Advertising promotes innumerable products and services that purport to relieve all the fear, suffering and pain of being human, promising us a perfect life if only we buy what is on offer. Many New Age teachings contain the same ego-enhancing distortions disguised beneath layers of spiritual glamour and enticing illusion. The prevalence of unrealistic claims and promises in so-called "spiritual" offerings attests to just how deeply this "quick fix" distortion pattern rests within the Western collective unconscious.

Within the spiritual marketplace, there is always the next "big thing," and those who have been on a spiritual path for some time will have watched many fascinations and spiritual celebrities rise and fall. Typically, an initial burst of collective excitement is soon supplanted by the realization that this new tool or technique, this alluring new personality, doesn't have all the answers and is incapable of alleviating 100% of our suffering. Behind the bright, promising front may lurk shadows that, once the newness has worn off, are then revealed, like a shiny new toy that is not well made and soon breaks.

Some people approach the Transmissions of Grace hoping they will be the "magic bullet" they seek to eradicate their earthly pain and suffering. But the Transmissions of Grace aren't the "quick fix" many spiritual seekers are looking for these days. Nothing is. The part of us that feels unable or unwilling to engage our suffering in an authentic way wants to believe that someone will give us a potion, say the right thing, or touch us on the head, and we will be instantly enlightened and never have a painful feeling or tormenting thought again. When we learn through our own direct experience that suffering can be met and transcended through being present to it, we no longer need to feed the dream of escaping it altogether.

We will probably never discover a spiritual "quick fix" that perfectly fulfills our egoic fantasies. Nonetheless, an amazing level of grace is, in fact, pouring onto the planet and increasing by the day. During the decades the two of us have facilitated awakening, we have observed this grace dramatically compressing the time transformation takes, making the process of awakening far easier, gentler and more joyful for the human self, and propelling ever more of us into advanced states of freedom that might have taken enormous, sustained effort during any other historical epoch.

That said, we are aware of no path, practice, or gift of grace that can eliminate the journey entirely. Even when a sudden, startling awakening takes place, months, if not years of integrating the openings in consciousness typically follow. Quantum leaps may occur along the way, but even they cannot replace the journey itself, because the evolution of conscious being does not happen all at once. It must be lived into. We wake up, come to truth, discover ultimate reality, and unfold our divine nature -- all within the day-to-day human experience.

How unsatisfying and hollow it would feel to skip to the final scene in an epic movie, the penultimate moment when the protagonists sail off into the sunset, without traveling along with them through all they endured to arrive at that point. In a compelling film, it's the journey itself that engrosses us. Seen from an overarching perspective, God is an evolving experience of Self-discovery. The One is eternally coming to know and realize its Self through a myriad of expressions and experiences that unfold over time. The evolution that occurs throughout that ever-unspooling story line is what we are here to experience; this is what being alive on Earth is all about.

As with the heroine who makes her way through a minefield of obstacles to at last reach her destination, finding our way through resistance and suffering is central to our journey. Just as pressure is required to turn carbon into a diamond and heat is needed to anneal steel, the fiery furnace of transformation is essential to turn the "lead" of our humanness into the pure gold of divine being. Whatever we need to experience in the alchemical process of birthing our Luminous Self is vital and precious to the journey.

Awakening is about facing and embracing all that we encounter along the path. This is the way "self" and "i" become "Self" and "I." We seek instant solutions when we believe we are unable to be with what is arising within us. We feel in desperate need of relief when we have not yet cultivated the ability to meet what comes with full, willing presence. It is this process of learning to be with What Is, not the quest for a magical fix, that forms the heart and soul of the journey of awakening.

Finally, the Transmissions of Grace do not offer a "quick fix" because there is nothing about us that is broken or in need of repair. Rather than presenting a shortcut to the finish line, the transmissions offer a balanced, integrated approach to the entire journey of awakening -- which, for most of us, occurs one step at a time. Addressing and including all three of the primary focal-points of the soul, the Transmissions of Grace support an awakening that incorporates all major aspects of the Self and is sustainable over time.

Transmitting the Grace of Contagious Ease

Grace is always present, just waiting for us to turn inward and upward and ask the Source of all things to pour it into our lives. This is how Ilahinoor, Love~Oneness and Spotless Mind came into being. The Transmissions of Grace and all that they engender within us attest to the level of blessing-grace that is flowing onto the planet now. This grace is not meant for just a few; it is available to us all when we open to receive it and invite it to pour in.

Whenever a true desire or need of the soul arises, Source is there to provide. As the interdimensional veils thin and the planetary vibration uplevels exponentially, the immediacy of the Divine's response increases with each passing day. Grace descends when we surrender our struggle and suffering and ask for help from Beyond.

Has there ever been a time on Earth when grace was needed more? And has there ever been an evolutionary moment when more of us were energetically available to receive and transmit the grace of the One?

All spiritual paths and religions, all movements for social justice and freedom have begun with one catalytic being or a handful of people with a vision. At first these pioneers are rejected for acting on what they know to be true. They and their followers may be tortured, imprisoned, or killed. But in time, their ideals spread, until they become the accepted baseline of human dignity and sovereignty.

These momentous paradigm shifts depend on the power of the exponential function. While the number of those who are currently awakening may seem to constitute a small percentage of humanity, consider how dramatically interest in all things spiritual has grown during the last few decades. Then contemplate the mass uprisings for freedom and self-determination that are occurring across the Mideast and Europe as we write. Each began with relatively small, isolated protests during previous years, actions that seemed all but ineffectual at the time. Yet the momentum of change has continued to gather energy, until now many thousands of people are willing to lay their lives down for what they can no longer live without. Imagine what might happen if the numbers of such humans doubled every year for the next few years. It wouldn't take long for an all-pervasive collective awakening and uprising to unfold.

Grace is suffusing our planet right now, in this very moment, and this grace is enabling humanity to awaken and realize its unity, both as a species and with every other form of life. As considerable research by the TM Movement, David Hawkins, and others demonstrates, it takes just a small percentage of awakened beings to catalyze a shift in the populace as a whole. These few "lift" the others into the awareness of greater clarity and truth.

The grace that is pouring forth all across the planet seems more than sufficient to catalyze such a massive, collective shift. And the "contagious ease" of this grace can also spread in an exponential way. Consider this: If one person were to share the Transmissions of Grace with one other person each month, and each person who received them did the same, in a little less than three years everyone on planet Earth would have experienced the transmissions. In the process, they would be far more in touch with their three primary soul centers. The corresponding consciousness shifts would most likely be catalyzing a considerable reduction in mental and emotional suffering across the globe. Most importantly, each of us would know, through our own direct experience, that we are, in our essential nature, conduits for the Divine -- agents of grace who are co-creating Heaven on Earth.

Whatever we are experiencing tends to be passed on, so as this collective effect takes hold, we can expect far more "contagious ease" to characterize human interaction than any of us has ever seen. Each of us will participate in this ever-expanding field of grace in the ways we are prompted, the ways that feel right to us. Some are drawn to receive and thus become initiated in the Transmissions of Grace, and will delight in sharing them. Others may find themselves having, and then catalyzing, direct experiences of the soul and its vast, infinite Source. In calling for the awakening of the true, eternal Self through grace, each of us feeds the momentum of the exponential wave of awakening. When we consecrate our work and creative efforts, they, too, become imbued with grace. We can invite any of the transmissions to "program" or infuse whatever we do or consciously create with this intention. What is possible is limited only by our imaginations.

Whenever one of us consecrates our life to awakening, the momentum of the exponential curve of evolution and the ease with which others may join in are likewise enhanced. The power of the group field cannot be overestimated. Each person who exists within a collective field of awakening finds his or her own journey made easier, as every obstacle that once seemed formidable is revealed as just another stepping-stone along the way to full Presence and freedom.

If we were to envision the pace of planetary awakening on a graph, for millennia, the rate of awakening would be represented by a slow, very gradual upward curve. During each era, while a few awakened ones visited the planet to spark whatever could be kindled in the available souls, the resulting changes were often imperceptible to the masses. But now, at this unprecedented time on Earth, more of us are awakening than ever before -- and this is just the beginning. Imagine the quickening that will occur as awakening builds upon awakening, and the curve on the graph climbs straight into infinity.

PART FOUR

✧ ✧ ✧

The Full Flowering
of Grace

✧ ✧ ✧

14

The Three Dimensions of Awakening

Through years of facilitating sessions and groups, we had come to respect the importance of the seven major chakras in the awakening process. They are the seats of consciousness through which our interface with everything in creation occurs. Our capacity to receive what Life is offering us and express our unique contributions to the Whole directly depends on the energetic health of these centers. Through the five senses, the information held within the chakras is stepped down so we can interact with physical reality, which is but one dimension of the multidimensional universe in which we exist. Many awakening sessions had spontaneously turned into in-depth explorations of one or more chakras and the issues connected with them. We were well aware that as the mental~emotional patterning within the chakras is addressed and transcended, the chakras become clear, open filters through which the light of the soul can project onto the screen of life without the distortion that had once colored it. As the chakras empty of all that had occluded them, it becomes possible to move through life unencumbered by past patterns of suffering, as day-to-day existence aligns ever more fully with the true Self.

Now, we were being taken deeper, to a level of being more fundamental than even the chakras. With the advent of Spotless Mind, we realized the Divine had provided three Transmissions of Grace, each of which activated a corresponding soul center. The three soul centers with which we were becoming intimately familiar -- the head, heart, and belly centers -- clearly played an even more important role in the awakening process than the chakras. How perfect that the three transmissions functioned to awaken each of these pivotal focal-points of consciousness!

Awakening: An Overview

As our immersion in the three transmissions became a central feature of our lives, we researched a variety of spiritual cosmologies that discuss the centers of being that are more fundamental and causal than the chakras. Many spiritual traditions hold that the absolute One expresses through three primary dimensions of being: the pure spirit aspect, the material or form aspect, and the fusion of the two, or embodied divinity. For instance, the trinity of Father, Son/Daughter and Holy Spirit is a central tenet of Christianity, while Hindus revere Brahma, Vishnu and Shiva as the three primary aspects of the Divine.

The three dimensions of being correspond to the three loci of the soul, or soul centers. As mentioned above, these are not to be confused with the chakras, which are the means by which the soul experiences and expresses within creation. Because the consciousness locus of each soul center resides at a much deeper and vaster level of being than the chakras, the soul centers form the very foundation for the soul's unfoldment as an aspect of God/One/All That Is.

In its fullest expression, awakening involves the conscious unfoldment of the three primary dimensions of the soul-nature, resulting in the realization of the Self as a holographic, fractal essence of God. The full development of each of these three centers corresponds to the paths of Enlightenment, God-realization, and conscious union with the natural soul or psyche, the mother/feminine aspect of the Divine. We often refer to these three dimensions of awakening as En-Light-enment, En-Love-enment and En-Life-enment.

Ilahinoor lays the foundation for the unfoldment of the hara or belly soul center and the dimension of En-Life-enment. Love~Oneness awakens the heart soul center and the realization of En-Love-enment. The head soul center and its corresponding En-Light-enment flower through the grace of Spotless Mind. Together, the three transmissions synergize to call forth our fullness as holographic fractals of the One through perfected human expression.

For most people, the term "holographic fractal" may be an unfamiliar mouthful. What do we mean by it? As souls, we are completely identical to God. Because there is no essential difference between our nature and that of the Godhead, each soul is a holographic aspect of the One Great Being. The everyday lives of most humans don't demonstrate this because we are, to one degree or another, asleep to this fact. It is also true that while we are identical in nature to God, we are not the *totality* of the One, but a subset, or fractal -- identical in essence, but operating with a much small domain of reality. We can become Godlike within the small room of God's house we inhabit, but, however grandiose our egoic fantasies, we will never be the master of the house.

Depending on our spiritual orientation, each of us is probably more familiar with the purview of one or possibly two of the soul centers, while feeling less connected to the remaining one(s). Organized spiritual methodologies have tended to focus primarily on one or the other of the soul centers, but not all three. Enlightenment paths such as Buddhism, Advaita Vedanta and other non-dual approaches focus on awakening the soul center in the head, the Cave of Brahman. The heart soul center is central to paths that hold God-communion as their goal. Christians, for example, focus their loving devotion on Christ, Sufis on the Beloved, and the Bhakti yogis of India on Shiva, Krishna, Kali and other Hindu deities. The awakening of the belly soul center features prominently in earth-based religions that honor the fecundity of the goddess and Divine Mother. Taoist, shamanic, and "pagan" paths, among others, exalt union with the feminine source of all life and revere Her earthly manifestations.

Although each of these approaches to spirituality is imbued with sublime beauty, power, and truth, few, if any, offer a complete, comprehensive experience of the Divine; nor do they support the all-inclusive realization of our own nature as aspects of the One. The full flowering of the human being occurs with the realization of the true, eternal Self as the composite expression of all three dimensions of awakening. This forms the evolutionary vector and imperative of this time. The fullness of the One is coming forth in and as individual and collective humanity. As the Earth and humanity complete this evolutionary cycle, ever more human beings will express all that they are here to bring forth as aspects of the Divine.

As this Garden of divine humanness erupts into bloom, everything wants to be included in the flowering: the clear emptiness of the Absolute and the soaring, transcendental realms of light; the presence of God moving as love through all of Creation; and the depths of the subconscious in which the luminous dark light enfolds and births life's multitudinous forms. To embrace all three dimensions of being leads, ultimately, to fully awakening and realizing each of them. This is why any path that embraces one dimension and singles it out as the only, or the highest, way eventually becomes a limitation. Proponents of the path of enlightenment or nonduality, for example, often eschew realizing one's God nature and perfecting the human nature as of little, if any, ultimate importance, since, in their view, enlightenment takes one beyond it all.

Yet living as a divine human, a Luminous Self, necessarily includes all three vectors of consciousness.

In the emerging divine human species, all three soul centers will be fully activated. Head, heart, and belly soul centers will synergize in the ever-evolving, all-inclusive dance of life. This is the nature of complete Self-realization, the Christ consciousness that great beings such as Buddha, Krishna, and Padmasambhava demonstrated to varying degrees. As the fullest manifestation of this state of being, Christ Jesus is the foremost icon of possibility for this time. Now, complete realization will no longer be confined to a few way-showers; collective humanity will realize its true nature, in a radical, never-before-seen unfoldment of divinity.

The Ultimate Gift of the Transmissions of Grace

As the old adage reminds us, we mustn't confuse the finger pointing at the moon for the moon itself. The Ilahinoor, Love~Oneness and Spotless Mind transmissions are all "fingers" of grace. Our divine Self is the "moon" we seek -- that which is not somewhere high above us, but always and forever central to who and what we already are. Realization of the Self inevitably flowers in its right time, just as all things come to fruition at the appointed stage of their development.

The first group of evolutionary prototypes is now entering into a rapid acceleration in the process of Self-realization. Vast, cosmic forces are propelling us forward into the fulfillment of our destiny, the overarching reason we took embodiment at this pivotal time on Earth: to know ourselves as members of a luminous human species. Many of us will serve as the midwives for those to follow as the planetary birthing process unfolds.

As ever more conduits of grace walk the Earth, igniting the fire of divinity in those we meet, we will, in effect, initiate countless others so they can also serve as agents of awakening. Each of us has a particular role that will be activated at the perfect time. A planetary divine symphony is unfolding, and within it, we are each a unique and irreplaceable note.

Through discovering our note in the planetary symphony, the seeming gap between our humanness and God dissolves. We come to know that every one of us is directly connected to Source -- that we are actually floating in and imbued with All That Is. In the process, our capacity to access the "flavor of God" required in a particular circumstance will grow until it is total and complete. This is the basis of all prayer: A need is perceived and a request is made of God.

Ultimately, whatever paths or practices we pursue, our desire for union will us lead into conscious communion and ultimate reunion with our absolute nature. We arrive at the end of all paths once we have reconnected with the fountain of divinity at our core. The ultimate guru is within, and regularly communing with this inner divinity is the fast path home. Just as, decades ago, Barry first became aware of the intelligent and loving presence arising just above his heart and followed it into his awakening, the mysterious, pathless path will carry each of us into full divine communion when we want that more than anything else.

As we work with them over time, the Transmissions of Grace activate and awaken each of the three soul centers. The energy~consciousness stimulation the transmissions provide heightens our awareness of the three fundamental aspects of our being that correspond to the soul centers. We refer to these aspects as **enlightenment**, **enlovenment**, and **enlifenment**.

A working knowledge of the three soul centers and the facets of awakening they focalize can be tremendously helpful on the journey of realizing the fullness of the Self. It is much easier to align with what is unfolding at each stage along the way when we understand how our current experience fits within our overall unfoldment. When we are familiar with the "territory" of each soul center, we are more likely to recognize which of them is at the core of our current process. In the same way, as we become acquainted with the energetic "flavor" of each aspect of the awakened Self, and include them all in a balanced approach to Self-realization, our evolution proceeds in a comprehensive, well-rounded way.

In the sections below, each facet of awakening is presented in turn. We begin at the top of the subtle anatomy, with the head soul center and the aspect of enlightenment, and proceed downward through the heart to the belly.

ENLIGHTENMENT

Transcendental Being, Oneness, Non-dual Awareness, No Definable Self

The soul center deep within the center of the head, in the hollow surrounded by the corpus callosum, pineal and hypothalamus, is known as the Cave of Brahman in the Vedic tradition. Here, awakening to the absolute Self as that which is both transcendental and prior to all manifestation is experienced. In Judeo-Christian-Islamic cosmology, this is most comparable to the domain of the

Father, the pure spirit aspect of the holy trinity.

Awakening into conscious union with this soul center results in the experience of the luminous realms of light that are the Source of everything in existence. The full merger into the pure light of the One is synonymous with complete unification with God as the Absolute, in which there is "no-thing" perceptible. Consciousness detaches from Mind, using the Buddhist version of the term, which refers to the sentience that originates and permeates all subtle and manifest forms. When consciousness comes back to its root, all is resolved in the void or emptiness that is the indescribable source of All That Is. The sense of all manifest reality dissolves as the Self or larger "I" is subsumed within pure consciousness. Even the sense of God or Source ceases to exist in that which is indescribable, even beyond "experience" itself. Vedic texts refer to this state as nirvikalpa samadhi.

The above forms a traditional definition of enlightenment or unity consciousness, for the oneness of all things is directly apprehended. It is classically termed "non-dual awareness," since subject-object consciousness dissolves. There is no longer a "me" here and "you" or the world "out there." Attachment and identification are destroyed by this awakening, for it is seen that there is no "self" and nothing "other," nothing outside of Self to become or obtain. At this level, relationship, as we have previously experienced our dualistic connection to others and life, does not exist. Until this is directly experienced, such statements will seem confusing, if not completely mystifying.

Identification with the contents and processes of mind and ultimately with mind itself is the very veil that obscures awareness of the pure, spotless nature of mind. In this realization, the illusion of the self as a separate, fixed being dissolves in the ocean of pure consciousness, in which all things arise as but temporary modifications of consciousness itself.

Diving into Enlightenment

When the head soul center awakens, consciousness rises into the transcendental spheres. Experiences may include expansion into realms of endless vastness, limitless Presence, an indescribable Void, geometries in otherworldly colors tumbling through Infinity, and/or encounters with nonphysical, higher-dimensional presences including world teachers, ascended masters, and angelic beings. Light infuses the head soul center and upper chakras, dissolving the veils of mind. The term illumination is often used to describe this level of soul unfoldment.

The Three Dimensions of Awakening

One time-honored way toward illumination is the path through the mind. This involves becoming aware of the attachment to and identification with the subtle forms that arise in mind, whether they be thoughts, feelings, judgments, images, or patterns of personality. Each is examined to determine whether what is arising is based in absolute truth or reality. When investigated, every construct of the mind is seen to be arbitrary, based in illusion. No thought or belief is found to be ultimately true, including the core thought behind all others, the sense of an individual "i."

The totality of all the structures and processes of mind constitutes the sense of the finite self or "i." As the layers peel away, the core illusion of mind eventually emerges: the sense of "i/me/mine." Turning mind back upon itself to look at the root origin of the "i" thought eventuates in the realization that there is no "i" or definite self to be found. All that is discovered is mind looking and the thought of an "i." This constitutes liberation from the illusion of self, the source of all suffering.

Suffering arises when the self sense is threatened -- when there is a challenge to the attachment to and identification with the body, possessions, other persons, circumstances and conditions, cherished thoughts and images, or, most fundamentally, the idea of "me." When all is given up, when all attachment and identification dissolve, what remains is freedom. When there is no one left to suffer, there can be no suffering.

While instant awakening does occur, the separate ego~personality self sense typically dissolves gradually. This usually begins with dis-identifying with the contents of mind, as mental patterns are examined and discarded. The mind begins to quiet; fewer thoughts arise, and unconscious reactivity based on threats to patterns of thinking diminishes.

Next, as the eternal witness becomes established, one is no longer caught inside the labyrinth of the contents of mind. Experiences of free awareness, prior to the arising of the ever-changing landscape of the mind, begin to occur. All is seen as temporary modifications of the mind-stuff; it becomes clear that none of it supports the perception that there is a self.

Whether gradually or all at once, the dynamics of mind reveal themselves. The modus operandi of the mind is seen to center on categorizing, projecting/blaming, analyzing, controlling/directing, and so on. It becomes clear that the separate self sense experiences fear and aversion to whatever it deems threatening, while it seeks that which it views as life-enhancing. Seeking and avoiding are recognized as the cornerstones of the ego's constant activity as the "doer."

The subsequent loss of subject-object orientation can also be described as the realization of oneness. The experiencer and that which is experienced melt away into pure experiencing. What remains is the direct experience of Self as pure consciousness, pure beingness, the light of consciousness apprehending itself. Throughout the ages, this state has been called enlightenment. It is accompanied by an apparent paradox: As self, or separate being, is seen to be an illusion, the realization of Self occurs.

Although beings from all traditions have experienced enlightenment, for thousands of years this has been the preeminent goal of the classical Eastern path. Hindu and Buddhist yogis and monks devote decades to austerities and stringent practices all aimed at one thing: to get off the wheel of rebirth, to escape the world of samsara through moksha, or liberation. Typically, the primary focus has been to go beyond the ensnarements of the world and physical embodiment altogether. This quest often sits atop a judgment on matter and embodiment that can have a potent impact on consciousness. Therein lies the traditional shadow of the Enlightenment path.

The Limits of Enlightenment

The attempt to awaken any one soul center without a corresponding inclusion of the other two centers can result in limitations and imbalances. One possible cul-de-sac of overly focusing on the head soul center can be an attachment to and identification with ascent, dissolution and emptiness. In the extreme, this can manifest as an addictive craving for anything that leads to a spiritual high, whether it be a meditation practice, channeling, a catalytic transmission, or another spiritual tool or technique that focuses exclusively on projecting consciousness into the realms above the body. Getting high and feeling free and detached are not synonymous with experiencing the fullness of Self-realization, which unfolds in unison with the heart and belly soul centers. Nor should we mistake spiritual highs and blissful states for true awakening or enlightenment.

The glorious bliss of consciousness soaring free of the body-mind can be particularly intoxicating for those who are especially sensitive to the harshness of embodied existence. Seeking after transcendental bliss at the expense of earthly grounding, however, tends to imbalance the subtle bodies and chakras so that our being becomes spirit-polarized. We may value experiences of disembodied vastness over the delights of earthly embodiment and find it challenging to deal with the responsibilities of incarnated life.

Virtually everyone carries at least some unresolved pain. Human beings tend to want to escape the pain in any way possible. And we live in a culture that endlessly encourages and reinforces the escape from pain. When the diversions of the world are eventually revealed as inadequate to assuage the suffering, many embark upon the spiritual path in response to the pain of earthly embodiment. Consciously or unconsciously, and understandably so, a prime motive is to escape the suffering. The way beyond the pain is through it, but many do not understand this. The attempt to avoid the pain is further reinforced by spiritual paths and practices that preach that one can transcend or go beyond it all, never having to fully face and embrace the wounding. These paths of ascent promote the idea that one can rise above the lower chakras and the pain they hold. During years of facilitating soul-awakening, we have never seen this work. It only tends to create a split or attenuation in energy~consciousness, which gives a temporary sense of relief but leads to even greater long-term suffering when what has been denied eventually roars to the surface, like a torrent of water breaking through a dam.

The more spirit-polarized a person becomes, the greater the likelihood s/he will withdraw from a robust, engaged involvement in life, for the daily round of earth-plane existence may be perceived as not only painful, but also meaningless, limited or illusory. The personality nature can become dry, cold and austere, with a detached indifference to others, even when they are suffering. The warmth and aliveness of everyday life can diminish, along with the desire to heal and make whole the wounded, fragmented parts of the psyche.

All is seen as the source of suffering, something to go beyond. *It isn't even real,* a spirit-polarized person may say, *so why engage with it?* Yet outer life circumstances may be crying out for someone to deal with them, to accept their relative reality and actively participate in their resolution.

In extreme cases, the lower three chakras can become shut down and virtually inaccessible to the individual's consciousness. This results in a lack of connection with and ability to foster basic human well-being, an inability to manifest resources, and a loss of interest in or an aversion to sensual and sexual experiences. Sometimes, consciousness becomes so spirit-polarized that it becomes almost impossible to engage warmly and authentically with others, or with life in general.

What drives spirit-polarization is a deep fear of loss of self in the "maya" of everyday life. In its extreme form, this may manifest as a fear of being swallowed up and engulfed in the "darkness." The deep feminine attributes of life may be judged as negative, dangerous, and to be avoided; darkness can be equated with evil rather than seen as the enfolding womb that gives rise to all matter. Many patriarchal ways of being and perceiving have arisen from this skew in consciousness. Great destruction to life has resulted, as the current state of the planet reflects.

The more spirit-polarized and disembodied we become, the less we experience communion with the innate intelligence of life. The connection with that which nurtures and causes life to flourish may be severely attenuated, if not lost. In the Hindu culture of India, for instance, the realm of matter has traditionally been viewed as impermanent; the goal of life is to get off the wheel of rebirth and suffering. It is the spiritual realms that are sought after. The result: buildings decaying, rampant poverty, millions homeless, and death in the streets.

Just as the quest for enlightenment may not translate into embracing physical, embodied life, a head center awakening does not guarantee that the heart soul center will open. As strange as it sounds, it is possible to be awakened to oneness and not be particularly loving. Some who have come into radically clear states seem to exist in an austere, dry realm, largely devoid of human warmth -- quite a different experience of awakening from that of those whose hearts are blossoming.

In addition, opening to the absolute, non-dual state doesn't necessarily lead to the purification or transformation of subconscious shadow aspects. While consciousness rests in the unifying emptiness prior to all manifestation, there may be very little awareness of the wounds and fragmentation that have impacted the human self. Shadow material may continue to play out in the person's life, despite a seemingly high state of consciousness.

An interview with a well-known non-dual teacher graphically illustrated this. Although the teacher's spouse had been involved in an ongoing affair with a student, the teacher had apparently been oblivious to this for some time. When asked how a purportedly enlightened being could be unaware of such a blatant rent in the fabric of the relationship, the teacher's response was that the awakened consciousness had not completely transferred to everyday life. Here is a classic case of a head-centered awakening that hadn't been fully integrated in the heart and especially the belly.

EXPERIENCE~ACTIVATION: Head Soul Center

Invite your body to assume a comfortable position, preferably sitting with the spine vertically aligned. Become aware of your breathing, and allow the breath to be as it likes. As you sink into the breath, feel your body relaxing and your awareness traveling into the center of the brain, to the head soul center. This seat of consciousness is also called the Cave of Brahman in the Hindu tradition.

Breathe into this center and feel your awareness resting there. Notice any sensations that are present, breathing into them and releasing them on the out-breath.

From the head soul center, allow your awareness to travel up the vertical channel to the oversoul levels and ultimately to Source. Invite Source to pour into the head soul center the frequencies of energy~consciousness that will assist it in opening further, as appropriate. Rest as pure awareness in the center of the head and feel energy~consciousness moving freely.

Become aware of all that arises in consciousness, allowing it to appear, pass across the empty sky of the infinite mind, and pass away. Whether it be a thought, feeling, or image, allow all to have its brief, temporary existence, as each small wave arises in the ocean of the Infinite only to pass away. As this witnessing continues, feel the mind relax its grip on the subtle mental forms that cross the field of pure consciousness.

A second inner process that is also effective is to ask oneself, "Who or what is witnessing?" Then look within for the "i" or "me" that is the witness. Scour the inner domains of mind and consciousness to locate the self, the locus of origin of the sense of the "i" that is behind it all.

The head soul center is a place you can return to as frequently as you like. The more regularly your awareness rests there, the more fully it will reveal itself over time.

ENLOVENMENT

God and Self as Love and Oneness with All That Is

A few inches above the heart chakra and deep within our being lies the Cave of the Heart, the heart soul center. Entering this center, we come into a deep, profound stillness, the "peace that passeth all understanding." Those who are absorbed into this sacred stillness often say that this is the soothing balm they have longed for but did not know how to find.

The disconnected, frenetic striving of modern life is brought to rest in the peace of the soul. Once it is experienced, the thirst for living in this peace becomes a central focus in our lives. The more we merge with that peace, the more fully our daily lives outpicture it. Discord and disagreement diminish, both within ourselves and in our relationships. The addiction to the adrenaline rush of stress-filled living falls away. In more and more moments, we experience joy and happiness instead of suffering and conflict.

This newfound joy arises out of being itself; it has no specific cause or reason, and is unrelated to outer circumstances and conditions. We may have spent decades attempting to find and secure whatever we think will bring us the peace and happiness that are our native condition. When we realize this serene inner stillness forms the core of who and what we are, all seeking subsides, and we discover a deep, quiet joy in even the most mundane circumstances.

Once this authentic joy has been tasted, we find ourselves drifting away from the activities of the personality's quest for happiness, which begin to feel empty and false. As the realization of innate joy, peace and happiness deepens, it increasingly underlies and even consumes feelings based in separation, such as anger, fear, guilt, and despair. Resting within a foundational sense that all is okay, just as it is, our inner Mona Lisa smile gently remains present through the ups and downs of life.

As we deepen in the heart soul center, the realization that love is not only our nature, but also the nature of all things, eventually pervades every aspect of our experience. Love and oneness are no longer experienced as distinct, but merge and join as a unity best expressed as love~oneness. The deeper our immersion in love~oneness, the more fully we experience it as a universal constant, underlying even appearances that would seem to contradict this, such as "accidents" and feelings such as fear, anger, and hatred. All such states are eventually seen as temporary aberrations or distortions in the omnipresent field of love, arising out of believing the illusions of the mind.

The more deeply we merge with the love that is our innate beingness, the more thoroughly we come to know that love is All That Is, the very fabric and essence of the Divine. We become exquisitely aware that love~oneness eternally emanates from the living God Presence that forms the core of our being. The God of Love that the Sufis and Christ Jesus extolled is now a directly apprehended, living reality. This realization might be simply stated as *God is Love, Love is All That Is, and I AM That.* We like to call the full, embodied realization of these fundamental truths Enlovenment.

Whereas enlightenment is typically experienced as oneness with pure consciousness -- a oneness of mind -- enlovenment is a felt experience of love as the nature of God and Self, the very fabric of Being itself. This realization is powerfully transforming. Now we, as individuated beings, know that all of Creation is based in love and that love is omnipresent. Ultimately, such an awareness dissolves away all fear and separation, and imbues us with a loving, compassionate embrace of all life.

Diving into Enlovenment

Unification with the love~oneness aspect of the Divine becomes the path to the unification of all that is unlike itself. Each and every piece that is not woven into the fabric of our wholeness will eventually be brought back Home, where it will take its place within our totality. This process carries us right into the middle of the ego~personality, where each of us will certainly find much that has been held outside the embrace of love~oneness. The foundation of the separate ego~personality self sense is the core illusion of separation, and the innate existential fear this perception evokes.

Our primary childhood woundings, involving those who, because of their own wounding, were unable to consistently hold us in love~oneness, convince the non-reflective, infantile mind that the illusions of fear and separation are real. It is terrifying to be cut off from the love and unity with the Godlike figures our parents or caregivers represent. When we do not perceive this love~oneness as present in our world, we recoil, contract and shut down in existential pain. In response, a separate ego~personality develops in order to survive in this "hostile" environment.

Because its basis is fear and separation, the self goes about the task of sculpting a personality by building a mask that best gets its needs met, while suppressing in the subconscious whatever it believes threatens its safety and survival. Gradually, this personality becomes who we think we are. Of course, it is not in the least who we really are. At best, it is a fragmented assemblage of identities, few of which are in harmony with one another, much less the larger sphere of Life. This fundamental disharmony manifests at all levels of being -- spiritual, mental, emotional, and etheric/physical. The separate ego self is really a perception of mind, a false sense of self that is not in the least real. Yet when we think it is who we are, it becomes the fundamental basis for our experience.

There is only one true source of healing and wholing: the truth of our core being as the living presence of love~oneness. When the fragmented and dis-eased aspects of the psyche are brought into the unifying presence of love, they begin to be restored and resurrected to their innate, soulful nature. Those parts of our being that were fearfully exiled to the basement of the unconscious rise up to be expressed as whole, love-infused, integrated aspects of the personality. Shame and guilt dissolve in the knowing of our true sinlessness and eternal, unquestionable value as divine souls. Where withdrawal, contraction and blockage once prevailed, life energy flows and healing occurs.

As mentioned above, God-realization and love~oneness are intimately connected, for universal love is the fundamental emanation of Divine Presence. Going ever deeper into love, all that remains is the living presence of God the One; to separate or even clearly differentiate this from love and oneness becomes impossible.

Enlovenment, the realization of saints and lovers of God throughout history, is exemplified by Christian mystics in their fervent adoration of Jesus the Christ, God-intoxicated Hindu saints, and Sufis drunk on the Beloved. The heart aflame with a passionate love of God possesses a willingness to give all, surrender all into the fiery, all-consuming presence of the Divine. In the end the separate self is immolated, reduced back into the nothingness that it has always been.

The frequencies of energy and consciousness within ourselves sooner or later, one way or another, outpicture as our outer reality. Whatever we hold most near and dear -- whatever we "love" the most -- becomes what we create, whether our experience is challenging or seemingly miraculous. When we love God more than anything and yearn for nothing but God, manifestations of the Divine begin to crop up all around us. In one in whom enlovenment is blossoming, siddhis and spiritual gifts may unfold. So much love flows through such a being that outer reality can rapidly shift to reflect the truth of the divine nature of whoever or whatever is experiencing dis-ease. In this way, miraculous healings occur.

As the heart soul center awakens, it increasingly coordinates the functioning of the head and belly soul centers from its central location between them. Just as the heart chakra unites the lower and upper chakras, so, too, does the heart soul center mediate the integration of non-dual, transcendental awareness with the earthy, life-engaging consciousness of the hara/tan tien or belly center. True oneness flowers through loving and including all parts of the journey, as well as all parts of ourselves, and this ongoing process of opening ever wider to embrace All focalizes in the heart soul center.

To deny the oneness of the imminent expression of God as our bodies and the Earth while seeking union only in the transcendental realms can lead to imbalance. Awakening to the heart soul center, we become able to love and include all parts of our humanness as wholly holy aspects of our true nature. In the soul's "heart of oneness," all is embraced, loved and made whole.

As previously suppressed and denied aspects of the psyche are welcomed into the "heart of oneness," it expands and enfolds even that which we have viewed as irredeemable. Realization of this center is synonymous with knowing that every part of us is an intrinsically worthy, inextricable facet of the One. We no longer need to try to fix, change or get rid of even our most difficult shadow aspects. All are seen as parts of the Divine that have become distorted through judgment and exclusion. As they are welcomed back into the spiritual heart center, they transform and reintegrate as essential aspects of the soul.

The Limits of Enlovenment

When the heart soul center has awakened without a corresponding level of head-centered enlightenment, dualism or separation between self and God can remain. A higher power or Source may be perceived as residing exclusively above and beyond oneself. Even while miracles may be common in the individual's life, they seem to emanate from an external God.

If the head soul center has not yet been sufficiently activated, the great love that flows from an awakened heart of hearts may be expressed without a corresponding presence of intelligent clarity. Others may take advantage of the kindness and generosity that flow from such a person, for discernment is lacking. The desire to give as much as possible to everyone in need may or may not express mature wisdom. Without it, burnout can result.

If the spiritual heart has been blasted open without a corresponding awakening of the belly soul center, the enormous love that is experienced may not have sufficient grounding to support it. Overwhelm at feeling such extreme love for everyone and everything, and confusion about how to live such love, may be present. Being in the presence of anger, hatred and other seemingly love-alienated emotions can seem too painful to bear. As the belly soul center comes into balance with the heart opening, the great, all-pervading love can then find expression in grounded, sustainable ways. The life pattern increasingly provides a sturdy, trustworthy container in which the love can be lived. Overwhelming tsunamis of ecstatic love give way to a gentler, subtler, ever-present undercurrent of love that is deeply known to be the unifying fabric of one's life, and is expressed in practical, truly helpful ways in one's everyday interactions.

The heart soul center may be quite developed, and love and intelligence may be evolving toward a healthy balance, yet one's outer life conditions may reflect a lack of attention to the belly soul center. This may manifest as persistent poverty, physical dis-ease, particularly in the belly region, frequent changes of address or homelessness, and feeling world-weary. Although one may be able to access the soul's wisdom with ease, a sense of joy in living on Earth in a physical body may seem elusive. The simple, sensual pleasures of incarnation may seem distant and out of reach, available to others but somehow inappropriate or not even important for oneself.

EXPERIENCE~ACTIVATION: Heart Soul Center

Invite the physical body to find a comfortable position that can be maintained for a while, preferably sitting upright with the spine vertically aligned. Become aware of your breathing; feel the breath breathing you in exactly the way it likes, breath by breath. Feel the body relaxing as surface tensions melt away.

Invite awareness to travel on the breath as it flows into the center of the chest, a couple of inches above the physical heart. Feel any sensations that you meet along the way, releasing their energetic charge on the outbreath. Devote a few minutes to this simple practice of feeling whatever is present and inviting it to flow out of the body on the exhale.

At some point, the physical sensations may become mixed with or give way to emotions arising.

Again, meet each layer of feeling with full presence and participation, feeling it on each inbreath and releasing it on the outbreath. Allow this process to continue until everything empties out and what remains is a calm stillness. This is the essence of your being beginning to reveal itself.

From this place of quietude, call to the soul, the true Self, inviting the heart soul center to unfold into your awareness and experience. Continue to breathe and feel whatever is present in the upper chest area, inviting the experience of your true nature as love~oneness to be amplified by the breath. Melt into the living reality of love~oneness as it manifests within you.

From here, multiple pathways can open out. Directly experiencing love~oneness may call to the surface that which has not yet been enfolded within this all-encompassing vibration. If such material arises, simply give it into the heart of love within your chest and ask that it be loved into wholeness. If challenging feelings arise, feel them and then turn them over to the heart of love, too.

You may also be taken ever more deeply into the heart of love itself. Go with this wherever it takes you. You might find yourself welcoming the love of the soul into places in the physical body that would like to receive an infusion of its healing acceptance and compassion. You can also invite love~oneness to suffuse the emotional and mental bodies, particular issues and challenges you currently face, and other levels or facets of your being that come into your awareness. You might also simply let the love flow as it will, enjoying the freeform journey it takes throughout your being.

The love you access in the heart soul center may rise up so strongly within you that it overflows, wanting to be shared. It may want to bless those you know, humanity as a whole, or the planet and the larger universe. Again, let the love itself guide you in how this wants to unfold.

Often, the inner pathway takes us through a variety of sensations and experiences. It may wind from painful feelings to exalted spaces in consciousness and back again, as it gathers all facets and aspects of being into the heart of wholeness. Bring full presence to each part of your experience as it unfolds, allowing it to segue into the next. What occurs may not make much sense to the mind, but this is the way the heart soul center modulates and balances all aspects of our being.

Allow the love to expand outward beyond the body, merging with all that it meets. Feel your oneness with the love and all that the love enfolds. Becoming one with the love, release all sense of a self separate from the ever-expanding love. The love now continues to expand out beyond all that you perceive, beyond this planet into the galaxy, universe and beyond. The love that is the essence of your being, of all being, pervades All That Is.

Now, invite the vastness of all that has been experienced to gradually travel back through infinite space, condensing through the dimensions until our planet is once again in view. Let awareness continue to descend until the limitless love that has been experienced settles within the heart soul center, its natural home within your being. Savor the awareness of your true nature as that love that knows no bounds.

As your inner journey comes to its natural completion, feel your gratitude for all that has transpired. Gratefulness amplifies the presence of love~oneness and helps it permeate every aspect of our existence. In the state of gratitude for All, love~oneness blossoms into ever more beautiful expressions. Pouring out love and gratitude to the soul, the Divine within, strengthens our soul-alignment and enables the true Self to govern our lives in more and more moments.

~~~

ENLIFENMENT

God and Self as Form, Body, and Life

We may have been blessed with tremendous upper chakra activations and see the world through crystal-clear, awakened eyes. Our hearts may have been blasted open, and we may feel nothing but love for everyone and everything. Enlightenment and enlovenment are flowering, and we are filled with gratitude.

Many would conclude that this is it -- the journey is complete. Yet even this exalted state is not the end of the story. How well are we able to *live* our realization? To what degree does our daily life express an integrated, full-bodied awakening that has become rooted in the lower chakras? How fully are the masculine and feminine principles integrated within us?

Many traditional paths of awakening have centered on cultivating either the clear, stainless mirror of enlightened mind, or the fervent, heart-opened states of God-realization. Because the body, along with earthly life itself, has often been viewed as an impediment to awakening, many paths have advocated giving the physical form the bare minimum of food, sleep, and other requirements necessary for its sustenance. Any further comforts were viewed as distractions from the real work of getting and staying awake.

Yet many of us now hunger for an integrated, full-bodied experience of awakening, one that not only includes but actively celebrates physical embodiment and allows us to participate actively in any way we are called to do so. Thus, we are brought into the third dimension of awakening, which, for lack of a better word, we call Enlifenment.

When, after years of stringent practices, austere schedules and demanding disciplines, spiritual life begins to feel arid, parched, and severe -- if not downright punishing -- enlifenment is needed. If our spiritual path has focused on the upper chakras, the spiritual ego may have convinced us that the human self, with its messy feelings and inconvenient needs, should be controlled, reined in, or transcended altogether. We may have judged ourselves for not being beyond unfinished emotional business; we might have labeled legitimate human needs as "not spiritual." If we have withdrawn from the outer world because we find it too coarse or harsh, if we feel unfulfilled in manifesting our soul purpose or in simply enjoying life, the earthy, embodied dimension of being is likely crying out to be embraced and allowed to unfold. In our quest for the pure, rarefied realms of spirit, the enlifenment aspects of awakening may have been neglected.

If life in the body feels like an endless round of suffering, it's often because we've overlooked the embodied side of waking up. An inner perfectionist may hold us to impossibly high standards of spiritual mastery; we may have trouble forgiving our human selves for their imperfections and unresolved issues. The physical body may be shouting at us, through a variety of symptoms, to include it in our loving embrace.

Enlifenment is about putting more life in our lives. When this aspect of ourselves is well-nourished, life feels juicy, delicious, and satisfying. Our bodies are well, our energy is sufficient for all that we want to experience, and our emotions are allowed to freely rise up and move through. When enlifenment is present, we feel as if we have "dropped in." We're not hovering somewhere above the ground in an ethereal, disembodied state. We're right here, in this dimension, actively engaged in physical-plane existence. We feel competent to do what needs to be done in our daily lives. And most of the time, at least, we enjoy being here.

In the ultimate expression of a happy, healthy belly center, we see that all of life is divine. It is God's body, and we are one with that. All forms are one at this level of consciousness. All of Creation is seen as one unbroken, totally unified web of life. To affect one aspect is to immediately and directly affect it all. Everything in the manifest realm is perceived as alive, sentient, communicating, and loving. Not one iota in existence is seen as an object, separate from us and everything else. When the belly center is awake, we know that if we harm the Earth, we harm everything that lives, ourselves included. The preciousness of all embodied experience is obvious, revealed exquisitely in a richness impossible to apprehend with an unawakened belly soul center.

Diving into Enlifenment

Deep within the torso, just below the navel, lies the belly soul center. It is known by many names in various spiritual traditions, but the most common might be the hara or tan tien, the seat of grounding in Taoist practices such as Tai Chi. In this center, we access the unified consciousness of life itself -- the innate, omniscient omnipresence that pervades all manifest forms. The prime purpose of this intelligent presence is to further life: to see all of Creation flourish and become more abundant.

When we are aware of this inherent intelligence at the heart of form, we see it at play everywhere, within and without. Walking through a forest, we witness the symbiosis of the plants and animals that live within it. We watch a bee gather pollen for its hive, knowing it simultaneously pollinates the plants it visits, allowing them to flower, bear fruit and reproduce; this, in turn, feeds other forms of life, including humans. We marvel at the innate intelligence that tells migratory birds when to fly south for the winter, and the unerring guidance system that leads them to their destination. Who hasn't experienced the sensations of hunger that signal it is time to eat, or the instant reaction that tells us to flee in the face of danger? We all know how to cuddle and stroke a frightened baby, and to sleep when the body needs rest.

We are born with this intelligence as part of our embodied being, our natural soul. Although it remains within us all our lives, our communion with it may diminish. Emotional and psychological traumas can lead us to judge, deny and separate from aspects of the psyche that might have helped us to stay in touch with the innate intelligence of life. Attempting to find the comfort that has become elusive, we may succumb to addictions and other life-damaging behaviors.

When we are disconnected from the hara center, it may seem as though there is an insatiable hole within us that continually asks for **more** -- more food, more drink, more things, more experiences, more of whatever it believes will finally fill it up. For this reason, those who have lost touch with the belly soul center tend to be on the lookout for what might fill that inner hole. Because they are not in connection with the subtle realms of soul-essence that surround us in every moment, they are unable to receive nourishment that is nonphysical. And because they feel such a gnawing emptiness within, the authentically generous, giving nature that characterizes healthy souls remains elusive.

Our multidimensional sensory perception sees, smells, tastes and feels the subtle realms, making daily life a rich, multifaceted experience. But when we fall asleep to our true, vast nature and become physically identified, we lose connection with those dimensions, and our soul cannot get what it needs. Since the physical world has become all-important, we try to replace this sense of loss with material things, but this can never work. Disconnected from the life intelligence of our soul, we do not even know what we need on the physical level. We stuff ourselves with things that don't provide the nourishment the physical body, much less the emotional and spiritual levels of our being, requires. Thus we are starving and malnourished, even while our bodies swell and our lives become bloated with possessions. Surrounded by more of everything than has ever been available, we nonetheless hunger for what can never be bought and sold. How much of humanity has become a bottomless psychic pit, attempting to suck in whatever it can to fill that hole?

To reverse this process, we must go beyond the search for solace in the material world and rediscover what is real and lasting. When 500 books or pairs of shoes do not succeed in filling the hole, we must eventually admit that our search is futile. The lost, fragmented psyche awaits being healed and made whole through recovering wounded aspects and bringing them back into conscious union with the soul. When all parts of ourselves can be held within the loving arms of the internal mother who lives in the belly soul center, we at last find the unconditional acceptance we have sought without.

In the absence of this inner healing, our human expression will be distorted in some manner, no matter how fully the mental and spiritual dimensions are developed. We witness this in some who have widely been considered "enlightened." While claiming to be beyond all human illusion, they may have concealed a long-term relationship, a taste for luxury, a child born to a devotee, or other "shadow" or "belly" aspects of their lives. Such beings may have wide-open head centers, but they have not fully experienced the healing solace and embodied authenticity the belly soul center offers. When evolution has focused on one vector at the expense of others, Life will eventually redress the imbalance, one way or another.

Cultivating Belly Wisdom

Enlifenment brings us in touch with our "belly wisdom" -- that deep-down, gut feeling that tells us what we need to know about something or someone. It's our belly wisdom that, despite all evidence to the contrary, cautions us and protects our best interests, even while other parts of us may be ready to jump into a situation that would not be beneficial for us at all.

When we are listening to our belly wisdom, we know how to care for our bodily temple. We know what to feed it, when it can handle an occasional indulgent treat, and when that might not be such a good idea. We care for the body and do what we can to make life pleasurable for this soul-vehicle, without overdoing that and losing touch with the other aspects of our totality. We respect our own particular life rhythms; when the body needs rest, we rest. When a walk would feel good, we lace up our shoes and go.

Belly wisdom also helps us out emotionally. When it is strongly engaged, we know how to nurture ourselves in many more ways than just through food. We are able to be sweet to ourselves, so we don't need to feed the body as many sugary treats. We actively cultivate ways to expand our self-nurturing repertoire, from admiring the beauty of nature to lighting a candle at dusk and basking in the quiet glow. As we develop true intimacy with our human self, it responds with an increasing sense of feeling at home and comfortable in its own skin. When it knows it is loved and cared for, our humanness relaxes and settles into itself, releasing the habits and addictions that were merely unsatisfying substitutes for an authentic sense of well-being.

All that we need to physically heal ourselves is also found in the innate life intelligence that unfolds from the hara center. We are drawn to the foods, modalities, healing practitioners and all else that is needed to support the healing of our body. Even more fundamentally, when the belly soul center opens, the blocks and breaks in the web of life within our being are revealed. We become conscious of the ways in which our natural state of health and wholeness has been disturbed, allowing them to be addressed at the true level of cause -- our own consciousness.

Endarkenment

In our spiritual quest, we may have become so fixated on merging with the light as the ultimate goal that we pursued en"light"enment at the expense of our humanness. Years into the journey, we may receive a wake-up call in the form of an illness or other imbalance that lets us know we've left our human selves lying in the dust, forgotten in the rush toward our image of the ultimate spiritual accomplishment. The degree to which we've pursued enlightenment through severely structured, "disembodied" spiritual practices and disciplines may turn out to directly correspond to our need to surrender to the complementary aspect of wholeness: endarkenment.

Endarkenment asks us to drop down, to sink into the depths of being, to surrender all striving to remain "above it all." This can take the form of a "dark night of the soul," as St. John of the Cross termed the experience of finding that God or the Light has abandoned us. Our most cherished spiritual ideals and truths suddenly seem empty, devoid of meaning or substance. We may feel shattered, taken apart; with our carefully constructed edifice dismantled, we find ourselves utterly confused, clueless, and lost.

Much has been written about the Dark Night experience, and our own voyages through this passage are described in *Soul Awakening*, so we won't go into it too deeply here. Suffice it to say that all that we have been avoiding typically comes flooding into our consciousness and experience. We can no longer evade or rise above it; now, our task is to accept, allow, and acknowledge every last bit of it. Eventually, through grace, we find we can even love it all. As a loving embrace replaces hatred, resistance, and denial, the intensity recedes and we are carried into the next phase of our journey.

Another kind of endarkenment can follow years of holding in or pushing down a lifetime of feelings and traumatic memories. So much emotional and even physical pain may have accumulated in the belly that, when it is finally allowed to move, it erupts with volcanic intensity. We may find ourselves "blowing up" at people, situations, or ourselves. Beneath the rage lie deeper layers of emotional pain -- the tears, the grief, the fears that were never acknowledged. Through allowing it all to be what it is, we gradually master a third way of dealing with emotions, between the extremes of venting and holding in: simply being with and feeling whatever arises.

While endarkenment asks us to face and feel what has been ignored or pushed down, it is not necessarily a painful experience. Diving into the depths of our being can be revelatory in ways we had not imagined possible. Many who make the descent find themselves melting into a velvety darkness, enfolded in rich, moist nurturance. Some access the infinitely deep, feminine Source of all fecundity, which appears in our outer universe as the black holes out of which all matter and light are extruded.

It is now widely accepted that the universe is filled with dark matter. This discovery coincides with the increasingly widespread metaphysical realization that it is just as important to access the darkness as the light. Through inner explorations into the realms of both light and darkness, we come to embody the realization expressed in the yin-yang symbol, in which light and dark eternally spiral, each containing a bit of the other. As Taoist philosophy reminds us, everything is eternally and continually reverting to its opposite. Just as light could not exist without the darkness and vice versa, nothing in manifest Creation would be present without the infinitely mysterious union and alternation of these fundamental aspects of the One.

Conflating darkness with unconsciousness and even evil has created a split in the collective unconscious that tends to skew much of contemporary spirituality. The Judeo-Christian and Islamic religions contain many allusions that demonize the darkness. During an age when the male sky gods and the solar principle have reigned supreme, we have lost touch with the rich, enlifening fecundity of the divine feminine. Icons and images held as sacred within goddess cultures, such as the serpent, the symbol for the kundalini force, were spurned as the current male-dominated spiritual age replaced matrilineal societies. In the process, the terrestrial Mother Earth that holds and nurtures all of life became a threat to overcome, control, and plunder. This primal schism in the collective unconscious must be healed if we are to go beyond the life-destroying tendencies that have become ubiquitous on planet Earth.

Our human judgments prevent us from seeing what is truly so, within and without. It helps to remember that *all judgment is optional*. Darkness is not evil unless we judge it so. Similarly, consciousness is not exclusively found within the white light of spirit. The clear light of consciousness emerges from the union of the white and dark light -- the marriage of the masculine, bright light and the luminous darkness of the Divine Mother. When we are able to access both of these realms, we become capable of seeing all aspects of reality as they are.

Union with the dark feminine ultimately takes one into the absolute, ineffable reality that is prior to all manifest being. Many have found their illumination occurred as an endarkenment, an experience of finding the absolute truth or reality through merging with the deepest darkness of the pre-manifest reality of the divine feminine. Sri Ramakrishna, the great Hindu saint, was one of these beings. His overwhelming love of the goddess Kali took him the whole way to the ultimate realization, as he expressed thus:

> *My Mother is the principle of consciousness. She is Akhanda Satchidananda; indivisible Reality, Awareness, and Bliss. The night sky between the stars is perfectly black. The waters of the ocean depths are the same; The infinite is always mysteriously dark. This inebriating darkness is my beloved Kali.*

Enlifened Spirituality

Tribal cultures and insulated indigenous groups exemplify consciousness focused at the belly soul center. The realization of the Self that occurs from this focus expresses in shamanic capacities such as shape-shifting, interspecies communication and healing abilities. A strong connection with the Earth and her animate and inanimate inhabitants is central to such traditions.

Taoism is another path of Self-realization with a strong emphasis on the belly soul center. Taoist martial arts and practices including tai chi and chi kung aim at unifying body, mind, and spirit. Some tantric lineages also primarily focus in the belly center, as do a wide variety of contemporary paths and practices that facilitate getting in touch with spirit or soul through body awareness and movement.

Women's spirituality groups often begin with creating a safe, sacred container -- an energetic womb-space -- in which participants can get in touch with "belly wisdom" and other feminine ways of knowing. In an endless variety of formats, women and men also gather to create ceremony and ritual to honor one another, the Goddess in her various forms, and Life itself. In the countless books and web sites devoted to the newly emerging feminine spirituality, a ubiquitous unifying thread is the emphasis on nurturing and celebrating the rich diversity of Life in all its forms.

A dimension of the soul that has largely been lost in Western culture is our innate connection with the Earth as a living being. James Lovelock's Gaia hypothesis was widely ridiculed when, several decades ago, he first proposed that our planet and all its inhabitants coexist as one interconnected web of life. Such views are gaining widespread recognition as humanity reawakens to its oneness with all other life-forms. This sacred awareness has been passed down and fiercely protected by indigenous groups all over the globe. It is taboo, for instance, for Aborigines to discuss the intricacies of the song lines and other aspects of their spirituality with outsiders. Although some Native American rituals can be shared, others are reserved for those born into the tribe. Guarding such knowledge is considered essential for the survival of not only the tribal group but also humanity and the planet. Tribal wisdom emphasizes that every task in life must be performed in a sacred manner that honors our Mother, if we wish to receive Her beneficent abundance.

When we are out of touch with the sacredness of all life, we may act in ways that disrespect the Mother and her myriad forms of offspring. Those human beings who have lost the sacred knowledge clear-cut and burn, poison and pillage, and show no remorse for their actions. They would no more recognize a sacred place than they would honor the accumulated wisdom of a tribal elder if they heard it.

In contrast, in the state of conscious union an awakened belly soul center furthers, we instinctively and naturally know how best to interact with all forms of life and all places on the planet. Giving and receiving occur in perfect balance, in a horizontal figure 8, aptly called the eternity symbol, that links our own soul with the soul of another being or place. When we perceive the energetic grids of sacredness that surround the planet and the essential soul-qualities of particular places, our actions honor all of Life.

When the two of us lived on Kaua'i, we frequently visited the island's ancient, sacred places, called heiaus. We loved to open our awareness to each place and invite it to reveal itself to us. Tourists often happened upon these holy places, oblivious to their true, inner nature. They talked loudly, snapped pictures, smoked, and even drank, their discordant energies harshly reverberating within the beautiful, sacred stillness of these places imbued with mana, or spiritual energy. At times we could almost feel the earth shudder after these intrusions. We understood the inadvertent visitors were unconscious of the sacredness of the heiaus, and had no idea how their energies were affecting the place and the others who were present. We wished that somehow, they could be brought into a recognition of and a receptivity to the special gifts of these places, but we knew that would only occur as they awakened to the sacredness of all of life.

As we awaken, many of us feel drawn to visit the Earth's widely recognized sacred places, for their unique frequencies provide particular consciousness-raising effects. Like the tourists we observed in Hawai'i, some of us get our first taste of such places when we are still relatively asleep. Perhaps a seed is planted that will later sprout and play a role in our awakening. Often we are not made aware of the sacredness of earthly life until at least some of our attachments and addictions have been surrendered, either by choice or through outer events that conspire to remove them from our lives. As the veils that have clouded awareness lift, we begin to see what was formerly invisible to us, and entirely new realms of earthly delight open up to be enjoyed, protected, and held sacred.

When Barry quit working at a large bank in L. A. and left behind a life pattern that he now sees was abusive to himself and life on many levels, he eventually landed on the moist, enveloping north shore of Kaua'i. There he spent many months dying to what he had been and experiencing a rebirth into a whole new way of being. During that time, he discovered the wet cave. Getting to the cave entailed walking through the jungle to a sheer rock wall, and then, in stark blackness, descending to the cave. Once inside, he'd immerse in the cool, clear water, floating in utter serenity for hours on end. Sometimes he swam beneath little rock ledges into small pockets and rooms. Each visit to the wet cave was a much-needed immersion into the dark feminine and nurturing so deep it seemed to have no end. It felt as though he was returning to the womb. In that sheltering, feminine space, Barry knew he was being totally, multidimensionally reborn.

Directly above the wet cave stood an enormous rock pinnacle called Bali Hai that resembled a Shiva lingam, while the wet cave was the yoni, its energetic complement. Together, they formed a perfect symbol of the cosmic masculine and feminine in eternal union. No wonder this sacred place on the planet draws so many awakening souls to experience its healing, wholing gifts.

In addition to becoming more sensitive to the energies of well-known, traditionally revered sacred places, as we awaken to the belly center we also feel the sacredness that is present at every point on the globe. In this consciousness, wherever we find ourselves on planet Earth becomes sacred ground. This awareness may express through honoring the Earth wherever we go, as we come to view the entire planet as our home. If we are rooted in one place, our dedication to making our little spot on the planet as beautiful as possible and doing whatever we can to protect it may increase. Sinking into the belly soul center often manifests as a simultaneous dropping into the place where Life has positioned us, and a new appreciation of *home* as far more than a physical shelter; our abode becomes a sacred place of refuge.

As belly wisdom awakens, we discover joyful new ways to meet our most basic human needs. Earlier in our own lives, when we existed within the layers of padding provided by secure jobs and more than enough income, would we even have noticed the abundance of food free for the taking that surrounds many of us? By the time we found ourselves living in Ashland, Oregon during the 1990s, all of that had been stripped away. But although our financial resources were slim, free food kept showing up. On our daily walks through the neighborhood, we discovered trees full of nuts and fruit that fell onto the pavement within public domain. Down the street lived a woman with a yard full of windfall apples, only too happy to see us gather as many as we wanted. Around the corner grew an ornamental artichoke bush whose owners gave us permission to harvest the delicacies they had no interest in eating. The blackberry bushes behind our home overflowed with juicy berries that soon filled the freezer. We never would have discovered any of this plenitude if we had been insulated in a car every time we went someplace. But as we walked and bicycled through town, a world of opportunities opened up.

Living simply, we notice primal aspects of life we become inured to when existence gets to be too complex. We become intimately familiar with the earth beneath our feet and the other beings who share the space we inhabit. Our senses are heightened, tuned in to the energies around us, acutely aware of the subtleties just beneath the surface. At the beach, we know whether it is wise to go into the ocean today, or whether it might be better to give her a day to herself. In the mountains, we remember to ask if this is a good day for a walk through territory bears also inhabit, or not. Sometimes Nature invites us into her splendor, while other days She prefers to be alone.

Just as the Inuit language contains dozens of names for snow, indigenous peoples and others who live close to the land are aware of a spectrum of subtle energies that simply do not exist within modern, "civilized" awareness. They know exactly how to interact with places of power. They have to -- their survival depends on it, if not in a literal sense, then in a spiritual one. Martin Gray, a lifelong chronicler of sacred places through his stunning photographs and perceptive writings, asserts that throughout human history, communities sprang up in particular locations not based on the supply of food or water or other necessities of life, as we might imagine, but instead around points of power. It was the spiritual energy of a place, rather than material needs, that determined where early peoples settled. That same spiritual energy, in combination with our own, inexorably draws us to some places while others have no attraction.

The White Light and the Dark Light

While the head soul center is illuminated by the white light of pure spirit, in the hara or belly soul center we tap into the luminous "dark light," the deep, primordial substance that gives birth to all of life. The dark light provides the yin complement to the yang nature of the white light; they are inextricably intertwined, for one cannot exist without the other. At the most fundamental level, it is the merging of the white and dark light that unfolds the clear light of pure consciousness. Only when the two are in balance does a human being truly flourish.

This basic yin/yang equilibrium underlies all other energy balances in the subtle anatomy. Polarization toward either vector influences all the subtle bodies, and eventually precipitates into dis-ease in the physical form. Someone who tends toward what is termed manic behavior, for example, is identified with and polarized toward the white light, whereas a depressive inhabits the dark side of the spectrum. Cancer is of a dark or negative polarity, while inflammation reflects a skew toward the positive vector of white light.

The vitally important point here is that the balance of the white and dark light is the key to awakening. As explained in a previous section, awakening occurs as the balanced flow of the white and dark light ascends through the human subtle energy system, vivifying the chakras. As the combined spiral exits the crown of the head, the illumination of enlightenment occurs. Many spiritual seekers have concluded that increasing the stimulation of the higher centers -- through more and more energetic transmissions, for instance, or hours of meditating per day -- will quicken awakening. Others believe that if they focus the bulk of their attention on the higher chakras, their emotional issues will somehow go away on their own. In truth, going after more and more white light and ascending spiritual energy only leads to greater imbalance, which can actually slow the spiritual evolution of the soul.

The Limits of Enlifenment

As mentioned above, if our spiritual quest focuses on accessing the light from above, our evolution may unfold in a skewed manner, since the dark light component of being is not receiving corresponding attention. Conversely, if we put too much focus on the hara center, we are apt to lose touch with the transcendent aspects of our totality, and may not perceive our capacity to evolve beyond the physical level of being. As our veneration and adoration of the sacred web of life deepen, we may become so identified with it and our embodied humanness that we forget that, as souls, we are ultimately free and untouched by anything that takes place within the physical realm. If the belly center is overemphasized, we might feel mired down in matter and overly affected by what unfolds within the realm of 3-D, for spiritual liberation and ascension occur only when the head and heart soul centers also awaken.

When the hara center becomes our primary focus, the bulk of our energy might be poured into physical-plane activities such as shopping, preparing meals, decorating our home, and hosting social gatherings. At a larger level, we may become identified with our role as a crusader on behalf of the Earth, and attached to saving the planet above all else. This third-dimensional focus of consciousness can easily eclipse or exclude other levels of reality. Consequently, we may feel bogged down with material-plane considerations and to-do lists, or become despairing and hopeless over the perceived state of humanity and the planet.

Overemphasizing the belly soul center, we may find ourselves pursuing sensual and sexual practices without a corresponding level of heart-centering. The many distortions of ancient sacred practices currently marketed as "tantra" exemplify this overemphasis on certain facets of the belly center. Ultimately, we may feel emotionally empty after encounters that center in the belly center at the expense of the heart.

Another manifestation of belly center overindulgence occurs among those who are fascinated by, and possibly addicted to, the realm of the emotions. Relationships become the ground of being for such belly-centered people. They may spend hours dissecting every nuance of a situation, probing the inner workings of everyone involved, and reliving or anticipating important encounters. Without the detached clarity of an awakened head center and the calm wisdom of the heart soul center, things can seem very muddled indeed.

In tribal groups throughout history, awareness remained embedded in the consciousness of the Great Mother, while differentiation and individualization were sacrificed to group cohesion. This is akin to what happens to those who never leave home and depend on their families the rest of their lives; they may never fully mature into complete, self-responsible human beings. A similar state occurs when we are unable to spiritually mature and transcend our group identities, whether they be religious, political, cultural or national. In this ouroboric merging, the love~oneness that forms the underlying truth of all existence is not known, much less the absolute experience that everything is, after all, a fleeting dream in the mind of God. Safety and security considerations win out over explorations that might reveal other, more inclusive aspects of human experience.

EXPERIENCE~ACTIVATION: Belly Soul Center

Invite your body to find a comfortable position it can maintain for a while, preferably sitting upright with spine straight. As your eyes close and your consciousness travels inward, become aware of your breathing, feeling the sensations as each breath comes in and goes back out. Let the breath breathe you just as it likes. Allow a few minutes to breathe and feel whatever is present, letting it all go on each outbreath. This practice helps surface tensions melt away so your interior state of awareness can deepen.

When you feel ready, invite the breath into the center of the belly, deep within your torso, a couple of inches below the belly button. Breathe into this area of your being and feel whatever sensations are present there. This is the realm of the hara or tan t'ien, also known as the belly soul center.

Nearly everyone in the modern world carries some tension and tightness in the belly, and if this is true for you, the first sensations that arise may be uncomfortable or even painful. Breathe into the sensa-

tions, allowing them to spread our and take up more room. In this way, you are inviting the energetic contraction to expand back out and eventually dissipate. If the tension and tightness are chronic, many sessions of breathing into it and feeling it may be needed before it diminishes in a significant way.

As you breathe into the belly, invite this soul center to continue to reveal itself to you. While you breathe into the sensations that are present, you can also invite any feelings within them to come forward. Fear, sadness, vulnerability, guilt, and other feelings may arise. You may also encounter a younger you, who is holding feelings that cannot be fully felt and released without your adult help and support. For most of us, the belly center is the home of the inner child. That little being may be so young it cannot even talk about what is going on. Open to receive its communication in whatever form it takes place.

Breathe into each layer that arises and feel whatever sensations and emotions are present. On the exhale, give the feelings back to Life, or to Divine Mother, who can absorb it all within her vast, loving compassion. With the tender innocence of a child, you can implore, "I don't know what to do with these feelings -- but you do, Divine Mother. So instead of holding onto them, instead of letting them go on festering inside, I'm feeling them now and turning them over to you."

Allow plenty of time for each layer of feeling to be fully felt and released. As this process continues, you may reach a point when you sense that everything that wants to empty out for now has done so. Your belly may feel blessedly quiet and at peace. Now, the deeper essence of the belly soul center begins to reveal itself. Breathe into the sensations of peace and serenity, and fully enjoy them. Invite them to spread out and take up more space within this soft, tender part of your being.

Welcome the belly soul center to continue to unfold in your awareness in its own ways. You may become aware of sensations of warmth, contentedness, and nurturance, and other physical-emotional *experiences may occur. Breathe into each of them and invite it to be fully present.*

At times, Divine Mother may come forth and express her unconditional, endlessly nurturing love. She may invite you to crawl into Her infinitely welcoming lap to be cuddled and enfolded within Her beckoning arms. Allow yourself and all that concerns you to be absorbed into Her loving embrace. Listen as She shares Her compassionate perspective on your life.

You can also invite the wisdom of the belly soul center -- the wisdom of your embodied divinity -- to emerge. If there is a life issue you would like to ask it about, do so now. If you want to know how you can become more aware of the belly center, ask it to show you how to cultivate a greater sense of belly-grounding. Open to receive the emanations of belly-wisdom that are ready to come forth at this time.

Finally, you can allow your belly soul center to begin to expand. Feel it extend out beyond the confines of your body to encompass the room you are in. When you sense everything in the room is included as part of your beingness, allow the soul's deeper presence to continue to expand out from the belly soul center, into your community, bioregion and beyond, until it includes the entire planet. Feel and directly know the oneness of the web of life, within which you are an integral whole. Sense the same life in everything that courses through your own body. Now feel that presence expanding out to encompass the solar system, galaxy and universe. The entire universe is your body and your body the universe in this oneness.

Float in this oneness for as long as it is palpably present. At some point, the experience of existing at this vast level will give way to a return through all the strata of being, until awareness once again rests within the belly soul center at the core of your human form. Feel the simultaneous presence of all aspects and levels of being within the limitless oneness that is your true nature.

*As your experience comes to a natural comple-
tion and your awareness returns to the outer world,
know that the belly soul center is always there within
you, awaiting your return. It offers an unending source
of nurturing warmth, emotional healing, and feminine
containment for your process of awakening. You might
like to give thanks to the belly center for all you have
learned about it during this experience.*

The Three Soul Centers: A Summary

Cultivating a balanced, integrated awareness of the three
primary soul centers may be the work of a lifetime, if not many embodiments. In some ways, our journey resembles that of an airplane pilot. Although a pilot is, in the big picture, striving for balance, most of the time s/he is making subtle corrections to keep
the wings of the craft level and aloft. There is rarely a moment
when it can honestly be said, "This plane is flying in perfect balance." So it is with us as we evolve. Countless daily adjustments
are made beneath our conscious awareness as the three fundamental aspects of our nature work out their intricate, ever-changing
dance.

One facet of the Self may take precedence for a time as the
keynote of our spiritual development, while others seem to be ignored or undervalued. Only by taking the long view does some
semblance of balance reveal itself. For instance, decades may be
devoted to learning about love through relationships with a partner,
children, extended family, neighbors and friends. As that cycle
completes itself, a desire for solitude may arise, and within that
spacious aloneness, head-centered awareness may blossom into
awakening. This may lead to a yearning for a simple, earthy way of
living, in which the belly-center pleasures of gardening, raising
one's own food, and fine-tuning awareness of the yearly round take
precedence.

Of course, this sort of progression can occur in any order.
And in the larger sweep of our evolution as a soul, one of the three
primary soul-vectors may prevail throughout an entire life. Perhaps
in the next, another will come forward. Or all three may be incorporated into a life pattern that honors the triune aspects of the soul's
nature in a fairly equivalent manner.

But there is a phenomenon that transcends this sequential,
or even simultaneous, mixing of the three vectors of the soul into a
life pattern that ultimately embodies them all. An alchemical blending can occur in which we find ourselves in a fourth state: that of

the unified soul. When this takes place, we realize the soul rests within a beingness that is far larger than itself. As this awareness flowers, we experience a vastly expanded level of existence that we refer to as resting in the True, Eternal Self.

15

The True, Eternal Self

During our groups and teleconferences, the two of us had often referred to living as the True, Eternal Self as the "goal" of the awakening process. But we didn't know that people would spontaneously find themselves immersed in that vast beingness as a result of experiencing the Transmissions of Grace over time. When the first reports of this began to come in, we felt delighted at this unexpected unfoldment. It clearly indicated the powerful synergistic effect that can take place when all three transmissions have been received, integrated, and invited to deepen gradually and organically. This effect superseded the sum of the individual transmissions and reinforced the vital importance of focusing on all three soul centers within an integrated, holistic approach to awakening. While it is true that, as all three soul centers awaken, we experience a unity of mind, a realization of our divine nature as love, and the healing and wholing of the human psyche, something beyond all of this was going on. The transmissions were initiating the birthing of the Luminous Self, the radiant beingness that shines forth as we realize our true, eternal nature.

We had begun to notice that sometimes, as we prepared to offer a transmission to someone, it did not come through as either Ilahinoor, or Love~Oneness, or Spotless Mind, but as a vaster, more formless infusion of divine energy~consciousness. We assumed God was pouring in exactly what the recipient needed at that time, and rested in that certainty, enjoying the sense that something far more comprehensive was being transmitted.

Although we didn't mention anything about this new phenomenon during our regular teleconferences, it wasn't long before a woman who had participated in just about all the calls over a two-year period brought it up. During the question and feedback time on a call, Maryval asked, "Do you ever find that the transmissions become less distinct and blend into something beyond their individual natures?" She went on to reveal that this had spontaneously begun to occur as she called them forth. She no longer felt the need to ask that one or another of the three transmissions come through her; she simply trusted that this bigger amalgamation of frequencies would pour in and offer whatever was appropriate in each situation.

We next heard from Kathleen, who had also joined a number of calls over several months. She had easily and naturally incorporated the three Transmissions of Grace into her life in an active, everyday way. Wherever she found herself during her daily round, she often offered the transmissions to others, including more than a few people she had never before met. In one example she related, when a checkout clerk mentioned a headache, Kathleen did not go into a long explanation of the three Transmissions of Grace; instead, she simply offered to give the woman a "healing blessing." Within a few moments, the clerk felt the pain and contraction release, and thanked Kathleen profusely. Kathleen had shared many stories of such encounters during teleconferences. The process and the results of these spontaneous sharings were often touching and sometimes life-changing.

After many months of focusing on the three Transmissions of Grace during our calls, we offered a teleconference devoted to calling forth the True, Eternal Self. Soon after this call, Kathleen e-mailed to share her experiences with us. Here is how she expressed what occurred:

> So I was thinking...after all the classes and all the workshops and all the healing work and modalities and trainings...there came the day when I experienced a state of pure love...eternal, unconditional, where I knew that "this" was all I had ever wanted in my whole and entire life -- this moment when I adored myself...the way I look, the way I feel, the way I act...I adored me and knew why I am the way I am, and the perfection that I am.
>
> And then I lifted my vision to the world outside of me and I adored everything...and knew the perfection of EVERYTHING!! All I ever wanted...all I ever bought, acquired, chased, envied, wished for and dreamed about...was a pale, shallow form compared to THIS moment. I can die happy...I have experienced heaven

and it is real...it is here...and beyond anything I ever imagined !!!!

I understand the drug addicts now...those few moments which felt like an eternity of bliss...I would do ANYTHING to have more of that...another experience of that...nothing else matters more than that...I would surrender anything I own for that...so I open to my eternal Self every night as I go to sleep and I awaken in bliss, loving myself, adoring myself, appreciating myself and you too.

And in that same moment I sang songs of gratitude for Barry and Karen who had stretched out their hands to take mine and say...come on...it is right here...fear not...it is soooo easy...just open to it...and they took me through the process called the True Eternal Self...oh joy!! OH JOY!! I searched my whole 64 years of life...and right here, in my own living room on the other end of the phone...it came...OH JOY...Oh Exultation...Oh Sweet Divine.

There are no more questions in my mind, no more concerns in my heart, no more pain in my soul, no more dither, no more drama...just joy JOY JOY!!!

No matter what we human beings are doing, what we almost always secretly hope is that whatever we are doing will bring us back to the place we never actually left, the place called Home. We may spend our lives looking in all the wrong places for the enfolding solace we are sure lies just around the next bend. We seek it in food, alcohol, substances, purchases, and all manner of outer diversions and distractions, unaware that no matter how hard we look, what we seek cannot be found out there. What we seek is not an activity or possession we will someday locate at last -- it is who we truly are, and it is never further than a heartbeat away.

Once we are on the path Home there is no turning back, for we come to realize that everything we seek without is really a misplaced attempt to find what can only be found within. Asleep in the dream, we believe the dream to be real and have no remembrance of the awakened state. Just as a sleeping child relies on a parent or an alarm clock to awaken her for school each day, we are incapable of awakening ourselves. Yes, we can apply ourselves to whatever inner spiritual work calls us, but in the end, all that even the most intense sadhana, or practice, can do is prepare us for that which our human self is incapable of bringing about. Only through grace, only through That which always, already resides above and beyond the dream, can we be awakened.

As we awaken through grace, each of the three dimensions of being naturally begins to unfold. We continuously toggle back and forth, developing one dimension for a time and then moving on to the next, only to circle back on a new level of the spiral to an aspect we had focused on before. At one point we may be ardently attempting to deepen our communion with the innate intelligence of the body. We find ourselves wanting to understand what it takes to heal ourselves physically. We spend time deepening our connection with the body's wisdom, getting in touch with what it's trying to tell us. We may explore body-practices such as yoga, chi kung and massage. During another phase, we feel drawn up and out into the highest realms of spirit. The body seems to be the least of our concerns as we seek absolute transcendence of earthly limitation and suffering. At a different time, we feel inexorably pulled ever deeper into our heart and soul, wanting nothing more than to commune with the God within.

Where do these impulses originate? What contains and orchestrates the yearning to know all three of these dimensions? We seek an experience of ourselves that is absolute and comprehensive, that includes everything about us. We want to know ourselves totally and completely, on every level, in every dimension. And we want to know that which lies beyond all levels, dimensions and aspects -- that which cannot be described or encompassed.

This is the path of Self-realization that every human being treads, discovering one facet after another of our true nature, until we arrive at the moment when the direct apprehension of who and what we are simply occurs. This experience is so simple and natural, so effortless and inevitable, we wonder why we thought we needed the immense effort we put into seeking for so many years. The Self is magnificent, luminous, whole and complete, yet simultaneously absolutely normal and natural. It is everything we would inherently expect ourselves to be, except that we have come to accept the abnormal, the limited, and the painful as our experience.

The sincere desire to realize the Self takes us on a mysterious, always surprising journey in which all three dimensions of being open and evolve until the moment comes when our true nature stands apparent and clear. In that moment, the journey ends: In a way, there is nothing more to know about who and what we truly are. The essential Self is revealed. But this is also when the journey truly begins, for before that time we have been more or less asleep in a hypnotic trance, and much of who we are has not been living at all.

Now, we embark upon the adventure of exploring the nature of the true Self within the context of Creation. As we devote the rest of our lives to this exploration, we find that it may include long inner periods where we bask in the glow and deepen in the eternal Essence. Intelligently and lovingly, this inner presence gradually transforms every aspect of our being to align with its nature. As we commune with it, the greatest -- the only -- remaining desire is total absorption: to be dissolved into the Divine Presence. Simultaneously we become aware of the myriad ways the true Self is reflected through physical embodiment and the world around us. Contemplation reveals what it is like to realize the Self in every human experience, continually deepening our experience of its inherent nature. While the essence of the Self never fundamentally changes, the variety and creativity of its expressions are without limit. Evolution and constancy coexist in an eternal Mystery; what we are, once realized, never changes, yet its extensions endlessly manifest in new ways.

If the three soul centers are the focal-points within the subtle bodies for the three fundamental aspects of being, imagine an even deeper focus of being, a unifying point where the True, Eternal Self can most easily be accessed. Deep within the heart soul center lies the Soul Lotus, which, as its name implies, is the flower of our true beingness awaiting its time to blossom. Within it resides the Divine Presence that animates the physical form, the flame of the One that burns within for as long as the soul inhabits the body.

As our Self-exploration and discovery deepen, the Soul Lotus gradually unfurls, revealing more of the Divine Presence within. Throughout that unfoldment, the infinite intelligence and love of that Presence orchestrate the awakening of the three soul centers. The True, Eternal Self blossoms into our awareness when the Soul Lotus has opened sufficiently so that its essential nature can be experienced through the three soul centers. This enables us to apprehend the totality of who and what we are.

~ ~ ~

In the interior of the heart-cave,
the one Reality shines alone
as "I-I," the Self.

Ramana Maharshi

While the eternal Self resides within an apparent center within us, it is by no means limited to that locale or defined by it. The True, Eternal Self is infinite and indescribable; it is both empty and full, at once the Source and an extension of it, itself omnipresent and unlimited. The Self can in no way be described or truly understood. "I AM" might be the only two words that can ever adequately describe the indescribable. The Self is a pure experience of existence itself; to know the Self is to apprehend that one's own nature *is* that consciousness and existence. This realization is also an explosion of that pure I AM-ness into a kaleidoscope of divine qualities and characteristics that are its nature unfolded. And that is the evolutionary part of the journey.

The opening of the Soul Lotus involves a coordinated awakening of all three soul centers as the pure beingness of the Self experiences its existence through the three primary dimensions of being. As the Soul Lotus opens, the three dimensions of the Self unfold. When Self-realization becomes the primary focus of spiritual practice, attention increasingly centers upon the Soul Lotus, which resides at a level deeper than the heart soul center. Here, we are truly at the altar of our being. The love emanating from our sacred core invites and allows all dimensions of being to take their place within the total oneness that is our essential nature. Within the Soul Lotus, we merge with the "ground of being," that which encompasses the absolute and transcendental as well as the imminent and physical. The Soul Lotus envelops all seeming polarities -- the upper and lower, the personal and transpersonal -- within its vast field of being. This final stage of the journey continues to ripen as the three primary dimensions of being awaken.

A conscious experience of the Self can occur at any point in the journey of awakening. It may be precipitated by a specific event or action, stimulated by some type of spiritual input or transmission, or spontaneously arise when conditions are ripe. Here, Barry describes an experience of Self that occurred in India in 2005.

Barry: Remember the Self

Karen and I had traveled to the little town of Tiruvannamalai, in South India, to visit Ramana Maharshi's ashram. As I walked into the ashram compound, the depth of the peace was immediately palpable, and the aura of the departed sage embraced me. A sense of energy and presence magnetically drew me to the temple, which was largely empty this early in the day. A few dozen people circumambulated the altar area chanting mantras, fingering malas, and walking in meditative silence. Finding a seat against a wall, I dropped into the peace.

Within moments, I saw Ramana Maharshi's face before me, as though it were but a foot from mine. With a loving smile, he said, "Remember the Self."

His words were a transmission. As I received and considered them, I became aware of what was and always had been. Since receiving the first deeksha the year before, I had become subtly identified with the emptiness or void state, seeking to dissolve all elements of individualized consciousness that arose. A subtle "i" that was trying to eliminate itself remained.

It was now apparent that, while the prior nature of consciousness was profoundly empty, always *This* remained -- the Self, indescribable, yet forever present, the only perpetual truth or reality. How simple and obvious it was! It had always been there, even before I embarked upon the spiritual path. In fact, this was the *only* thing that was truly there, yet to define it in any way or call it "me" was also not accurate. Words or thoughts could not define this Self, but there it was, the only thing I knew to be ultimately true.

I laughed out loud. It was as though I had, for the first time, fully noticed something so obvious that it seemed absurd I could ever have missed it. It was as if a hand had been right in front of my face for eternity, yet somehow I had managed to ignore it. It seemed totally preposterous that I could have missed the absolutely obvious -- in fact, the only -- thing that is really there.

As the laughter continued, I opened my eyes and saw the people still marching around the "altar," which I later found out was really Ramana's maha samadhi, or bodily tomb. It all seemed so absurd -- all their practices, chanting, and pacing for God. I wanted to jump up and shout, "Stop! Sit down and look. It's right there in front of you!"

As I walked out of the temple, the feeling arose that I had gotten what I had come to India for.

∽∾∽

One of the great paradoxes about realizing the true Self is that the experience of self, and all that we have known the self to be, must first dissolve for the true Self to be experienced. The paradox is further extended in that the true Self can be simultaneously experienced as absolute emptiness and void, utterly nonexistent, while also as pure being, I AM, or Sat-Chit-Ananda -- existence, consciousness and bliss, as described in the Vedas. The Self is ultimately without attribute -- indescribable, almost indiscernible to the mind except in the cognition of existence itself and the presence of bliss. This is why the experience of no-self is always an essential part of the process of realizing the true Self. As Ramana Maharshi himself put it:

The "I" casts off the illusion of "I" and yet remains as "I."
Such is the paradox of Self-realization.

The self that seeks the Self is the illusion that must die so that the Self can stand apparent as What Is. It is the seeker that must be revealed as the final barrier to realization. The seeker can never find. The seeker can only cease to exist.

And when the separate self sense dissolves, even for a moment, the magnificence of the true Self stands revealed. As it is first apprehended, the moment of coming Home has arrived. There is nothing else we could want than what we are.

It can seem utterly, stupendously spectacular to realize the true Self, for this is the pinnacle of all searching and questing, the "pearl of great price" that has long been sought. There is nothing more to achieve or attain, spiritually, than this. Yet it is also the most simple and natural thing that can ever occur. Once it takes place, living in conscious communion with who and what we really are is all that is necessary for Heaven on Earth to begin to appear all around us. In fact, there is no other way that this can ever happen.

All we have to "do" is to live in this truth and give no power to anything that would seem otherwise, in ourselves, others, and the world at large. We may temporarily leave our ultimate resting place within, but as we come back home to our true nature, which shines within the Lotus of the Soul, Heaven unfolds within and before us as a movement of total ease and grace. Our unique role on Earth is then fulfilled. This is our ultimate service as agents of grace -- to be fountains of infinite grace through simply realizing who and what we really are.

There is a light that shines beyond all things on
Earth, beyond us all, beyond the heavens, beyond
the highest, the very highest heavens.
This is the Light that shines in our heart.

Chandogya Upanishad

The True, Eternal Self

The Process of Awakening the True, Eternal Self

The experience of the True, Eternal Self spontaneously emerges as the natural fruit of the desire for full union with God/ One/All That Is. The processes to consciously connect with soul, oversoul and Source presented earlier in this book are practical ways to ground a practice that will lead to this realization. As we go higher we will also be carried deeper, while the figure 8 of wholeness weaves all aspects of being into its eternal return. Each ascent into the oversoul realms is inevitably followed by a corresponding descent into the subconscious domains. Over time, energy~consciousness expands and the three dimensions of awakening flower, as do the subtle bodies and chakras.

The core of the Self-realization process lies in making contact with the God Presence within, feeling Divine Essence flowing into and through ourselves as a spiritual substance -- highly refined, yet palpable and perceptible to our subtle, higher senses. Once this contact has occurred, we are in touch with the essence of the True, Eternal Self. Now, we are Home; we have returned to our essential nature and are once again in communion with it. From here on, an organic process orchestrated by the God within us unfolds. It typically centers on continually returning to the altar of being within the Lotus of the Soul. There, we supplicate our outer-acting, ego~personality self sense to the inner divinity that knows exactly how to choreograph the psycho-spiritual and physical conversion or transformation that must occur for all the soul centers and chakras to bloom, revealing our true nature as a luminous, divine being.

Contacting the indwelling presence is accompanied by the direct knowing that the essence of God and the essence of our true nature are identical, for they are One. In a matter of moments, everything falls into place; now, we no longer feel the sense of a subtle separation between the human self sense and the numinous presence we have deeply desired to merge with. As Barry and Kathleen described in their accounts above, what emerges is an absolute realization of our true nature as who we really are.

This moment is not something we can make happen. The one who is seeking is the one that stands in the way. It happens at the right moment, the moment of ultimate ripeness, through grace. When we connect with the divine essence within, we can then commit our spiritual journey to fully merging with it until no sense of self separate from it remains.

The core of the journey is the inner process of realizing our divinity. There is nothing that can take the place of devoting inner time to making the connection and deepening in it. That is something we can and must commit ourselves to. The way the true Self comes forth into our awareness and further, into full realization, is, as we have said many times, a process of surrendering the "doer" and allowing the Divine to do the work. Grace is always the active agency that makes it happen, even though we can do much to prepare and purify ourselves so the doors will eventually open wide.

Grace is now showering down upon the human species because collectively we have come to the point where we are ready to receive it. The three Transmissions of Grace were given to serve as vehicles of grace to help awaken the three dimensions of the soul's beingness. As the three soul centers and dimensions unfold and the Soul Lotus opens, our truest, deepest, vastest and most inclusive nature stands revealed as what has always been.

When we want God and our true Self more than we want our next breath, we stand at the doorway to our sacred Home within. Everything we want more than God is what stands in the way of full Self-realization. Honest self-scrutiny is a vital aspect of the journey Home, for to the degree that we are preoccupied with the things of the world, we miss the signposts guiding us inward to the abode of our eternal sacredness. When we hold union with the Divine as the only thing of ultimate importance, and are willing to die and die again to all that we are not, then as surely as energy follows intention, what will stand revealed is who and what we truly are.

PART FIVE

✦ ✦ ✦

GraceWork
at the
End of Time

✦ ✦ ✦

16

Planetary GraceWork

I saw them cross the twilight of an age,
The sun-eyed children of a marvelous dawn,
Great creators with wide brows of calm,
The massive barrier-breakers of the world,
Laborers in the quarries of the gods...
The architects of immortality.
Into the fallen human sphere they came,
Faces that wore the Immortal's glory still...
Bodies made beautiful by the spirit's light...
Carrying the Dionysian cup of joy,
Lips chanting an unknown anthem of the soul,
Feet echoing in the corridors of Time.
High priests of wisdom, sweetness, might, and bliss;
Discoverers of beauty's sunlit ways...
Their tread one day shall change the suffering Earth
And justify the light on Nature's face.

Sri Aurobindo

Agents of Grace to Center Stage

The end of the age is upon us; the time of the great transformation is here. Those who have come to Earth to catalyze the
shift of the ages are being called to take their places at the center
of the stage. This is the moment we have waited for, the fulfillment
we have returned yet again to this planet to realize at last. The
Earth and our brothers and sisters look to us now to step forward
and carry out our part of the divine plan.

As our souls expand beyond the small sphere of ego and
personality and our self sense widens to encompass the world, we
are called into this larger context and brought into our service. A

divine impulse arises from the core of our being to serve on the highest level possible to heal, alleviate suffering and spur awakening. This is the natural culmination of the soul's unfoldment, an organic process that impels us into the fulfillment of our soul destiny and purpose. As the Soul Lotus blossoms and our heart opens, we naturally want to know what our brothers and sisters around the planet are experiencing, because "they" are us. We are inexorably drawn into relationship with everyone, everywhere; the planet herself becomes a beloved family member.

Weaving the webs of planetary awareness, the mass media, internet, and social media are outer manifestations of the blossoming of unity consciousness. These technological advances reflect our need to know what is happening beyond the confines of our personal lives. Within seconds, we can pull up information on what is occurring anywhere we wish and join energies with anyone we like to further life's unfoldment. As individual consciousness merges with the Whole, encompassing ever more of the totality, the neurons in the planetary brain interconnect in ever more intricate patterns. The limiting identities -- religious, cultural, racial and even that of the nation-state -- that formerly circumscribed our sense of self can no longer contain our ever-expanding sense of who we are.

In a myriad of ways, we are discovering that we are cells in the body of God. Within the human body, each cell is in communication with every other cell through subtle energetic transmissions that convey an exceedingly complex flow of information. Through the DNA, the intelligence contained in every cell, each individual unit is tuned in to all others. This bio-informational wifi allows each cell to know what is going on within every other cell so it can biochemically adjust to stay in harmony with the whole body. Like the cells in the physical body, we are each cells in the collective body human. As we awaken to our oneness with every other form of life, we feel an increasing desire to connect, to respond, and to assist others wherever we can. This evolution sets the stage for our service as planetary agents of grace to expand and deepen.

Just as we've learned that we can be agents of grace in the interpersonal realm of everyday life, we can shift the scope of our attention and intention to focus on the global situation. Everything we've learned, all the skills and tools we've acquired in this and previous lifetimes, and most importantly the grace we are capable of accessing, find their ultimate potential application at the planetary level.

Stepping into our larger role, we discover what quantum physics and spirituality have revealed: There is no such thing as separation. Beyond the veils of third-dimensional, physical reality, time and space collapse and everything exists in complete inter-connectedness with everything else. There is no here or there, no distance to be crossed or obstacles to be overcome. That's why it is just as easy and equally potent to share a Transmission of Grace whether the recipient is physically present or on the other side of the planet. If a subconscious belief lingers that a transmission is not as powerful when we can't touch someone, this illusion quickly dissolves through experience.

Just as distance is not a limit, the size, order, and scope of the grace we are capable of actualizing are likewise unbounded. As *A Course In Miracles* reminds us, there is no sense of scale or magnitude when it comes to miracles. This illusion only arises in the materially bound, intellectual mind. Accordingly, our focus and intention can be equally effective with a disturbance involving thousands of people on the other side of the planet and one person sitting in our living room. When we connect with the energy and consciousness of the soul and beyond, all human considerations of distance, size and scale of difficulty collapse. These understandings vastly extend the scope of our service, and allow us to function as agents of grace for the Earth herself, at local, regional, and planetary levels. Now, opportunities to serve arise in any situation that is present, no matter how large, complex, distant, or entrenched it may seem.

As our interactions with the world become ever more virtual, our roles as agents of grace within it follow suit. Accordingly, our service may well become largely non-local. In the course of functioning as divine conduits, igniting the desire to serve as agents of grace in those we meet, the capacity of grace to affect the planetary situation can easily and quickly go viral.

The two of us were introduced to planetary gracework before we were brought together in 1989. Each of us was utilized in particular ways by the Divine, as the following accounts illustrate.

Barry: Conduit for the Christ

As Chapter 5, "Our Grace-Note in the Planetary Song of Awakening," relates, expressing my unique soul purpose as an agent of grace really began when I was asked to serve the Office of the Christ. This grouping of higher beings could work through me very easily, because few of the human skills I had developed were relevant to what they asked me to do. I came to understand that this was quite purposeful; it nullified my ego's capacity to drag up patterns of thought and behavior from the past and forced me to stay present and surrendered in every moment. This perfect setup allowed the Office of the Christ to utilize me more effectively as a conduit for the universal Christ energy~consciousness.

Over the ensuing years, many applications for this were revealed, including the Chrysalis and other forms of planetary gracework discussed later in this chapter. But the real gift of grace had very little to do with the various forms in which it was utilized. I think this is true for most conduits of grace. Every one of us is connected to a particular matrix of higher beings who will work with us when the time is right. Each of us also has a unique frequency pattern, both in our embodied humanness and at the level of our oversoul and higher Self. This pattern of energy~consciousness we bring to the planet is the essence of the grace we are here to bring through. Whether it be through an art form such as music or painting, through a particular focus of healing energy or awareness, or simply through our presence, the unique frequency pattern that makes us who we are becomes what we pour forth, catalyzing personal and planetary awakening.

Karen: Praying for the Planet

When I lived in Montana during the 1980s, my friend Cynthia and I met each week for planetary meditations. We began by putting aside all personality concerns and going within to connect with our true Selves. Then, as we sat facing each other, we'd envision the "beautiful blue marble" of our globe between us, surrounded by the streaming presences of the countless angelic beings and higher energies that are continually working to lift what is happening on Earth. This was always an exalted experience; no matter what had preoccupied our human selves as we began to meditate together, we invariably felt uplifted by it.

We perceived these beings as individualized presences whose scope and size were far vaster than that of human beings. They were unified within a shimmering golden web of light and energy. Their consciousness clearly floated in a realm far beyond the petty considerations of human life, yet out of their great love, they did whatever was possible to relieve the suffering of humanity, uplift our minds and hearts, and inspire us to act from our better natures.

Resting in the awareness of this angelic realm, we then consciously connected with the golden web of presences surrounding the planet. We made ourselves available for this vast, nonphysical grouping to work through us in any way they saw fit. We felt their gratitude for our willingness to be "used" in this way.

Often, Cynthia and I inwardly scanned the planet for "hot spots" -- places where higher energies were greatly needed, whether to counterbalance geopathic stress in the natural world or the human miscreation that results from egoic amnesia and forgetting. Once one of us had identified such a location, we'd focus our consciousness on it together, briefly sharing what we each sensed about it, and then calling to the higher beings to do what they could through us. We added our energies to the expanded frequencies we felt them pouring in.

As we felt a sense of completion with one area, we'd scan the globe to see where our attention was drawn next. Then we repeated the same process with the next location or situation that seemed to be calling out for help. We continued this process for an hour or more, until we felt complete for that day. At the close of our sessions, we once again connected with the vast, loving presences who comprised the golden web of light around the Earth. We thanked them for their assistance and for the great blessing of working with them.

This was my first experience of transcending the human level to work for the betterment of the planet and its inhabitants. During a time when my personal world often churned with turbulent emotions, this larger service lifted my consciousness to an altogether new level. Joining energies with a dear friend provided a template of what is possible when our own frequencies combine with those of other beings for the greater good.

Barry: "Let's Get to Work!"

In 1989, shortly after Karen and I were brought together, we were introduced to another type of service involving the nonphysical realms. During this time, we often attended late-afternoon meditation gatherings at the home of Pearl Dorris and her assistant, Bill Gaum. There, we learned about the I AM Teachings, which had originally been delivered to the planet through Guy Ballard, who later referred to himself as Godfre Ray King. His books, especially *Original Unveiled Mysteries* and *The Magic Presence*, had galvanized our attention ever since we had begun to read them.

One October afternoon, the group's meditation was interrupted by the ringing of the telephone. Bill jumped up to answer it, and listened intently to the caller. Suddenly, his body pivoted toward us all. To our great surprise, he then said, quietly but with great urgency, "Turn on the TV!"

Within another minute, Bill had hung up the phone and resumed his place in the circle. By then, we all had seen the visual evidence of what he had just been told: A major earthquake had occurred in San Francisco. Bill had often emphasized the power of "making the call" for divine assistance during times of need. The Ascended Master teachings emphasized the importance of directing all requests and commands for a specific activity of grace to the I AM Presence, the aspect of Source that resides above each soul. Now, Bill turned off the TV and exhorted us to put into action all that we had read and learned. His gentle yet insistent voice said, "Let's get to work."

He then suggested that we bring our awareness into the area of the heart soul center and feel the vertical connection up to the I AM Presence above our heads, something we had regularly practiced together during the groups. After facilitating our reconnection with the I AM Presence and Source, Bill prompted us to commune with the Presence and ask with all our hearts that the divine light pour down on the San Francisco Bay Area and everyone there. As each of us made the call, the room was infused with light. Bill then continued to lead us in making the calls for particular divine energies and qualities to descend into the situation.

Working as one, everyone in our little group made the request with Bill, sending it up from our hearts to the Divine Presence above us and asking with sincerity for It to respond: "I AM the presence of divine grace and assistance, pouring forth to minimize injuries and loss of life."

Steeped as he was in the Ascended Master teachings, Bill effortlessly spoke one clear, potent decree after another. His refined voice now affirmed, "I AM the presence of divine peace, descending over the entire area." We had witnessed many people in fearful, agitated states during the TV news report. As we joined Bill in making the call, we imagined divine peace calming the frayed composure of all those under severe duress. Remembering the video footage of buildings listing or on fire and bridges collapsing, we asked for assistance for the people who were hurt, trapped or otherwise challenged: "I AM the presence of divine healing for all who are injured or afraid."

Making the calls became a self-guiding process propelled and directed by our innate empathy and our desire to lessen suffering. Each time we made a call, we felt the corresponding response from Above. As the grace-filled energies we were requesting descended upon San Francisco, we also felt them within ourselves, and knew our request had been answered. Feeling the power being released, we also knew the blessing-grace would have a deep and profound effect.

The two of us walked out of the meditation gathering that evening radically transformed. A whole new dimension of service had opened to us, and now we knew exactly how to engage with calamities and disasters around the globe. In his simple, natural manner, Bill had imparted a direct, immediate, and powerful way to make a difference. We knew now that we could offer a strong, positive contribution to any crisis, anywhere on the planet. This opened a new realm of possibility, making us aware of opportunities to serve that were far more expanded than our individual sessions and group work. Acknowledging and embracing this new role was a significant initiation, a step into a vaster scope of service.

Our shared experience during the immediate aftermath of the Loma Prieta earthquake engraved a template within us that became part of our everyday lives. This began our combined role as planetary agents of grace. During the years to come, we have often referred to what we learned that evening, and have just as often put it to use.

Karen: Synchronicity Strikes Again

Since that formative experience during the meditation gathering with Bill and Pearl, planetary gracework has been an integral part of our lives, something that naturally arises in response to whatever crosses the screen of our awareness. Yesterday, as I was editing the preceding section about responding in a sacred manner to an earthquake, a striking synchronicity occurred: A massive earthquake occurred in Japan. We spent the day going back and forth from our laptops to the TV to watch the breaking news about the 8.9 temblor, the fifth-biggest quake on record. Writing and editing alternated with making calls for the safety and well-being of all those in the areas affected by the quake and subsequent tsunami.

Later in the day, the situation in Japan took an even more ominous turn as it was revealed that several nuclear reactors threatened to overheat and possibly melt down. Although radioactive cesium was leaking from one reactor, Japanese authorities insisted this posed no risk to inhabitants. Barry and I looked at one another in disbelief.

Once again, we got to work, calling to Those On High for help to stop the overheating of the reactors, if it were in the highest to do so. We prayed that everyone involved, from the rulers of nations to the citizens now homeless and possibly badly injured, would receive the evolutionary messages this catastrophe had manifested to deliver. If the cooling towers continued to malfunction, the news report continued, the radioactive cloud released during a meltdown would waft across the Pacific to the West Coast of the U.S. We live just a few hours' drive from the Pacific Ocean, so this latest news considerably ramped up our possible personal involvement in the catastrophe. Our calls to our Friends Upstairs became more fervent as we asked for divine intervention for the reactors, for the people of Japan, for our beloved planet, and for us all.

Before we went to sleep, it occurred to me that there was a possibility, however remote, that this could turn out to be our Last Night. I recalled the film by that name that Barry and I had happened to see years ago. As the story began, the governments of the world had just announced that a massive solar event would wipe out life on Earth within the next 24 hours. The movie followed a variety of characters as they lived out their last night of this incarnation. While some sought meaning and connection, others, in futile attempts to divert their attention from their imminent demise, resorted to superficial pastimes and addictive behaviors.

As I lay in bed, the inquiry arose: *Would I do anything differently if this were, in fact, my Last Night?* The immediate response was a clear and definite *No*. My life is as it is, I realized; there is nothing to change, add, or complete. I'd like to finish writing these books, but even if that is not to be, all seemed to be in order, within and without. Our lives rest in the Great Mystery. What will be, will be.

We dissolved into sleep not knowing what morning would bring. When we awakened, we learned that several nuclear reactors remained threatened. Again we sat together and made the calls: *I AM the presence of Infinite Intelligence, providing the answers to these pressing dilemmas. And I AM Divine Love, blanketing Japan and all who are suffering there, soothing the land and the seas and the reactors.*

When our calls felt complete for the time being, Barry revealed that during the past few days, before this crisis began to unfold, he'd erected an etheric Christ pyramid over our house and energized it. Now, we both tuned in to it and asked its protective power to become even stronger. From the Christed pyramid overhead, I felt a golden mantle spreading out from our home on the farm toward the Pacific coast. It reached down to southern California to cover friends there, and up to Eugene and Corvallis, Oregon to envelop loved ones in those areas. I asked it to shelter friends in towns between these far northern and southern reaches and felt it settle over them all.

As we did our morning yoga, Barry said, "These kinds of events do more than almost anything else could to help us release our attachment to our human selves and these physical bodies." Right now, our sisters and brothers in Japan are living into this as we write. Tomorrow, it may be our turn.

By the following day, the estimated death count had risen to at least 10,000. Hearing this, the words *migration assistant* popped into my mind. During the purchase of a new laptop the day before, the salesman had recommended a software program by this name; it would handily move everything from my old computer to the new one. Now, the words took on new meaning. I, myself, could serve as a migration assistant, offering my love and blessings to all those making their Great Migration from Japan to the realms Beyond.

As I sat in meditation, a vision arose: a huge gathering of souls gently fluttering up and out of their earthly forms, heading on to their next Divine Assignment. I asked that any confusion about what had happened to them be lifted so they could release all remaining attachment to this life. Wishing them well, I felt nothing but eace and grace surrounding their migration Home.

During the times ahead, many of us may be offered opportunities to serve as "migrations assistants." We may find ourselves sitting with loved ones as they prepare for the Great Crossing, or sending out prayers and blessings on behalf of those we have never met who are in the process of returning Home. The possibilities open to agents of grace are truly unlimited.

Aligning with Our Purpose

That evening more than two decades ago, during the San Francisco earthquake, we were suddenly and unexpectedly shown a larger aspect of our soul purpose and destiny. As we sat in Pearl's little living room, nothing could have felt more right than joining with others to call for divine assistance for those in need. In that moment, the consecration to our next level of service was made.

Recent events have deepened that consecration. And the numerical synchronicity is striking: While our initiation into this level of planetary service began in 1989, it went to its next level during what was initially reported as an 8.9 earthquake. The 8 and the 9 create a potent pairing -- the intense, life-or-death transformation of the 8 joins with the possibility for transcendence symbolized by the 9. The same outer events can lead us into both.

It wasn't too long ago that Earth changes and "natural" disasters occurred with far less frequency and severity. Intervals of a few years often separated the great disasters of our time from one another. But now, they arrive within months or even weeks of each other, challenging us all to keep pace with the energetic shifts that set them into motion and follow in their aftermath.

And "natural" cataclysms are not the only events we are all pressed to encompass within our consciousness. Alongside the outer earthquakes and tsunamis, a tidal wave of awakening is roiling through humanity's awareness, impelling untold numbers of human beings to rise up in solidarity with one another in a united call for freedom. Sometimes, this coincides with a shift in the ruling class, which recognizes the evolutionary opportunity in the uprisings and works together with the people to bring about change. But when the soul-calling for freedom encounters the reactionary forces of tyranny, much hardship and bloodshed can ensue.

As all of this takes place in an increasingly simultaneous unfoldment, ever more of us are stepping forward to further humanity's evolution. Occasionally making the calls for higher assistance transitions into regularly tuning in to world events and asking how we can be utilized for the greater good of All. As our consecration to being of service to the Whole deepens, our willingness to be used by larger forces may eventually become the bedrock of our daily meditations.

Each of us is brought into this consecration as we identify and agree to fulfill our role as a planetary agent of grace. Through our own particular avenues of expression, this service unfolds. At the right moment, the knowing in our hearts and souls comes forth: *This is why I came to Earth; these are the gifts I was made to offer to the Whole.*

When we totally commit to our unique purpose, the universe is set into motion to support us in fulfilling it. The doors open for Life to bring us everything we need, including the opportunities that invite us to make our contribution. Our inner commitment and alignment magnetize these possibilities to us, and they arise in the everyday flow of our lives with absolute ease and grace, for this is the natural direction in which our souls want to travel.

This process of consecration and inner alignment is further enhanced when we consciously ask the Divine to use us to the highest degree possible for all of Life. When this is what we hold most dear in our hearts, it becomes a living prayer. The two of us have found it deeply meaningful to begin each day by offering ourselves to the Divine to use us as It will to assist the Earth and humanity to awaken and ascend into the new Golden Age. Over time, this intention instills a watchfulness, just below the surface of the conscious mind, that helps us to be attentive to the soul's calls to service. As we learn of challenging outer situations during the course of the day, we pause a moment to "make the call" to the

Divine. We add our energies to those of the higher beings who are working to alleviate earthly suffering and help us all to evolve.

When, for instance, the people of Egypt rose up during early 2011 to claim the self-determination that is the birthright of all souls, we found ourselves ending each day of writing with eating dinner as we watched Al Jazeera news, joining with our brothers and sisters across the globe in their transformational journey. Our oneness with people everywhere had never been more palpable. We felt deeply called to be with our family members half a world away as their actions bore witness to what we knew was a major activation of the planetary soul.

As we watched what was unfolding in Tahrir Square, impulses to offer ourselves in service spontaneously arose within us, just as they had during the San Francisco earthquake of 1989. Through consciously making the vertical connection to the Divine, the words to our calls and prayers formed themselves with no thought or effort: *May all unfold in peace. May this nation be lifted to its next level of sovereignty and human dignity. May the ruler recognize he is no longer aligned with the evolution of the people and step down. May all work together for the betterment of humanity!*

When government-backed attacks on those peacefully camping in Tahrir Square began, our hearts and souls were profoundly affected. This distressing turn of events deepened our call to service. Divine intervention was needed! As flaming bottles of gas flew through the tense air and protesters were shot by snipers while family members looked on in shock, our souls unified with the Divine and we called for help. We asked that the forces of hatred and separation be contained so they could do no further harm, and that all those who were peacefully following their souls be protected. *May the infinite power and intelligence of the Only One That Is pour down strength and courage into their hearts and souls, so they can persist despite these trials.* Finally and most importantly, we prayed on behalf of those acting out of soul-forgetting and ego blindness: *May they awaken to the love and wisdom of their souls. May they recognize their fundamental oneness with those who are rising up for sovereignty!*

This evening ritual soon became a much-anticipated, deeply gratifying interlude within the flow of our day. As is always the case when our soul purpose manifests, we felt uplifted and fulfilled to take part in this great transformation as conduits for grace to pour through where it was so obviously needed. This fulfillment arises out of the knowing that our presence, along with any particular actions we feel guided to bring forth, is contributing to Life. When we act from our inner essence, we rest in the awareness that there is nothing of greater importance we could be doing than serving in this way.

As the ground of our being shifts from ego to soul, the voice of doubt may arise at any point along the way. The mind can ask a thousand questions: *Do I really have the capacity to bring forth the Divine to bless earthly beings and situations? Is my contribution truly making a difference?* The most powerful antidote to the mind's fear and doubt is the sure and certain response the Divine makes to even our smallest request. This comes as an inner knowing, a clear feeling that the All in All has registered our plea. A felt sense of a movement or descent of divine energy also typically occurs in response to the request. As we gain experience in this sort of gracework, our ability to perceive that the Divine is there and responding in a real, experiential way strengthens. When we register that God really does respond to our fervent entreaties, the knowing in our hearts and souls that we do matter -- that we are, in fact, an integral aspect of the One Great Being -- grows ever stronger.

At times, we receive direct confirmation at the outer, physical level that bolsters our faith and trust. During the uprising in Egypt, when the conflict between armed, pro-government forces and mostly unarmed protesters reached a critical crescendo, we received a knowing, before the issue was discussed in the media, that the key to resolution was the Egyptian military. They held the physical-plane power in the situation, and whoever they decided to support would largely determine the outcome of the protest. We found ourselves making prayers and requests that those in the upper echelons of the Egyptian military be awakened to the truth in their souls and feel their oneness with the Egyptian people.

Within a day, the army had sided with the people and the tyrannical regime had been toppled. Our prayers, along with those of many others, had sent a psychic message and impulse to the Egyptian military leaders. Those prayers had also actuated an influx of grace from Above to cause the shift, allowing the highest possibility to come forth.

The transition to a more democratic system of government is not unfolding as smoothly as it began in Egypt. In that nation, where the people have been ruled by autocrats for decades, if not millennia, the military has not firmly sided with the people in all cases. The subsequent struggle for freedom in neighboring nations has often been met with brutal repression. We continue to pray that the initial impulse for liberty and self-determination that arose in the hearts and souls of millions throughout the Mideast can be sustained through the challenging times that may well lie ahead. The simplest of prayers can have the biggest impact: *May peace prevail. May all awaken.*

The Power of "I AM"

Pearl and Bill taught us to make decrees using two simple words whose power is unstoppable: I AM. This irreducible phrase declares the absolute, essential truth about us -- that we exist and have being. They are the same two words God spoke to Moses when he asked who it was that gave him the Ten Commandments. In Exodus 3:14, the voice of God replied, "Tell them, I AM that I AM."

Christ Jesus also used these words in key statements that referred to his unity with God. In John 8:58, Jesus says, "Truly, truly I say to you, before Abraham was born, I AM." Later, in John 15:1, he elaborates, "I AM the true vine, and my Father is the vine-dresser." Just as the voice of God had expressed aloud to Moses, at times Christ Jesus spoke as this voice and presence.

In the Vedic tradition, awakened beings including Ramana Maharshi and Nisargadatta Maharaj have articulated their understanding of the power of the truth in the words I AM. From Wikipedia -- "I Am":

> In the Hindu Advaita Vedanta, the South Indian sage Ramana Maharshi mentions that of all the definitions of God, "none is indeed so well put as the biblical statement 'I am that I am.'" He maintained that although Hindu scripture contains similar statements, the Mahavakyas, these are not as direct as given in Exodus. Further, the "I am" is explained by Sri Nisargadatta Maharaj as an abstraction in the mind of the Stateless State, of the Absolute, or the Supreme Reality, called Parabrahman: it is pure awareness, prior to thoughts, free from perceptions, associations, memories. Parabrahman is often considered to be a cognate term for the Supreme Being in Hinduism.

The true nature of each one of us is I AM. These two words contain the most fundamental frequency pattern of the core essence of who and what we truly are. Whatever we add to them is qualified by the pure light of God that continuously pours through us. In its all-loving spaciousness and allowance, the Divine agrees with whatever we deem true about ourselves. For instance, if we say, *I AM sick* and believe this to be true, the amount of the unlimited power of the Creator we are capable of channeling through our being then energizes that statement, making it true in our experience. Conversely, when we add positive qualifiers to the two fundamental words, we affirm our awareness and agreement with the highest and best it is possible for us to experience. Feel the potency in this classic decree as you say it out loud: *I AM the great omnipotence of God, made visible in my use, right now!*

Using I AM truth statements or decrees is not limited to petitioning the Divine on our own behalf. This form of communication with Source can also be used in situations affecting others -- indeed, the entire planet. In such cases, we need only add two more words: Instead of simply stating *I AM* and following with whatever we are affirming, we declare, *I AM the presence*, followed by the qualities or conditions we would like to see manifest. During the initial stages of the uprising in Egypt, for instance, the calls we made included *I AM the presence of peace in the Mideast* and *I AM the presence of freedom for all.* When we use our life energy to make calls on behalf of others, we are setting energies in motion that must inevitably outpicture at some point unless they are recalled, cancelled or overridden by a higher, more truth-aligned being. As we feel the Divine empowering the words we are given to utter, our decrees have the ability to directly affect the unspooling of human evolution. Not only that -- whenever any one of us makes a call, the divine qualities we are invoking on behalf of others also deepen within us, accelerating our own soul-evolution.

We tap into the unlimitedness of God's grace and power to whatever degree we can subconsciously allow when, either silently or aloud, we say "I AM" and follow with a statement that we wish to be demonstrated as truth or reality within manifest creation. At first, we may be operating on faith as we give voice to decrees; trust in the Divine may alternate with the ever-present fear and doubt that consume the human mind. As results begin to appear, our shaky faith turns into knowing, which engenders even greater faith that we are, in fact, one with the infinite power of the All in All.

Barry: From Victim to Victor

One wintry day during a visit to Karen's family in Indiana, I found myself driving out into the country to visit an old-growth hardwood forest, an environment I hadn't experienced since my childhood on the East Coast. Enjoying the drive through miles of farmland dotted with rows of trees and cornfields covered with snow, I was in a state of bliss until I became aware of a pervasive sense of dis-ease all around me.

As I tuned in to the stressful energy, I noticed it was arising from the fields on either side of the road. When I pulled over to meditate on what I was experiencing, I received the message that the fields had been treated with particularly harsh pesticides and had become depleted due to overuse. The stress I was feeling was the toxicity and dis-ease of the earth itself.

I wasn't sure what to do, or even whether I was supposed to do anything at all, so I brought my awareness deep into my core and asked whether there was something that wanted to happen through me. The response was a strong *Yes*. I immediately opened up the vertical axis from my heart and soul upward, connected with the Divine, and asked what could be done to balance and rectify the situation. I was shown that Ilahinoor would be a powerful way to give the land a strong burst of healing and enlifenment.

I immediately chanted *Ilahinoor* three times and began to feel its soothing energetic signature descend through my own body. I raised my hands and directed it first to the fields to the left of the car for a few minutes. There came a point when I could feel that the land had absorbed the Ilahinoor and that what was needed had been done. I then directed the transmission to the other three directions until the 360° radius had been covered. Within fifteen minutes, the entire energy of the area had substantially shifted. The sense of toxicity and stress was still present, but less so, and it was accompanied by the knowing that the infusion of Ilahinoor would continue to reduce it.

Now, as I look back on that day, I recall that when I felt the toxicity in the earth in Indiana, my first reactions included anger at the farmers for poisoning and abusing the land, fear that the toxins would affect me, and the immediate desire to get away as fast as I could. It would have been easy to ignore or deny these feelings and get back to focusing on enjoying my trip. I could have simply depressed the gas pedal to get out of there. Instead, I watched all the thoughts and feelings arise and didn't give them power. This can be hard to do when we are bombarded with events and cir-cumstances that can engender powerful feelings of fear and over-whelm. Staying conscious of what is arising instead of falling into unconscious ego-reactions is an important skill to cultivate, if we are to translate our desire to serve into the arena of everyday life.

Over time, we find our way into a dynamic balance that al-lows us to stay centered within ourselves, yet connected with the world and all who inhabit it. The belly soul center tells us when this balance is present. Resting within an ouroboric oneness with all other life forms, it reminds us that the person demonstrating for freedom in the Middle East, the homeless man watching people in thousand-dollar suits pass him by, the emaciated child dying in Africa...all are us. The reality of our oneness is coursing through our beings with increasing intensity with each passing day. Not much longer will we be able to turn our heads in denial out of fear of what is asked of us, or the subconscious belief that we are incapable of answering the call.

It can be tempting, viewing the state of the planet, to give way to feelings of helplessness and overwhelm at the size, scope, and number of crises humanity faces. We turn away from what we see when it seems we can do nothing to mitigate the suffering, much less the lack of awareness that spawns it. We avoid facing and embracing what is going on because we don't know how to deal with what it brings up within us. We want to know, we want to help, yet we don't want to be overwhelmed by what we find out or what that awareness might ask of us.

How can we consciously meet this sense of hopelessness and victimization? Nothing less than a fundamental perceptual reframing will bring about a potent shift in our response, turning victimization into a victory for all. The process begins with the realization that in this beautifully, lovingly intelligent universe that only wants to further life, each of us is given the perfect opportunities to awaken, realize our divinity, and, in turn, serve Life. This means that whatever we are facing, including both the outer circumstances and our inner reactions to them, offers an evolutionary doorway that will catalyze our own awakening and allow us to serve as agents of Grace. That is, if we walk through it.

There couldn't be a more potent call to expand our awakening and provide service then when we're feeling fear, doubt and overwhelm and want to run away or ignore it all, as I felt like doing in those fields in Indiana. Karen likes to say, "Our emotional stuff is not *in* the way -- our stuff *is* the way." This simple reminder is true of both our awakening and our service. That day in Indiana, it was relatively easy to move through the feelings, because the emotional charge wasn't too strong. At other times -- for instance, when we witness aspects of Life being horribly mistreated and feel others' pain as our own -- it may take time to move through all that is present, for the feelings are painfully deep and intense.

While our human selves are challenged to feel and release the pain that injustice and cruelty stimulate, at the soul level, realizing that everything that comes our way offers an opportunity to awaken and fulfill our purpose as agents of grace is a victory of the highest order. Cultivating this perspective fuels our capacity to face and embrace more of what shows up in our world, however difficult it may initially appear. Life is an equal opportunity provider. Every event and circumstance we encounter offers us another chance to meet it with eyes and hearts wide open.

It can be helpful to condition ourselves to be aware of when we are being triggered by something we are experiencing. In the moment we realize emotions are stirring and the mind is kicking into gear with thoughts of wanting to distract, run away, or fall into a downward spiral, we can decide to take another path. When we recognize we are being gifted with the opportunity to become conscious of what has always been there, hidden in the subconscious mind, we can participate in its transformation and transcendence.

As hard as this can be to believe, the outer events are not the issue. In every situation, our response to what arises in us as a result is the point of power. If we unconsciously fear we will be overwhelmed by whatever is buried in our subconscious, the ego will take over. When it does, the results are never the ones we would choose. Whether we go into denial, run away from the situation, or get caught in the negative, limiting thoughts and feelings that paint us as victims of a terrifying world, in the end the unconscious power and presence of the separate ego increase. That is the exact opposite of what we are here for, which is to awaken and serve as agents of grace.

We can reframe every single thing Life brings our way as an opportunity to awaken, a chance to transform another chunk of the subconscious mental and emotional material that has kept us asleep and living in denial of our inherent wholeness and divinity. People sit on the couch and stuff themselves while they watch the latest episode of their favorite TV show, or go out and buy more things although their closets are already bursting, because they don't know they can embrace their fear, doubt and suffering as a path to awakening and transforming their lives. As agents of grace, we can show the way to be present to whatever arises, face and embrace it all, and turn it over to the Divine. We can also agree to be surrogates for the rest of humanity until more humans learn how to meet whatever comes with full presence. When we are willing to feel all the potent emotions, and look at all the limiting thoughts that tend to imprison and disempower, we not only free ourselves but also contribute to the awakening of all.

When "stuff" arises and we ask for divine help with a sincere, humble desire, the gates through which grace can flow simply open. The strong negative charge of the emotions in the lower chakras acts like a magnet, drawing positively charged spiritual energies down the central channel and into the body to merge with them. This is especially pronounced when we are consciously asking for help in transforming feelings, and when we are functioning as an agent of grace on behalf of a planetary situation. The more emotion that it stirs up in us to want to see things change, the stronger the desire behind the request we make of the Divine. Again, the greater the desire, the stronger the response.

The first step in this process is to reframe crisis as a doorway to awakening. In so doing, we make a choice that takes us beyond victimization. The next step is to face and embrace whatever is arising, without and within, as the path through and beyond the crisis. By being willing to experience all that we were unable to previously be with and then to turn it over to God, we release whatever has caused us to live in a limited, distorted way. This invites the superconscious levels of being to descend and transform it into a manifestation of our true, divine nature.

Developing the ability to meet whatever comes as described here allows us, as embodied souls, to participate in human evolution in a way that ascended masters and divine beings cannot. Because we inhabit a human form, we are attuned to the collective unconscious, the pool of unresolved thought and feeling that keeps humanity asleep and in bondage when it is seen as real and true. The thoughts and feelings rising up within any one of us are the same as those present in the whole of humanity, for they are stored in the collective unconscious. This huge pool of psychic "stuff" lies buried, unfelt and unseen until something triggers its eruption. When our "stuff" is set off, we have a chance to transform it -- not only for ourselves, but for everyone else. Each time we face and feel what is arising, the consciousness we are able to bring to it all leaves an imprint in the collective energetic field, making it that much easier for the next person to respond with awareness instead of reaction. And every little bit of that sticky emotional charge that is transformed and dissolved reduces the remaining charge in the collective unconscious. When we transform the shadow material that has limited us, we are creating an imprint in the planetary mind fields of a new way for human energy~consciousness to function.

The process we go through acts something like a transformational homeopathic remedy that enters the global mind fields. It sends out a seed crystal of truth that can shift not only ourselves, but, since we are all fundamentally one being, humanity as a whole. Because the truth is far more powerful than illusion, it takes only a little bit of truth to recrystallize the collective consciousness into its next level of realization. This makes it easier for the next person to do what we have previously done. Having observed the course of soul-awakening sessions for many years, we see that people are able to process unconscious material much more quickly today than when we began in the late 1980s. That's because agents of grace -- including you, the reader of this book -- have been willing to perform their functions.

As planetary grace workers, we have the potential to be the small percentage of collective humanity that transforms countless limiting patterns, replacing them with the seed crystals of coherence and truth that enable major, collective shifts to occur. What a powerful way to fulfill our soul purpose and destiny as agents of grace, while accelerating our own awakening! This, in turn, makes us even more effective at what we came here to do. As we empty ourselves of all that does not need to be within us, we become superconductors for the Divine to flow through us, and function ever more elegantly and efficiently in our God-given roles.

Fear of the "Negative"

For all the reasons presented above, our experience indicates that it is not possible to awaken or be an effective agent of grace unless we become adept at facing and transforming our own shadow. In our groups and workshops, we have heard a number of viewpoints that argue against doing this deep inner work. One line of New Age thought advocates simply rising above all seemingly negative conditions, both external and internal, in the belief that engaging any so-called negative content only feeds the negativity. While this would be true if we believed we were victims of the negative conditions, it is not the case when we take an empowered approach to them.

The first step is to realize that all discordant or non-life supporting conditions have no basis at the level of absolute truth or reality. They are, instead, relative realities created through human consciousness in the illusion of separation from the love, life and perfection of Source. Most life-limiting conditions and crises on Earth are spawned by human thoughts and emotions that are experienced and embraced as truth or reality. That includes psycho-emotional material that is suppressed because of the belief that it is real and has power. The act of suppressing it is also the testimony that we believe it has reality and power over us. We empower our discordant inner experiences by believing they are real and reacting to them accordingly. The infinitely creative fabric of Life then mirrors our actions back to us as the circumstances and conditions in our lives.

When we bring disturbing thoughts and feelings into the light of consciousness and question their truth or reality, we take a position of power through directly confronting them. Rather than denying their existence, we stand firm in the truth that they have no basis in ultimate reality. When examined, all are seen to be illusions of the separative ego-mind. In more than two decades of facilitating inner explorations, not one person has ever discovered a negative thought, feeling or perception that was ultimately true.

We only fear looking at disturbing elements in ourselves and the world because we think to look at them gives them power and truth. When we believe the illusion is real, we are temporarily asleep, forgetting our true, divine nature. Nothing anyone can do at an outer level can change this eternal truth. To turn away because we subconsciously believe the energies or actions of another have some innate basis or power is to actually give them power. In most cases a subconscious fear of being engulfed and overwhelmed by negativity is present, which again attests to a belief in one's own powerlessness and the power of something that has no basis in absolute truth or reality. Even to fear Earth changes or human-created threats to physical life is to give power to the relative level.

As souls, nothing can harm us, and nothing can befall us that is not in our best interest. This is especially true when we've given our lives to God. The greater our surrender and attendant faith, the more we are lifted out of the chaotic processes of the collective karmic unfoldment. Surrendering to whatever arises is far easier when we know the loving hand of the Divine is behind it all.

That said, observing the many tragedies of the human experience, especially our mistreatment of one another and our beautiful planet, can stimulate a lot of emotion. At times, the sadness at all the suffering can feel overwhelming. Similarly, facing the specter of a planetary apocalypse caused by climate or other Earth changes can surface intense fear. But when we turn away because we think we are giving power to something that seems to betray the truth of our inherent divinity, we are creating exactly what we fear.

Instead of fearing we will empower the negative or cause further harm by even witnessing it, there is another path. We can instead be with our inner reactions, observe what arises in feeling, thought and perception, and bring it to the light of truth. When we face and embrace our own pain and suffering, fear and doubt, we free ourselves to be fully present with whatever arises. We are then able to experience things as they are, instead of through our unconscious filters. Then, we can stand as a clear witness, shining the light of the soul onto whatever we encounter.

Simply being present in this state of consciousness is a creative act, and a blessing in and of itself. When we witness sleeping souls forgetting their oneness and harming one another through the fearful illusions they project, the light of truth enters the collective mind fields. The trance state of all involved is lessened by even one person witnessing from an awakened state. Thus, facing the world's negativity is a profoundly empowering act, a gift of grace to all, when we stand firmly rooted in the light of absolute truth.

Transcending the Spiritual Ego

As discussed above, the spiritual ego often tries to convince us that there is no need to examine our shadow material; we can simply turn toward the light and all that it deems negative will dissolve into that radiance. Another "spiritual" perspective insists that everything that happens in the world of form is just illusion. According to this mindset, all that awakening asks of us is to transcend into the unmanifest domains and reside in and as the emptiness. While that may be true when viewed from the absolute perspective of the undifferentiated, pre-manifest states of being, it excludes all other dimensions of being -- and most importantly, that of incarnate divinity, our embodied, human life. If God is All That Is, the human realm cannot be excluded; the truth is a oneness that is absolutely inclusive. As all three dimensions of being awaken, these issues ultimately resolve themselves, for the evolutionary vector is propelling the soul into including all facets of its existence -- unmanifest and manifest, transcendent and imminent, form and formless. In the oneness of the soul and its larger Source, all finds its natural place.

An additional "spiritual" belief system holds that higher beings or the evolutionary forces of the cosmos are going to take care of everything, so there's nothing for us to do at this level. While it's true that great assistance is being rendered to the Earth and that the evolutionary vector is toward awakening, we are integral parts of the process. Each soul is an aspect of the One, moving through grace to transform and awaken its many facets. To a large degree, the transformation of this planet happens through us. The light becomes fully embodied only as it descends into the depths of our lower chakras and even further into the chakras in our legs and below our feet. As the light descends and the belly soul center awakens, our consciousness becomes increasingly connected to all of life. We feel the reality of what is happening to those who are starving to death in Africa, being slaughtered in the Middle East, or dying alone and homeless in the streets of America. They are us, and we cannot escape this reality when we are awake all the way up and all the way down.

Ultimately, our species as a whole must find its way through and beyond its experience of limitation and fear, if we are to birth a new EarthHeaven. Each one of us must go through this process of awakening and transformation. Attempting to escape any part of it would be counter to the evolutionary impetus that grows stronger by the day. We cannot look to our leaders, higher forces, spiritual beings, or extraterrestrials to do this for us. The collective awakening foretold in countless prophecies means that each element within the Whole must consciously participate!

The Exponential Power of Groups

As we have all probably experienced, an individual call for grace can have potent effects. Who among us has not, in a moment of extremity, sent forth a call for help from Beyond? When things get tough, even atheists and agnostics find themselves hoping there is, despite the firmest doubt and disbelief, a greater power that will intercede. To their great surprise, their calls are often answered in ways that are impossible to miss.

When an individual is centered in the Divine and humbly, sincerely asking for help, the call for assistance will be answered with corresponding spiritual potency. This effect is multiplied when people join energies around the highest intentions they can summon; the level of spiritual power and grace that comes forth automatically increases exponentially. Jesus expressed the principle behind this in declaring, "For where two or three are gathered together in my name, there am I in the midst of them." (Matthew 18:20)

The exponential function that occurs when groups of people join energies makes the effect far more than the sum of the parts. For this reason, the ascended masters have always prompted the two of us to do as much group work as possible. They have repeatedly told us that, from our perspective, we can't see the immense effect it has. They have also said that groups of people strongly attract the ascended host because of the opportunity their combined consecration creates. When we offer ourselves as conduits through which higher beings can pour their exalted energy and consciousness, they are, in essence, overlighting us, and their power can be transduced through us to the planet. We need them and they need us, creating a situation of perfect synergy.

Each of us has a unique energetic pattern, consisting of our astrological imprint at birth, our genetic and familial matrix, our soul experiences in this and previous lifetimes, and all the other imprints such as race, nationality, and so on. When people come together, the collective energy~consciousness mandala they create becomes a fractal hologram of humanity as a whole that is exponentially more resonant with the totality than the energetic pattern of any one of its members. The grace they can access as a group is nearly always far more powerful than that which an individual can call in. In addition, the divine blessings can be more effectively transmitted to the planetary mind fields when many beings are receiving and distributing them in synchrony.

The fundamental key to group effectiveness is a strong heart and soul alignment of all involved. When the two of us facilitate groups, we begin by inviting everyone to join energies to create a group soul. During teleconferences, we start by asking participants to state their names and locations. We then suggest that everyone visualize each of us on the call as a point of light on the planet, and then envision the pattern created by all the points scattered across the globe.

Another way to foster group coherence is to ask each group member to visualize a stream of light coming out from the heart soul center and joining with the light-stream from each other person's soul, as though we were standing in a large virtual circle. As the individual streams of soul energy merge, a group soul presence that is a composite of all souls involved is created. We then connect our individual soul centers and the group soul to Source through the vertical channel. Next, we consciously connect with all of humanity, asking that everything that occurs during our group work, and particularly all the blessing-grace that pours in from Above, be instantly transmitted to all souls everywhere.

As planetary evolution accelerates, teleconferences and webcasts dedicated to global gracework are proliferating. It can be highly meaningful to join in such group endeavors for the betterment of all. But simpler, humbler means are also effective. We can get together with friends by phone or in person, or even set a predetermined time to meditate together for a specific purpose such as world peace. Any time a group gathers for the purpose of awakening and transformation, the principles discussed here can be consciously utilized to greatly enhance the effects for collective humanity.

17

GraceWork with Gaia

The Earth is a living, sentient being. While we humans, along with the cetaceans, may be the highest evolutionary forms on the planet, we are but part of the Earth's higher consciousness and being. This places us in a unique position to act as conduits for spiritual energies to infuse the planet. We are the lightning rods that bring spirit into matter.

The planetary awakening and unfoldment is not limited to humans. Since all species and the planet herself are going through a dimensional shift process, we human beings can't make this shift on our own. Our evolution is integrally connected to that of Gaia, the great mother that holds all life on planet Earth within her loving embrace. Our planet's awakening and ascension are the larger story of what is happening to us as human beings.

When we step into advanced levels of planetary gracework, we directly connect with the great living, sentient being we call Earth. In our capacity as agents of grace, we serve as bridges uniting the highest levels of spirit with our beloved planet, assisting the Earth to awaken and make her ascension. This is the larger evolutionary process that is unfolding.

Local Planetary GraceWork

Gaia's being includes all the species that reside on and within her. Each is an integral part of her conscious beingness. For our planet to take her next evolutionary steps, each species must be healed and made whole again so that it, too, can evolve as part of her all-encompassing being. We humans take part in this process whenever we consciously connect with the nature kingdoms and act as an agent of grace on their behalf. We are surrounded by opportunities to function as planetary conduits of grace. From the house plants that enliven our interiors to the animals with whom we share our environs, we can begin right where we live.

The primary dimension of our being that connects with the life of the Mother of All is the hara or tan tien soul center deep within the belly. When this dimension of being awakens, we naturally connect with the unified intelligence that unites all species into the vast, interwoven fabric of Life. The two of us, along with many others, have found that the more we work with Ilahinoor, the more this dimension opens to us. As we become increasingly aware of what is going on in the web of life that surrounds and interpenetrates us, we are more open and available to receive communications that let us know our help is needed.

An example of this ability to tune in occurred years before we had ever heard of Ilahinoor. In 1992, we were living on the island of Kaua'i. One afternoon, a couple we knew who had established a spiritual center on the island visited us. While we meditated together, Donna received the message that we needed to do some energy work together to protect the island. She added that a number of people she knew had recently felt the presence of some sort of threat to the island. We, too, had noticed a sense of something ominous lurking right behind the seemingly serene surface of our everyday experience. We joined with Donna and Robert in invoking divine protection around the island and offering prayers for the highest possible outcome of any future threats.

About a week later, the divine plan was revealed. One early September day, a Category Five hurricane, the strongest possible, made a bullseye strike on the island. Despite the extensive damage, few injuries occurred and not one death could be directly attributed to the storm. If this was not a miracle, it was the closest thing to it we had ever witnessed. Many others must have felt the same, for a book of stories by those who had weathered the hurricane was given the title *Miracles of Iniki.*

Our own account of our profound experiences during Hurricane Iniki can be found in our first book, *Soul Awakening.* After the storm, we learned that others, like us, had felt that some kind of crisis was imminent on our beloved island. Just as we had done with Robert and Donna, they had devoted themselves to going within to call for grace. How all of this inner work affected the unfoldment of outer events is impossible to know for sure, but many of us felt sure it was an important component in the grace-filled experience that transpired.

Barry: Looking Out

The potent effects of spiritual presence have been brought home over and over during my fifteen summers at Eddy Gulch fire lookout, which sits atop a half-million acres of wilderness in the coastal range of northern California. Eddy Gulch is the sole lookout on the Salmon River Ranger District of the Klamath National Forest. When I arrived in 1997, I immediately felt an immense sense of love and stewardship for this magnificent country. As I sat on top of a mountain in the very center of this majestic landscape, I felt my auric field expand to encompass it all, as my being became a component of the larger Whole. I studied the streams, canyons, ridges, peaks and gulches of this place, wanting to know her intimately. A deep love and adoration for her beauty and magnificence has always spontaneously flowed forth from my being.

Due to excessive fire suppression and a climate that is warming and drying, the coastal ranges of northern California have endured some of the most dramatic wildfires on the entire planet. In 1977 and 1987, the Salmon River District experienced two massive, catastrophic fires, each around 100,000 acres. These fires became the stuff of local legend; nearly everyone who lived in the area during one or the other has stories to tell. This history, along with the severity of the landscape and the few roads into and out of each settled area, makes the specter of fire a serious, ever-present concern to everyone who lives and works along the river.

In 1999, a very large fire started just south of Salmon River country on the Shasta Trinity National Forest. It began in August and raged until the snow came in October. At its peak, it roared up to the boundary of the Salmon River District, a high ridge all along its south and west sides. Everyone felt certain it would spill over and burn right through the district.

That never happened. The fire burned right up to the forest boundary along a perimeter of 10 miles or so, but never jumped across. Firefighting efforts alone could not explain this uncanny outcome. On either side of the district, 150,000 acres burned, but nothing caught fire on Salmon River. At the time, it seemed as though the divine hand had moved; through grace, this beautiful, pristine land had been spared.

In 2002, a large fire started to the northwest and burned southeast toward the heart of Salmon River. Again it stopped, without a lot of fire suppression activity. Everyone knew we had "dodged the bullet," and I became aware that something profound was going on.

In 2006 another large fire started on the Shasta-Trinity Forest and moved rapidly north, this time to the east of the 1999 fire. Again, it came to the edge of the Salmon River district and stopped. In 2008, massive fires started everywhere in the coast range, from just north of San Francisco to the Oregon border. More than half a million acres burned between the summer solstice, when they began, and sometime in October, when Mother Nature finally put them out. On a map of the fires that summer, the Salmon District conspicuously stands out as one of the very few relatively untouched areas. The mountainous northwest and southeast corners of the district burned, but the heart of the Salmon River drainage that is so vital to dwindling salmon and steelhead populations remained intact. Usually a number of significant lightning storms result in fires throughout the summer. That summer, there were none. That was an amazing blessing, since heavy smoke covered the entire area, making detection of any new fires nearly impossible. Everyone in the U.S. Forest Service Fire Suppression group knew that if fires did start, it would be almost impossible to detect them before they became entrenched and rapidly grew.

Sometime during that year, I was awakened in the middle of the night by a flash of lightning to the west. I prayed that the thunderstorm would not come onto our district. It traveled northward along the western boundary, stopped just where it would have crossed over, turned around and went backward, and finally dissipated. This is just one of many stories I could tell.

At first I didn't really grasp the effects of my daily meditation and spiritual communion. It took the first two major fire years to really register what was going on. One day in meditation, I was shown that all the mornings and evenings spent communing with the Divine, coupled with my conscious, loving communion and sense of stewardship of the entire area, formed an energetic canopy of harmony over the district. I knew my role was to watch over and protect the entire expanse of thousands of acres, and every bit of my being was dedicated to carrying out this "assignment." Often during meditation I felt my aura spread out to encompass it all, as I communed in love and gratitude for her nurturing presence and beauty. At times I consciously called in divine energies to protect and benefit the entire region.

During my first few seasons on Eddy Gulch, I wasn't consciously focusing my inner work on preventing fires from ravaging the district, but I later understood that everything I was doing and where it arose in consciousness contributed to this result. I don't want to imply that what occurred through me was the only or even the predominant source of grace. Many other souls who live on the river and elsewhere were praying with me, and the assistance of angels and other divine beings cannot be overlooked. Still, the knowing remains that the spiritual presence I called forth and my role there as a steward for this blessed country made a difference.

While I am very grateful for being utilized in this way, I am even happier to know, with the certainty that direct experience alone can give, that the power of our divinity to harmonize destructive transformational processes is far more immense than the human mind can conceive. During these pivotal times, we sincerely hope that many who read this book will become conscious of just how powerful a catalyst each of us can be in birthing a new age in beauty and harmony instead of through the passage of chaos and destruction.

Karen: Blessing the Waters

During the early 1980s, I took part in a series of women's gatherings centered on Native American teachings and practices, all of which honored the land and the natural world. One Fall, our group traveled from Boulder, Colorado to Ojo Caliente Hot Springs in northern New Mexico. There, we made a large medicine wheel on the earth, to which each of us added the stones we had been guided to bring to the circle. Feeling the power of the intentions and prayers participants voiced as they placed their stones and watching the medicine wheel come together in a sacred manner brought us all into a deeper relationship with Creation and its Creator.

We then went into the indoor pool to give back to the waters that had nurtured the many thousands of people who had visited the springs over the years. Lorraine, our leader, began by pointing out, "Most of the people who come here are stressed out, in need of healing and balancing. They *take* from the waters without giving back. Over time, this depletes the life energies of the waters. We are here to give thanks for this great service, and to ask the Creator to replenish the energy of the waters through us."

She then invited each of us to share a poem, a song, a story, or a simple, heartfelt prayer for blessings with the group. The intention of all that would be shared was to give back to the hot springs many of us had come to love through previous visits. As each woman spoke, sang, or chanted, what came forth not only blessed the waters, but all of us, as we drank in the beauty and soulfulness of each contribution.

I had always felt a deep connection with the natural world, and had often felt profoundly grateful for the nurturing sustenance I've always received from nature. But I had never consciously expressed my gratitude as we were now doing. At this very early stage in my spiritual journey, it had never occurred to me to call forth blessings for a place I was visiting or even inhabiting. Our co-created ceremony at the hot springs provided a template for giving back to the land, the waters, the trees, and all other aspects of Life on countless future occasions.

As wonderful as it was to join with a large group of beings to bless the hot springs, it can be equally meaningful to invite blessing-grace to shower a place on our own, or with just one or two others. On our journey through life, Barry and I often join energies to bless the places we love, or locations that seem in need of loving care. When we visit the coast of northern California, for example, if we detect tension along a fault line, we ask the Divine to balance and harmonize the energies there. If we sense that human miscreation has left a residue of discordance, we ask that it be lifted and replaced by healing and purity.

Transmissions of Grace for Planetary GraceWork

Since the Transmissions of Grace entered our lives, they have proven to be easily accessed, user-friendly, and very effective methods of inviting healing and upleveling into any situation on the planet. Our friend Skandar, whose stories are featured in the chapters devoted to each of the transmissions, has been a pioneer in this area. At one point, Skandar received the guidance to construct an energetic grid in the Owens Valley, on the east side of the California Sierras. In the center of his grid lies Owens Lake, which flows into viaducts that carry water to Los Angeles. The grid continuously pulses the energies of the three Transmissions of Grace, in turn encoding Owens Lake. Every day, this highly charged water flows out of the taps of homes in the L.A. basin, catalyzing unknown, untold awakening in the City of Angels.

Skandar has had a powerful influence on us, opening up all kinds of possibilities to use the Transmissions of Grace with plants, animals, and the Earth. His example has heightened our awareness of the immense field of possibility for sharing the Transmissions of Grace with the flora, fauna, and mineral lifeforms we meet along our way. This has become something we do wherever we are, for very few areas remain where the Earth is not diseased and stressed.

One of our favorite ecosystems is the redwood forests along the coast of northern California. We feel a deep soul connection with these great, ancient beings who have anchored the energy fields of this entire region for millennia, yet have been logged until just 3% of their original number still stand. One of the most pristine remaining areas is right below the Oregon border near Crescent City, California. One day, as we drove through a remote section of these precious groves, we felt called to give Ilahinoor to certain trees along the way. Every few hundred yards, a particular tree would call out to receive the grace. Gradually, a chain of Ilahinoor-infused trees stretched across the entire forest. We sensed that this not only provided a barrier to wildfire and disease, but also infused the major stream in the area, which nourishes the entire ecosystem. We felt grateful to be able to give back in this way to a place that has provided soul-nurturance to us for decades.

GraceWork with Gaia's Subtle Energy Systems

As the planetary awakening gathers momentum, ever more human beings realize the Earth is, like ourselves, a living, sentient being. Just as our subtle anatomy contains major and minor vortices, or chakras, and a system of energy lines and meridians through which subtle energies flow, Gaia possesses a similar subtle energetic system of power points, vortices, and lines, embedded within a geometric network that has been called the Earth Grid. This subtle energetic system contains and conducts all of Gaia's energy~consciousness processes. In the same way that an acupuncture needle placed in a meridian point stimulates energy shifts throughout the entire human body, conscious infusions of grace produce significant effects when directed into the Earth's subtle structures. As with acupuncture, these effects are not merely local, but affect the planet as a whole.

The human subtle anatomy contains many thousands of small energy passageways called nadis. They permeate the entire body with a finely woven web of channels for life energy or prana. Similarly, minor energy passageways and nodes, which are the crossing points of the passageways, exist everywhere on the Earth's surface. Many of us have had the experience of walking through a forest and being drawn to a particular place within it, for no outer reason. The place simply feels good to us. We might find ourselves climbing onto a boulder or sitting under a tree to absorb the energetic blessings of this spot we inexplicably like. At other times, a sense of unease or an ominous feeling propels us away from a location. The energy feels "off" and we cannot wait to distance ourselves from it. In these places, the flows of energy have been blocked or distorted, often by toxins or other life-alienating human activities.

If someone digs a large hole in the ground and fills it with cement, metal, or other energetically opaque materials -- or worse, toxic substances -- these materials don't just sit there. Their presence creates an effect, one that most of us would deem negative. The health of the ecosystem, along with the energy of the entire area, may be affected for many miles in all directions. Conversely, if we infuse a transmission of higher-dimensional energy and light into the earth or a living being such as a tree, the energy radiates through the energetic passageways that honeycomb the planet's subtle anatomy. Many of these pathways are physically obvious -- they follow the course of rivers and streams or form the backbone of mountain ranges. Others are not as easily detected, for they lack an overt physical counterpart. The more sensitive we become, the more likely we will feel them as places where the energy is enhanced, nurturing, peaceful and often sublime. Harmonious energy tends to center within the planetary body in places like a glade in a forest or a jewel-like lake in the mountains. These kinds of locations can be excellent places to practice planetary gracework.

In addition to the countless smaller oases of grace that dot the planet, the Earth is also covered with more significant power points and sacred sites, places where some of the most potent of Gaia's spiritual energies are concentrated. Think of Mt. Fuji in Japan, Kilimanjaro in Africa, Denali in Alaska, Ayer's Rock in Australia, the Dead Sea, and the Great Pyramid; these storied places figure in countless legends over the millennia of human history. Writer and photographer Martin Grey has devoted decades to traveling the planet in search of sacred sites. In each place he visits, he deeply connects with the spirit of the land and its sacred features, and then captures its sublime beauty in extraordinary photographs. His website, http://sacredsites.com/ offers a doorway into the exquisite realm of sacred sites the world over.

Virtually everyone has some type of natural or human-created sacred site within driving distance of home, and many of us enjoy traveling to such special locations. The opportunities to receive and contribute grace-filled energies are particularly heightened in these places. Since, throughout the ages, human beings have intentionally visited these places of power, a potent cross-resonance between the collective human soul and the soul of Gaia has taken hold at these locations. Consciously weaving the interdimensional and terrestrial realms together at these points greatly accelerates the spiritualization of the Earth and humanity, the essence of the personal and planetary ascension process.

Other planetary energy~consciousness matrices encompass larger areas of the globe. Many contain sacred geometric structures or other designs that cause them to naturally resonate with the planet's energetic bodies at many levels simultaneously. Most have been discovered by individuals receiving higher-dimensional communication from spiritual beings. A few are particularly important for those living in North America, and include some that the two of us have personally experienced.

The Earth Star North America grid was discovered by Dorothy Leon and consists of a latticework of 19 power points in a large circle that covers a significant portion of the upper intermountain states, with the Grand Tetons at the center. The Tetons, according to information received through Alice Bailey from the ascended masters at the beginning of the twentieth century, are where the first of the seven root races of humanity entered the Earth's domain long, long ago. The Tetons are also an ascended master retreat. The 19 points on the grid are geographic features, many of which are power points in their own right. They include Mt. Shasta, Mt. Whitney, and Lake Tahoe in California, and the Platte and Arkansas Rivers in Nebraska and Kansas. We learned about this grid from Dan Shaw, whose company, Vortex Maps, offers a treasure trove of information on planetary gridworks. Information on this grid appears on his website: http://www.vortexmaps.com/.

During the 1990s, two friends of ours were guided to travel from their home in Hawai'i to the mainland, buy an RV, and visit all 19 of the grid points. At each one, they did Earth activation work involving prayers, ceremony, and multidimensional light work. For most of a year, they journeyed around the intermountain states, guided by higher-dimensional beings, to help light up and activate this grid. Their spiritual odyssey included many amazing experiences as they wove their path of grace over the western U.S.

We, too, have been given many similar assignments during the years we've been together. One involved a trip to the eastern U.S. to travel from North Carolina to Vermont to help activate the Arkhom grid, which Peter Champoux has documented in detail in his book, *Gaia Matrix*. Information on this grid can be found on his website: http://geometryofplace.com/gaiamatrix.html. We traveled the gridline from one nodal point to another to awaken each of the points. At each location, we opened our vertical channel to Source and the higher-dimensional beings guiding us, in order to infuse and encode each point with particular energies and geometries we receive from Beyond. We functioned as interdimensional bridges, "acupuncture needles" grounded to the Earth through which divine energies could enter and encode the planetary grid with subtle, antenna-like geometries that continue to download spiritual energies into the Arkhom grid to this day.

The Planetary Grid

The elegant, geometric structure of the Planetary Grid both contains and overlights all the other subtle energy passageways, power points and vortices that crisscross the Earth. We can interact with planetary consciousness on a causal level through this macro grid structure that surrounds and interpenetrates the globe, weaving together all levels and dimensions of Gaia's soul. The Planetary or Earth Grid is the form-patterning template for the entire planet, the causal energetic matrix through which Gaia connects, interfaces with and organizes everything that occurs within her being. This grid provides the means for unfathomable quantities of multidimensional energy~consciousness to be communicated instantaneously to the myriad lifeforms that comprise Gaia's being. As has often been said, when a butterfly's wings flutter in the rain forest, a grain of sand on a beach on the other side of the world responds. The Planetary Grid is the structure through which this communication occurs.

The current grid is operating at a fourth-dimensional level, while also being anchored to the third-dimensional, physical Earth. This grid is often referred to as the Becker-Hagens grid after the researchers who documented it. Many books have been written about this grid, and an excellent website is devoted to it: http://www.bibliotecapleyades.net/mapas_ocultotierra/esp_mapa_o cultotierra_12.htm

Within the grid are twelve macro grid points through which the most significant flows of energy~consciousness occur. They are also the points through which the planet receives the most potent influxes of higher-dimensional energy from the galaxy and beyond. This makes them the most effective points for infusing Gaia's subtle energy structure with spiritual frequencies of grace. These twelve grid points are in the center of the twelve pentagons that form the dodecahedral aspect of the grid's energetic structure. The second primary formation within the grid's crystalline pattern is an icosahedron composed of twenty equilateral triangles. These two facets combine to form the icosadodecahedral structure of Gaia's foundational gridwork.

Within this larger pattern lie many other grid points of varying degrees of significance. For instance, the points in the center of the twenty triangles on the icosahedron portion of the grid's framework are very important, but have a masculine, yang nature. They are therefore not as receptive to inflowing energies as those within the dodecahedron, whose nature is feminine or yin, but they are still of major importance for planetary gracework, since they are the next most potent points on the Planetary Grid. Many other grid points are created where two or more lines cross, and the power of each point is proportional to the number of grid lines that cross to form it. The larger the number of intersections, the more potent the point. The lines themselves offer ways to key into the planetary soul-sphere, though less potently than the crossing points.

We have been doing gracework with the Planetary Grid for decades, and it remains central to our planetary service. We begin by connecting with the grid on the inner planes, and then project our consciousness into one of the grid points we are intuitively drawn to connect with. We then tune in to that locus, just as we would with a person or situation, to see what, if anything, is required.

As always, the inner alignment from soul to Source facilitates accessing both the highest, clearest information and the levels of spiritual grace that provide what is needed. We can invite the soul and beyond to convey all necessary guidance about whether there is something we are to contribute as an agent of grace, and the nature of that service. We need to be vigilant so the ego-mind does not step in and mislead us or inflate our personal role. It is vital to leave any sense that we are doing anything on our own outside the sacred cathedral of the inner planes when we embark on this level of planetary gracework.

Locating the power points on the planetary grid is now very easy, thanks to the Google Earth application on VortexMaps.com, http://www.vortexmaps.com/hagens-grid-google.php. This application superimposes the Earth Grid onto Google Earth, so any of us can cruise around the planet, panning in and out to find grid points close to where we live or travel, as well as more inclusive points we can travel to via Google Earth on the inner level. We can also physically journey to points near us to delve into how we experience these energetic vortices, and whether our input would be helpful there. In addition, we can locate grid crossing points near places anywhere on the globe where challenging situations exist. These are ideal places to relieve environmental, social or geopathic stresses, for they are analogous to acupuncture points in the physical body. The points closest to large cities and toxic conditions such as nuclear reactors, polluted rivers, and so on tend to be congested or blocked. Points in the vicinity of human crises such as wars, epidemics, and famines offer other opportunities to consider focusing our energy. Being able to zoom in to the grid points and connect with them visually greatly increases the "phase lock" that can be made. Dan Shaw's VortexMaps application offers us all a major upgrade in our planetary gracework tool kit.

The Christ or Unity Consciousness Grid

While many sacred scientific researchers and others are aware of the Planetary Grid, relatively few have as yet become conscious of the higher-dimensional Unity or Christ Consciousness Grid. Since it exists at and beyond the fifth-dimensional level, part of the reason it remains obscure is that few human beings have been capable of accessing those realms of Creation. This exalted grid is becoming increasingly interwoven in, through, and around the Earth Grid. It operates at the fifth- and sixth-dimensional level.For a beautiful image of the Christ or Unity Consciousness Grid, go to:
http://www.luisprada.com/Protected/the_planetary_grids.htm·

This luminous and numinous matrix of divine consciousness has been coming into existence for a very long time and significantly coalesced with the first coming of the Christ through Jesus two thousand years ago. Since then, it has gradually become increasingly defined as more and more people awaken to their true nature. The great ones who have become enlightened and God-realized, and especially those that have ascended, are both the major contributors to this energetic field and the ultimate stewards of it.

The formation of this grid has been the principal energetic focus of the divine beings who have been working to facilitate the dimensional shift and personal and planetary ascension. As humanity and the Earth ascend, the Earth Grid and the Christ Consciousness Grid interlock and fuse, resulting in the translation and merger of the existing grid into a more complex, higher-energetic Unity Consciousness web.

Each of us strengthens the Christ Consciousness Grid whenever we consciously connect with our divinity, for our God-nature directly resonates with its frequencies. Because we are in physical bodies, which are connected to the existing Planetary Grid, our beings become the interface between the two grids. Thus, our very presence on Earth helps the two to interlock, progressively grounding the Christ or Unity Consciousness Grid into the planet.

From a macro energetic perspective, this is the ultimate function of those who are here to be planetary agents of grace. Because we are self-reflective and thus capable of consciously realizing our true nature, we, along with the cetaceans, are the species capable of fusing the two grids. This is why awakening souls are scattered all over the planet, rather than living together in isolated enclaves. We are each like little grounding rods, placed at very specific points on the planet to interact with the Planetary Grid and ground higher frequencies. Sitting at home quietly connected to the Divine, we are subtly, unobtrusively transducing higher frequencies into the Earth's causal energetic grid. Instantly, the unified crystalline structure carries the energies all through the latticework, sparking awakening and Self-realization everywhere.

Awareness and intention provide an even stronger connection and flow of energies into the grids. As we consciously connect with the planetary gridworks, visualizing them and feeling into their energetic nature, we are, in effect, logging onto Gaia's main "server." Once we are in the system, we are capable of conscious, direct reprogramming. Any intention, thought, image, or energetic configuration projected into the grid is quickly distributed to all points that compose it.

Major service can be rendered through consciously connecting with the Christ Consciousness Grid, for it forms the stronger, more causal energy web surrounding the planet. Its level of consciousness also represents humanity's next evolutionary step. The manner in which the grids merge determines how the dimensional shift will occur. As the fourth-dimensional grid disintegrates, it is important that the more inclusive pattern of the Unity Grid be in place, so that the planetary energy field can immediately recrystallize around it. If the two weave together seamlessly, all the matter~energy~consciousness of the old grid will easily translate into the new octave, and an orderly, peaceful shift will result. To the degree that this does not occur, the planet will experience chaos in the form of Earth changes and human-generated catastrophes. The good news is that the energetic differential between the grids is decreasing every day as the grids are rapidly merging.

Each of us has the capacity to affect the energetic ease and coherence of this shift. Consciously joining with others to receive energies for the Earth exponentially increases the effects. Four people may have sixteen times the effect of one, for the exponential function multiplies our effectiveness when we join energies.

As mentioned previously, at the beginning of our teleconferences we invite everyone to share their names and locations. We then collectively visualize each of the participants as a point of light beaming out from that part of the world. Next, we join to envision all of us linking up and forming a web of light and energy. This automatically creates a connection between the existing Earth Grid and the Christ Consciousness Grid and offers blessing-grace to all beings everywhere, as well as to the Earth herself. Our intention is to serve as energetic witnesses for all of humanity, so that the higher infusions of grace that pour in during our time together and the resulting transformations in consciousness will spread throughout the Planetary Grid with "contagious ease."

Any of us can also deeply ground the Christ Consciousness Grid into the planet by doing Earthwork that links the physical dimension with the higher realms and the energetic templates of perfection. Earthwork can assume forms as varied as the souls who undertake these endeavors. Many beings have been guided to create etheric energetic structures over vast expanses of the planet. Indigenous peoples have created medicine wheels and other sacred structures to link the spiritual worlds with the Earth since the beginning of time. Many of us feel called to travel to sacred places and use sound frequencies -- generated by the human voice, gongs, crystal bowls, or other instruments -- to uplevel the energies in these locations. Our very presence, especially when we are consciously connected to the spiritual realms, acts as a human acupuncture needle, and a "treatment" with our particular frequencies may be needed in various spots on the globe at specific times. This energetic need for our vibrational gifts is often behind the mysterious inner promptings we receive to travel to places we may never have been interested in visiting until now.

Barry: The Christ Consciousness Pyramid

Over the years, the two of us have participated in many planetary grid projects under the direction of the Office of the Christ. Our first assignment was to build a 50-mile-high Christed etheric pyramid over a grid point in northern New Mexico that is crucial to grounding the incoming evolutionary program for the awakened human species. (For more about the pivotal role of this energy center, see *The Keys of Enoch* by J. J. Hurtak.) The story of this project offers a living transmission of Planetary Grid gracework, and contains many elements that those who feel called to this type of service might find helpful to know about.

First, my Friends Upstairs "enrolled" me in a higher-dimensional, multiyear educational program to prepare me for this project. It involved lots of reading and research, punctuated by many conversations with the Christ, ascended masters, and other higher beings. Gradually, it was revealed that the project would include sacred geometry, crystals, pyramidal technology, and knowledge of the Planetary and Christ Consciousness Grids.

As described earlier in this book, many aspects of my soul's lifestream of incarnations were coming together during this time, as the knowledge gained during past lives came forth. What I was learning -- remembering, really -- were technologies and principles I had worked with in ancient Egypt and Atlantis. One of the principal technologies involved the use of large quartz crystals. Beyond the gift of their beauty, crystals are interdimensional doorways through which we can more easily link awareness with the universal energy network. Crystals function like "servers" to help us access the multidimensional "inner net." They can also be programmed to store and transmit energy~consciousness programs and frequencies. When programmed, they function as remote generators that continuously emit the frequencies with which they are encoded. This is particularly helpful when a specific energetic program needs to be sustained over long periods of time.

All members of the mineral kingdom are capable of functioning in this way, which forms the basis for the effectiveness of medicine wheels, standing stone alignments such as Stonehenge, and cathedrals and temples. Quartz crystals, though, are exponentially more effective because of their transparency and perfectly aligned molecular structure. For these very reasons, pure silicon is also the stuff computer chips are made of. Although physical crystals are wonderful to work with, they are not vital to planetary earthwork. Through visualization, it is possible to create etheric crystals, which can substitute for the real thing. As always, it's important to trust guidance and respond to what is asked.

Placed in sacred geometric configurations, crystals access certain archetypal harmonic frequency bands that create linkages to particular domains and octaves of Creation. The sacred power of geometry is central to the ability of medicine wheels to bridge to the spirit worlds, and likewise governs the effects of planetary aspects in astrology. The importance of geometry is currently emerging within contemporary chemistry and physics, especially quantum physics. It is now understood, for example, that the configuration of subatomic particles has a geometric basis.

Pyramids also create linkages with the higher dimensions. The Great Pyramid of Giza and the Mesoamerican pyramids were designed to function as initiatory chambers. Inside a pyramid, awareness can easily entrain with an interdimensional spiral of white light that lifts energy~consciousness into the higher realms. A circular array of crystals, when set on the ground and angled upward so that their points all focus on a spot above the exact center of the circle, creates a pyramid based on the geometry of the crystals placed in the grid.

All of this knowledge would play its part in the mission I was given, which was to place a very large etheric pyramid over the Taos Valley in northern New Mexico, where I was living at the time. The primary purpose of this pyramid was to fortify and anchor the Christ or Unity Consciousness Grid being created around the Earth by many beings, both in and out of body. This grid contains the holographic pattern~intelligence for the new, higher-dimensional planet into which the Earth, along with all its species, is rapidly evolving.

To further prepare, I was guided to read the book mentioned at the beginning of this section, *The Keys of Enoch,* which was channeled from Ascended Master Enoch through Dr. J. J. Hurtak. This sacred scientific text had been written to assist humanity in making the dimensional shift or ascension. In it, key planetary grid locations that function as interdimensional vortexes are shown in maps of the world and particularly the North American continent. The Brotherhoods of Light are most powerfully able to communicate through these portals, assisting humanity in every step of its evolution. These spots also function as doorways for ascension, for they are places whose special energetic nature allows this process to happen most easily.

Christ Jesus and Martin had been telling me that America had a special purpose in birthing the new EarthHeaven; in fact, they emphasized this nation would serve as the cradle for its unfoldment. In *The Keys of Enoch*, the USA is referred to as the New Jer-USA-lem. The descent of the New Jer-USA-lem energy field is to occur through the "Return of the Dove," a holographic energy matrix created and governed by the Office of the Christ, consisting of certain energy vortices that cover North America. The Taos Valley and the surrounding area from Santa Fe up to Southern Colorado is under one of the most important, the place where the right foundation of the "Dove" is anchored. This may help to explain the many consciousness-raising impulses that have come out of that area.

Building the huge, etheric, six-sided pyramid over this area, I was shown, would occur through the creation of six smaller grids at points all around the Taos Valley. Each of these would function as an angle or energy vector of a pyramid extending forty miles skyward, phase-locking with the Christ or Unity Consciousness Grid high overhead. When fully erected and activated by the Universal Christ Presence, this pyramid would anchor the Christ or Unity Consciousness Grid at one of the most important grid points on the planet.

Constructing such a massive grid sounded like a daunting prospect. I needed crystals and a plan for where to put them. Back in the Tire House, my humble little adobe outside of Taos that was constructed from worn-out tires and wire, I studied a Forest Service map, hoping the pattern would be revealed.

I knew the pyramid was to be created in a Star of David configuration, the energetic pattern symbolizing the marriage of spirit and matter. The six geometry is also the basis for the Merkaba, the light body field through which it is possible to travel interdimensionally. Studying the map, I wondered where each of the six grid points would be located.

Slowly an image emerged. The northernmost point would lie near Lama Foundation, a spiritual community and retreat center with a very high vibration which, for decades, had served as a meeting place for many of the "children of light." That made perfect sense. Since the six sides would need to be about sixty degrees apart, I began to plot out the sixty-degree angles from this point on the map. I noticed that Blue Lake, a sacred site for the Taos Pueblo people, lay exactly sixty degrees from the northern point near Lama Foundation.

Now I had what I needed to lay out the grid, and the rest easily fell into place. A central grid would be placed on a remote mesa west of Taos that just happened to be on the property of a very awake inventor of new technologies. He would understand this project, and a close friend knew him well.

A few weeks later I was in Hot Springs, Arkansas with the owner of the only mine that sold crystals large enough to be effective in the grids. He "just happened" to be the friend of a new friend from Hot Springs who was now living in Taos, and gave me a great deal when he found out the intended use of the crystals. But my wallet was still $5,000 lighter as the little Subaru strained to haul hundreds of pounds of quartz crystals back to New Mexico.

Intuitively, I saw that there needed to be a balance of the masculine and feminine when certain of the grids were constructed. I was going to need help, and from just the right women, since Karen and I had not yet been brought together. As luck would have it, a wonderful being named Glenda owned the land on which the Tire House stood. Robin, who would later assist with another assignment, had recently rented an apartment below Glenda's house. The team was in place.

I was still nervous about the whole thing. The task would require getting up before dawn, traveling out into the rugged mountains or remote desert mesas, and finding the exact point at which each grid needed to be constructed. Who knew what I would run into? Visions of angry, protective landowners, rattlesnakes, and even assaults by the forces of darkness ran through my mind.

But I couldn't deny the aura of great power and significance around the whole project. Clearly it was way, way beyond Barry to accomplish this through his own devices. As always, I was forced to return to the same place I'd been brought back to on many previous occasions -- the point of absolute surrender. There was nothing else to do but turn the whole thing over to the Divine, trusting the Christ would carry me through.

One morning around 4 a.m., Martin, my higher-dimensional aspect, came into consciousness along with the knowing it was time to get up and go to the northwest grid point. Constructing this first grid was to be a solo adventure. As I shuffled around groggily, somehow the shovels, crystals, compasses, protractors and other tools found their way into the car, and off I went. A blend of excitement and nervous jitters vibrated through my being.

Yellow rays of light illuminated the spectacular tapestry of rugged earth and sky that seemed to stretch out to infinity as I headed out onto the vast mesa west of Taos. The sun beckoned in the new day, removing the chill without and within. Its warmth assured me that all would go well.

The sun was cresting the Sangre De Christo Mountains as I crossed the Rio Grande. Soon I was approaching the spot on the map marked with an X. All around stretched a vast expanse of desert, seemingly roadless, and the spot where the grid was to be planted lay a few miles from the main road. *How will I carry all the crystals and tools for miles up and down ravines and over those harsh mesas?* By the time I got there, the sun would be high in the July sky. I didn't relish the thought of the trip back on foot. In the midst of that train of thought, I noticed the first dirt road I'd seen for miles, at exactly the point where I thought I'd have to begin my desert march to the site.

A sigh of relief mixed with laughter erupted from my being, and I thought I heard a chuckle from my invisible guides upstairs. It was all wired in, taken care of from a much vaster, infinitely intelligent level. *Relax, Barry,* that level conveyed, *and enjoy the ride.*

Bumping along the dirt road, I came to the spot straightaway. There was no doubt about it, no thought process involved. It was an unspectacular piece of land, but an unmistakable energy led me right to the spot.

Soon I was standing in the middle of that first grid point, engulfed with awe and gratitude that this was happening. The joy was so great I broke into tears. *What a gift to be able to serve in this way.* I turned my eyes upward and gave thanks, and offered my being as never before into Their service.

I felt my soul center open wide as "Barry" was subsumed by the larger presence of my higher or Martin Self. As Martin, with compass in hand and protractor on the earth, I laid out the six points on the grid. Little stones were placed on each point, and soon the Star of David geometry lay before me. The small army shovel dug six small holes for the crystals, which, when placed at a precise angle, would connect the etheric pyramid with the Christ/Unity Consciousness Grid. Six clear generator crystals each communicated where they wanted to be placed in the grid, and soon they were nestled gently into Mother Earth, their points directed at an angle skyward, converging over the middle of the grid. A slightly larger crystal chose itself to be the "pillar of light" crystal and was placed vertically in a hole in the very center of the array. There was no thought involved in any of the construction.

I stood back and looked at this cosmic pyramidal medicine wheel in a trancelike state. All orientation to anything other than what was going on at that moment in this most sacred place had disappeared. Just as the thought arose about what to do next, a particularly strong current of a very familiar energy began to descend. The Christ energy streamed down through my crown chakra, out through the heart soul center, and down my arms. I knelt down and gently embraced the crystal directly before me. The Universal Christ energy flowed into it, imbuing it with a brilliant but soft golden-white glow. I knelt before each of the other six crystals forming the perimeter of the grid in turn and allowed the energy to infuse them. Finishing the last one, I noticed a silent humming or ringing coming from the glowing grid of light.

Finally, after asking permission, I entered the grid and placed my hand on the center crystal. The Christ energy flowed into it and almost instantly shot out the top of the point skyward. As this occurred, each of the other six crystals also emanated a beam of golden light, all converging with the central beam about five feet off the ground, forming a six-sided pyramid. Sitting in the middle of it, I felt the splendor of the vast, Universal Christ with its immense clarity and purity, its subtle yet enormous power.

I'm not sure how long I sat in the pyramid, but there came a moment when I found myself getting up and walking outside of it. Once again eyes turned skyward as gratitude arose for the opportunity to be utilized in such a profound way. All that was left to do was bury the crystals, so they would not be found and removed. Soon, with the sun now high overhead, the little Subaru rolled back onto the asphalt road heading toward Taos. Even though my stomach now churned with hunger and there were good places to eat all along the way, the car wanted to go straight to the little adobe.

Exhausted on a level beyond the stresses of the day and lack of sleep, I crawled into bed, only to awaken in the late afternoon to the sound of thunder clapping in the distance. Punctuating the harsh, dry midsummer heat, it was a sweet sound. The thunder came closer and soon rain and hail were rattling the corrugated metal roof as cool, wet winds blew through the window. What a perfect ending to the day!

A week or so passed with no more contacts from Beyond about the work. One afternoon on the way to the pool for a swim, the inner knowing arose that tomorrow would be the day to build the next grid, and that Glenda needed to go along. That evening I told her of the prompting and she gladly consented. That was a great relief, as Glenda, a long time Taoseno, knew the country well. I was certain she would be helpful on every level, for she was very spiritually connected.

Again I was awakened before dawn with the prompting to get moving. Soon Glenda and I, along with all the gear, were bouncing down the rutted dirt road. My guts were churning as we wound up into the mountains through pines and aspen groves on a labyrinth of Forest Service roads. But sure enough, we arrived at the place where the X marked the map with relative ease. As if an invisible cord was anchored to my soul center, a homing beacon drew me right to the point where the grid wanted to go, a beautiful place in a meadow at what must have been over ten thousand feet in elevation.

Glenda and I got busy and soon all the crystals were placed in the ground, just as in the last grid. This time, though, our participation was required to a greater degree. We were asked to consciously call the energetic geometry of the six-sided etheric pyramid into being. To do this, we connected with each crystal, honoring it for its service and asking that it help us in this mission, to which we felt each one gladly consent. We asked them to join their energies to form the six-sided pyramid and then visualized the pyramid coming into being with the pillar of light in the middle. Immediately it came into place as it had the time before, but now we functioned as co-creators. We knelt on the ground and held each crystal in turn, again asking the Christ energy to come into one after another. The energetic downpour came as quickly as the request, and soon golden-white light was filling each crystal as we made our way around the circle, finishing with the crystal in the middle.

After this was complete, we stood there knowing the grid was in place. We buried the crystals so no one would find them, gave thanks, and were headed toward the car when we realized there was one more piece. We had to connect this grid of crystals to the first one, located across the Rio Grande more than fifty miles to the northwest. As we made the linkage by visualizing the other grid and projecting our consciousness to it, a palpable energetic connection formed between the two.

By the time we drove into Taos, the sky had turned dark again and signs of an imminent thunderstorm were building. Within an hour the skies opened up. Thunder and sharp flashes filled the air as the rain pummeled the dry earth. I began to wonder: Was it a coincidence that a thunderstorm occurred after both expeditions?

Summer moved on toward fall, and three of the other points on the outside of the grid had been put in place. Two of the times I was with Glenda or Robin, and once on my own. These, too, happened with absolute ease. We drove to the spot, the pyramid was created, the Christ energy came in and the grid was connected with all the others. Each process was punctuated by a strong thunderstorm within a day or two after we completed the grid.

Usually one of the driest places in the country, northern New Mexico was the wettest spot in the continental U.S. during that summer of '88. This, despite the worst drought in America in 50 years, during the major La Nina of 1988-1989. Mother Earth seemed to be balancing and cleansing the area to support the new energetics.

Now there were only two more grids to finish -- the one in the center, which was to be last, and the one at Blue Lake, which was high in the Sangre De Christos and on sacred Indian land. How would that work out? What else but to go inside and turn it over to the ones behind this project.

Within a week my friend Marcy told me she knew one of the medicine men at Taos Pueblo and that she would contact him about helping out. After being infused with the Christ energies, a crystal was given to Marcy to take to the Pueblo. Within days, the medicine man had journeyed to Blue Lake and deposited the crystal in the very middle of it.

Only the center grid remained. I wondered when I could complete the whole grid and energetically erect the fifty-mile-in-diameter pyramid formed out of all the smaller ones. The answer to this question would not come until another major turning point in my life occurred, when Karen and I came together at Lama Foundation, just up the road from Taos, in perfect timing for the project to be completed.

The day she arrived, I got the message it was time to place the last, central crystal grid into the earth and ignite the entire pyramidal grid. This, I now knew, could not be done without Karen, for the process required our twin souls to be united for the full spectrum of energy to be released. Off we went the next morning to complete the larger mission.

Constructing the grid felt different this time -- much more powerful, and a sense of finality was in the air. Even as we started to dig the holes and place the crystals, thunderstorms began to build on all sides of us. By the time everything was in place, lightning was piercing the sky within a few miles of us. The Christ energy flowed through both of us strongly, and soon it was time to erect the entire Christed Pyramid.

I connected with all the other grids that had been created, including the one in the waters of Blue Lake. I asked that each send up a ray of Christ Light to a point about forty miles above us, encompassing all layers of the Earth's atmosphere. A pillar of light ascended, gently at first and then accelerating in speed and power, into the middle of all the angling rays from the other points, and the entire pyramidal energy matrix phase-locked into place. Karen and I stood there together in great reverence, little knowing that we had just begun a lifetime of service together, assisting the Office of the Christ in birthing the new, luminous human species that would live on a higher-dimensional Heaven on Earth.

～ ～ ～

Earth Grid work provides a very potent way to unify the existing Planetary Grid and the Christ Consciousness Grid. Creating a physical grid as we did in northern New Mexico can be particularly effective because the energetic gracework is anchored very deeply into the third dimension. Whenever we take a walk on the earth, our multidimensional energy system is connecting both upward into the light and downward into the earth. The energetic acupuncture needle of our presence functions as a bridge between the realms, and this is enhanced when we ground the energies in a ceremonial manner, as was done during the creation of the crystalline pyramids over northern New Mexico.

During our work with the Arkhom project, we left nothing physical behind. In fact, we picked up a few stones at each grid point so we could meditate on the points when we returned home.

At times while traveling we have found ourselves drawn to pick up a stone and hold it while higher frequencies of divine grace were poured into it. The stone would then be placed in the precise spot that "lit up" or was shown as the point where the energies needed to ground into the planetary body.

The examples of planetary gracework in this chapter are but a small sampling of what is possible. May reading about them vibrate open the field of possibility in your own consciousness so that your particular contributions to the Whole can more easily come through.

18

Planetary Holocaust
or
Planetary Pentecost?

Our Choice: Ego-Death or Eco-Death?

As we write this chapter, the questions that begin it have never seemed more pertinent. The nuclear catastrophe unfolding in Japan after the earthquake and tsunami there threatens not only the well-being of the Japanese land and people, but all of life on Earth if the disaster cannot be stopped. The human race has now entered uncharted territory, as the potential threat of the situation at the now-famous Daiichi reactors surpasses the level of the world's worst nuclear disaster at Chernobyl.

Humans the world over wonder *What lies ahead?* There are no clear answers, no experts who can reassure us about how this will work out, for this situation has never existed before. To compound matters, governments everywhere are downplaying the severity of the threat to stave off what they believe would be mass panic if the true situation were known. Unwilling to pursue the kinds of solutions that might actually reflect a shift in the prevailing paradigm, not to mention effectively work to mitigate our crises, those in power seem to feel it is best to act as though there are no problems.

Millions the world over are sending prayers and blessings to the Japanese people as they face the unthinkable. Hopi elders remind us that they have known this time of purification was coming, and advocate envisioning the world returning to a state of balance. Spiritual teachers recommend focusing on our inner life and returning to the eternal values and qualities at the heart of true awakening, as the ubiquitous crises propel us beyond superficial preoccupations and back to our sacred cores.

Agents of Grace

The current apocalyptic scene in Japan would seem to present enough evidence of humanity's forgetting, but it does not stand alone. Countless other situations, from the 2010 massive oil spill in the Gulf of Mexico to the ongoing poisoning of the land through the unregulated use of chemical pesticides and fertilizers by agribusiness and the destruction of ecosystems, including the crucial Amazon basin, cry out for our attention.

A recent news article indicates the sixth massive extinction may be underway, a theory that is hard to dispute in the face of the current mass disappearance of bees, bats, birds, and many species of sea life. The article states that "over the past 540 million years, five mega-wipeouts of species have occurred through naturally-induced events. But the new threat is man-made, inflicted by habitation loss, over-hunting, overfishing, the spread of germs and viruses and introduced species, and by climate change caused by fossil fuel greenhouse gases, says the study."

This list of threats to life doesn't include deforestation, desertification, acidification of the oceans, overflowing pollution sinks, potential catastrophes from genetically modified organisms, and the danger that we will destroy each other through wars over dwindling resources. The way things are going certainly presents overwhelmingly convincing evidence that we are headed for some sort of planetary holocaust.

Scientist James Lovelock is the originator of the Gaia Hypothesis, which purports that the Earth is a living, sentient being. Using the word "hypothesis" to refer to this idea may seem a bit cautious to those for whom it is an easily observable fact. Lovelock advocates seeing our planet as the larger living being of which we are but a subset, one species among many that are all part of her body. In contrast, how many human beings see the Earth as a material object, here for our needs and perfectly all right to exploit and plunder?

Lovelock scoffs at the idea that we will be able save the planet, pointing out that this attitude is rife with arrogance. The Earth, he points out, was doing just fine until the Industrial Revolution and the massive upleveling in resource use that accompanied it. More audaciously than ever before, a small but powerful percentage of the human species acted as though it was the ruler of the planet, entitled to do whatever it wanted to her and take whatever it liked from her bounty, with no thought of subsequent generations or the devastation being wreaked upon our terrestrial home.

A hundred fifty years later, this wanton carelessness having multiplied exponentially, we find ourselves in a fine mess. How are we going to "save the planet" when we are the ones who are putting it in jeopardy? Every scientific breakthrough humans have ever made has resulted in damage to the Earth. Long, long ago we stumbled onto the awareness of how to create and use fire. While this, like all such pivotal discoveries, has been a boon to human survival and advancement, its repercussions have also slowly, steadily eroded life. From fire came not only warmer caves and the ability to heat our food, but also explosives and modern warfare, along with the internal combustion engine and coal- and oil-fired power plants and factories, all of which have heavily contributed to potentially catastrophic climate change.

The story goes on, with a million permutations. When we learned how to split the atom, what did we do first? We built bombs and destroyed two cities, instantly incinerating hundreds of thousands of human beings. Later, when we didn't know what to do with the "depleted" uranium left over from nuclear reactors, we realized it could be used in rockets and tank shells to kill more human beings. And it kills them more cruelly than almost any other method, for DU weapons create maximum damage to living tissue and cause very long-term health issues for the "enemy," which all too often turns out to be innocent people who are simply living their lives.

Humans create one new chemical medicine after another, only to find out many of them harm more than they heal. We use more chemicals to grow our food and then wonder why the earth becomes depleted and those who eat the food develop a host of mysterious new ailments. Now, we claim we're going to solve global warming by filling the atmosphere with sulfur, barium, aluminum and other toxic compounds. Would you hire someone with humanity's track record to fix your planet?

More than a few of us wonder what it will take for humanity to reverse its migration away from the Divine and return Home. The current planetary situation is a stark reminder that the train of ego acting in separation from all of Life is coming to the end of the line. It's time to get off the train before it crashes -- time to seek alternate transportation into the future.

The Solution: Planetary Awakening Through Grace

Since the world "out there" is a direct reflection of our state of consciousness, it seems the height of delusion to believe we are going to fix our self-created mess without first "fixing" ourselves. In the egoic state, the little "me" sees itself as separate from other human beings and all of life, and arrogantly thinks it can play God. The small, egocentric self is only out for one thing: to take care of its own needs and desires. Everything that is threatening life on planet Earth has its roots in this separative human consciousness.

When we contemplate a toxic waste site, for instance, often the first thought that arises is *How do we clean up this mess?* While that's a natural and important thought process, it doesn't deal with the core of the issue: *How did that place become filled with deadly toxins?* Something was created that was inhospitable to life. Those responsible for this miscreation then felt it was okay to deposit the deadly material into the ecosystem. Only beings disconnected from their own souls are capable of stealing from nature and harming life. If they were in touch with their true nature, they would recoil at the thought of desecrating life. They would feel the wounds that result within themselves. They would love life so much that it would be impossible to deliberately harm it in any way.

The Environmental Protection Agency or any other governmental or nongovernmental organization will never stop this kind of behavior through legislation, education, or imposing penalties. Even direct force would probably have little or no impact on the awareness of the sleeping souls perpetrating the destruction. While imposing laws and penalties can indirectly bring awareness to the need for change, ultimately, our outer problems will only be solved through a collective shift in consciousness. Self-forgetting is the root cause of virtually all the problems we face. Soul awakening is the solution that leads to the resolution of them all.

The prospects of nearly seven billion people awakening in time to avert all-out catastrophe may look dim, from the human perspective. While some humans have consciously stepped onto the path to freedom, many more appear to be largely asleep and entrenched in life-destroying ways of being. At times it may seem that even the brightest of beings are like tiny candles floating in the dark sea of humanity's self-forgetting, which at any moment might wash over them. Fortunately, the outlook brightens when we realize that at the deepest, most fundamental level, there is only one being here, one collective human soul that is awakening, and that immense grace is pouring in as never before to catalyze the evolution these times require. In addition, a recent study demonstrated that the tipping point at which a new level of awareness spreads to the whole is actually quite small. Amazingly, when only ten per cent of a population makes a significant shift, the rest inevitably follow. The point of power for planetary lightworkers and agents of grace is to focus on these basic truths.

As we awaken, we naturally serve as conduits of grace for others. Our consecration to awakening and the inner work we dedicate to that end are immense contributions in themselves, for they increase the light and consciousness on the planet. The soul-spark at our core that we fan into an ever-brighter flame with our loving attention in turn kindles the radiance of the collective human soul. In the oneness we share, the illumination that grace bestows upon one member of the human family is directly transmitted and inducted into the soul of each of the seven billion beings that form its totality. Thus, our consecration to furthering our awakening is an investment that will eventually bear fruit for all of humanity.

As the planetary awakening gathers momentum, the collective unconscious will inevitably be purified of the widely shared distortions that are contributing to the multitude of planetary crises. We individuals tend to entrain to these shared patterns of thought and feeling and act them out in our lives as if they were uniquely our own. While each of our minds contains our own thought patterns conditioned by our experience, genetic factors, the planetary energetic matrix at birth, and so on, each seemingly individual mind is but a drop in the ocean of the collective mind. As Bhagavan and other awakened beings have pointed out, the vast majority of what passes through our consciousness is not really our own, but merely a download of selective perceptions from the unified field of the collective consciousness, more than 90% of which resides below conscious awareness. Whatever we have stuffed into the subconscious, individually and collectively -- the fear, hatred, greed, guilt, shame, aggression, and the attendant limiting beliefs and illusory images of ourselves and life that we don't want to face and own -- is the real issue and the source of all outer problems. When we are not aware of our own hatred and anger, for example, we project it onto others. They become the "bad guys" we then attack. The unconscious aggression we attempt to hide eventually sneaks out when we kick the dog, cheat someone, or abuse ourselves. When it plays out on a collective level, one country rises up to attack another. This dynamic explains why separation, hatred, war, and the myriad anti-life behaviors that threaten the Earth and all of life persist.

De-clutching from Ancient Mind

The mental~emotional patterns in the planetary mind field are so ancient and deep-seated that they have powerfully influenced the consciousness of each human being. Because of this, humanity individually and collectively repeats the same kinds of anti-life behaviors again and again. To students of history, our progress as a species can seem unbearably slow.

The collective egoic subconscious is behind most, if not all, of the life-destroying activities taking place on planet Earth. The distortions it contains cause otherwise peaceful people to morph into deranged mobs and commit atrocities, including genocide and ethnic, religious, and other forms of violence. The strength of the collective egoic subconscious also accounts for the wanton use of natural resources to provide things the ego convinces us we must have in order to be happy, none of which is truly necessary to the soul.

Bhagavan had made us aware that humanity had entered an age of exponential grace. The deeksha he transmitted and initiated thousands of people to pass on was clearly a manifestation of this grace. Bhagavan repeatedly stressed that the major impediment to awakening is the physical entrainment of the brain to the dense domain of the collective unconscious, which he called the Ancient Mind. According to Bhagavan, since we have been asleep for thousands of years, humanity has generated a huge, dark field of mind whose base frequency is separation and fear. We have all been subconsciously connected to this field for so long that the consciousness of separation has created aberrations in the physical tissue of the brain itself. In effect, we can become "hardwired" into destructive ways of being.

As we awaken, the downward pull of the Ancient Mind can impart the feeling that we are taking two steps forward and one back, and that we are held hostage by the deeply entrenched mental~emotional patterns that repeatedly show up in our lives. Its regressive allure explains why it can be so hard to overcome addictions and other harmful habits. Just about everyone on the spiritual path has experienced a burst of illumination followed by the strong backlash of the subconscious to the new level of awareness. The brain's neural networks act like antennae that phase-lock our consciousness with the field of the Ancient Mind, causing its contents to be continuously downloaded, whether we like it or not. This mechanism is also implicated in the difficulty of maintaining a sustained, illumined state. Over many years of sustained inner work, we can clear the subtle imprints from our past traumas and karmic patterns, which lessens the cross-resonance with the collective unconscious. We can, indeed, clear our own inner reservoirs, but since we are still connected to the vast ocean of unconsciousness of billions of souls throughout the ages, we may feel as if we're attempting to empty this ocean with a teaspoon. Few beings throughout human history have managed to completely disconnect their consciousness from this collective stew of suffering.

Yet Bhagavan declared what spiritual teachers have insisted for millennia: *We are meant to be awake. Enlightenment is our natural state.* As Bhagavan promised of the deeksha and we have found with the Transmissions of Grace, these gifts from Beyond contain omnipotent, infinitely intelligent and beneficent programming that unhooks the distorted neural networks from the collective unconscious or Ancient Mind. In the process, the brain's structure and functioning return to their divinely intended design. This changes our inner programming from the frequency band of a tragic melodrama of pain, suffering, darkness and illusion to a wavelength that vibrates with truth, illumination and love. When the brain shifts and our awareness becomes free of the obscuring veils of Ancient Mind, we experience what Bhagavan called the "de-clutching" of the mind.

Because all souls are part of the collective soul of humankind, the "de-clutching" of one mind directly and immediately affects the consciousness field of humanity as a whole. As enough of us experience the "de-clutching" of our minds from the collective separate ego-mind, it rapidly loses its power since all other souls begin to disconnect from it. Of itself, the collective unconscious has no energetic basis or ultimate reality; only when we get caught in our shadow patterns of fear and separation do we feed energy back into Ancient Mind. If we don't feed it, it dies.

As more of us become capable of accessing the superconscious realms, the vaster energy~consciousness of the multidimensional domains pours in to illumine and dissolve what was previously subconscious. A few souls who are capable of accessing these realms "lift" humanity as a whole, for we are all part of one great being. As more and more of us bring consciousness to what was previously veiled in illusion, the spiral of awakening accelerates exponentially, far beyond anything the linear mind can comprehend. Gradually and inexorably, the collective consciousness becomes illumined.

When we send transmissions to groups of people, situations, geographic areas of the Earth, and the Planetary Grid and power points around the globe, we directly catalyze the awakening of the one mind, one soul -- the collective soul of humanity and ultimately the Earth. In the process, we contribute to the dissolution of the major impediment to planetary awakening, the collective separate ego-mind. Seeing our earthly situation from this larger perspective as planetary agents of grace is a key shift in consciousness that has the potential to enable humanity to awaken in time to avoid the major catastrophes prophesied in the world's spiritual traditions. Those predictions of destruction are predicated on humanity's remaining asleep and in the clutches of the collective separate ego mind. Most, if not all, of them add that if enough of us awaken in time, we can mitigate the intensity and severity of what unfolds.

The majority of both ancient and modern-day prophecies, from native peoples, spiritual traditions and visionary prophets,agree that humanity is approaching the time of a Golden Age. Predictions differ on just when this will occur, and undoubtedly the greatest question is what the journey will be like from here to there. Considering the state of the planet and humanity's plethora of unresolved issues, it's easy to see the need for what most prophecies describe as a great purification and probably some level of cataclysmic activity prior to the birthing of this new age.

Hopi elders, for instance, insist that it is no longer possible for humanity to continue to "live with two hearts," meaning we must be wholly dedicated to living from the Divine. Hopi prophesy depicts one portion of humanity awakening and walking the upward path homeward, while the second continues on the path of separation, illusion and certain destruction. This message is consonant with what countless other traditions emphasize: We can't go on living a split life, convincing ourselves we are acting according to the will of the Divine when, in actuality, the ego's will and desires are in control.

The primary purpose of the Transmissions of Grace is to help people shift the focus of their lives from self to Self. The transmissions were given to assist us all in releasing who and what we are not so that we can directly experience and then live from the essence of who we truly are. Whether we utilize the transmissions alone or share them with many others, as agents of grace we have the capacity to help shift the field of human consciousness from the limitations of Ancient Mind into the freedom and clarity of the Mind of God. Imagine what the world will be like when all human beings sincerely and humbly echo the words of Albert Einstein: "I want only God's thoughts."

Transcending Apocalypse

The grace that is flowing forth onto the planet is already having a significant effect. One way we can see this is by comparing the predictions of ancient and recent prophets with how events have played out so far. Another is to peer through eyes of current seers who are being shown a different reality for humanity than prophets of the past foretold.

It's also helpful to understand the nature of prophesies themselves. Many people view them as utterly certain to occur, as if they were inscribed in stone. Despite the stunning congruity that unites many prophecies, though, it's important to remember that none of them is cast in concrete. Although some believe prophecies, particularly religious ones, come from God and are therefore immutable, history has demonstrated that this is simply not the case. There are probably far more prophecies that don't happen as predicted than those that do. Recent discoveries in quantum physics indicate the universe is a place of possibilities and probabilities, and the only certain outcome of any event is revealed at the moment something actually occurs.

Thus, prophesies are nothing more than possibilities. Prophets are shown the probabilities that are most likely to outpicture at the time they receive a vision. St. John the Divine, for example, was given a vision of the end of time two millennia ago. His context, like that of all prophets, was the field of consciousness of his time. Prophets are shown what the collective consciousness is dreaming up as possible futures; they see the probabilities that exist *at that time*. Based on the current vector of evolution, prophets foretell what looks most likely if that vector continues to unspool as it is currently doing. The images they see are the ways the collective consciousness field can portray what is likely to unfold if the current trajectory continues unchanged. Because the universe is unceasingly evolving, some possibilities become probabilities and then manifest realities, while others fade away.

In its unfathomably mysterious, never-ending unfoldment, the One continually dreams an infinity of possibilities into existence. As it weaves in and through all levels, domains, and configurations of being, we can never know what the endless creativity of the One will come up with next. And since each of us is an inextricable aspect of that One, we, too, are part of that creative process. What do we want to dream into being?

Decades ago, Karen's therapist, Pallas, gave her a simple inquiry to help her get in touch with her inner world. "Ask yourself," Pallas suggested, *"What do I want now?"* Of course, the reply depends on whether the ego or the soul is responding to the question. When we invite the inquiry to be answered by the true Self, we learn about what it loves. And we can trust that all that it enjoys, all that it feels prompted to bring forth, is good not only for itself, but for the Whole.

In light of humanity's current evolutionary situation, we might consider a variant of this question: *What do I want now for the Earth and humanity?* When we focus on what we'd like to see happen, it has a far better chance of occurring than when we give way to fearful, doubting thoughts and scenarios. Since a spark of the One lives within each of us, we are co-creators with the Divine. Moment by moment, what do we want to set into motion?

This is a lot more creative -- and a lot more fun -- than giving power to the endless litany of doom-and-gloom prophesies of the past. There's no way that the prophets of old could see the possibilities that would emerge a century or a millennium after their visions, because that reality and the possibilities related to it literally did not exist. God as Creation, which includes each of us, is evolving through and as the universes, galaxies, solar systems, stars, planets, and myriads of life forms. Each day it is born anew, a different Creation than it was the night before.

Not only does Creation keep evolving, making many of yesterday's prophecies obsolete, but the nature of time is also changing, making the prophecies of the past even less relevant to the present and future. Our minds tend to think about time as a linear phenomenon, traveling in a straight line from past to future, bisected by the present. Our calendars depict time in this way; other than leap years, every year has the same number of days and months, each decade the same number of years, and so on. This leads to the impression that our life experience should be relatively the same from one year to the next, in terms of how fast time goes by and how we and our world change.

But we know that's not the case -- the world is changing faster than ever. Carl Calleman has produced an interpretation of the Mayan calendar that seems particularly relevant to the way time is changing. The Mayan calendar is very different from any other calendric system in that it depicts time not as a constant, but rather as *the rate at which* events or evolutionary impulses flow through our experience. The last age in the current cycle of the calendar, which began in 3115 BC, is made up of a number of smaller segments of unequal lengths. Each succeeding increment becomes shorter, indicating that the nature of time itself is changing. Imagine our Gregorian calendar suddenly having 27-day months and 45-week years, dwindling until months were 1 day long and years consisted of 3 weeks.

According to Carl Calleman, the Mayan calendar indicates that time, or event flow itself, accelerates as human evolution gathers momentum. Simply put, the Mayan calendar depicts a rapidly accelerating evolution for the Earth and humanity. The last days of the current cycle, which he believes ends in late October of 2011 rather than the commonly accepted date of December 21, 2012, will, Calleman believes, turn out to contain as much evolution as did hundreds of years at the beginning of the cycle 5000 or so years ago. Whether the end-date of the calendar falls in 2011, 2012, or sometime beyond, the major point is that the evolution of human consciousness is accelerating at an exponential rate.

The galactic weather report provides considerable support, along with a causal foundation, for this idea. According to many space scholars, the solar system is moving into a different sector of the galaxy, in which there is considerably more energetic perturbation. The size of the heliopause, the leading edge of the solar system's energetic shell, has increased tenfold over the past few decades, which validates that our energetic environment is heightening. Hard scientific evidence indicates the Earth is not the only planet in our solar system experiencing global warming; our neighbor planets are undergoing an energetic upleveling as well, as their own forms of planetary warming manifest. Evidence strongly suggests the source of this energy is the galactic core.

Waves of energy appear to pulse through the galaxy at regular intervals to seed and uplevel evolution. Just as many of us now view our planet as a sentient being, it is helpful to think of the galaxy as a living, evolving being to comprehend this. Periodically, the galactic core sends a wave of physical and higher-dimensional energy and light out into its body, which carries the information and programming that enable the galaxy to take its next evolutionary step.

It appears that our solar system has already entered into one of these waves. To envision the impact of this impulse, imagine you are bodysurfing in the ocean. Here comes a big swell. You feel yourself being slowly lifted by the rising ocean. The swell gets closer, and turns into a wave. As its face gets steeper, you rise ever faster toward the crest. You catch the wave perfectly, and now you are zooming toward the shore, propelled by the energy in the water. What a rush!

Now imagine a wave of illumination, an evolutionary activation of galactic proportions. As this higher-energy wave hits the planet, some people will catch it and ride it for all it's worth, into the fourth dimension and beyond. Others will not be able to match the level of energetic intensity and will "wipe out." These souls will leave their bodies for other locations in the cosmos where they can continue to evolve within a third-dimensional vibratory field. But this isn't a pass/fail situation. Each one of us surfs into the next, totally appropriate evolutionary matrix for our souls, whatever and wherever that may be.

The influx of this galactic wave of energy is expanding not only planetary consciousness but also the field of possibilities available to us all. As our consciousness frontiers expand, we become ever more cognizant of the larger nature of things, allowing us to perceive even greater possibilities. The inpouring higher frequencies explain why our levels of understanding in all fields of human endeavor, from the sciences to the healing arts, are expanding so rapidly. As a result, innovations and advances in technology are coming forth with exponentially increasing speed.

We human beings are likewise compressing evolutionary leaps into shorter and shorter increments of time. A thousand years ago, even the most advanced member of homo sapiens would have found it impossible to think of leaving the surface of the Earth. Just a hundred years ago, few envisioned the possibility of flying machines, let alone intercontinental aviation. It wasn't until after the Second World War that we could have dreamed of leaving the planet in a spacecraft. Soon, we will collectively dream of leaving the solar system, and even of ascending into celestial realms of being.

Our true nature as infinitely intelligent, powerfully creative beings is being revealed ever more rapidly. The consciousness of more and more human beings is able to access the vast, spiritual dimensions of the higher mind, containing infinite creative potentials and even more importantly, the knowledge that oneness and love are the true nature of things. Evidence suggests we are evolving so quickly that many prophesies are being transcended, rendered outmoded by shifts in the collective consciousness. It wasn't long ago that nuclear holocaust looked like a highly possible, if not probable, outcome for the human experience. During the 1950s and 60s, when the two of us grew up, the likelihood of thermonuclear war was front and center in the collective consciousness. During air raid drills, we had to crouch under our desks at school or hide in our basements at home. No one ever explained how this would protect us against the threat of nuclear annihilation. So we lay awake at night, wondering if the plane we heard overhead might drop a bomb on us while we slept.

But some time during the subsequent decades, humanity seems to have figured out there are absolutely no winners in this scenario. Game over, everyone loses -- even the global elite in the most advanced underground shelters money can buy. While no one knows what the future will bring, and our collective unresolved fears could yet bring about a nuclear war, there's evidence that we have evolved enough to recognize the consequences of such folly. For several decades now, ever more citizens of nations the world over have risen up as one to say *NO* to nuclear war, nuclear energy, and all other applications of this frightful technology.

There are other indications that humanity is evolving rapidly enough to, in effect, transcend the prophesies of massive destruction. California has not fallen into the ocean, as many believed was inevitable by now, and Edgar Cayce's prediction of a physical pole shift before the year 2000 has not occurred. Many predictions pointed to the last part of the twentieth century as a time of total global upheaval. While some infer the prophecies were simply wrong, or have not yet come to pass, many contemporary seers insist our rate of evolution is sufficient to nullify or at least lessen the need for large-scale catalysts to wake us up. For a decade, we have received the same inner message, that the highest probability is that Earth changes will be less intense than previously expected due to widespread shifts in consciousness.

Humanity must still need some shocks, though, for the massive quake in Japan certainly indicates the time of intensive purification and cleansing has arrived -- if much later than previously predicted. We may have outdistanced the possibility waves of particular prophesied outcomes, but the Earth and her people seem still to need potent reminders that our way of life is seriously out of balance. And the crises themselves serve as extreme evolutionary catalysts for those who can meet them on that level. The degree to which humanity uses these opportunities to evolve may well determine how many more severe events are needed to rouse us from our ego-lulled slumber, and how quickly the curve of our evolution accelerates upward.

The evolutionary feedback loop appears to be approaching an infinite slope, matching the contour of the incoming wave of galactic light. As the influx of illumination accelerates, so too will our consciousness expand proportionally. Thus, it is possible that we will leapfrog right over many or most of the scenarios of doom long foreseen in prophecies. Our skyrocketing consciousness will catapult us into futures we cannot even imagine today. We are unable to envision the possibilities that are about to unfold, because we are creating them as we go, based on each choice we make.

When we look at the state of the world and attempt to project what is possible for humanity as we evolve beyond the path of crises, our human minds cannot grasp the exponential rate of change that is now unfolding. Only the higher mind can fathom the infinite possibilities that lie before us. The ancient Mayans understood how rapidly things could change, and their calendar provides testimony confirming the acceleration of evolution into a dimensional shift.

It is time to join all of our sister races in the galaxy as part of the galactic family. As we awaken sufficiently to no longer be a danger to ourselves and others, immense assistance will be offered us by our more-evolved brothers and sisters from distant worlds. They have been visiting our planet with greater frequency since we demonstrated our increasing mastery of higher-dimensional physics by stepping into the atomic age.

Our more illumined galactic neighbors stand ready to help us evolve and go beyond our limitations. First, though, we must demonstrate that we have evolved into a soul-awakened species, living in the knowledge of oneness. Before that moment arrives, we would only use their advanced technologies to harm one another, as we have used every bit of earthly technology so far. No longer can we look to war and domination to solve our differences. When all human beings have the basics needed to further life, when all are seen as worthy of honor and dignity, integral to the human family, *without exception*, our exo-planetary friends will know that they can finally offer us the help required to turn our situation around. There is no limit to how much they can aid us in resolving our issues of climate change, pollution, energy shortages, and so on, when we are ready to use the technologies they possess for constructive purposes.

The Ultimate Possibility: A Planetary Pentecost

In the wonderful film *La Belle Verte*, or *The Green Beautiful*, a woman from an advanced civilization volunteers to visit Earth to check in on how human evolution is progressing. As soon as she arrives, Mira is thrust into the maelstrom of earthly existence. Shocked at the state of things, she chokes on the polluted air, gets sick on what passes for food, and is deeply dismayed by the ugliness of urban life. Even more confounding are the limitations of human consciousness. She seems unable to find even one other soul with whom she can talk without major misunderstandings and suspicion arising.

Whenever a conversation seems headed for trouble, Mira pulls back her hair, shakes her head, and "disconnects" the Earthling from the sociocultural matrix, the Ancient Mind that prevents true connection and understanding. Suddenly freed from mental restraints, the recipient of the "disconnect" then wanders off, rapturously smiling, besotted with the newly revealed beauty of Life.

In the film, this sudden shift not only removed the filters of the mind, it also reconnected its recipients with the ultimate truth of the core Self. People were no longer interested in enforcing the rules and regulations of a death-dealing culture. Now, they only wanted to live and let live, if not actively seek out ways to enhance the lives of those around them.

Imagine what would happen if hundreds or thousands of us were capable of delivering such a "disconnect." This is not as far-fetched as it may sound; in fact, human history contains a model for just such a radical discontinuity. Something happened two thousand years ago, at the beginning of this age, that provides a glimpse of how the next age might be birthed. Before Christ Jesus ascended, the fullness of the Divine Presence descended into his twelve disciples, empowering them to be icons of possibility for a future time when many more souls would be ready to follow in their footsteps. Through grace, they experienced something never previously seen on Earth, a descent of the Holy Spirit that is called the Pentecost in the Christian Bible. An inexpressible Something from

Beyond entered twelve human beings and transformed them into the ultimate agents of grace, imbuing them with superhuman capacities. They suddenly found themselves speaking in many languages, healing the sick, raising the dead, and catalyzing powerful awakenings in all who witnessed the Presence expressing through them.

At this supremely pivotal time on the planet, we don't have to be Christians to find meaning and relevance in the idea of the Pentecost. Imagine what might unfold on the modern-day Earth if many, many people suddenly found this level of grace flowing through them. We might not only avoid the massive destruction that has so often been predicted, but also participate in the new era of awakened co-creation and peace that so many of us have long envisioned.

In a planetary Pentecost, the kinds of miracles the twelve disciples suddenly realized were possible might occur through hundreds, thousands, or even millions of people. Some might be prompted to visit toxic waste sites, where their intently focused prayers would transmute the poisons. Others may pray for an end to war, helping to bring that about. Many would discover that healing energies come through their hands, eyes, and intentions, benefitting untold numbers of suffering beings.

As Utopian as it sounds, this is not some distant dream. The incipient stages of a planetary Pentecost are already unfolding, as growing numbers of human beings uncover heretofore unknown abilities to catalyze change as agents of grace. The levels of grace now manifesting through a few beings, along with a cornucopia of transmissions of divine energies, offer a preview of what is likely to soon go viral as the luminosity of the collective soul grows ever brighter. Avatars and gurus including Sai Baba, Ammachi, Mother Meera, and others known and unknown have brought many into awakened states through their very presence. An Eastern European light being named Braco is touring the planet, awakening many through his eye gaze, while Panache Desai simply touches people, sending them into an inner transformation that deepens communion with the true Self. Mahendra Trivedi, whose potent healing and empowering capacities have been corroborated through hundreds of scientific experiments, transmits blessing-grace to more than a thousand people at a time through teleconferences.

These and other examples offer convincing evidence that the possibility of the instantaneous "disconnect" the woman from another planet demonstrated in *The Green Beautiful* may not be that far out in the future. Bhagavan's deeksha or Oneness Blessing, Sai Ma's deeksha, and Ilahinoor and the other Transmissions of Grace contain the capacity to shift consciousness and spark awareness of our inherent oneness with all of life. The deeksha and the Transmissions of Grace alter the brain's structure and functioning, resulting in a disconnect from the negative aspects of the collective unconscious that is similar to that in *The Green Beautiful*, although it may occur over time rather than all at once. The planetary Pentecost is already unfolding, as a rapidly expanding group of disciples of the Only One That Is walk the planet as agents of grace, just as the disciples of Christ Jesus did 2,000 years ago.

The number of these beings will continue to increase exponentially, as will the spiritual power that comes through them. The possibility field will inevitably birth ever more manifestations of the luminous, divine consciousness that is infusing the globe as the galactic en-light-enment unfolds. A great, rising wave of awakening is washing away all that is unlike itself as it streams across the face of the planet.

As the planetary Pentecost unfolds, more and more human souls will awaken and realize they possess spiritual capacities that transcend the inner and outer obstacles that block our advancement and threaten our existence. Stepping into our full dominion as souls, we will no longer look to those in power to do what we alone can bring forth en masse. The polarization of the current world scene, with its "leaders" and "followers" -- which all too often translates into "perpetrators" and "victims" -- will steadily transition into a way of being in which all have equal power and presence. Individually and collectively, we will consciously access the infinite creative intelligence and transformative power of the One and call forth the solutions we need to heal and raise the planet into the Edenic state we know we are here to birth. Joining energies with others awakening to their divinely infused wholeness, we will take action as one -- soul-awakened action that flows from our inner core of truth. Moving as one unified being, we will dance the new EarthHeaven into existence.

The time for agents of grace to step forth is now. As a Mayan elder recently expressed, "Now is the time to awaken and take action. Everyone is needed. You are here for a reason, a very important one. Everyone who is here now has an important purpose."

The way our planet's story unfolds will be greatly influenced by the consciousness and the actions of each one of us. The degree to which we experience a planetary holocaust or Pentecost will be determined by how many of us step into the divine purpose our true Self indicates is our reason for being, and how deeply we consecrate our lives to acting as agents of grace to benefit the Whole.

Planetary Holocaust or Planetary Pentecost?

A Vision of a New World

Sometime in the not too distant future, we all notice that something palpably different is occurring on planet Earth. There's a sense of hope unlike anything we've ever felt, and it is based on an unshakable inner knowing that we've made it; life has thoroughly transformed. Many challenges still face humanity, but every day brings new discoveries and breakthroughs in virtually every aspect of human life.

A number of zero point or free energy technologies have been developed and will soon supply all our energy and transportation needs. Within a few years, virtually no hydrocarbon emissions will foul the air. Fossil fuel depletion is rapidly becoming a non-issue, now that the technology exists to recycle all plastics and other petroleum byproducts back into their original hydrocarbon molecules. Advanced lasers are being used to neutralize radioactive waste worldwide, shortening its half-life from thousands of years to a number of days. Now that we no longer need nuclear energy, all fissionable materials on the planet are scheduled for this deactivation process within the next few years. Numerous other "alchemical" transmutation technologies look likely to eliminate concerns about resource depletion for good.

The United Nations has become the planetary stewardship organization it was always meant to be. All major nations have signed a declaration agreeing to bring about complete environmental sustainability within the next decade. Under discussion is another commitment to abandon all aggressive action -- war, covert activities, drones, and so on -- at national and international levels, since it is now clear that such methods do not, in fact, resolve conflict. The World Court has at last been given the authority to mediate all disputes to peaceful and mutually agreeable resolutions. Nuclear and conventional armaments are rapidly being dismantled. They seem a tragic nightmare from a past that no one wants to see persist.

Our galactic family has made public contact with humanity. Since the human species has reached a level of collective consciousness that enables peaceful interactions among ourselves to be the rule, not the exception, our interplanetary neighbors have begun to assist us, spiritually and physically. While many of the new technologies have come through the expanding consciousness of humans, our off-planet friends advise and provide whatever else is necessary to get us through this challenging time of transition.

More important than even these extraordinary events is the planetary Pentecost that is gaining momentum. All across the

Earth, souls are waking up and stepping forth as prototypes for the new, emerging species. They walk among us as beings of light, emanating frequencies of grace to bless all of humanity. With each passing day, larger numbers of people are attracted to them to be raised in consciousness so they, too, can bestow blessings to all.

Around the planet, the frequencies of light and love are increasing exponentially. A great wave of joy, happiness, bliss, and love is melting away all the old pain and suffering. The consciousness of separation is now virtually nonexistent. When its residues surface, they are more a memory than a present reality.

More and more people now live to give and serve. Those who yet carry remnants of selfishness and greed are seen as unfortunate beings who are still asleep. They are no longer revered, let alone given positions of power. It is now understood that this common past condition was really a spiritual illness. Humanity's material needs have rapidly declined as people find true nourishment within the spiritual dimensions of existence and communion with the natural world and all who live within it.

Sharing has become one of the greatest joys of life. Everyone knows the day is rapidly approaching when this field of love, oneness and light will increase until everyone is fully awakened and living as their true Self. It is understood by all that focusing on spiritual awakening is what really matters. Blessing one another with our spiritual gifts, we are actively co-creating a true Heaven on Earth.

Walking among our fellow beings, we see the gleam of light in one another's eyes. We feel the love pouring out to each other from our hearts. When we meet, we offer a salutation that acknowledges the divine essence glowing within us all:

Namaste: I honor the light of the Divine in you!

or

Salaam Aleikum: May God shower you with blessings!

Often we stop to touch or embrace, for sharing this state is the most joyful part of life. All of us know now that we are unique, irreplaceable facets of the Divine, fully worthy of receiving love and everything else we need to thrive and manifest our souls' purposes.

It is the advent of the time we have all hoped for, the possibility that every race, religion, and culture has held, that someday the Messiah would come and humanity would be saved. Now we know the long-awaited Messiah is not confined to just one being -- it is descending into, through and as each one of us!

Knowing ourselves to be agents of grace, we walk this Earth dispensing divine blessings to all we encounter. Together, we are creating the new world we have all envisioned for so long. The words to a much-loved Sufi dance are finally coming true:

> In my lifetime, love in every heart.
> In my lifetime, peace...peace on Earth.

Resources

To receive our monthly emails, please join our mailing list on our website. These newsletters include information on our teleconferences, books, CDs, and more, as well as articles by us and others about the process of awakening. Our monthly emails also include links to register for teleconferences and read or hear more about our offerings.

Birthing the Luminous Self www.luminousself.com

Please visit our website store:
http://www.luminousself.com/store.html to purchase copies of:

> *Agents of Grace*: Fulfilling our Destinies, Blessing the World
> *Ilahinoor CD* featuring music by Mary Angelico and Ilahinoor
>   transmission by Barry and Karen
> *Soul Awakening: The Journey from Ego to Essence*
> *Conscious Soul Communion* CD
> Other books, CDs, and mp3s as they become available

We have also created a *Birthing the Luminous Self* Facebook page, where you will find postings that evoke the many facets of awakening. You can "Like" the page and contribute to it!

PART ONE

Chapter 2

This chapter recapitulates the primary message in our first book, *Soul Awakening: The Journey from Ego to Essence.* To order, see above.

To order our *Conscious Soul Communion* CD, go here:
www.luminousself.com/catalog/item/6570152/6425525.htm

The Dawn Horse Testament Of Heart-Master Da Free John by Adi Da Samraj

The Book of Knowledge: The Keys of Enoch by J. J. Hurtak

PART THREE

Chapter 11

The Rumi poem that begins the chapter is from Coleman Barks' *Like This.*
The poem on page 168 is a Kabir Helminski translation of Rumi from his *Ruins of the Heart.* Thanks go to Duncan Mackintosh for his help in sourcing these Rumi gems.
We were unable to find out the author and source of the poem that ends the chapter. Please e-mail us if you can help!

Chapter 12

Unless otherwise noted, the quotations that evoke the condition of Spotless Mind were sourced from the Internet. These include "After the awakening...", "I am the Boundless Sky" and the words of Ramana Maharshi and Hui Neng.

The Thomas Merton quote appeared as a caption in an exhibit in Chicago several years ago of Merton's photos of the Abbey of Gethsemani.

The lines from the *Astavakra Samhita* are from a hardbound version Barry picked up in India in 1983.

Chapter 13

The phrase "God pouring God into God" is from a J. D. Salinger short story called "Teddy" that appears in *Raise High the Roof Beams, Carpenters.*

PART FOUR

Chapter 14

The Ramakrishna quotation expressing his all-consuming love for Kali was found at wikipedia.com.

Chapter 15

The Ramana Maharshi quotations are from *Abide as the Self: The Essential Teachings of Ramana Maharshi*, Inner Directions Publishing, 2003. We highly recommend this book, which includes many wonderful photos of beloved Ramana Maharshi.

PART FIVE

Chapter 16

The Sri Aurobindo quote that opens the chapter is from his epic poem, *Savitri*, pages 343-344.

The central importance of I AM is elucidated in the following books:
Step By Step We Climb To Freedom Volumes 1-3 by Pearl
Original Unveiled Mysteries and *The Magic Presence* by Godfre' Ray King
The I Am Discourses by Ascended Master Saint Germain through Godfre' Ray King
Available through: Saint Germain Foundation:
www.saintgermainfoundation.org

The quotation on the importance of I AM in Advaita Vedanta is from Wikipedia:
http://en.wikipedia.org/wiki/I_Am_that_I_Am.

Chapter 18

Richard Ingham and Laurent Banquet: "World's Sixth Mass Extinction May Be Underway," *Science Nature Journal*, March 2011

The information on the tipping point for ideas to go viral comes from NHNE, http://nhne-pulse.org/todays-news/. The article begins: "Scientists at Rensselaer Polytechnic Institute have found that when just 10 percent of the population holds an unshakable belief, their belief will always be adopted by the majority of the society": http://nhne-pulse.org/scientists-discover-tipping-point-for-the-spread-of-ideas

Acknowledgements

Our eternal gratitude goes out to Kiara Windrider, who introduced us to Amma/Bhagavan and the deeksha. Experiencing the deeksha in India and subsequently sharing this transmission with hundreds of people made it unmistakably clear that a new level of grace is now available on planet Earth. Kiara also opened the door to the Transmissions of Grace by sharing Ilahinoor with us. Thank you, Kiara!

We are grateful to all the participants in our groups in America, and everyone who has joined our teleconferences from countries the world over. You are the pioneers who first stepped forward to experience and share the Transmissions of Grace. We continue to learn so much from your feedback, questions, and stories of how the transmissions have changed your lives. May you continue to spread the blessings far and wide!

Special thanks go to DeeDee Schneider and everyone who has participated in the Love~Oneness group in Corvallis, OR. This gathering of souls began during a weekend group we facilitated in May of 2007 and has continued to meet monthly ever since. You have demonstrated the way the Love~Oneness transmission brings people together and strengthens the bonds of caring, creating an embracing, allowing space that supports all aspects of soul-evolution.

Thanks, too, to Skandar Reid and Maryval McCoy, who have contributed to our teleconferences in so many ways. With adventurous spirits and playful creativity, each of you has added to the collective body of knowledge about the Transmissions of Grace. You have inspired us, and no doubt many others, to experiment with new ways of opening to and sharing the transmissions with plants, animals, people, and places.